ENTRANCES

Alan Schneider

ENTRANCES

An American Director's Journey

PREFACE BY

Edward Albee

VIKING
Viking Penguin Inc., 40 West 23rd Street, New York, New York 10010, U.S.A.
Penguin Books Ltd, Harmondsworth, Middlesex, England
Penguin Books Australia Ltd, Ringwood, Victoria, Australia
Penguin Books Canada Limited, 2801 John Street,
Markham, Ontario, Canada L3R 1B4
Penguin Books (N.Z.) Ltd, 182–190 Wairau Road, Auckland 10, New Zealand

First published in 1986 by Viking Penguin Inc.
Published simultaneously in Canada

Grateful acknowledgment is made to Samuel Beckett for permission to reprint a portion of his letter.

Drawing by Al Hirschfeld: © Al Hirschfeld, 1961. Reproduced by special arrangement with Al Hirschfeld's exclusive representative, the Margo Feiden Galleries, New York.

Frontispiece photograph by George de Vincent.

Portions of this book first appeared in *The New York Times Magazine* and *American Theatre*.

LIBRARY OF CONGRESS CATALOGING IN PUBLICATION DATA
Schneider, Alan.
Entrances.
Includes index.
1. Schneider, Alan. 2. Theatrical producers and directors—United States—Biography. I. Title.
PN2287.S335A34 1986 792'.0233'0924 [B] 83-40643
ISBN 0-670-80608-0

Printed in the United States of America by
R. R. Donnelley & Sons Company, Harrisonburg, Virginia
Set in Electra

For my wife

CONTENTS

THIRD ACTS

PREFACE

When Alan Schneider received his killing injury in the late Spring of 1984 he was in England, about to begin rehearsal of *The Home Front*, a splendid new play by a very gifted young American playwright, James Duff. Of course Alan was in England, for that is where the challenge was, where the new talent was at that moment, where the chance was to help and realize, where a young American playwright needed guidance, encouragement and realization.

And I am certain that had Alan lived to direct the play, both in London and subsequently, in New York, it would have received a far less superficial and insensitive production than it suffered in other hands. Certainly, it would have been precisely the play the author intended, undistorted. Alan was that kind of director.

He almost never directed a play he did not respect, and on those occasions when he persuaded himself that one was worthy when it was not, the results were often calamitous.

Alan understood that the director (indeed the entire production—actors, sets, costumes, all) is at the service of a worthwhile play. Alan was meticulous, detailed and exhaustive in his examination of a text, and woe to an author who could not answer the hundreds of textual questions thrown at him. Indeed, woe to the author who does not have these answers even if they are *not* thrown at him.

I have learned more about the craft of directing—and not a little about the craft of playwriting—from watching Alan work on a play of mine than from any other source, though I must give Peter Hall a nudge of credit, too.

I am told that moments before he was struck down Alan had mailed a letter to his friend Sam Beckett. I'm sure that letter was filled with enthusiasm, news . . . and questions—enthusiasm about the world about him, news of the outside and questions about others, for Alan was an intensely private person for all of his engagement.

This detailed memoir—cut off, alas, in mid-career—is a fascinating document. It provides us with extraordinary insights into Alan's childhood and early struggles as well as careful, exhaustive notes on work process and response to outside stimuli. It is invaluable in its miniature portraits of myriad theatre and literary personalities—Beckett, Buster Keaton, Harold Pinter, for example.

I would be sure to read the book very carefully if I were you, for Alan's prose does not change its tone no matter the event, and if you are rushing through the inconsequential you may very well miss the momentous.

I have a few quarrels with the book: Alan remembers things about our professional relationship that I do not, no matter how hard I try, and he occasionally omits mention of a number of mitigators, and even in so horrid a place as the commercial theatre in the United States, the number of people who betrayed Alan is staggering. The number of people who disappointed him is even larger, but, given his standards, it is not surprising.

The book chronicles in enormous detail an intense, prodigously busy, useful and creative life. Anyone interested in the theatre—in the history of a theatrical times—will find this book invaluable. Those of us who knew Alan and worked closely with him are grateful to discover something of the man behind the dynamo, the emotion behind the mind.

Edward Albee
New York City
June 7, 1985

ACKNOWLEDGMENTS

On April 26, 1984, my husband, Alan Schneider, delivered the completed manuscript of this, the first volume of his autobiography, to his publisher, Viking Penguin. Nine days later, Alan died after being struck by a motorcycle in London. During the editorial preparation the following acknowledgments were found among the papers Alan had on his desk:

> This book would not have happened had not Franklin Heller, my old directorial colleague and friend, pushed and goaded me all along the way, and held my hand while he did that; had not Edwin Kennebeck and Alan Williams, my editors, been so long patient with me and guided me; had not Mark Hofflund, my smiling actor-to-be and word-processing genius at the University of California at San Diego not led me through the labyrinths of the English language, coaxed and cajoled and clarified and corrected (I owe him special thanks); had not Jean, my loyal wife, heckler, tea server, sandwich maker, peerless Manhattan mixer, not loved me so much that she forgave my intrusions, extrusions, and total lack of grace. I thank all of them, especially Jean, through whatever printings the Fates take this book.

It is important to add to the above our gratitude to Samuel Beckett for his kind permission to include excerpts from his letters to Alan; for the generosity of George De Vincent in providing his unique photographs; to Walter Bode, who followed Alan Williams at Viking Penguin and pulled this all together; to Joy Small; and by no means least to the

University of California at San Diego Department of Drama, where Alan was teaching, which provided encouragement and facilities. If anyone has been overlooked, it is inadvertent, and our appreciation is no less fervent. Alan left a great many notes and materials for a second volume, and it is planned to assemble that material in a companion volume in the future.

Jean Schneider

WHAT'S PROLOGUE IS PAST

Unlike most directors or actors who set out to trace the true and yet unpredictable story of their wanderings, I'm not sure I ever belonged in the theater. All my life I've wanted order, continuity, connection, and a measure of sanity. Instead, the pattern of my theatrical life has been scattered and unpredictable, a combination of chance—happy or unhappy—confusion, and irony: "organized chaos." For so long as I could, I remained rational and avoided the theater. When I finally stumbled onto the profession of director, I never intended to go to New York or to Broadway. I pursued the holy grail of artistic leadership of a regional theater yet have managed to escape that dangerous prize. For most of my working life, I have managed to earn my living at what I have liked doing the most: directing plays on the stage with actors. Whether this happened to be in the New York theater or elsewhere did not affect my attitude or manner of working. I've directed plays on almost every size and shape of stage, from those with a proscenium, now almost a historic form, to theater-in-the-round, the use of which I helped to pioneer, as well as three-quarters round, thrust stage, and almost everything else in between. I have held rehearsals in attics, lofts, storerooms, washrooms, boiler factories, gymnasiums, churches—and, occasionally, even in theaters. I have put on plays in tiny auditoriums where the actors tripped over the first rows of spectators and in amphitheaters that would have been too vast for Reinhardt. I have worked indoors and out, on classics and inexperienced first drafts—the best and the worst—and the only virtue in all this is that I kept on working.

Always I have persisted, regardless of reception or results. On. Which is what Samuel Beckett in particular has taught me, through his plays and the example of his life. In spite of everything, one goes on, with or without sand in the bags. In the theater, as well as in all artistic endeavors, the only thing that counts is the work itself and the need to go on with it to the highest possible level, with the most intense personal concentration. It was Beckett who taught me not to be distracted or disturbed by success or failure, by praise or blame, by surface or show, analysis or distraction, self-criticism or the criticism of others.

When I was in high school, in Baltimore, I wrote a short story (unpublished and probably unpublishable) about an actor who, at the last moment, walked off the platform where he was to accept the Academy Award and vanished into the Hollywood night, to think. I've forgotten what happened to him, or perhaps it was never in the story.

All in all, I consider myself to have been more fortunate than most people and, on most days, I would not trade my state or my troubles for anyone else's. We are each, as someone has said, the sum of all the signatures that life and times have written on us. I, for one, cannot complain about my autograph collection. I have worked with some of the most wonderful and some of the most impossible people in the theater. I have myself worked wonderfully well and impossibly badly. The inflated egos and the nasty dispositions, I've forgotten about very quickly; the real artists and people are there to be remembered forever.

As Thornton Wilder's marvelously wise Fortune Teller in *The Skin of Our Teeth* tells us, it's easy to know the future, but who can tell the past? All I know for certain about what happened to me is that I am the only American theater director who ever went from the avant-garde to the Old Guard without having passed through the Establishment. I have always favored the poetic over the prosaic, siding with instinct over reason, swayed by the power of symbols, images, metaphors, all of the substances lurking behind the closed eyelids of the mind. To me, these are more faithful signs of essential truths than all those glossy photographs that seek to mirror our external world. I've always preferred Chekhov to Ibsen, Tennessee Williams to Arthur Miller, and Dostoyevsky to Tolstoy; but Beckett's metaphors reach deepest into my subconscious self.

In the past quarter of a century and more, I have discovered a great deal about the world of the theater, as well as about myself. These discoveries are not always easily described, easily transmitted, or even understood. The theater, like all of life, is—in a way never dreamed of by Heraclitus in his philosophy—always in a state of flux, always in transition, always excitingly changeable and changingly exciting. One cannot work in it and stop discovering, investigating, learning, finding out, experimenting. To me there is no such thing as a uniquely experimental theater; everything in the theater—every production, every play, every rehearsal—is by its very nature experimental. There are no absolute standards or absolute truths, either theoretical or actual, including this one. You have to take your own chances on your own tastes and your own instincts. And you'll never know whether you are right or wrong—only whether you are successful or unsuccessful, and rarely why.

Today when the American theater, because of the decline of Broadway and the rise of the nonprofit theater movement, gives promise, more than ever in its history, of attaining not only its majority but a meaningful and unified national identity, this account of hopes and confusions is dedicated to the future of the American theater. Some of what is herein set down may have a modicum of meaning and truth to those who are now—and will be in the future—laboring to establish that identity more strongly.

Almost the first words about the theater I ever put into print, some four decades long past, were in an essay entitled "One Theatre." Those words were a plea for essential unity, for a kind of theater we were then far from having. Today, now that we are several steps closer to that goal, every word contained in the personal chronicle that follows speaks, I hope, of a life spent searching for the impossible possible theater; and of a life that occasionally, in rare moments and places, finds it.

First Acts

FROM ROSTOV WITH LOVE

1917–1923

The first thing I remember was the soldiers. I never saw them, but I remember them. And the sundial. I was not yet four years old, making up my own games around that great golden globe in the yard of my mother's father's house, a decaying Chekhovian mansion on the outskirts of Rostov-on-Don in what was not yet the Union of Soviet Socialist Republics. And my big German shepherd—"police dog," I always called him, his actual name long lost in the mists—racing with me through the hot summer dust, hiding somewhere in the house's welcome coolness and dark.

I remember the sun's intense reflection on the sundial, but not the face or the name of the "babushka" who was desperately running down our sun-baked cobblestone street and through the creaking pine gate into the house. She was our housekeeper, maid, grandmother's helper, middle-aged peasant "girl," who gave me sunflower seeds when no one was looking, and hugged me to her smelly but comforting breast.

"The soldiers are coming!" she was shouting, in that harsh, nasal, peculiarly Russian scream of a voice. "Hide! . . . They're taking the women! Quick! Down in the cellar! Hide!"

Quickly, from wherever she had been, my mother the doctor, Rebecka Samoilovna ("Revecka")—always as determined as she was tiny—grabbed me; we hid, huddling together in that damp, cool cellar with the thick walls and the heavy smell of potatoes. My sad, serious maternal grandmother, Rose, her hair up in what I would now call the Gibson Girl style, quiet as always, listening; my mother gently rocking me to a semblance of reassurance. Where was my father, Leopold Victorovitch ("Lyova"), the other doctor, tall and strong, built like a Don Cossack himself though he was only a peasant and a Jew? Where was my maternal grandfather, Samuel, with his great oval beard, his soft voice, and his repertoire of physical parlor games that would keep me breathless and laughing for hours?

I still remember the coolness, the smell, the dog's barking faintly from outside—interrupted by the single shot. Then, the pounding of fists on the big wooden door, the rough men's voices, the loud laughing. And then silence, for a long time.

To this day I do not know for sure who those men were, from which of the many armies, "White" or "Red" or in-between, crisscrossing the countryside and our daily lives. I know only that my German shepherd, my companion from the first day I could walk, was no more. Even his body was gone, taken away for whatever purposes. I cried for days afterward and could never look at the sundial again without crying. Until the tears just ran out. To this day, I have difficulty with dogs—and soldiers.

There were other armed men, too, a year or so later in Moscow. Food was even scarcer there—the farms were farther away, as was the war—and there were still sporadic outbreaks of shooting. There were ration cards for everybody, but not necessarily any rations. And every evening after he came home from work—at the clinic or the railroad yard (he was the physician on the Moscow-Smolensk line)—my father would grab me, hold me up to stand unsupported on his outstretched right palm, then laugh, plant me on his broad shoulders, and tramp the streets with me for hours, looking for a public soup kitchen, a "*stolovaya*," that might have some soup left.

Mine was a fine perch for a chubby yet somehow frail four-year-old. My father was carrying me out of the third or fourth empty soup kitchen, making me recite some of the yards of Pushkin's poetry I then knew by heart to assuage the growing emptiness inside. Suddenly a truck roared out of a side street, its open wooden top packed with leather-coated, Lenin-capped, unshaven militiamen, laughing and shouting and letting loose barrages of gunfire at whatever or whomever they were passing.

Without a word, my father grabbed me and practically threw me into the first sheltering doorway, crouching over me with his large body. The bullets and the laughter ricocheted down the street, under us, over us, past us. The truck and the leather coats rounded a corner and disappeared. We got up, not saying anything, and went on walking. My father held onto my hand as we continued our search for the ever-elusive soup.

One midnight many years later, I left a Greenwich Village loft party with Ruth Mayleas, director of the theater program for the National Endowment for the Arts, and Edith Markson, special trouble-shooter for San Francisco's American Conservatory Theatre and general godmother of international theater exchange with Eastern Europe. As we ambled down the street, past dark and deserted warehouses toward my car, Ruth and Edith lagged farther and farther behind, talking and laughing, continuing the party. I realized that we were drifting away from each other; shadows loomed more menacingly and warehouse doors seemed more dangerous. *The New York Times* that morning had been full of the usual accounts of the previous day's muggings.

With my eye on an especially dark doorway, I retraced my steps and urged the ladies to pick up their pace. "It's dangerous out here," I said, as politely as possible. "Let's get to the car. Then we can talk."

"Oh, Alan, stop!" came Ruth's amused and slightly contemptuous response. "You're always doing that. Always being a Russian peasant."

That's what I am, I guess: a Russian peasant. As not only Ruth Mayleas but my ever-patient and ever-loving wife, Jean, an elegant and gracious lady of somewhat patrician French-German-English background, often remind me. The Russian peasant, my mother used to say, gets to the station on the stroke of seven, by the station clock, in order not to miss the train due in at ten.

I was born, it says on my somewhat faded Certificate of Birth, which my father managed to bring with him out of Russia, in a suburb of Kharkov, a large industrial city in the Ukraine, on November 28, 1917. Actually, since the calendar was changed from Gregorian to Julian (or is it vice versa?), the true date should be thirteen days later, December 11. My mother, bless her, miscalculated, so we always celebrated my birthday on December 12. By the time we realized her mistake, I'd gotten so used to December 12, I couldn't change my thinking, much less all the records. Besides, I had already sent in an item to Ripley's "Believe It or Not" cartoon stating that I had been born on the twelfth day of the twelfth month and was now aged twelve. Ripley didn't care. I wound up marrying a girl who was born on the real November 28, so the coincidence makes a good story, though it does confuse a lot of people who don't understand all that fooling around with calendars.

What remains clear—and occasionally creates difficulties when I want either to establish, or to escape, my venerability—is that the year in question is indubitably 1917, a year that remains fairly notorious in the twentieth century. The Russian Revolution and I are the same age, give or take a few days, and of similar temperament. I am an imperfect perfectionist, predictably mercurial, a confusing combination of skeptic and romantic, consistently inconsistent, disorganized and yet organized in my disorganization.

My paternal grandfather, Victor, looked like King George V of England. He was a skilled gentleman's tailor who in another time and place would have done well on Savile Row. As a young man he had left his hometown of Vilna to settle further south, in Taganrog. After moving to Rostov from Taganrog soon after my father was born, Grandfather Victor spent his days sitting cross-legged beside a samovar, sewing a bit, napping a bit, and drinking sixty or seventy glasses of lemon tea daily. He sent his kids out to work—there were ten of them, sharing each other's beds, pants, and shoes as they grew up. Four, including a set of twins, died very young, of malnutrition. The youngest, sisters Fanya and Raya, lived the longest, Fanya never stirring from Rostov except to hide from the Nazis in neighboring fields and forests. Two brothers became physicians—my father and the next of age, Isai, who could have come with us to America but chose not to. Isai spent the Stalin years going to cafés after work, to avoid being at home in case someone came to arrest him. He died, peacefully, the ship's physician on a steamer plying the Volga, leaving my one remaining Russian cousin, Lyuba, now a practicing psychiatrist in Moscow.

An older brother, Anyanya, was an assistant cameraman on a 1930s Soviet film, *Gypsies*. He survived the siege of Leningrad, was awarded a medal for "heroism," and then after the war was stabbed to death by a fellow inmate at the prison camp where he was serving an eight-year term for "borrowing" a movie camera. The oldest brother, Abram, was the pride of the family and my father's idol. Gentle, handsome, dark, a kind of slavic Rudolph Valentino, Abram studied engineering, achieving such high marks that despite his Jewishness he was awarded a university scholarship. Shortly after graduation he died in the influenza epidemic of 1916. It was his name that I was given, Abram, subsequently Anglicized to Abraham and later theatricalized to Alan. My original name was Abram Leopoldovitch (son of Leopold) Schneider. The Lithuanian version on my father's Lithuanian passport refers to Abram Lippmanis Schneideris, which would have looked good on one of today's marquees.

My other grandfather, Samuel Malkin, was a middle-class Rostov businessman who looked like Stanislavski's partner, Nemirovitch-Dantchenko. A kindly teddy bear of a man, he should have been a scholar, a teacher, a patron of the arts. Nothing pleased him more than gathering a group of intelligentsia, hiring a few musicians, then lubricating the conversation with wine and informal dancing around his large Victorian living room. He played the violin, not badly, and was an amateur theater enthusiast, putting on short plays of his own composition at one end of the room, playing—my mother often told me—all the roles himself. He would dangle me on his well-pressed knee while reciting from Hans Christian Andersen or my favorite, Pushkin, sometimes getting down on all fours to give me rides to Banbury Cross. Best of all I liked "*Pshchk,*" a peculiarly Russian type of tag in which he never failed to catch me, point his thumb at me, shouting "*Pshchk,*" and then hug me hard, his beard deliciously tickling my face. He was Chekhov's Gaev to the hair. When I began to read Chekhov, I understood what life in his house must have been like.

My grandfather, through various connections, managed to do well with a wholesale building-supply business. That accounted for the large house and the well-pressed knees. One night he cosigned a note for the gambling debt of a casual acquaintance. The friend went home and shot himself, leaving my grandfather responsible for the entire amount. As a man of honor and standing, he could not avoid the obligation, in the process losing his business and almost bringing his family to bankruptcy. Chekhov certainly would have understood.

Eventually, my grandfather opened a small kefir factory, manufacturing something like liquid yogurt, which was supposedly possessed of medicinal virtues—and which I rediscovered, years later, having a West Coast revival as a health food. The factory employed only eleven people, which did not prevent the Bolsheviks from expropriating it a few years later. With whatever resources they could scrape up, the Malkins fled to the Caucasus Mountains, where they bribed a local guide to lead them across the Turkish border. They stayed in Constantinople—one of my aunts played the violin in a nightclub there—before reaching Palestine. Two of my mother's brothers, Mikhail (called "Uncle Vanya" by everyone) and Syoma, and her youngest sister, Rachel, settled in Tel Aviv, where they opened a pharmacy. Mother's oldest sister, Celia, remained in Rostov until the war; she died at Auschwitz.

My mother and my father evidently met when they were young and living near each other in Nakhitchevan, the Armenian and Jewish section of the commercial Don River city of Rostov. They went to school together and were always very close—ice-skating, walking, going occasionally to the theater. Although their two families were strongly divided by class and education—with neither side happy about their relationship—the political and social position of the Jewish population, parlous at best under Czarist whim, kept them together. When my mother's humanitarian impulses led her to fall in love with another young man who was almost totally paralyzed and bedridden, her horrified family suddenly accepted poverty as preferable to paralysis.

With superior grades, my mother overcame the obstacles of both sex and origin, and was accepted into medical school, while my father was still unsure of his life work. She encouraged him, soothed his insecurities, and made him seriously consider a medical career. Hippocrates guided my mother, the humane, healing, humanitarian impulse. Economic opportunity led my father. For him, humanity was not nearly so important as security, the human desire to wear his own pair of shoes.

The details of my parents' wartime experience remain confused in my mind. I heard so many versions that I can no longer determine the actuality. Some of my recollections, I'm afraid, tend to resemble some of the Russian novels of the period, which I later read.

I do know that they got married in 1916, in the midst of the war. I have no idea where the wedding took place, who was there, if anyone, and what sort of ceremony it was. It must have been, under the circumstances, simple, inexpensive, and quick—although they seem to have gone off to Tsaritsyn (now Volgograd and once, in between, Stalingrad) for a brief honeymoon.

Accelerated by the war, my father's medical career overtook my mother's. He was off serving in the Czarist army—without facilities, equipment, or proper medicines—when the First Revolution came in February/March 1917. In the chaos preceding the Second Revolution in October/November, he got himself transferred to Rostov, nearer his wife, who was pregnant with me at the time.

My mother had not yet taken her final medical examinations, which were given only occasionally in selected locations. As the Bolshevik forces, newly established in Moscow and Petrograd (later Leningrad), were extending their power into the provinces, my mother received notice that examinations would be given in Kharkov, some two hundred miles away. If she didn't take them now, there was no telling when there would be another opportunity.

Against almost everyone's wishes, my five-foot-one-inch mother—as brave as Anna Karenina—boarded one of the few irregularly running trains to Kharkov. Almost seven months pregnant, she rented a room in a student boarding house and proceeded with her higher education. In the meantime, a ragtag collection of soldiers and political commissars known as the Red Army was closing in from the North.

Somewhere between the tensions of answering questions about anatomy and physiology, and the panic and confusion infusing a fragmented civilian population, my mother's water bag broke. Only the presence and peasant knowledge of her roommate, a childhood friend, kept my mother and, I suppose, little premature me alive. I came out weighing less than five pounds. Without incubators, proper sterilization, milk, or even much water—or the facilities to heat it—the two ladies somehow managed: propping me up on a pillow in a bureau drawer and feeding me from their collective breasts, the only milk that revolution and civil war had not denied them.

The roommate, bless her, got off a telegram to my father, who wangled leave, "borrowed" a motorcycle, rustled up some unobtainable fuel, and zoomed up to my mother's boarding house. In spite of a crush at the Kharkov railroad station that would have made the crowd scenes of Eisenstein seem deserted, my father, abandoning his hard-won steed, bought tickets for the train to Rostov and got us into a first-class carriage. First class at that time meant a couple of hard benches to sit on. All that mattered, though, was that we were aboard what turned out to be the last train to leave Kharkov before the Bolsheviks arrived—the last train for months.

My mother later explained how tenderly my father cradled me on the train floor, padded by whatever clothes or bedding she had brought along for her exam period, placing his 220-pound body between me and random Bolshevik gunfire.

That huge frame had gone through a few traumas of its own, and was destined to go through more before succumbing to emphysema (he never touched a cigarette) and leukemia in a U.S. Veterans Hospital in West Haven, Connecticut, some forty-six years later. In 1916 he had contracted typhus, then raging across Russia. His family, afraid he might infect someone, insisted that he be put into a hospital. Without proper medicine and care, however, neither of which were available, hospitals were places to die in. My mother decided to tend to him at home—

begging, borrowing, and stealing extra linen, which she had to wash by hand several times each day because of the constant perspiration. She moved two beds together and rolled my father, mostly unconscious with high fever, from side to side in order to keep the sheets changed. After six weeks, he recovered completely. My mother weighed less than one hundred pounds; her determination, as always, was immense.

As a physician, direly needed by both sides in the civil war, my father managed to survive the constantly changing political and military fates endured by Rostov, which was strategically located and a promising target for occupation. While the Whites were gradually relinquishing their control of the Don region to the Reds, Rostov changed hands half a dozen times in the two or three years we lived there. Whenever the Reds took over, they rounded up all the men they could find between the ages of sixteen and sixty and shot them, especially if they happened to be wearing epaulets—a sign that they had served as officers in the White army. Then when the Whites recaptured the town for a few hours or days, they in turn lined up all the men they could find between the ages of twelve and seventy and shot them, sometimes (as in the film *Chapayev*) offering a slim—and rare—Czarist cigarette to a condemned man before shooting. After a while, there were few men left in Rostov.

When the White armies melted away on the Don front, my father was attached to a front-line medical unit consisting of a horse and carriage, three or four nonmedical assistants, and whatever medicines and bandages they could dig up. One day he woke up to find himself alone with the horse. Eventually he made his way back to Rostov and went to work in a civilian clinic alongside my mother.

The closest he himself ever came to being shot by either side was one day when he had just returned from work. My mother was cooking supper. I was playing on the kitchen floor. Suddenly, there was a loud banging at the back door of my grandfather's house, where we were staying. Looking out the kitchen window, my mother glimpsed a red star on one man's cap.

"Bolsheviki!" she managed to spit out between her teeth. "Hide the epaulets!"—still on the uniform my father was wearing.

He ripped them off, lifted a kitchen floorboard specially prepared as a hiding place, and shoved the telltale pieces of cloth inside. My grandmother, wearing a babushka and looking as much like a peasant as possible, let the men in.

Guns in hand, they came, found a bottle of cognac, and started prowling around. "We're looking for a White officer the people have seen here," they explained, looking at my father, who was sitting down, trying to look small and unimposing.

"Not here," answered my mother, stirring the soup. "My husband and I are physicians. Have some soup with us."

They kept looking at my father suspiciously, but evidently the prospect of the borscht, as well as my mother's apparent calmness, got to them. They stayed to eat the soup and some black bread, and finished up the cognac. My father, for the moment, was saved. I often wonder what would have happened to me if they had noticed the epaulet threads on his shirt.

My father's most serious trial by fire came a year or so later when the civil war was simmering down, Rostov firmly in the hands of the Reds. In 1921, when I was barely three, an order appeared for all Rostov physicians who had ever served in the White army to report to a central headquarters to explain. Anyone discovered not reporting would be shot.

After much discussion, my father decided he had to go and try to explain. After all, he came from a clearly proletarian family. He had never volunteered for army service but had always been drafted. His record at the civilian clinic in Rostov, including the period of Soviet occupation, was good. He had friends. He reported to the designated location and was informed that he had to go to Moscow to explain.

The next morning, my father and thirty-two other physicians—seven of them women—arrived at the Rostov railroad yard. They were loaded into a closed boxcar, the car was sealed, and the train started off for Moscow. In one corner of the car stood a barrel of herring, in the other a barrel for bodily functions. There was nothing else except some dirty straw on the floor. Normally, the trip from Rostov took two nights and a day. With trains not yet running exactly on schedule, it might take a bit longer.

Sixteen days later, the boxcar—still sealed—arrived at Moscow's Kievskaya Station. Of the thirty-three physicians who had left Rostov, only eleven were still alive, one of them a woman. Both barrels were still there, neither one approachable. By this time, my father understood that, in his present situation, no explanation would insure his survival.

Once off the train, his legs revived, he took a bus to the apartment of an old college classmate, another physician. His intention was to recover and hole up for a while without reporting to any authorities. The classmate was there, sympathetic; my father was able to go to bed for a week.

By week's end, somewhat recovered, he decided that the only way to stay alive was to make himself in some way valuable to the regime. What advances in medical science might set him up in a special category? His friend suggested something called roentgenology (X-ray techniques) as the most important medical field in need of trained personnel and a certain professor who was the country's leading expert. My father, having learned that everyone else from the train who had reported to the Moscow authorities had been either shot or jailed, at once sought out this man and told him his story.

The professor turned out to be not only understanding but most compassionate. More important, he happened at the moment to need an assistant, having been unable to get one through the usual bureaucratic channels, then more confused and inefficient than ever. My father was apprenticed to the study of Dr. Roentgen's new and vital discovery. As soon as he could, he telegraphed my mother in Rostov, explaining indirectly what had happened.

My mother, meanwhile, left alone with me in Rostov, had been ordered to leave her work at the clinic in Rostov, to become chief physician at a nearby camp for young "orphans of the Revolution." She soon endeared herself to the entire camp, coming home each evening with enthusiasm for each day's new achievements—and, on rare occasions, a bottle of cod-liver oil for me. Once, I remember, she or I broke a bottle of that precious cod-liver oil, and there were bitter tears.

Just when she felt she was getting established in the minds of the local authorities, she received an order to evacuate the camp immediately to make way for a new contingent of youngsters—sons and daughters of Communist Party officials. What was to happen to the orphans of the Revolution? No one cared.

When she protested that she could not evacuate such a large group in the time given and that there was no other place where the children could be reasonably housed and fed, she was called before the camp's commandant, a new Party member, and sternly informed that she was herself being replaced as chief physician. More than that, her orders—military orders—were to report immediately to another camp several thousand miles eastward, in Siberia. No reference to anyone accompanying her; no provision for her four-year-old me.

It was just at this time that my father's telegram arrived from Moscow. My mother, torn between love and duty, Moscow and Siberia, felt that she could not, at whatever cost, go off without me. Hoping that the general bureaucratic confusion might let her fall through a chink in the structure, she decided to ignore the orders. She grabbed me and a few personal belongings, and got on a train to Moscow.

In accordance with Murphy's Law, I was just then recovering from an intense bout with acute dysentery, the result of my paternal grandfather's inability to resist his grandson's appeal. One Sunday afternoon, he had taken me out for a stroll in Nakhitchevan, having received strict instructions not to feed me anything. These orders notwithstanding, the moment we were by ourselves, he gave in to my pleas for a street vendor's cream puff filled wih delicious gooey custard. The cream puff was far from sanitary, and I had no sooner gotten home than I became violently ill. I remained flat on my back and hardly able to move for weeks, unable to hold down food or to control my bowels. Only my mother's regular ministration of coarse oats, intended for her father's horses, served to save me. By the time we got off the train in Moscow, I was barely able to walk.

I remember my father's face when he met us at the station and saw that something had happened to me. My mother hadn't had the nerve to tell him. He had brought me a welcoming present, a miniature tabletop croquet set. I was too weak to sit up with it on the table, so I wound up pushing the little wooden balls past various patterns on the slightly faded rug on the floor of our one room. I could just barely hold the tiny six-inch mallet. It was the only time in my life that I remember my father coming close to tears.

He had gotten us a small apartment on Yermolayevski Pereulok (alley or lane), number 19. Fifty years later, when I came back to Moscow, I tried to find the apartment house. But the street name had changed, and my inquiries for the old name so disconcerted taxi drivers and even my theater friends that I finally stopped asking. Again, I have no recollection of the house itself, but I do remember a curved and polished wooden staircase over which the son of our closest neighbor, Georgi Mikhailovitch, was wont to throw his pet cat. And I recall that every Wednesday night, my parents—by then both productively employed—went to the Moscow Art Theatre with free tickets supplied by a patient. As my mother later explained, theatergoing at that time was not entirely a matter of aesthetic experience, but a means of achieving a measure of warmth, color, and social contact. They had to go.

Lacking babysitters, my parents pushed a bureau in front of the window, locked the door—heaven forbid there should be a fire!—told me to be a good boy, and went off to the MXAT, the Moscow Artistic and Academic Theatre, whose director was Constantin Sergeyevitch Stanislavski. I cried when they went, not because I wanted to go with them but because I didn't like being left alone.

My first theater came elsewhere. On Saturday mornings, my mother took off on shopping expeditions with the then equivalent of Moscow's present-day "maybe bags," those hopeful harbingers of culinary or other material delights that might be accidentally encountered en route to wherever one was going. Maybe. Maybe she would find some bread or potatoes, a piece of cloth, some thread. The search would go on each Saturday.

To deal with the problem of my short legs hampering her few available hours of searching, my mother would take me not to one of the neighborhood day-care centers, which were inevitably sad, bedraggled, and dull. She left me instead at the Moscow State Children's Theatre, just opened under the auspices of seventeen-year-old Natalya Zats, later world-famous for her work with an adult children's theater, employing some of the finest actors in Moscow.

Here I spent my formative Saturdays in a magically colorful fairyland, inhabited by such engaging creatures as Mark Twain's Tom Sawyer and Huckleberry Finn, Kipling's Mowgli and the marvelous animals in his *Jungle Tales*, and—best of all—Hans Christian Andersen's enchantments. My favorite always was *The Emperor and the Nightingale,* which seemed to me at the time grander and more spectacular than would *Oklahoma!* or *The King and I* when I saw them much later, on a different planet. The flight of that fragile freed bird moved me beyond tears and transported me to a world infinitely more glowing and comforting than the peeling, impersonal facades of Moscow. My sundial had come to life.

Years later, as a theater student at Cornell University, I was to read about that theater I had attended so regularly, some of its productions, and Natalya Zats herself. The photographs revealed ordinary settings, improvised costumes, an impoverished theater akin to the makeshift of off-off-Broadway. Those photographs were lies. What I had witnessed were wondrous creations of a fantasy world redolent of rainbows and golden castles, true evocations of a child's need for imagination and adventure. I was to see Natalya Zats once again in Moscow, in 1973, when the Arena Stage made a triumphant visit with *Our Town* (which I directed) and *Inherit the Wind* (directed by Arena's Zelda Fichandler).

While I was discovering the wonders of Asia, Africa, and the mysterious Mississippi, my parents were struggling to keep their heads above the swirling currents of daily life in the Soviet Union of 1921 and 1922. My mother worked in various clinics—keeping an ear open for word from that camp commandant in Rostov—and tried to find cod-liver oil for a frail four-year-old. My father had learned all that could be learned about X-rays. As a physician on the railroad line between Moscow and Smolensk on the Polish border, he discovered that while such staples as butter and flour and salt were unavailable in Moscow, they were plentiful in capitalist Smolensk. Every now and then he'd bring some back with him, keeping both our own family and our relatives in Rostov slightly more comfortably alive.

My father once treated the wife of a middle-echelon Party functionary named Krassnov and received in recompense a pair of well-made women's shoes, which my mother wore for a long time. Krassnov, who had connections all the way up to the Politburo, liked my father and began to assist him in getting food, medicine, and that elusive cod-liver oil—which I dreaded but swallowed regularly.

As the months passed, my father's train trips to Smolensk and certain plans of Krassnov coalesced. Each trip saw my father bring back more bags of flour and salt. Sometimes, three or four men met him at the station in Moscow to carry the bags and put them in a storehouse. Something was going on, of what exact nature no one else in our family was entirely sure.

The fear remained in my father's constantly churning mind that his White army past would return to confront him. There had already been one occasion when he had denied knowing a "female Dr. Schneider" from Rostov who had, some years back, not responded to a military order that she report to Siberia.

At about this time, Lenin was inaugurating his New Economic Policy to encourage the production of more and better-made material goods and deal with the growing unhappiness about what the new Soviet regime was doing for the ordinary citizen. The New Economic Policy represented a partial and temporary return to the principles of supply and demand—that is, to free enterprise.

Such enterprise flourished in the most surprising places, including the Kremlin itself. Krassnov, with close connections to Minister of Agriculture Yenukidze, was organizing a group of people to stockpile industrial and agricultural equipment, and he offered my father a job coordinating this operation, permitted but shady because some, including some higher-ups, were benefiting. Krassnov assuaged my mother's fears by slipping us extra ration coupons—sometimes a matter of life and death—for an occasional pound of sugar, a bit of cooking salt, or that awful cod-liver oil. The more active and successful my father's involvement became with his powerful and ingenious patron, the more he worried. It was a trait that was to descend, in some measure, on his son.

For the first time, my father began to think seriously of emigration as the only solution to a lifetime of uncertainty. Legal emigration was, of course, impossible. My mother's parents were planning to slip out of the country illegally and find their way to Palestine. My dear tender mother, like the lady in *Othello* who loved the handsome Lodovico, would have walked barefoot halfway for a touch of the Holy Land; but my father would have none of that. If he were to go somewhere to spend the rest of his life—he was in his early thirties—it would be only to America. And that was neither legal, possible, nor walkable. It would also take money.

Quietly, on each of his trips to Smolensk, he contrived to bring back a few parcels of his own. Especially salt. Salt, almost unavailable in the U.S.S.R. since before the war, was worth its weight in American dollars and British pounds. In less than a year my father managed, parcel by parcel, to assemble three hundred dollars. He never told me where he kept it, but I have a feeling he never parted from it, sewn into a lining or imbedded in a heel. If he had been caught, that would have been the end.

Without warning or preparation, the Soviet government, increasingly pressured from outside and anxious for stability, recognized the independence of the recently seceded territories—now countries—of Poland, Lithuania, Latvia, and Estonia. The Soviets were even prepared to grant emigration visas to persons who could establish their citizenship in these countries.

Looking at his internal passport one day, my father discovered to his intense surprise that he was listed as coming from Vilna, a place in Lithuania on which he had never set either eyes or feet. The registrar in the town of Taganrog in the Ukraine, at the time of my father's birth in 1890, had evidently copied the Vilna information from my grandfather's passport. My father suddenly could see the eyes of the lady in the Statue of Liberty looking into his. A light shining in his eyes, his passport held tight in his hands, he took himself quickly to the newly arrived Lithuanian consul in Moscow, a gentleman who had no staff and no clear understanding of his job.

He showed his passport to the consul, at the moment sweeping up the place, and asked if it would entitle him to Lithuanian citizenship.

"Do you speak Lithuanian?" the consul asked, putting down his broom, I suppose.

My father hesitated, not sure how to answer. Knowing that Lithuania hadn't been a country since the fifteenth century, and wondering who, if anybody, spoke Lithuanian, he finally answered, "Do you?"

The consul laughed and looked closely at my father, who at thirty-two must have been a convincingly impressive young man, excellent potential for the new Lithuanian society. Then he wrote in the passport, "Lippmanis Schneideris qualifies for Lithuanian citizenship" and stamped it with his official seal. We were off.

Although not quite. My father, as usual, was checking all ends against all middles (as I still do). He was determined not to settle permanently in Lithuania or even to subject himself temporarily to the whims of a Lithuanian Division of Immigration and Naturalization. He wanted to go directly to America, and for that he needed not only money but an American visa, more difficult to get than the money. A visa required an affidavit from someone in the States who would guarantee to support us if necessary. Besides, there was a new quota system for immigrants to the U.S.A., placing numerical limits for newcomers of each national or ethnic origin. The Lithuanian quota was full.

My father remembered that we had distant cousins, related to his grandmother, somewhere in the depths of a territory called Brooklyn. We dug through some attics, got the address, and wrote to them, asking them to please send us an affidavit, fast. The new law said that persons claiming rights of citizenship in the newly created countries had to be out by a certain date, or they had to remain Soviet citizens.

Increasingly anxious, we waited for one or the other to come. Which was it going to be: the deadline or the affidavit? We waited. With my father growing increasingly unsure of the whole affair. With Krassnov and his group making more demands on his time and energy, openly engaging in underground capitalism on a larger scale. With my mother hesitating about going to America while the rest of her living relatives made plans for their midnight dash across the mountains. I was preoccupied with Natalya Zats and Georgi Mikhailovitch's battered cat.

The next few weeks brought good news and bad. The bad: no answer came from our American cousins, even after another urgent telegram. The silence was not entirely unexpected. These particular cousins were distant and unknown, and the Schneider family in general was not celebrated for its great cohesion or boundless compassion. How did they know that we might not indeed become financial burdens? Two doctors, yes, but one was a woman. The good news: we discovered that the new quota system did not apply to doctors.

The deadline was almost upon us when my father decided he had had enough. By renouncing his Lithuanian opportunity ahead of time, he could, perhaps, strengthen his position with the Soviet authorities. Not telling my mother, he filled in the required forms, took them to the proper office, and breathed a sigh of relief. Naturally, when he came home that night from a hard day with Krassnov and the salt parcels, a letter with an American stamp was waiting for him in my mother's anxious hands. Not from Brooklyn, but Manhattan's Avenue B. The answer was yes, grudgingly.

Silent and literally white with tension and despair—I remember the moment vividly because I had that afternoon drawn a reasonably good sketch of a cat that I wanted him to see—my father turned and ran down the stairs, the signed affidavit in his hand. Not knowing why my father had so sharply rejected me, I started to cry. My mother held on to me, but she was crying herself.

Apart from his undoubted prowess as an administrator, my father was also a diplomat and a keen student of human psychology, especially bureaucratic psychology. Before heading back for that office where he had handed in his document of renunciation, he found—heaven knows where—a large box of Estonian chocolates. With the candy prominently displayed, he appeared before the glass door of the office just after it had closed. Several female assistants were already cleaning up the desktops. He knocked, gestured to the chocolates, and implored entrance. One of the assistants let him in.

He explained his predicament. The young woman told him that if his papers had already gone into the next office, there was nothing she could do. If they were still on a particular commissar's desk where they had been placed for signature, my father might be able to "amend" them.

She walked over to the commissar's desk and began to sort through stacks of papers. Minutes went by, my father trying not to reveal the intensity of his concern too openly.

"Schneideris?" A maximal pause, à la Samuel Beckett. "Yes, here it is."

My father took the precious pages, kissed the lady who had saved us from the tiger, gave her his Estonian treasure, and ran all the way back to his anxious wife and tearful son.

The next morning, an application for Lithuanian citizenship was brought by hand to the same office, together with a request for exit visas for three proper Lithuanian subjects. Two weeks later—after my father had procured American entrance visas, a copy of the Constitution of the United States, and a map of New York City—our Soviet exit permits arrived. We also were figuring out what else to take: my parents' university and medical-school records, a few family photographs, a set of my grandmother's hand-painted china plates, the silver-plated tea-glass holders given at birth to every Russian child, two beautifully laminated blond wood stethoscopes, and the Czarist double-eagle emblem my father once wore on his captain's hat.

My father's main concern was the three hundred dollars, discovery of which would not only stop us at the frontier but get us clapped into prison. He discovered an American businessman who had diplomatic credentials and was going to Riga, Latvia, the following week, and prevailed on him to take the money in a plain envelope, to be returned to my father when we passed through Riga. At the last minute my father retained several large bills, about one hundred dollars, "just in case." My mother stuffed a few into the stays of her corset, one or two into new heels on my father's shoes. The rest my father wrapped in newspaper and, just before we left, inserted in a private section of his anatomy.

Our great day of departure, deliberately or otherwise, fell on May 1, May Day, the biggest holiday in the Socialist calendar. I had chosen that morning to have a sore throat, with high fever. My mother, concerned that I might get stopped at the border by either the Russians or the Latvians, kept me submerged in cold water until we left for the station.

Regrets were expressed in behavior more than words. My father, a most unsentimental man, looked back at every street we passed. My mother tried to distract me by reading from a child's book. I was feeling terrible and didn't understand why we had to go anywhere that day.

When the train stopped at the border for the crossing formalities, my mother rushed me into the station's toilet to wash my face and hands with cold water. The border guards, it seemed, were busy celebrating. They stamped our papers, barely looked at us, and certainly didn't bother themselves about my temperature. In hardly any time we were across, silver glass holders, fever, and dollars. My father bought a bottle of wine from someone on the train, and we celebrated our own May Day. We were off to Avenue B.

There was an old Russian expression, "to take a trip to Riga," which meant to vomit. We planned to stay just long enough to get a night's rest—and the envelope with my father's money. In the morning I went with him to the office of the American firm to ask for the gentleman who had our envelope. "Oh, yes," we were told, "he was here, but he's gone back to New York."

Our spirits, refreshed by the Latvian sunlight, suddenly sagged.

"Oh, yes . . . he left this envelope for you. It has your name on it. Schneideris." Indifference and innocence, that wonderfully American combination we've encountered many times since. My father took the unsealed envelope, quietly counted the two hundred dollars, and thanked everybody, including the fellow who had gone back to New York. By midday we were across the German border and on our way to Berlin.

In May 1923, the capital of the Weimar Republic was glittering with light and the excesses of runaway inflation. It was also full of Russian émigrés, all urging my father to make his medical career there. Berlin was civilized, clean, and beautiful, full of good things to eat, including bread and salt. Everybody seemed to be working hard. Theater and the other arts were flourishing. And they needed all the doctors they could get. We would be mad not to consider staying.

My father and mother spoke very little German, but it didn't matter. Russian-speaking pedestrians stopped us in the streets to make a fuss over me—something that had never happened in Moscow. I don't remember much that month except the zoo and a lot of bread with generous portions of sweet butter and salt. The hotel and food bill for all three of us, with some extras thrown in, was less than a dollar a day.

Berlin certainly offered a temptation for two young physicians, still Europeans and not quite sure what was to greet them on that other continent. My father, however, remained determined to get to America. Early in June I found myself on the North Sea, in the middle of a storm, taking many trips to Riga, and asking—through my wails—why we were not going to Southampton on a train. We finally debarked on the semi-enclosed Southampton docks with a few thousand other immigrants, all waiting in line for the next boat west. I didn't mind those docks. There were all sorts of interesting places in which to run and play. And the floor didn't move with the waves.

We remained there for several weeks, moving up a few feet or yards as ships to America came and went. We didn't pick our ship. Eventually, the White Star Line's S.S. *Homeric* picked us. The *Homeric* was a beautiful ship, but we soon discovered that our living quarters—in the lower end of what was not even tourist class—were little different from the Southampton docks, except hotter and darker; and, after we got going, smellier. I went back to my usual question: why couldn't we take a train?

Two days out—the trip was to take seven days—our living conditions improved radically. The *Homeric*'s medical staff soon discovered that not everyone had been properly examined before being piled aboard. There was serious risk of infection and disease, even an epidemic. The ship's doctors looked for assistance and found it in the form of two Russian doctors within one family. They enlisted the services of both, moving us up to first class, which was largely empty except when it was being used for hospital space. From the lower depths we were transported to the sundeck and given a clean, bright, airy bedroom, with real beds, not wooden bunks—as well as real stewards and stewardesses to take care of us.

In the dining room the waiters rolled carts containing practically the entire menu to our table and had us point to the dishes we wanted. My knowledge of food and drink was minimal. I hadn't encountered an orange before, nor ice cream, which we had with almost every meal, including breakfast. I was determined to make up for lost time.

One morning, about halfway out, I started to talk to an attractive, dark-haired young girl of about eighteen or nineteen, who was from Rumania and on her way to join her childhood sweetheart in Baltimore. In spite of the considerable difference in our ages, we hit it off immediately. She was lively and bright, with a marvelous sense of humor. I not only introduced her to my parents but also invited her to the first-class dining room to eat with us. More than sixty years later, Baltimoreans Betty and Leon Moss, now grandparents, remain my oldest friends in America. Their good cheer and good humor often kept me going through the toughest portions of my up-and-down existence in the theater.

My father, who had a habit, which I share, of collecting bits and pieces, saved the dinner menu from the night before we landed. His name, as the main speaker, was included; his topic: "Remarks." I don't remember a word of those remarks, but I do remember the ice-cream cake sitting resplendent on a table in the center of the room. I ate most of it.

Exactly fifty-nine years later, in a Westchester, New York, hospital for surgery, I discovered that my roommate had been on that same ship with me. His name, I. Kritchmar, was on the menu, although I had not remembered it until we compared stitches. The coincidence was almost unbelievable—and unbearable.

After a week at sea, the S.S. *Homeric* steamed into New York harbor shortly after dusk on July 4, 1923. Its excited passengers, crowding the rails to observe the sights, especially the Statue of Liberty, were more than startled to find the harbor suddenly ablaze with explosions. My father's first thought was that we had left one revolution to find another taking place in New York City. One of the ship's officers calmed everyone down by explaining that no one was shooting at us; it was just a birthday celebration for America. We were also informed that we had to spend the night at Ellis Island getting examined, questioned, and fumigated. Nothing was going to discourage us, though. We were at the end of our journey and the beginning of our new life. We thought.

Our carefully made arrangements with those Avenue B relatives had been fussed over in detail via several exchanges of letters in Berlin and in Southampton. One of those relatives, now known to us as the Mittersteins, was supposed to meet us and take us to a small hotel, where we would stay until either my mother or my father found work.

When we got to the waiting room, however, there were no Mittersteins. And even though we waited throughout the hot and impossibly muggy New York day, there was still no one, and no messages, either. My father, trying to master the New York telephone system without proper language or change, didn't know what to do. My mother, as usual at such moments of familial crisis, took me to the closest available bathroom. She made a mistake and went into the men's room, luckily without too many of them there at the moment.

However, in the men's lounge there was a middle-aged man on one of the wooden benches, reading a Yiddish newspaper. He must have heard my mother addressing me as "Avotchka," my usual diminutive. Looking up from the newspaper, he asked if our name could possibly be Schneider, pronounced by him Schneyder. It was our missing cousin. Why he chose the men's room for our family reunion remains as mysterious to me now as it was to us then.

His subsequent actions were no less mysterious. Despite the humid heat, he absolutely refused to let us waste our money on a taxi, insisting that the subway was easier and faster. He also let us know that we were going to stay with them on Avenue B. Several hours later and years older, having lugged all our worldly possessions up and down endless steps and in and out of countless doors, we arrived at a small walk-up railroad apartment on Avenue B at Second Street. The street, with its seemingly thousands of people walking back and forth, was as grimy as we were. The apartment, hotter than the street, hadn't been swept or cleaned in weeks. Dishes were piled up, practically rotting, in the cracked, stained—and only—sink. Flies buzzed in through torn and baggy screens. We were in America.

My mother, who had always prided herself on her neatness and cleanliness, tried to clean up the place. She bought clean new bedspreads for the iron military cots they were using, but at night the mattresses sagged so much and the tiny unventilated closet of a bedroom was so hot that we could not get any sleep. My mother stayed inside, washing me in the sink when there was water while my father walked outside.

Grandfather Malkin in Rostov had once told me that the difference between Europe and America was that in Europe horses were used to transport people and in America they only transported goods. It seemed to us in those first few hectic, humid days that those American horses were pulling everything right past our dirty windows. We wondered why we had come here and where we might go. Several times, in desperation, we thought of moving to a hotel, but that envelope with the dollars was getting too thin. And there were no jobs, yet.

My father took out an ad in the Russian-language newspaper *Novoye Russkaya Slovo* (still in existence and still accepting similar ads from similar newcomers), asking to hear from anyone who had lived in Rostov or knew either the Schneiders or the Malkins. We immediately discovered that we had friends in New York and even some additional, more sophisticated, relatives. We were invited to homes in more palatable sections of the city, fed from time to time, and given advice about jobs.

In a few weeks my parents got jobs, helping to care for the sick people at the Jewish Home for the Aged in Brooklyn. We moved to Brooklyn, to a clean room on Blake Avenue—a street with trees on it. Come September, I started first grade at a nearby school. The teacher, though sympathetic to a little lonely foreigner, was cross-eyed, and it took me a long time to get used to her. I wanted to run away but wasn't sure where to run. We wound up great friends, and as my English got better, I felt more at home.

On Sundays we would go into Prospect Park and roam around, or ride down Fifth Avenue in the open double-decker buses and look at the expensive shop windows. A real treat was an occasional ride across Forty-second Street, sitting sidesaddle on those old streetcars that once traversed the city from river to river. And once or twice we went out to Staten Island on the ferry to see the grand old lady of Liberty—without accompanying fireworks. Everything was a nickel: the subway, the bus, the streetcar, the ferry, the hot dogs, and the ice-cream cones.

My parents were studying English at a night school for adult foreigners, but somehow they never met up with Leo Rosten's H*Y*M*A*N K*A*P*L*A*N. My own English was improving daily, and I refused to speak any Russian at home. I started to stay up nights till all hours, hanging around little corner candy stores and egg-cream stands that also sold cigarettes and newspapers. I loved seeing the Sunday *Daily News* printed and out on the Wednesday before. I tried to look like, sound, and be as much like an "Amurrican" as possible. To me, America was New York.

Toward the end of the year, my father got an offer to serve his internship at Mount Sinai Hospital in Hartford, Connecticut. I tearfully discovered we were off again. My first birthday party in New York, on December 12, 1923—I was six—was a total disaster. First, my mother took me to see the film *Peter Pan*, with silent screen star Betty Bronson; but when Tinker Bell died, I cried so hard that she had to bring me home. Second, I had expressed a great wish for an electric train, and in the midst of neighbors, relatives, and birthday cake my father proudly presented me with a mechanical windup one. Lubricated by Tinker Bell, my eyes started again, and I ran into the bathroom, locked the door, and was not dislodged until my mother—equally tearful—promised me an electric train in the morning. My father couldn't understand what all the fuss was about. A few weeks later we were in Hartford, train and all.

GROWING UP ABSURDLY

1923–1929

Hartford—where, as it happened, some thirty years later I opened my first Broadway-bound show, *The Remarkable Mr. Pennypacker*—was a friendly, busy, clean town. I loved it. We lived in a slightly rusting neighborhood and a house, New England wooden, with a big yard. That backyard has stayed with me, because on many afternoons I filled it with a road-company version of the Moscow State Children's Theatre. Draping someone's used sheets over clotheslines and tree branches, my schoolmates and I performed all sorts of skits, sketches, and musical revues that soon made us famous—and infamous—throughout the neighborhood. We charged one or two pins and, later, pennies, usually winding up with enough to buy strawberry ice cream sodas of the type immortalized by Thornton Wilder in *Our Town*. Once I spent some pennies to see Conan Doyle's *The Lost World* at the Princess Theatre, in downtown Hartford. That was a marvelous visit to a world of wonders, terrors, and uncertainties. I can still see that rope bridge trembling over the chasm, those dinosaurs battling each other on the jungle cliffs.

My father's internship at Mount Sinai brought him only twenty-four dollars per month, plus room and board. In order to get us through that period, Mom stuffed rag dolls, sewed, and made herself useful in community organizations. I was becoming Americanized. My English was getting better, my Russian worse. I learned to play baseball and Red Line, and I was part of a Treehouse Club, although the treehouse was on the ground. I had more difficulty with American slang, especially the concept of "cut it out!"—a favorite at the time. My reply, "I don't have any scissors," always produced gales of laughter. It was a pleasant growing-up time, and I grew up—fast.

My father was doing well at the hospital and would have stayed on had he not taken notice of a flyer about State Board Examinations especially for foreign physicians being given in Baltimore. Baltimore was where Johns Hopkins Medical School was, and even in Russia he seemed to have heard of Hopkins. He took the exams and passed them, even though his English was sketchy and his school years long behind him. He also walked around Baltimore a lot and liked what he saw.

In the spring of 1925, he accepted a job with the Maryland State Tuberculosis Association, but somehow, instead of Johns Hopkins and Baltimore, we wound up in the village of Henryton, a place which made Nakhitchevan look like New York. Treatment for tuberculosis was then less understood than improvised, usually consisting of mountaintop air, rest, and hope. The Henryton Tuberculosis Sanatorium, having white doctors but only black patients, was tucked even further away from civilization than all the other sanatoriums; it was also my introduction to segregation. In Brooklyn and Hartford I had had black friends and schoolmates. Here I had none. I walked to the all-white school, a tiny ramshackle building at the end of a long trail through the woods. Classes were ramshackle, too, and my parents began to question our move south. One month later, my father was able to transfer to a larger (all-white) sanatorium at Mount Wilson, an hour from Baltimore. But no sooner did we begin to feel comfortable at Mount Wilson than we had to move again, this time to a remote country village called Sabillasville, down the hill from what is now Camp David.

The Sabillasville "San's" superintendent was Dr. Victor Francis Cullen, a bluff but kindly Teddy Roosevelt look-alike who was both statesman and visionary. The sanatorium had been his idea and was now his baby. It was expanding and needed new doctors. He met my parents, liked them both, and immediately offered them separate but equal jobs, my mother receiving the same salary as my father—something like forty dollars weekly.

Although I didn't realize it then, the sanatorium was *The Magic Mountain* brought to life. A large main structure, which looked like a twenties resort hotel, housed the more seriously ill patients, and a collection of smaller, longish one-story bungalows, called "the shacks," housed the ambulatory patients. In between were administration buildings, a post office, a general store, and the doctors' quarters.

My father's responsibility was to take care of the men's shacks, and he often had to move beds onto the porches at night so that the patients awoke with a coating of snow on their blankets—the combination of snow and fresh air was supposed to be the best cure. My mother took care of a portion of the main building and the entire children's section. She loved her work, her only problem being then—as throughout her professional life—to stop everybody, including some of the patients and other doctors, from calling her Mrs. Dr. Schneider or even Mrs. Schneider, while they were, of course, addressing my father as Dr. Schneider. She won many battles in her life but not, I'm afraid, this one. Dad liked the place, too, especially after Henryton and Mount Wilson. So did young Abram (who had long since Americanized his name to "Abraham"), even though he was upset when everyone continually assumed that he would become a third Dr. Schneider.

The only drawback to this idyllic existence was that the sanatorium was seven miles from the nearest town, Thurmont (a considerable distance in those car-less days), and more than sixty miles from Baltimore. Sabillasville was a bit over two miles away, and consisted of a cluster of small wooden houses, a general store, a Polish tailor's shop, and a clapboard one-room schoolhouse, all of whose seven grades were taught by an elderly schoolmaster named Mr. Monahan.

Mr. Monahan had a bristly black mustache, wore a starched collar and string tie, and looked very much like a more severe and heavier Brooks Atkinson. He owned a shiny black horse that pulled his black leather and iron carriage to school every morning, occasionally allocating his students the honor of picking them up if they were doing well in their lessons. If not, he'd pass them right by.

Most mornings, I took a shortcut through the fields, picking fresh tomatoes or radishes in season to munch along the way, navigating through the San's gigantic open sewage disposal site, and occasionally dipping my shoes into the creek—pronounced, of course, "crick"—and having to dry my toes, as well as my socks, in the wonderfully warm pot-bellied stove that sat amid the seven rows of the schoolroom. When the fields were too wet or covered with snow, I had to go by road, always hoping that Old Man Monahan would feel kindly toward me that day.

Because no other housing was available, we lived in one large room in the bachelor doctors' quarters, which included a recreation room where I learned to sharpen the fiber needles of an old windup Victrola, whistle "Ramona" and "Stars and Stripes Forever," and shoot pool well enough to beat most of the doctors—and fool a lot of people in subsequent years. My parents ate their meals with the medical staff, and at first I had mine with the children patients. But my mother became worried that I might get infected, so I walked about a mile down the hill to have meals at the Browns' place, a sort of informal neighborhood boardinghouse. My breakfasts came out of our old ice-box, which was literally that, with great chunks of ice chopped out of the sanatorium's sawdust-covered icehouse. At the Browns', I discovered the great American Sunday dinner: roast chicken wih gravy, mashed or sweet potatoes with more gravy, and peas as big as marbles, and sometimes as hard.

I also discovered that the Browns' son, Jimmy, didn't really want to play with me afterward because I had killed Christ. Not knowing exactly who Christ was, much less why anyone would think I had caused his demise, I asked my mother, who tried hard to explain but couldn't. Jews and Catholics were not welcome in Sabillasville; the Ku Klux Klan burnt crosses regularly. Taunting me for being Jewish became common for most of the local kids (and occasionally their parents). Sometimes the abuse was sincere, sometimes it came for the sake of inflicting cruelty; inevitably it resulted in tears, anger, and—whenever it got physical—flight. I never learned to use my fists well, especially against larger opponents, but I did learn to run fast, a skill that later helped me as a track man in high school and college. Nothing is without its compensations.

In a few months the bachelor quarters gave way to a small cottage of our own, with separate bedrooms and a real kitchen with a real screen door that slammed all the time. The staff gave a surprise American housewarming, with everyone bringing a useful gift for our new home. My parents were touched and happy; I was grateful that I no longer had to walk up and down that hill and "take it" from Jimmy Brown and the others.

Some months after we had come, a Polish boy of my own age, eight or nine, and related to the tailor's family, arrived in the village. Both outsiders, he and I hit it off. We ate our sandwiches together, shared secret fantasies, walked the creek's stones together. One day the boy was ambushed on his way home by a pack of schoolmates, beaten severely, and left helpless and crying in a ditch. When Mr. Monahan questioned him, he said that it was I who had beaten him, no one else. I couldn't believe he had accused me, but he would no longer talk to or even look at me.

My parents and Mr. Monahan knew I couldn't have been guilty. They explained that the boy was afraid to name the culprits and was complimenting me by accusing me, but I never recovered from what I considered a horrible betrayal. Friendship, already not abundant, became an even more cherished commodity, and betrayal, the harshest pain of all. My sense of separation from the local kids grew. When they weren't making fun of my Jewishness, they would mock me for being a "Rooshian," although most of them didn't even know where or what "Rooshia" was. "Did you have this in Rooshia?" "Did you have that?" From pencils to watermelon. Even under Mr. Monahan's relatively sympathetic tutelage, I had a tough time. So I concentrated on my schoolwork, improved my mathematical abilities—we were in the fourth grade just getting into fractions—and tried to read the entire contents of the Waynesboro, Pennsylvania, library seven miles in the other direction.

After about a year, the funny little one-room schoolhouse, gave way to a more imposing, and uglier, two-room plaster pillbox set in the middle of some fields on the far edge of town. No one was happy with the move. Mr. Monahan was replaced by two "normal school"–type cold fish named Harold and Marian Moser, Mr. and Mrs. The Mosers took a special dislike to my being Jewish and made no attempt to hide it. Mrs. Moser called everyone else by his or her first name, me by my last. When I remonstrated with her, she responded by mispronouncing it as A-bram, even though she was quite capable of correctly pronouncing the first name of our sixteenth President, whom I now considered my namesake. She sneered at my occasional trouble with certain English words. When I mispronounced "usury" during our morning Bible reading one day, she mocked me in front of the class and said that as a Jew I should know especially well how to pronounce that word. Once during a softball game, when a kid's bat flew out of his hand and hit me in the groin, she blamed me for standing in the wrong place.

Once when I was ten, I was walking home past the house of Paul Wise, a young man of about twenty-six or twenty-seven, known for his hostility toward Jews and Catholics. Paul was working on his lawn, and I was daydreaming as usual. Without a word of warning he grabbed me and, sputtering expletives, started hitting me as hard as he could. By the time I managed—bloody, bruised, and dirty—to scramble away, Paul had beaten me up fairly badly. I got my first trip to Frederick, thirty miles away, and the county court, where I testified at his trial; he got a six-month jail term.

The unfriendliness of my daily environment didn't so much embitter me as it made me withdraw into myself. I played by myself. I read every book available, from the San's own collection and from Waynesboro, where we went once a month to shop. I'd bring home a handful of books—adventure stories, history, romance, occasionally something that went deeper. By the time I was nine, I had read both *Ben-Hur* and *Anna Karenina*, crying copious tears at the latter. At twelve I got most of the way through *War and Peace*, especially appreciating the battle scenes. Usually, I read about Tom Swift and his various inventions, *The Rover Boys* or *The Boy Allies*, and, best of all, the campaigns of the British Empire in G. A. Henty's seemingly limitless succession of historical romances: *With Clive in India, With Montcalm at Quebec, The Cat of Bubastes*, et al. Henty is almost unread today, but his books were my equivalent of *Shogun* and *Hawaii Five-O*.

And, always, I spent the days acting out all the stories, populating the fields and caves around the sanatorium with the heroes of every period and clime. I quoted Kipling as I had once known Pushkin, by the yard, usually at the top of my voice and leading a charge against the enemy. I replayed most of the battles fought by Caesar, Hannibal, Alexander, and Achilles, usually knocking down lots of tall grass and wheat stalks.

Then there were the movies. There was no theater of any kind around Sabillasville. New York was on the moon, and even Baltimore was too far away, Washington somehow a foreign country. The "theater" of my impressionable youth was all in my mind—as well as on the silent screen. Sometimes we saw a movie on our monthly visits to Waynesboro, and three or four nights a week the patients and staff at the sanatorium saw the latest films free of charge. Three or four nights a week, for five years, I went to the movies for free, except when misbehavior or a slightly too sexy title kept me tearfully at home with Henty. And sometimes my friend in the projection booth let me carry the octagonal metal boxes, covered with tags proclaiming their previous travels. The sanatorium could afford only one projector, so I thought that all moviegoing was interrupted as many times as there were reels.

These interruptions—with the auditorium lights coming on and the patients wandering off—did not stop me from being transported to many magical places by all those magical names: Tom Mix, Hoot Gibson, Milton Sills, Chaplin and Keaton, Charles "Buddy" Rogers and Richard Arlen, Betty Bronson (of *Peter Pan* fame) and Billie Dove, Vilma Banky, and Rod La Roque. I also knew every feature and flicker of expression—or nonexpression—ever demonstrated by Richard Dix, Anna Q. Nilsson, Corinne Griffith, Thomas Meighan, and a thousand lesser lights and shadows. I dreamt of them and loved them all; they were what I wanted to be when I grew up.

Somewhere along the line, the Sunday supplement of Hearst's *Baltimore American* advertised a projector and several exciting reels of film to anyone who sold thirty packets of needles (plus $3.50 for postage and handling). For the next month, I sold needles to everyone at the sanatorium, with or without TB, especially my mother. The projector eventually came and eventually worked, although the film kept breaking. My colleague in the projection booth gave me some smelly banana oil with which to splice it, and pieces of films that had torn off during showings—or which he purposely cut off for me. I began to show the films, mostly to myself, projected on a wall in my bedroom, with my own sound accompaniment. I showed them so many times that my mother got concerned that I wasn't playing outside enough. When I was playing outside, she worried that I wasn't inside, reading. My father refused to have anything to do with the process because the jerkiness of the projector hurt his eyes. The smell of the banana oil drove both him and my mother up the wall; I can still smell it myself. We also came across packets of needles for years.

As my sanatorium stay continued, a few playmates did emerge—those who were either genuinely interested in me or else desperately lonely themselves. Joe Curfman, who became a teacher and social worker, had a mother who made thin, tasty pancakes on an old wood-burning stove in the middle of her kitchen. Harold Law had curly red hair, a sly earthy sense of humor, and—at the times when he was my best friend—a stack of cartoon strips, including Popeye, the Katzenjammer Kids, and Tarzan, which he had been clipping out of the daily papers for years. I think my later penchant for cutting out all sorts of things from newspapers must have been stimulated by the size of his Tarzan collection. Finally, there was my hero, Glenn Lewis, descended from an old-time farming family, handsome in a severe dark sort of way, simultaneously romantic and skeptical. Glenn was the only one of all of them at school who treated me as an equal, without condescension. Glenn was the one I wanted to be like.

Closer at hand, Mrs. Victor F. Cullen, a Baltimore society beauty some thirty years younger than her distinguished husband, our superintendent, arrived at the sanatorium after years of being wooed. Dr. Victor F. Cullen built her a beautiful stone mansion, containing what seemed to me every possible luxury and amenity, although it was probably less fancy than most postwar suburban houses in any large city—right next door to our more modest cottage.

Ethel Bell Cullen was without question as witty and as glamorous as any of my screen heroines: a Southern beauty, delicate and tough, sophisticated, educated, and alive. Once she'd had a baby girl and established her household, however, she became bored rigid. She needed not luxury but excitement, people, parties. The dull routine of life at the sanatorium, even as the superintendent's beloved and beautiful wife, couldn't satisfy her. To keep from cracking up, she withdrew into the quiet shadows of her living room, drinking moderately and reading excessively. She read mostly the lighter things—detective stories, mysteries, romances—anything to get her attention away from the respectability and predictability around her. She read night and day—scattering books all over the house—entertained the other physicians as required by her position, brought up her daughter as well as she could out in the sticks, and stayed completely loyal to her husband. And after she had read her books, she passed them along to me.

Mrs. Cullen was the only person at the sanatorium who never asked me whether I was going to be a doctor. She knew I wasn't. More, she didn't particularly think I should. If doctors were people who shut themselves up and spent their lives in places like Sabillasville, who wanted to be a doctor?

Mrs. Cullen had a niece, also an Ethel, also a Bell, about the same age as I. The younger Ethel became my secret love. When she visited the Cullens, I was invited in to drink lemonade. Once I sat with her on the steps of the Cullen house, speechless, for what seemed hours. She was as radiant as Vilma Banky, and as unattainable. Even Mrs. Cullen, friendly and understanding as she was about my intellectual life, did not entirely encourage any relationship. Books I was free to borrow, not nieces. It was a great lesson to me not only about my peasant status but on the whole caste system of the American South. After all, though I wasn't exactly black, it was pretty close.

There were other characters at the sanatorium, most of them happily forgotten, though a few remain in memory for whatever reason. The doctors on the whole seemed a strange bunch. Anyone who chose to salt his life away on this lonely mountaintop had to be a misfit of one kind or another. The nurses seemed more normal, including some very attractive ones; the sanatorium was a training ground that they left as soon as they could. The ones who stayed on became dowagers of a hollow empire, drinking tea and crocheting tablecloths and making a fuss over me at proper intervals. The staff included Miss Swain in occupational therapy, who taught me basket weaving; Alec, a refugee from the Ukraine, who tended the gardens, raised rabbits, and taught me to use hand tools; and Hans, a little German fellow, who, naked to the waist, baked the sanatorium's bread in long, narrow, underground ovens, and let me watch him once in a while.

Next door to us, there was another physician couple, Dr. Wilkins and his wife, Dr. Reese. He was a spindly, angular, and unshaven Dickensian character; she had a mulatto-dark complexion, a large physique, and an equally expansive personality. They had both been missionaries in India and had a vast collection of photographs, slides, and stories to prove it. In their dark and musty house—the blinds always drawn as if to keep out the hot Indian sunlight—they had me watch endless slides of holy men (including a very thin one called Gandhi), people washing themselves in the Ganges, and a whole class of people called Untouchables, who touched me the most.

Dr. Reese and Dr. Wilkins had an "untouchable" of their own, a daughter who was just a year or two younger than I, round-faced, cheerful, and very active. She was totally unmanageable, however, because she was what we now call brain-damaged. Today's doctors might label her autistic. Whenever her parents went off anywhere, the girl had to be tied up to a stake in their backyard, where I played with her, listened to her whines and gurgles, and tried to penetrate her aloneness. I spent almost as much time with her as her parents did, grew intensely fond of her, and felt that I was making progress in "reaching" her.

One afternoon, for one moment I almost did. We were sitting on the ground, touching each other. I was humming some ordinary Russian tune which I'd picked up from my mother. She was restlessly making her usual sounds. Suddenly, she stopped and looked at me. Her right arm came up and she touched my cheek. She smiled spontaneously and then began to laugh, not her normal harshly guttural sound, but a little girl's clear laugh, direct and untroubled. It was as though she recognized something and was trying to tell me something, her eyes under her soup-bowl haircut looking straight into mine.

Then the telephone rang, and we heard Dr. Wilkins' high-pitched nasal tones out of the depths of their shrouded living room. That voice seemed to pull the girl back to wherever her real self lurked, and it was all over. I never got her to look at me in that soft way again.

BALTIMORE BOY

1930–1939

My parents always told me that they left the sanatorium so that I wouldn't have to go to the second-rate high school in Thurmont. I'd had a look behind its peeling yellowed walls and watched some nervously bored students cut up a frog in a dingy underground dungeon of a biology lab, deciding immediately that I would hate everything about the place. My loving mother sympathized and began a subtle but persistent campaign to persuade my father to move to more civilized climes.

As it happened, my father's spirit of adventure—always lurking beneath the surface of his steadfastness—had been aroused after five years in Sabillasville. All those perambulating patients and overly cautious physicians were beginning to bore him. He had acquired a 1927 square-bodied Chevrolet, and our old crystal set—purchased in 1928 to hear Al Smith's nomination for President—had given way to a huge Atwater Kent radio with a round speaker and three dials that required meticulous synchronization. We listened regularly to Lowell Thomas, Old Man Sunshine, and Stoopnagle and Bud. One summer we drove all the way to a rural resort in Connecticut, where everyone spoke only Russian. After our citizenship papers came through in 1928, we even went as far as Quebec. Dad was exploring.

When the Playground Athletic League in Baltimore announced that it was looking for a physician couple to examine Maryland high-school students for TB and other diseases, Dad immediately expressed interest. The pay was more than both my parents made at the sanatorium, and somebody said that if we located in a sprawling suburb called Forest Park, I could attend a good high school.

We moved to Baltimore in the late summer of 1930. The Depression was on, and Dad had lost three hundred dollars in Cities Service gold bonds, but no sad thoughts remained. After Sabillasville Elementary, Forest Park High School was huge (2400 students), overpowering, and incomprehensible. I was lost, unsure, and alone, and afraid to share my concerns with my parents, who had abandoned their rich and fruitful lives for my sake. Reeling from the double task of adjusting not only to a large city but to a big-city school that taught Latin, literature, and something called "civics," I was also approaching my thirteenth birthday, with just enough time for a crash course in the ritual of a Bar Mitzvah. My family was not religious in any way; we were Jewish because other people felt we were. I do not recall a single occasion in Russia or Sabillasville where we even spoke of going to synagogue. Nevertheless, the fact of my Bar Mitzvah was neither discussed nor questioned. No one, certainly, ever knew how terrified I was of botching the whole ceremony. Having to memorize what seemed like half the Torah in a language that was utterly incomprehensible, I regretted more than once forsaking Thurmont's frogs.

On the day of my Bar Mitzvah, I awoke earlier than usual to find, most disappointingly, a fountain pen beside my bed rather than the usual birthday toy or book. A chemistry set eventually materialized, however, threatening my prompt departure for the synagogue. My reading of the Torah didn't shock anyone but myself. I was appalled at having to move the hand-pointer vaguely on cue from line to line, intoning words of whose meaning I had no idea, and realizing that I was in no way serving my religion or my country or my inner self, but only acting out an agreed-upon pretense. The rabbi—a staunch liberal, an orator of eminence, and a leader of the Baltimore Reformed Judaism community—shook my hand warmly and took off on a rousing sermon, of which I recall not one word.

What bothered me most, however, was the party afterward. Our middle-floor apartment was far from large, and my bedroom was minimal—a cot-sized bed, a small desk, some books, and a sort of stamp collection. Over the bed there was a small framed magazine print of a teenager reading in bed, the glow from his bedside lamp lighting up the kind of youthful idealized Norman Rockwell countenance I always yearned to possess. I kept that print for years until the plays of Thornton Wilder took its place in my heart.

The party was held in the living and dining rooms and attended by all my parents' friends. I spent the whole afternoon in my bedroom, among coats thrown over my bed, the door closed, playing quietly with my chemistry set and talking with the one friend my father had allowed me to invite. Through the wall, I heard the laughter and revelry of all those so-called adults celebrating *my* coming of age.

My mother did bring us some tea and extra-large portions of cake, but that did not dispel the dreariness of the occasion. She was radiantly happy and looked especially youthful and beautiful in a long white evening dress she had bought for the occasion. I could not bring myself to tell her how empty I felt. I have never, except on rare occasions, set foot in a synagogue again, although the day my son should have been Bar Mitzvahed—and wasn't—was hard to take. Away from him, in California somewhere, I watched the film *Sunday, Bloody Sunday*, with its moving Bar Mitzvah scene, and wept without stop.

Forest Park's child social lion was Marvin "Buddy" Hammerman. Buddy was a dark-haired, eternally cheerful kid, about my age but infinitely more adept at life. He was friendly with everyone, had money on Saturday nights, and knew which corners and which drugstores were most promising for which purposes. He was also enrolled in the Park School, a prestigious private institution containing the prettiest, brightest, and wealthiest Jewish girls in the Western hemisphere. Buddy was an "operator." Tom Sawyer's ability to get his fence painted was nothing compared to Buddy's prowess. In return for a silent-screen smile and some fluid goodwill, I raked his leaves, tended his garbage, and cheerfully ran his errands.

Many years later I was happy to learn that Buddy Hammerman, a wealthy businessman/lawyer, got tangled up in the problems of his partner and client, Spiro T. Agnew. Spiro, as it happens, also went to Forest Park, two years behind me. I always felt sorry for him. He seemed very scrawny, very sad, very mysteriously named—was it Spiro Agnew or Agnew Spiro? People made fun of his Greek ancestry and occasionally roughed him up. He was an underdog, my favorite kind of hero. What I most appreciated about him, though, was that he took some of the pressure off the Jewish kids, especially me, who were also mocked, chased, and even beaten on occasion. I could never understand how Spiro got so tall and broad by the time he became Vice President.

As my parents ran out of schools within a day's drive at which they could examine students, they had to venture into Maryland's backwaters, leaving the apartment on Monday mornings and coming back Friday afternoons. In between, they left their one and only to the mercies and services of a very ancient, very tall, very skinny, and very lovely black lady named Frances, whose last name I never knew as it was not then the custom to ask or tell. I adored Frances, confided in Frances, was loved and cared for by Frances for more hours than by my mother. I even thought Frances was a better cook—at everything but red cabbage borscht with a bit of braised beef thrown in. When Frances had to leave us years later for her own family problems somewhere down south, I cried a long time.

Surviving my thirteenth birthday was not the only shattering experience in my new role of "Baltimore boy." I had to get used to paying for movies, a rather difficult adjustment since my father had not yet learned the American word "allowance." In the thirties, Gable, Harlow, Shearer, Cooper, and Colbert were always on display if one had the price of admission—anywhere from a nickel to a quarter, depending on the elegance of the theater. I read every movie magazine I could borrow or abscond with, and kept copious scrapbooks of all the stars.

I saw more exotic films, such as *Metropolis* and *Dr. Caligari* at the Little Theatre, Baltimore's tiny "art house." I also saw the original *Frankenstein*, *The Bat*, and *The Gorilla* several times, preferring the first even though it haunted my sleep for months. Once, I even went to the downtown Hippodrome, the poshest place in town at thirty-five cents, to see not only *King Kong* but an hour of accompanying vaudeville. I sat there from nine o'clock in the morning until nearly six, and I must have seen Fay Wray's hairy friend five times, as well as a fellow who turned water into wine. My worried mother called the police and was relieved when I finally made it home on my own.

For variety, I went down to the Bowery-like environment of lower Baltimore Street, to invest my weekly riches in a freak show, whose obvious seaminess and fraud in no way diminished my enjoyment. I loved street entertainment: clowns, circuses, magicians, jugglers, card manipulators—any gathering of more than three persons immediately drew my interest. Once I held a lady's legs while a magician named Thurston sawed her in half. When my end slid out about four feet, I almost fainted, but I didn't let go. I was also enthralled by mechanical puzzles, gadgets, and intellectual conundrums. When we went to the Century of Progress in Chicago in 1933, I spent hours watching a machine demonstrate the law of averages by switching the location of a golden ball in the midst of a repeated pattern of several hundred steel balls. I was sure that if only I could watch often enough, the law would be repealed.

Eventually, as I discovered Einstein and the theory of relativity, I also discovered science fiction in the pulp magazines *Astounding Stories*, *Amazing Stories*, and *Wonder Stories*, which were read at one's peril. No one dared show an *Astounding* cover—with one of Hugo Gernsback's bug-eyed galactic monsters clutching a ravishing blonde—in his home, and to be caught in class with one inside the cover of a geography book was grounds for expulsion. This did not stop me from testing both these locales, and I built up quite a respectable collection of back issues.

Next door to the back-issue shop was a movie house that showed two horror films, a comedy, a Buck Rogers or Flash Gordon serial, and a preview of coming attractions—all for a nickel. I began to go every Saturday, spending another nickel on the heart-rending choice of either an *Astounding* or an *Amazing*, and then walking home because I'd run out of nickels. Usually, I wore out fifteen cents worth of shoe leather, as my mother used to remind me. My father, luckily, knew nothing of the affair. He was busy reading medical magazines or listening to newscaster Lowell Thomas declaim the day's events.

To camouflage my Saturday excursions, I developed a habit of mentioning that I was going to the library. My parents had the Russian-Jewish respect for the absolute eminence of print, no matter who the author or what the subject; reading was an educational experience ultimately connected to "making a living." So, my Saturdays began early in the morning at the Pratt Library, where I read through the entire files of *Popular Science* and *Popular Mechanics*, found everything I could on space and the atom, tried to read Einstein in the original math, and even discovered the Michelson-Morley experiment, which established the constant velocity of light. I also read about the Zulu Empire, the First World War, Theodore Roosevelt, the sources of the Nile—anything to keep me out of the house. I may have read a play or two along the way, but I have no recollection of it. So far as I was concerned, the contemporary theater was on film.

At school, I gradually emerged from my small-town cocoon of shyness and began to feel more at home. I tried out for the track team and got my letter, became a cheerleader, and eventually joined the honor society, the student court, the stamp club, and the debate team—everything but the dramatics club, the Masquers. Persuaded by my accelerated-English teacher, Miss Angela M. Browning, I participated in a citywide oratorical contest on the aims and merits of President Franklin D. Roosevelt's National Recovery Administration—a contest in which I rather surprisingly triumphed over thousands of rivals. Not even President Roosevelt's standing me up on a promised trip to the White House frayed my newly aroused spirits, though it taught me, at a relatively early age, to beware of the promises of politicians. At the suggestion of our principal, a cherubic Victorian gentleman by the name of Glenn Owens, who got to know me when I unflinchingly braved a football injury's fourteen stitches in his office, I got involved in student politics. This hubris vanished when I lost the election for president of the student body because, as a member of my homeroom class blithely informed me, I was Jewish.

Baltimore at that time was still a sleepy southern village with only a few cultural scenes: the Lyric Opera House, to which the Met came yearly; the Peabody Conservatory of Music, with its weekend concerts; Ford's Theatre, a beautiful old cello of a legitimate theater; the more modest Maryland, housing Broadway attractions; the Vagabonds, a fairly decent community theater; and the Greengots, Abraham and Sonia, who introduced me to the subculture of Baltimorean intelligentsia, none of whom I really knew until after I had read and seen Chekhov. In spite of this, I stuck pretty much to the movies, science fiction, and the Greengots' weekly issue of *Collier's* magazine, until one day, by accident, everything changed.

My oldest friend, Betty Moss—the girl I'd "picked up" on the ship from Southampton to New York—subscribed to the Theatre Guild series at Ford's, but she was some months pregnant with her first child and not feeling well enough to attend. Would I like to go with her husband, Leon, to see Ina Claire in S. N. Behrman's *Biography*? I had never been to Ford's, or heard of either Miss Claire or Mr. Behrman, but seeing a show free was still almost a conditioned reflex, not to be refused.

That accidental journey to a Ford's matinee set me, at seventeen, on my life's direction. The play did not entirely impress me, but Miss Claire's presence and performance did. I was overwhelmed by her voice, her acting, the way she spoke, walked, wore her clothes, and settled into the sofa. That afternoon, I discovered that theater at its best was more satisfying than movies, books, or even running the hundred-yard dash in ten seconds.

I started going to the theater as often as I could afford it, and sometimes when I could not—going without meals, or ushering for my admission. I saw Walter Huston and his wife, Nan Sunderland, in *Dodsworth*; Ethel Barrymore in Maugham's *The Constant Wife*; and Walter Hampden in *Cyrano*. At one point, the fledgling University Players occupied the Maryland, and the enchanting Margaret Sullavan and her handsome husband, Henry Fonda, were playing the leads in *The Farmer Takes a Wife*. When Miss Sullavan left for Hollywood to play in *Little Man, What Now?*, the ushering crew (myself among them), considering her departure a rank betrayal not only of her art but also her man, took up a collection for poor deserted Mr. Fonda, who, we heard, was living on rice.

I saw the Lunts in *Idiot's Delight*—even though matinee tickets in the balcony had zoomed to $2.20 each (my previous high was $1.10)—and took a date, my absolute idol of an unattainable WASP girlfriend, a peach-complexioned Annette Challis, on whom I'd had a mad crush since my first days at Forest Park. Annette, sorry to say, left me for a later date at five that afternoon, but the Lunts were worth any sacrifice.

Best of all, I was able to see the Group Theatre when its company came down to Ford's. Their first show was Lee Strasberg's production of Sidney Kingsley's *Men in White*. I admired the clinical precision and almost poetic ambiance of its hospital scenes, and thought that Alexander Kirkland and the company were marvelous in their reality and teamwork. The second production, however, *Awake and Sing*—with Harold Clurman's original Broadway cast of Stella Adler, Morris Carnovsky, Sanford Meisner, Roman ("Bud") Bohnen, Robert Lewis, and Art Smith—made me realize that Ina Claire was not alone. Nor was her way the only one. *Awake and Sing* evoked such a sense of human truth and character richness that I was completely taken out of myself. I laughed and cried, and wanted to stay to see it over again; if the show had been a circus, I would have run away with it. I ran backstage to get everybody's autograph.

Odets' titans seemed somewhat diminished backstage, more human and subdued, but not enough to lose their glamour. I remember Robert Lewis—who had played Uncle Morty—coming out of his dressing room, wiping his bald head with a towel and yelling in New Yorkese. They all gave me their autographs willingly but detachedly. No one said much or even smiled, including Stella, who never once looked at me while she was signing my program. The evening was ending with a dull, nonartistic thud.

I continued to go to the theater, although my autograph-hunting toned down considerably. I joined the Masquers, and at the urging of my unorthodox and irrepressible French teacher, Fred "Baldy" Moore, I played the title role in Hugo's *Hernani*—in French. I also organized a group of friends who toured one-act plays around Baltimore on weekends, myself adapting the scripts (and changing the titles so that we wouldn't have to pay royalties). I snared the coveted George M. Cohan part in our senior-class production of *Seven Keys to Baldpate,* and saved the show one evening when someone messed up a familiar cue and got us out of the first act and into the third. During my senior year, I also paid an elderly English actor—whose name, Phidelah Rice, lingers in my memory together with his profile and sonority—the not inconsiderable sum of three dollars an hour to teach me to say, "Around the rugged rock the ragged rascal ran." Under Ina Claire's enduring spell, I was beginning to enjoy being let loose, even a little lost, in the wilds of the theater.

Extracurricularly lost, that is. No thought of the theater as a career or profession had entered my mind. If it had, my father would have quickly removed it. From the time I could listen, my father had taught me that the basis of life was a regular income, no matter how small or how earned. "After all," he often said, "do I like everything I'm doing?" Everyone destined me to become a doctor, like my mother and father, but as an early believer in dialectic, I determined that this was the one thing I would not become. I knew too much about the backstage machinations in hospitals, remembering one incident in which a resident had masterfully removed a patient's lung, but removed the wrong one, leaving the diseased lung intact. Furthermore, with medical uncles and cousins on several continents, I figured there were too many doctors in the family already.

My favorite subjects remained mathematics and physics. I wanted to become a theoretical physicist, splendidly isolated, doing research in a beautifully equipped laboratory and collecting regular paychecks. I applied to a variety of colleges boasting high-ranking physics programs, and—because I graduated first in my class—received scholarships to the University of Chicago (known as the place where Jewish professors taught Protestant students Catholic theology) and Johns Hopkins University, in Baltimore. Johns Hopkins was much closer and also less expensive—even though I could no longer live at home since my parents had left Baltimore for better jobs at the Glenn Dale Tuberculosis Sanatorium near Washington D.C. (where my father became chief resident) during my senior year at Forest Park.

I entered Johns Hopkins in the fall, my adviser glancing at my scholastic record and assigning me to an advanced physics class mostly populated by six-foot, two-hundred-pound genius engineers and a projective geometry class taught by a professor newly arrived from a year with Einstein at Princeton. Glowing in anticipation of a brilliant scientific career, I also tried out for the first dramatic club production of the season, Edwin Justus Mayer's *The Firebrand*, and, surprisingly, landed a small role alongside another young hopeful, Stanley Prager, who also became a professional director. On the side, I wrote for the newspaper—including occasional drama reviews—and ran on the track team.

Not on the side, I struggled with math and physics, and to my continued amazement (and growing despair), I found that advanced physics was much too advanced. I hated the class more and more, especially the laboratory work, which never seemed to come out right. My adviser suggested that I start over again with beginning physics. I, however, struggled to an "H" (the equivalent of an "A") in the advanced course. On my projective geometry midterm, I salvaged—through Herculean effort—one and a half of the ten problems provided by our smiling ex-Einsteinian. Only four members of the class were able to solve any; one fellow, a genius named Strobel, got all ten. That same genius, however, was having trouble with freshman English literature, and I wound up writing most of his themes for him. I reveled in Marlowe's rolling metaphors in *Tamburlaine the Great*, read *Beowulf* aloud at midnight, and even enjoyed our professor's somewhat heavy renditions of *Hamlet* and *Measure for Measure*. Thoreau seemed more fun than thermodynamics. Something was seriously askew.

I thought of switching majors but had spent too many years focusing on physics to shed my intellectual skin that easily. I remember sitting in my rented room one evening—lights out and tears unstemmed by my mother's gentle but nonreassuring words—feeling the end of the world had come. My father didn't know what all the fuss was about. So what if physics didn't come easily. Nothing had come easily for him either.

That summer of 1936, I returned to Glenn Dale to think and read and play some tennis with Gladys and Sadye, girls I was courting. To save my sanity, as well as the peace of the household, I enrolled in a couple of English courses at the University of Maryland: "Writing" and "Play Production for Teachers," both taught by a witty and scholarly skeptic named Charles Hale. I wrote stories and essays in one class and had a ball, acting, directing, stage-managing in the other class. Hale took a liking to me and cast me in a one-act play by A. A. Milne called *The Man in the Bowler Hat*. He also encouraged me to face my own reality: maybe the world of theoretical physics was not my natural habitat.

I was ready to leave physics, but not yet ready to take on a career in the theater. Fed by the examples of Vincent Sheean and John Gunther,

I decided to become a newspaperman, preferably a foreign correspondent, complete with trenchcoat. All summer long I investigated other schools and other courses. I decided on the University of Michigan, large enough and far enough away to lick my wounds in privacy.

When practically on the train, I discovered that Michigan had compulsory ROTC, a requirement my compassionate, pacifistic self utterly rejected. The University of Wisconsin was, however, free of ROTC and also boasted a journalism school, and even though someone suggested that it really wasn't so hot, I had no more time for changes. As tearfully as Anna Karenina, I boarded the train and disappeared into the American heartland.

The tears continued for some time. I discovered that Madison—despite its fearless sifting and winnowing of truth—was a town in which it was tough for a Jewish student to find a place to live. I trudged the streets for days, to be asked over and over again if I was a Jew, and having the door slammed in my face after an affirmative answer. Eventually, I hit on the tack of answering, "No, I'm Mohammedan and I have my wives with me," getting a modicum of satisfaction from the looks I received.

After almost deciding to reboard the train and head for home, I found lodgings of sorts, a somewhat smelly furnished room and three smelly meals served out of a communal pot. The room cost $2.50 weekly, and the meals another $2.75. With subsequent improvements, in both rooms and meals, I managed my entire Wisconsin stay on less than ten dollars weekly, including laundry, movies, sundries, and an occasional date. Out-of-state tuition was one hundred dollars per semester.

I discovered to my dismay that the fellow who had warned me about the journalism department was correct; it wasn't so good. After a semester, I decided that I could learn more about journalism by working for the university's *Daily Cardinal*, and I began to look for a conveniently accessible new major. Now an expert at shifting curricula, I shifted my way into political science, a floor below in the same building, without a quiver. I was now going to steep myself in international relations—a propitious choice since it required the least number of hours—and still have all sorts of time left over for other quests, including a comparative literature minor and a flock of courses chosen for their instructors: comp lit's gentlemanly Philo Buck (who had the absolute gift of turning a page of prose into the most wondrous work of creation), Wallace Stegner and Helen White of the English department, Fred Burkhardt in philosophy, Harold Taylor in history, and Grayson Kirk in my own department—

the latter three gentlemen going on to eminent careers as university presidents, at Bennington, Sarah Lawrence, and Columbia, respectively. I also took a most enlightening course in contemporary drama from Samuel Arnold Greene Rogers, of the French department. In spite of his consummate shyness, Professor Rogers introduced me to the major works of the modern theater, including Georg Kaiser's *Gas*, Charles Vildrac's *S.S. Tenacity*, and plays by Schnitzler, Strindberg, Pirandello, and above all, Chekhov. I'm afraid I don't remember much of what he said, but I know that without him I would not have read and cared about those plays.

I also wended my way through the *Daily Cardinal* hierarchy as reporter, feature writer, book reviewer, and drama critic. A gentle and slightly unrepresentative New Yorker named Morton Newman was editor-in-chief. His reign, quiet as it was, precipitated a campus struggle over the supposed invasion of "loud New York Jews," culminating in Newman's dismissal, a strike by the staff, openly bitter and harsh words on both sides, and an all-campus referendum in which Newman's dismissal was confirmed by the slimmest of majorities. Prominent on our side, and distinguished by his sanity under fire, was Mort's brother, Edwin Newman, a lowly reporter who subsequently went on to great heights in broadcasting. On the winning side stood another New Yorker, Howard Teichmann, president of the Musical Comedy Society, whose chief claim to campus notoriety came when he suceeded in depositing our morning's supply of a protest *Daily Cardinal* into Lake Mendota.

The university had an active drama society, the Wisconsin Players, composed of majors in the speech department. Each semester, the Players took a larger portion of my time and interest, a drift not entirely unnoticed by the political science department. I tried out for numerous productions, certain that among the hundreds of candidates I stood little chance. I was right.

One fine day, however, C. Lowell Lees, as skilled a director as ever strolled academic halls, pulled me into his office and offered me a small role in William Gillette's *Secret Service*. He needed a couple of extra bodies to stand up straight and brandish Union army rifles. I could do that, and did, subsequently carrying every kind of gun, spear, and weapon in mankind's and our prop department's copious arsenal. Lowell later left for the University of Minnesota, where his abilities were given greater freedom, and I would have gone with him if I could have explained another change of venue to my already confused and concerned family.

After a while I started to get parts with a line or two, sometimes playing in two or three shows at the same time in different theaters. Once, with a final exam pending, I managed to study onstage while playing Hadji, the blind beggar, in *The Desert Song*.

In a production of *Macbeth*—directed by an absolute replica of Mr. Phidelah Rice, my sonorous mentor in Baltimore—I graduated to MacDuff and one of the witches, but still had to collect props, too. Rice's replica, Alexius Baas, wanted me to find a cauldron large enough to hold the witches, as well as their brew.

"How large would that be?" I ventured to ask.

About eight feet in diameter.

"Where can I get one that big?" I pleaded. "And how could I ever get it onstage?"

"That's your job, dear boy," he thundered back at me, flinging his elegant wool cape over his shoulders and stalking off into the night. "You're on props."

I was so angry that I determined to show him.

After an endless search throughout Madison for an eight-foot witches' cauldron, I discovered that the city dump burned its refuse in two large iron vats. With political pull and a team of borrowed horses, I moved one of the vats to the smallish theater in Bascom Hall. It took hours.

Alex finally came in and saw his cauldron, standing there in the center of the stage, the floor almost buckling under its weight. I expected him to reward me with a knighthood, or at the very least a kiss on each cheek. He provided neither.

"Oh, you found one . . . good," he said, and started to rehearse with Lady M.

Ever since then, I have always told any member of any prop crew who ever came to me with a problem: "If I could find an eight-foot witches' cauldron in Madison, Wisconsin, you can find anything."

Had I been a few inches taller, my life in the theater might have been different. Since all of Wisconsin's directors felt that I was too short for romantic roles—opposite those lovely, tall Wisconsin females—they cast me as a succession of young boys and bearded ancients. I eventually sought refuge in writing, directing, and radio. I acted in radio plays presented by a very fine and adventurous university station, WHA, a pioneer in noncommercial broadcasting, and wrote one or two of them myself. When the speech students were too busy to direct, I was drafted to do a "studio production." With faculty guidance, including some from

Joseph Fielding Smith, then on the drama faculty and later head of the Mormon church, I ventured forth on a Soviet comedy, *Squaring the Circle*, by Valentin Katayev.

No one had ever shown me how to direct a play. I just solved the problems as I went along: where people should sit, stand, and move. When I hit a roadblock, I went back to where the trouble started and tried something else. With *Circle*, I did the same, casting the show and plunging right in. I did have sense enough to read the play a few times, and I did talk about the characters, though obviously without any awareness of "action," "intention," "spine," or other useful concepts. I shudder to think of the objective results, but at the time the show didn't seem too bad. It was funny and not without some sense of life; no one bumped into anyone, the audience laughed in the right places, and everyone told me I was not a bad director. Mert Koplin, who played a humorous and imaginative commissar, became a serious and highly successful television producer. Bert Cummings, my girlfriend at the time, played the ingenue and looked pretty terrific, even if her acting didn't match. She later married a distinguished and solvent Harvard professor of government.

Flushed with my initial success, I tried a much more difficult text, Ibsen's *The Master Builder*. Ibsen has never been my strongest suit. I chose the wrong translation, cast the show badly, and made every possible mistake with the setting. Even though I sensed doom, I went doggedly ahead, until my colon rebelled and forced me to turn the production over to someone else. It became a disaster, and I learned that directing can easily turn into a roller-coaster ride. I had also decided to learn how better to express myself on my feet, and so I joined the debating team. During my senior year, in the finals of an extemporaneous speaking contest, I drew the topic "The Munich Pact," then in the headlines. I surprised my audience and myself—and won the contest—with an adlibbed seven-minute speech that started, "Four great lovers of 'peace at any price' had dinner in a Munich restaurant the other night; after the meal, Mr. Adolf Hitler, with his customary alacrity, took care of the Czechs." I also won the annual Frankenburger Oratorical Contest with the topic "The Dilemma of Democracy"—whether and how to set limits on those within it who would deny democracy to others—and represented Wisconsin in the Big Ten contest at the University of Iowa. Winning those contests, even though I picked up two hundred dollars in the process, proved less consequential than getting friendly with fellow contestant Mason Adams, who should have won. A transfer student from

CCNY and now a successful actor, Mason would eventually lead me to Eugenie Muckle, who became my wife.

As a sophomore, I had been elected president of the Apprentice Players, whose name suggests its role. By the time I reached my final year, I became president of the Wisconsin Players, the first time such an honor had ever gone to a nonmajor. This growing involvement in theatrical affairs increasingly alienated my superiors in the political science department. They grilled me more tenaciously than necessary, I thought, in my Rhodes Scholarship interview, where I tried to establish a connection between my extracurricular activities and my desire to read history at Oxford. Even my mention of Orson Welles' current strongly topical production of *Julius Caesar* did not convince them. My candidacy was aborted relatively early in the proceedings.

One particular incident, in another academic thicket, almost ended my Wisconsin career. The Wisconsin Drama Guild, a local amateur organization, held an annual playwriting contest, which I entered even though I had not written any plays. Faced with a deadline, I submitted a rough adaptation of "Blood of the Martyrs," a short story by Stephen Vincent Benét, about the relationship between an aging professor, martyred by a totalitarian regime, and one of his students. Benét, a combination of poet and story-spinner, was a writer I had long admired; and his *Martyrs* was inherently dramatic—the scenes already laid out and filled with large sections of dialogue.

My play, titled *The Young Men*, won the contest. The prize, in addition to a heavy plaster plaque, was a one-night production by a group of my choosing. I cast the actors—including a literature student by the name of Leonard Silk, now more prominent for his knowledge of economics—gave myself the juicy role of the dictator, and started rehearsals. Halfway through, I realized that I had never cleared the dramatic rights. Maybe Mr. Benét should know what I was doing with his story. I wrote him a letter in care of his publisher, explaining all. Nary a word came back. Two or three days before we were to open, a letter arrived—but not from Benét. It was from a playwright named Percival Wilde, one of the staples of the Dramatic Publishing Company, related to Oscar neither by blood nor by talent. Wilde's letter informed me that he had already procured the dramatic rights to "Blood of the Martyrs," and that he had no intention of sharing them with me—even for one night.

Instead of remaining silent—the damage almost done—and quietly finishing up the show, I wrote Wilde a passionately sincere, young-man-aggrieved letter. The performance would be seen by very few people, I informed him, in a remote corner of the American Midwest. The moment the curtain came down, I would tear up all copies of my manuscript and burn them. His dramatic rights would, therefore, remain intact. But I added,

> I much regret your lack of understanding of and sympathy for a young man's sincere devotion to the work of Stephen Vincent Benét. The tone of your letter has challenged not only my infringement of your legal rights but my idealism and good intentions. If I ever attain your eminent status in the American theatre, I will hope to be more tolerant of a young man's unawareness of the letter of the copyright law, nor will I ever respond so cruelly to such a plea for help. After all, wasn't that what the short story was all about: The role that our elders could play in shaping youthful consciousness?

Feeling very moral—satisfied that I was on the side of the angels—I mailed the letter.

No sooner, however, was the final performance over and the plaque hung on my peeling wall than I was summoned to the office of our formidable dean of men, one Scott Goodnight—"Rocking Chair" Goodnight as he was known by the entire undergraduate community for his one-time exploit of spending the night in a rocking chair outside the girls' dorm waiting for some errant young man to emerge. His voice quivering, old Rocking Chair asked me what I had to say in defense of my abominable behavior.

"What behavior?"

I had not only impugned the good name of the university by writing a scurrilous letter to an eminent man of letters, I had disgraced myself and the university by putting on a play without possessing the legal or moral right to do so. Percival Wilde was a man of honor and literary distinction, as well as a fraternity brother of his. He, Scott Goodnight, saw no alternative to expelling me (as he had that other errant youth) from the halls of the University of Wisconsin, forever.

He would have done so, had it not been for the good offices of my friend, adviser, and debate coach, Professor Andrew T. Weaver, head of the department of speech and as decent as Goodnight was petty. "Andy" took on my case, calling upon a variety of allies united in detesting Goodnight's restrictive policies. He waged a campus-wide battle to keep me in school, attacking the proposed punishment as not befitting my supposed crime, and threatening to carry the question of Goodnight's jurisdiction before the University Senate.

Although I was deprived of membership in the senior honor society (Phi Kappa Phi)—though fortunately, because of Weaver's efforts, not Phi Beta Kappa—I eventually stayed to walk the halls and sully the good name of the University of Wisconsin for another year.

Nor did I abandon the habit, good or bad, of writing passionately sincere letters that would get me into other troubles.

THEATRICAL STIRRINGS
1939–1941

Our commencement speaker, Hans von Kaltenborn, a peppery and popular national radio commentator, reassured the Class of '39 that there was not going to be a war. So I spent the spring and summer sending out feelers, though not entirely sure for what. Newspapermen, I was told, were being laid off by the hundreds. Even the local *Marshfield Herald* was cutting down on its stringers, of which I was temporarily one. The theater was an imperial and inaccessible domain. Radio seemed safer for the moment, because at least nobody could see me, or I them. I sat down and wrote what I considered a pretty professional radio script, modeled on what was coming out of CBS's *Columbia Workshop*. This one was four pages entitled an "Out-of-Workshop Production," which dramatized an imaginary interview between an indifferent gentleman by the name of T. H. E. World and a young idealist aspiring to radio fame and fortune, "Me," who could act, direct, write, and announce, thus combining the best qualities of Orson Welles, Burgess Meredith, and Jules (later John) Garfield. Somehow, I persuaded someone at station WHA to mimeograph one hundred copies of the script, sent them out to every radio station whose call letters I could dig up, and waited for the avalanche of responses to flow over me. No avalanche. No response. Silence.

There was always graduate school, but I had no idea where to go or what to take. Besides, I was tired of school, and my father was tired of paying for my schooling. Somewhere out there was a real world where guys wore trenchcoats and went to exciting, glamorous places, and stayed up all night drinking prior to staying up all night, the same night, making love to ravishing females. I was still very much a virgin, sad to say, although yearning not to be. Nor did I know a Martini from a Bacardi. Although I did own a slightly frayed, slightly fading gabardine trenchcoat my mother had once bought me in a moment of confusion.

The summer was spent mostly at Glenn Dale, reading Vincent Sheean and John Gunther (as well as T. S. Eliot's "Waste Land") and again playing tennis with a variety of ex-high school flames whom I was trying to seduce except that I didn't know how. All of them assayed my nonprospects as a nondoctor or nonlawyer—all of them coming from Jewish mothers—laughed charmingly whenever things got too intense, and carefully protected their virginity for someone else.

Somehow I discovered, in late June of 1939, that the Braddock Heights Playhouse, in a suburb of Frederick, Maryland, needed some non-Equity actors to complete its roster for the summer. I telephoned for an interview, much to my family's concern, and hitchhiked from Washington to Frederick. Surprisingly, after an interview and audition, I was hired; no one really told me for what, or for how much. I knew that I would be playing a small role in the next production now in rehearsal, *Post Road*, a potboiler thriller that every summer theater in the country always seemed to be doing (I was to direct it myself at the Falmouth Playhouse in Massachusetts a decade later). The management had neglected to make clear to me that I was also expected to serve as an assistant stage manager for the production, paint and build the scenery at night in somebody's filthy attic, work in the box office whenever I wasn't rehearsing, and sell peanuts and popcorn in the aisles during each performance once my brief stint on stage was over. There was very little time left for eating, sleeping, or enjoying the experience. The director of the company, incidentally, happened to be Elaine Perry, daughter of Antoinette Perry of "Tony" award renown.

After a few too many weeks—or was it only days?—of this experience, I was rescued by a letter from CBS requiring my immediate appearance in New York City. Gilbert Seldes, who managed to combine art and commerce and still stay ahead of everyone else, was planning to experiment with the new medium of color television. Earlier in the summer, at the New York World's Fair, I had been intrigued by the wonders of black-and-white television, and after reading about Seldes' venture, I had written asking to be considered.

In about ten minutes flat, I gave up what seemed an exceedingly unrewarding theatrical career to pitch my tent before the mirage of color television. I resigned from Braddock Heights and proceeded to New York City, where, much to my chagrin, I discovered that the "situation had already changed." My scheduled interview had to be postponed to "later" in the summer. How much later? Nobody knew, but they would let me know. Were they cooling on me, or on color television? I never found out.

To make a short story long, absolutely nothing happened. Returning to Glenn Dale, I sat and waited, rereading the original CBS letter, and wondering how *Post Road* and the American theater were getting along without me. The summer wore on. I tried the Washington newspapers. Nothing. I entered a local contest for announcers held annually by Washington's NBC affiliate, WRC, and won. The prize was five dollars but no job, nary an offer, sorry. A station in a small town in Virginia responded to my "Out-of-Workshop" missive saying they sure liked my script, but weren't hiring anybody this summer. It was getting to be September, and there seemed to be a war starting in Europe, but not much happening in my life.

Near Glenn Dale, in Bowie, Maryland, there was an all-black high school. One day I went over there to suggest that I was an experienced though temporarily out-of-work director who was willing to put on a play for them to celebrate the start of the school year, free. The answer came back: What's a play? I offered to show them, and did. I typed out some copies of Mr. Milne's *Man in the Bowler Hat*, a one-act I had discovered three years earlier, adapted it a bit to local conditions, picked some kids, none of whom had ever acted, and went into rehearsal. I worked as hard as though it were on Broadway, and to everyone's relief, it turned out to be funny, spontaneous, and therapeutic. The principal gave me five dollars and asked me when I could do another one.

Having run out of other ideas, I was about to take his offer when a letter arrived that changed everything. This one was not from CBS, but from WBAL in Baltimore, which had received my "Out-of-Workshop" production. They needed a junior announcer cum writer. Would I care to come in and see them? Would I? I practically ran to Baltimore, some forty miles away, where I talked fast, auditioned slowly, and wound up as a junior announcer with all sorts of promises of future consideration for copywriter, director, and everything else as soon as they got to know me. In the meantime, I was to be a catch-all disc jockey from 10:30 A.M. to 2:30 P.M. every day, doing everything from weather, news, and stock market to commercials, for things from Camel cigarettes to Schneider's

Old Home Bread, which "opened in the middle like a book." Twenty dollars each and every week, but no extra loaves from my namesake the baker.

I was delighted, even though the salary kept me with my parents in Glenn Dale, getting up before sunrise to catch a milk train to Baltimore, grab an expensive taxi to WBAL, and get there barely in time to go on the air. With the slightest breakdown in any part of this sequence, there would be radio silence emanating from station WBAL. But I was back home in my familiar "Ballimer," "in radio," ready to show the world—or that portion of it listening to WBAL—how good I was. Including all those girls who were off dating those doctors and lawyers. Orson, here I come. . . .

Under the circumstances, the days were exciting. I even got to the point where I enjoyed switching buttons and making it back from the coffee urn just in time to do my seventy-eighth spot of the morning. Things got rapidly duller after two o'clock, even though I tried to hang around the station after working hours to learn all I could about radio. What I picked up mostly was that the last junior announcer had remained in his job for years, at more money.

I tried spending a few hours daily at my old stamping ground, the Pratt Library, which wasn't too far from Baltimore's Union Station. Somehow those open stacks had lost their allure. I needed something else after a day spouting commercial clichés before an open microphone, something more exciting and productive. Washington seemed more active, especially with a war on. Trains ran every hour, and I would often go there from Baltimore after work, visit a government building or a gallery, or just walk around. At night, like Tennessee Williams' Tom Wingfield, I'd go to the movies.

One evening, after one of my regular excursions to Washington's Little Theatre on Ninth Street, which was the only place in D.C. where one could see a foreign "art" film, I was taking the bus home to Glenn Dale and reading the *Washington Evening Star* when I spotted an item about a local drama group, the Washington Civic Theatre, holding tryouts the following week for Kaufman and Hart's *Merrily We Roll Along*. The Civic's director was a certain Day Tuttle, who was coproducer of the summertime Westport, Connecticut, Country Playhouse with Richard Skinner. I had not heard of either Mr. Tuttle or *Merrily We Roll Along*, but anything that would help me to spend my evenings forgetting about a bread that opened in the middle like a book was most welcome.

The following week, complete with tie and jacket, I presented myself at the appointed place to read for a role. *Merrily* was a bittersweet comedy about the progressive corruption of a young writer who started out true to himself and ended up prostituting himself to the commercial system. It was not one of Kaufman and Hart's most original plays, although it had had a respectable run on Broadway in 1934 with Kenneth McKenna and Walter Abel. What made it interesting was that (like Harold Pinter's *Betrayal*, many seasons later) its many scenes were presented in reverse order—thereby making each scene more biting and ironic than its predecessor.

I tried out for the part of Jonathan Crale, the writer's best friend, an idealistic young artist who bucked the system and refused to sell out. He got neither the girl nor the money, but he suited my current mood, not to mention my entire image of myself and my career. I felt myself to be excellently cast, and was not inordinately surprised when I got the part. Rehearsals, with dozens of attractive Washingtonians, were a joy. And even the hours at WBAL were made much more bearable. Day Tuttle was not only a professionally experienced director but a charming gentleman, a Yale man, and a humane New England Brahmin who felt that all of life, including rehearsals, should be made as pleasant and as comfortable as possible. The leading lady, Mimi Norton, was Washington's most highly extolled dramatic actress. Since Mimi was otherwise engaged, I wound up dating one of the other attractive young ladies in the cast and had a couple of good scenes onstage as well. Although the Nazis and Russians were tightening their grip on Poland, it suddenly seemed a good time to be alive.

The only problem involved my travel arrangements. Taking the bus from Baltimore to Washington each afternoon was not so bad, but in order to get home at night after rehearsals, I had to sprint for the last bus, get off at the closest roadside stop to Glenn Dale, and walk the mile to our cottage. Then in the next day's dawn (which seemed to come almost immediately) I had once more to climb on the train to Baltimore and grab the taxi to WBAL. Years later, I defined success as walking to work.

I was beginning to fall asleep between scenes one evening when Day, who had developed a liking for whatever I was doing in the play, took pity on me. He suggested that I skip the Glenn Dale leg of my commuting and stay over with him in his D.C. apartment. At first I was a trifle nervous about Day's motives. My mother wasn't sure what a homosexual was, or else believed that there weren't any in the world. But my own few experiences had given me, at least, a glimmer. Once, earlier, after a backstage visit following a performance by a well-known theater company, one of the actors had invited me to his hotel room to talk—he said. There, he removed his coat and suggested that I'd be more comfortable without my jacket and then my shirt. When he helpfully suggested that I might also remove my trousers and started to hold out his hand to help me, I responded by backing away to the locked door and blurting out, rather tearfully, "My mother doesn't let me do that." I'm sure he chalked up the nonaffair to experience, but I left sadly disillusioned.

This time need won out over fear, as it often does. I decided to take advantage of Day's offer, tinged though it might be with whatever implications. If his wife, Lauralee, who taught at the Dalton School in New York, and with whom he spent occasional weekends, and his three children, were just a coverup for his real appetites, I felt myself quite capable of coping. I moved in, saving myself not only a lot of time and energy, but discovering immediately that I was all wrong in being suspicious of Day. As well as being somewhat lonely himself, he really cared about me. We both had someone to talk to and share rehearsal problems with; and I had what amounted to a surrogate artistic father. I'm not sure that I slept any more than I had the other way, but I certainly received a great store of understanding, encouragement, and—ultimately—a direct push upward for my career and life.

The play opened successfully, with everyone—cast, audiences, and local critics—pleased with my contribution. There were dozens of parties to go to, on opening night and afterward, with lots of girls who suddenly looked at me—and kissed me—differently. Mimi was going steady with a student at Catholic University's newly emerging department of speech and drama, a young fellow named Leo Brady. Through Leo, I came to meet a youthful and dynamic Dominican priest, Father Gilbert V. Hartke, who looked just like a combination of Spencer Tracy and Clark Gable. The head of the department, Father Hartke had recently added to his faculty a young writer and director from Chicago named Walter Kerr, and was bent on bringing Catholic University national attention. Leo and Walter were already establishing C.U.'s artistic stature with their coauthored productions of *Yankee Doodle Boy* and *Cook Book*, musical biographies respectively of George M. Cohan and Joe Cook. The Cohan musical had just been made into a movie, *Yankee Doodle Dandy*, starring Jimmy Cagney.

For the first time since graduating from school, I was beginning to find that there was a future for the world, even though H. V. Kaltenborn's confident prediction had been contradicted by events. Hitler's armies were in Warsaw, the Russians in the other half of Poland, and the phony war was on between the defenders of the Maginot and Siegfried lines. In the air was the question of whether the United States could stay out. We went right on with each night's performance.

With the excitement of my new-found Washington world, WBAL's early-morning brand of wake-up medicine grew more boringly unbearable. I was rapidly exhausting the pleasures of being a junior announcer and spending more and more time thinking of how best to advance myself, a subject that had not yet been mentioned by anyone else. I thought about quitting almost from the first day of rehearsal, but in those post-Depression days nobody—especially in my family—ever quit a paying job unless he was dying. Even then he had to have a doctor's affidavit. My father, the doctor, would have disowned me, even though my mother, the doctor, would have understood. But when Day—constantly concerned with my welfare and well-being—gave me a way out of my dilemma by offering me a post as the Civic Theatre's promotion director for thirty-five dollars per week, I quit WBAL and radio without a qualm. I wasn't quite sure what a promotion director did, but that didn't matter.

Mainly, I wrote releases to the papers—at which endeavor I wasn't too bad—and tried to raise money from various private donors—at which I was awful. I also addressed envelopes and stuffed them, usually at all hours of the night. There wasn't much time to try out for the rest of the season's shows. Although when Day persuaded the eminent German émigré director Erwin Piscator to come down from his New York post as director of the New School's Dramatic Workshop to do a production for Finnish War Relief, I made sure I was in that one. Piscator chose Shaw's *Saint Joan*, and brought film and stage star Luise Rainer with him to play Joan. Piscator was able to cast very well. Norman Rose, now one of television's most mellifluous commercial voices and a Broadway stage actor, played the Bishop; Ted Tenley, a fine character actor formerly with Maurice Evans, did the Dauphin, and I was cast as Brother Martin, another impractical idealist.

Piscator, a giant in the European theater, was not used to working in the American way with American actors. He came to rehearsal with about four assistants and his *Regiebuch*, which must have weighed half a ton, with everything already decided and written down in it—every move, every gesture, every intonation. None of us had ever seen anything like it before, although we'd heard that Max Reinhardt worked this way. Day Tuttle was appalled. Piscator also demanded that all the actors come to every rehearsal, whether they might be needed that day or not. I remember sitting outside the rehearsal room with the entire cast literally for four days listening to the first line of the play, "What, no eggs!" which was as far as he managed to get in that time. There was a revolution brewing, which Day headed off only when Piscator relented, got past the first line, and called in people for specific scenes.

We didn't know it at the time, but the production was pure Brecht, replete with platforms and signs and white light. And Luise was at least interesting, albeit difficult to work with. She never looked at or listened to another actor. Nor did she care about anything but her own appearance, vocal and physical, and the impression she made. Her accent itself left a lot to be desired so far as simple clarity was concerned, and she also had a strange way of intoning or rather wailing some of her lines.

I thought I was doing reasonably well in my several scenes as her passionate defender at her trial. Except in the matter of my moves, Piscator left me pretty much alone, and Day kept reassuring me, and himself. As the weeks went by, however, I came to see that something in my performance was bothering Miss Rainer. She kept whispering to Piscator during rehearsal of our scenes, obviously about me. And he kept asking me to be bigger, which I interpreted as louder. It turned out that he really meant "bigger" in the sense of being larger, taller, heavier. Luise evidently didn't think I had enough weight, physical or emotional, for the part.

About a week before we were to open, Piscator informed me that I was just not powerful enough; he had to replace me. He asked me to stay on as one of the monks, and, after some hesitation, I put aside my pride and decided I would, just to watch him work. I also wanted to see what Luise was going to do. At first, they replaced me with a New York actor they both knew, Nicholas Ray, who went on to become a cult figure as a film director. He was large, all right, but not much of an actor. After three or four days he was replaced by a local radio announcer, who wasn't much of a stage actor either but who was big and had a large voice. I sat there under my hood, suffering.

Piscator's *Saint Joan* was a great success with critics and audience, and raised a fair amount for the Finns, who were being invaded by their Russian neighbors and getting lots of sympathy from the West. Opinion was divided about Luise, who had won two Academy Awards in a row but had some limitations and idiosyncrasies as a stage performer, at least in English. In spite of my demotion, I continued to think the director's work brilliant, certainly the most theatricalist use of the stage, and the most imaginative manipulation of scenery, costumes, lights, and music I had ever encountered. My relation with Piscator continued, and years later I would visit him at the New School. When he went back to Germany in the early fifties to work at the Schiller and eventually to head the new Volksbiene, I saw his fairly spectacular productions of such plays as *War and Peace*, *Requiem for a Nun*, *The Rainmaker*, and *The Deputy*. Whenever I saw him, he would introduce me as his favorite Brother Martin. I think he simply forgot that he had ever replaced me. I never corrected him.

More important than *Saint Joan* or my job with the Civic—which didn't last long because the theater ran out of funds for promotion directors—was the deepening of my relationship with Day Tuttle. We shared our frustrations about Erwin and Luise. I felt that I should still be playing Brother Martin, and Day felt he should have been directing the production himself without all the confusion and havoc wreaked by our invaders from the Continent. He talked to me enthusiastically about his own New York adventures and misadventures, his discoveries of and connections with youthful talent. Tirelessly, hour after hour, day after day, he implored me to stop denying my own abilities and interest in the theater and commit myself to it fully. If I was really that fearful of the commercial theater and of Broadway why didn't I at least try my hand in community or university theater? It was possible to make a living there, and to get a great deal of satisfaction as well. For the first time in my life I began to think seriously about that possibility, although I was still reluctant to share my feelings with my parents.

I did share them with Walter Kerr—whose production of *The Comedy of Errors*, set on a giant chessboard, I had just seen and admired. Walter, in spite of his obvious talents, was basically something of a loner and must have sensed a kindred spirit in me. He listened to my problems and advised that I might indeed be able to carve out a career in university theater, especially with a good master's degree. He had gone to Northwestern himself but didn't exactly recommend it. Maybe Yale, or Cornell, or North Carolina.

No one at the time talked of working in what we now call regional theater. The reason was simple. With the exception of one or two theaters like the Cleveland Playhouse, there were none. Nor did a sudden sprouting seem likely, or even possible.

Sometimes, when the twilight is close, I wonder how different the pattern of my life might have been had chance not led me to Washington, to the Civic, and to Day Tuttle, with his particular brand of sensibility and personal generosity. Certainly, without Day's interest and encouragement, without those long hours we spent over late coffee talking about "Hank" Fonda painting scenery for him at five dollars per week, without his early acting appearances with Laurette Taylor and Jane Cowl and Katharine Cornell, my overcautious nature and lack of sophistication might have taken me elsewhere. Not that I've been unalterably grateful to Day for his urgings, especially after a set of poor notices or a particularly unhappy production experience. If our paths had not collided at that moment, I might have continued in radio or journalism or writing or teaching, or even something quite different. One never gets a chance to put one's foot in the same river twice, perhaps fortunately for the foot, or for the river.

When the promotion job came to an end in the spring of 1940, I had pretty much decided to put aside as much money as I could collect, choose the best graduate school that would take me in without an undergraduate degree in drama, and prepare myself to teach and direct in a university setup. Through my contacts at station WHA, I wangled an introduction to W. H. Boutwell, a cheerfully tough information officer for the U.S. Office of Education. Boutwell read some of my stuff very quickly, shook hands, and promised that he'd find something for me. I walked out of his office figuring I was getting a brush-off, but I didn't know "Bill" Boutwell. A day or two later I was back, with an assignment to write a series of speeches for Postmaster General James A. Farley. The U.S. Post Office had, for the first time, issued a set of postage stamps honoring figures in the arts, literature, and the sciences. Every time one of those stamps came out, with a picture of someone like Washington Irving or Mark Twain or John Greenleaf Whittier on it, Farley was to make an opening-day speech. And I was the fellow who was going to write it, at fifty bucks per speech.

Fifty dollars a speech was not bad in those days, and would get me through a lot of graduate school. Although I never actually met Farley, I quickly acquainted myself with his personal style, boned up on the subjects in question, and polished up my rhetoric. By that time I had finally gotten an apartment of my own in a modestly pleasant section of middle-class Washington. I got so that after properly doing my research I could turn out an acceptable draft in about five to six hours of concentrated privacy. I was told that Farley came to trust my speeches so much that he wouldn't always bother to read them until he was on the rostrum. More than once I was tempted to slip him some sort of mickey for the fun of it, but since I knew that some aide was reading it first, I managed to avoid that temptation. My happiest moment was when a speech I wrote for him comparing Booker T. Washington with that other fellow with the same last name rated a front-page story in *The New York Times* in addition to a double-take from smiling Jim while he was reading it.

When the stamp series ran out, Boutwell switched me over to writing radio scripts, semidocumentaries on such dramatic subjects as venereal disease, and car safety. As soon as I felt I had enough money put away to get me safely through graduate school, I stopped; preferring to spend whatever time I could now muster educating myself theatrically, reading plays, and going to the theater. By now I had a room of my own with a congenial family in northwest Washington. I had a life of my own, friends; spring was awakening in me. I was so well educated that when I saw a local production of Thornton Wilder's *Our Town*, I pronounced it a complete fraud and an evasion of the playwright's responsibility to structure a play. Little did I know the impact that this "fraudulent" playwright and this particular play were to have on my life and times.

The question of which graduate school to pick was not easily settled; most schools would not take me without proper undergraduate credits. But elder statesman E. C. Mabie, then in his heyday at the University of Iowa, knew of me through Wisconsin's Andrew Weaver as well as my success at the Frankenburger Oratorical the previous spring. Mabie offered me a graduate fellowship and a large measure of goodwill. I was tempted to accept, but decided I ought to try another part of the country. Yale, whose degree process took three years, told me there was no way to get financial support in my first year. In any case, three years seemed endless. Walter Kerr suggested Cornell, about which I knew little. Cornell's own version of Mabie, A. M. Drummond, immediately came through with a fellowship and a letter telling me he was glad I hadn't had any undergraduate drama courses. At least, he suggested, my mind wouldn't have to be then disabused of what I'd already learned. I put Cornell on the front burner.

My first choice, however, was the University of North Carolina in Chapel Hill, where "Proff" Frederick Koch and his Carolina Playmakers were solidly and prominently established, and which didn't seem too far away from Washington. Also at Carolina was Paul Green, a fascinating maverick of a poet-philosopher whose plays on the social and moral issues of the South I had much admired, from *The Rising of the Sun*, a one-act about prisoners on a chain gang, to *The House of Connelly*, a Chekhovian piece originally performed by the Group Theatre. Proff accepted me at once and invited me down to have a look at the place.

One weekend, I took an early Saturday morning bus to Chapel Hill. On my way across the campus to a performance of a new play in the old tradition-laden Playmakers Theatre, I passed a young man in his early twenties sitting on a low wall, crying his eyes out. He was wearing what looked like a sailor suit, slightly amended. In spite of what generations of actors or scene designers may have later said or thought about me, I am compassionate by nature, so I walked over to see if I could help.

Apart from being an ex-sailor, he was a student in Koch's courses and had just submitted a play about some of his experiences at sea, which were very important to him. Koch had dismissed his script on the grounds that it did not qualify as a "folk play" and therefore it suited neither him nor the department. "Folk play" evidently referred only to those dramas dealing directly with rural characters and rural themes, not nautical ones. Remembering Eugene O'Neill's early one-acts, I reassured my playwright friend that this was much too narrow a definition. My feelings a bit dashed, I proceeded to the production on display, a dull two hours of something about farmers and crops and mortgages. Certainly it was not in a class with either *Beyond the Horizon* or *Triple A Plowed Under*—the latter something I had seen the Federal Theatre perform before it was itself plowed under by Congressional suspicion and narrow-mindedness. Afterward, while I was wondering whether the sailor would let me read his play, a beaming Koch corralled me to explain how much the play I had just seen meant to him and to the future of the American theater.

I bade my farewells, took the next bus back to Washington, and sent a telegram off to Drummond at Cornell, thanking him for his offer and inquiring as to the earliest date I could start and the shortest amount of time I could spend there and still acquire an M.A. in dramatic art and literature.

The earliest, I was soon informed, was that summer session; the shortest time, a year and a summer. Meantime, in May, the phony war came to an end. Hitler's armies were knifing through Belgium into France, all the way to Dunkirk. All thoughts of graduate school went out of my head as I tried to organize my emotional chaos. I applied to the American Field Service for ambulance duty, but was turned down without any explanation. Was it my bad eyes or my being just too Jewish? All I knew was that Hitler was winning and we weren't doing much about it. I gave in and decided to go on living my daily life, oblivious of world events. And so that June, just as Hitler entered Paris, I was entering Cornell, never forgetting for a moment that the political and military fates might be conspiring against me.

From the day I arrived, I had difficulty adjusting to Cornell. The theater department was doing *Our Town*, and I assumed I'd be considered for George. Instead, I was unceremoniously assigned, sans tryout, to play one of the baseball players as well as serve as assistant stage manager. The one decent role I was given all summer was the bad guy in *What a Life* by Clifford Goldsmith, which was directed by the instructor in stage lighting.

Although I met him toward the end of what had been a pioneering career in the academic theater, Alexander "Boss" Drummond was a huge, dominating, and often terrifying personality, who had been on crutches most of his adult life. He could get from the back of the auditorium to the stage in three big leaps. And his irony and sarcasm could squash you like a bug when he got there. I was, in his description, "the boy orator from the river Platte" or "the Leaning Tower of Pisa"—these criticisms stemming from my tendency to ham up a dramatic scene, and to lean forward when I acted. Once, I think it was in a scene from *Of Mice and Men*, which I performed with a very talented older actor, Archibald McLeod (later head of the theater at Southern Illinois University), he referred to us, for some unknown reason, as "whited sepulchers." No scene for the Boss was entirely right, no moment completely truthful or fully expressed. We took the blame and went on.

In spite of the Boss's and Hitler's intrusions that summer, everyone seemed to have an absolutely gorgeous time, theatrically and sexually—except me. I remained cooped up in my hot and humid hole-in-the-wall, eating pounds of seedless grapes and typing out one term paper after another. I knew nothing and, lonely as a cloud, kept discovering more and more that I didn't know. Including something called phonetics, which required me to pursue and produce sounds I didn't even know existed in the English language, much less my own tongue and vocal cords. The speech expert at Cornell's vocal lab, more skilled than Shaw's Henry Higgins, informed me that my diction was full of peculiarly Russian foibles and tics; he was able to discern vocal mannerisms that revealed every geographical location I'd ever come near. And I discovered that my lefthanded manual ineptitude set a new world indoor record. I ate alone, slept alone, and suffered alone in a variety of places. Not even the Canadian army could have made me as wretched.

But after a few weeks' vacation at Glenn Dale I came back for more of the same. Drummond had picked my thesis subject which was about director-playwright-theorist Nikolai Evreinov, a wild Russian who had once staged a tenth-anniversary production of the original storming of the Winter Palace in Leningrad in which several of the performers had been killed. Evreinov's essential aesthetic doctrine had to do with the prevalence of theatricality in daily life. He called this phenomenon "the theater in life." I had never heard of him or it before.

Five seconds later, it seemed, I found myself dragged in as assistant director on the department's production of Evreinov's *The Chief Thing*, a play about a boardinghouse landlord who brings in a troupe of actors to solve the emotional problems of his tenants. The Theatre Guild hadn't been able to make it go on Broadway in the twenties, and the Cornell Dramatic Club was certainly not going to do any better with it now. The director, faculty member H. Darkes "Butch" Albright, decided that I was to stage the second act, which took place entirely in another time and location than the rest of the play. In the meantime, I was in Albright's directing class, some ninety percent of which, about stage triangles and rigid rules of focus and composition, I considered either ridiculous or stupid. It was his belief that because we read from left to right, stage left was per se more significant than stage right.

That second act, after some trial and tribulation on all sides, turned out reasonably well, but not the other acts, nor my relations with the director. Later in the year, I recovered my equilibrium by directing on my own a one-act play entitled *A Night in the Country*, whose chief characters were crickets. Although the local reviewer commented favorably on the director's comic invention, the play and the production passed into oblivion. In our final artistic adventure I played the juvenile lead without drawing out too many new epithets from the Boss. The boy orator from the Platte was growing up.

This was the year that I really got to study the hard terrain of the theater on my hands and knees, with Drummond's vision as my magnifying glass, enlarging every inch of ground. Apart from becoming familiar with the entire literature of the theater, I discovered the fascinating dichotomy of representational and presentational theater—the theater of the fourth wall, which basically pretends that it is representing life as though there were no audience—versus the theatricalist theater, which presents and demonstrates its own nature, that of putting on a show for an audience that is always and inevitably there. More than once in the interim my allegiance has swung back and forth between these two very contrasting fundamental views of theater. But it was at Cornell, I'm sure, that my subsequent enthusiasm for such theatricalist playwrights as Samuel Beckett, Harold Pinter, Edward Albee, and Bertolt Brecht had its origins.

It was there that I first came upon a penetrating exposition of the presentational theater in Alexander Bakshy's *The Theatre Unbound*, a book still languishing in the outer darkness. I discovered and reveled in the pronunciamentos of Gordon Craig and Adolphe Appia, those Siamese twins of the modern theater, beside whose ideas those of Richard Schechner and Richard Foreman seem flaccid. I found out about Jacques Copeau as well as Stanislavski; Meyerhold and Vakhtangov, Mordecai Gorelik and Robert Edmond Jones. It was Cornell that led me to exchange *Stage Magazine* for *Theatre Arts Monthly*, made me realize that Brooks Atkinson, as much as he loved the theater, was less to be listened to than the more literary Stark Young. And it was at Cornell that Henry Alonzo Myers, professor of English, gave me an insight into the nature of tragedy that went far beyond the boundaries of theater. Tragedy, he told us, has nothing to do with accident but everything to do with character; tragedy deals with the sense of limitation and loss that life inevitably brings, and with paying the price for whatever choices we make.

And Drummond himself, though always distant and gruff (obviously his defense against getting too involved with us), made us increasingly aware of the treasures contained in theatrical art and history. He demonstrated the importance of imagination and curiosity over triangles and stage left. "The best theater playing in New York right now is the Ice Show," he would tell us, thereby making us all want to shape a theater in which a play could be as beautiful and as moving as a spectacle on ice.

We did not always agree with Drummond, or with his means. But he led us, goaded us, even loved us—and made us love the theater outside of ourselves. I lived in the library, and wore out a dozen typewriter ribbons on Mr. Evreinov's exciting but sadly sprawling play, *The Theatre of Eternal War*, still—justly, I'm afraid—unproduced in this country. By the time I was ready for my orals, less than a calendar year from my first entrance, I knew that I had made the right choice and had paid the right price.

Second Acts

OUT INTO THE REAL WORLD

1941

As graduation approached, the question of the future loomed more darkly than the sudden intrusion of Hitler's might into Yugoslavia, the Lend-Lease plan, the bitter debate between the Committee to Aid the Allies and those who were strictly for America First. Seven of us were scheduled to receive our M.A.s, and there were few job offers trickling in from that uncertain world outside, none of them entirely thrilling.

I scouted the academic theater with no luck, then transferred my job-seeking to the real world, whose immediacy and general theatricality was increasing daily. The Committee to Aid the Allies didn't seem to want me, although a smaller outfit called the Friends of Democracy kept me dangling for a while. Then one night in late June, sitting in my father's Chevy in Glenn Dale with an old girlfriend, I turned the radio on for some "jitterbug" music and heard instead the first announcement of the Nazi invasion of my native soil. My father informed me, sadly but insistently, that the Russians wouldn't last six weeks.

I wound up getting hired, at a practically nonexistent salary, by the Loyal Americans of German Descent. With a name as German as Schneider, no one bothered to realize that I was really a Russian. (As my grandmother used to say, if a cat has kittens in an oven, it doesn't mean that they are biscuits.) I wrote speeches for a tough and not exactly brilliant fellow named Robert Wagner, who in later years managed to get himself elected mayor of New York City. Observing Wagner in closeup, I wasn't entirely impressed with our side. But the chance to do some real work in what I felt was something very real, gave me the impression—again, in Mr. Beckett's words—that I existed. I put my M.A. diploma away in a drawer, and started to look for a place down in Greenwich Village.

One afternoon, in August 1941, upon returning to the East Ninth Street pad I was sharing with Phil Cohen, a radio writer and producer I had met in Washington, I got a message that a Walter Kerr from Washington had called. He told me that Father Hartke was going off to Northwestern University in Chicago for a year to get his doctorate. C.U. had hired a nun from a seminary in Scranton to replace him, but at the last minute, her mother superior had decided the nun could not be spared. Catholic University was in a bind because they needed someone to teach Father's courses, direct a play, and be around. In an emergency, they were even willing to take a non-Catholic someone. Was I at all interested?

Truthfully, I wasn't. I'd convinced myself that I was single-handedly turning the tide of war, and besides it wouldn't be very long before we were all in it anyhow. I liked New York, especially Greenwich Village, and I wasn't too sure about teaching at a Catholic school. What would I do when the year was up? And did Father know that I was Jewish? (He did.) Ironically, that was a bit better than if I'd been a Protestant. C.U. had more Jewish faculty members than "renegade Catholics." I was about to decline with thanks, when Phil, who happened to be listening, let me know that he thought I was nuts. Here I was turning down a chance to join one of the strongest and fastest-growing drama departments in the country. Here was a great way of finding out, once and for all, whether I liked the academic life for which I had just spent a year and a summer preparing myself. Washington was my hometown, and a much more interesting place to live in than, say, Kansas or Alabama. And how long would Bob Wagner go on making my speeches?

"Okay," I told Walter, "I'll come down and talk to Father." The next day I was sitting in Father Hartke's office, getting the treatment from the greatest master of salesmanship I have ever met. The Reverend Gilbert V. Hartke, O.P., in his handsome Dominican white robes or in a T-shirt, had the unique ability to make whoever was listening to him believe that he, the listener, was the most important person in the world. For almost half a century, through every financial, political, emotional, psychological, legal, and even spiritual problem, Father was able to pull through. He managed to collect a circle of supporters that included doormen and presidents, fanatics and skeptics, every persuasion and creed. In the last hours of the Carter administration, he got himself invited by Jimmy for a farewell visit; he also attended Reagan's inauguration and first reception.

In about fifteen minutes, Father not only had convinced me that to spend a year as an instructor in the speech and drama department at Catholic University would be the most important move of my life, he had practically converted me to Catholicism. I forgot to ask about the salary, which turned out to be $1800 for the year. Father explained that the actual appointment would have to be approved by the dean, but he foresaw no problems so long as the Lord shone his countenance upon me. We shook hands warmly, Father assuring me that my life was made; and I went out to Glenn Dale to inform my folks that I was going to be in the neighborhood next year.

The following morning, I took the train back to New York to get my things together, as well as to tell the Loyal Americans of German Descent that I was going to be disloyal. On the train with me sat a friend of Walter's, an actor named Hugh Franklin. We chatted, I not mentioning my C.U. job, assuming it should be kept secret until official. Hugh proceeded to let me know that Walter, with whom he'd had dinner the night before, had told him that C.U. had just hired someone from Yale to take Father's place for a year. That four-hour train trip from Washington to New York—a ride I've taken literally hundreds of times—was the longest in history. Not only was I terror-stricken inside, I had to sit there and keep talking to Hugh without letting him know that anything was wrong.

The moment we hit Penn Station, I took off for a phone booth, with my meager supply of nickels, dimes, and faith. Walter wasn't home. I called Father at the department; no answer there either. I took the subway downtown, my hands colder in August than they had been the previous January on the ski slopes. When Phil Cohen asked me how things had gone, I tried to be both nonchalant and noncommittal.

Finally, close to midnight, I reached Walter. I explained that I had bumped into Hugh on the train, and that he had revealed all. Now, who was the guy from Yale? Walter laughed—actually laughed—and then explained that, yes, he'd had dinner with Hugh; yes, he'd told him about the appointment. Hugh had just made a mistake and said Yale when he meant Cornell. He'd been telling me about myself.

That planned one year at Catholic University turned into a twelve-year stay, with time off for a war, occasional forays elsewhere, and good behavior. At first, I taught all the crud courses, including phonetics, public speaking, and a research seminar—where I almost caused a mass revolt by requiring the class to assemble a complete bibliography on my old friend Nikolai Evreinov, whose name they couldn't even spell, much less pronounce. Later I was able to extend my acting classes, add directing, and even invent something called "Theatre, Art, and Civilization," in which we did nothing but talk about such fellows as Frank Lloyd Wright, Walter Gropius, and Lewis Mumford, and deal with various theoretical questions of space and form, hardly mentioning the word theater at all. It was the best course I've ever taught.

To say that I felt at home at C.U. was far from the truth, although I soon realized that the people around me and the quality of experience I was sharing were very special. Apart from often feeling like a fifth wheel because I was the only non-Catholic in the department, I found myself out of step with many of my colleagues and students about the war in Europe, since many of the Irish Catholics were more or less anti-British.

I also suffered something of an inferiority complex as far as Walter Kerr was concerned. After working as film critic and writer for Edgar Bergen, Walter had graduated, a few years earlier than I, from Northwestern. He'd read everything and had very clear-cut opinions, many of them stemming back to Thomas Aquinas or Aristotle, and his aesthetic point of view permeated and shaped the department. I found myself more often than not disagreeing with a great many of those attitudes.

Realism, Walter preached, was not a legitimate form because it sought to imitate rather than transform reality, and he was firmly opposed to the Stanislavski system or approach to acting, which I was just at that time attempting to understand through the various American followers and books then appearing on the scene. Walter preferred and practiced what we would now call the external or technical (British?) technique, which he had acquired from his Northwestern classes. Alexander Dean, teaching and directing at Yale, was his directorial mentor; and Dean was much more interested in those compositional triangles I'd resented at Cornell than in inner motivation or truth.

According to Walter, Chekhov—whom I worshiped—wasn't a playwright at all because the element of story, which Aristotle called the keystone of drama, was so minimized. Nothing happens in Chekhov, Walter used to say, and I'd go back and reread *The Cherry Orchard* and *Uncle Vanya* to prove how wrong he was. But until Walter left C.U., Chekhov's plays were never put on there, and I was never supported in my constant efforts to direct one.

On another level, Walter believed that truth, artistic as well as moral, was absolute. I kept thinking and saying that truth, of whatever type, was subjective, relative to a given situation or time. Walter would smile, listen to me, and then go on making the decisions about what was good or bad, right and wrong, for the department. Interestingly enough, our artistic and philosophical positions have reversed many times since, although it was even more difficult to disagree with the senior drama critic of *The New York Times* than it was to disagree with a senior colleague. At C.U., our disagreements were confined to numerous friendly—and a few not so friendly—intellectual discussions, with white wine and occasional musical accompaniment, Walter being most adept at parties with the piano works of Noel Coward and Dwight Fiske.

On the other hand, the department proved astonishingly liberal in its directing assignments. No sooner had I arrived than I was plunged into rehearsals of *Jim Dandy*, a surrealistically lyrical new play by William Saroyan, which the National Theatre Conference—the prevailing national organization of university and community theaters—had somehow succeeded in acquiring for a big splash of simultaneous nationwide premieres. *Jim Dandy* was a love story set in a stylized public library with a revolving door and a rambunctious set of characters. One of them, identified as having "one foot in the grave," walked around with a miniature wooden coffin for a shoe. The play mixed tones and themes without any preparation or logic. Some of it didn't necessarily make any sense at all, but most of it was poetic and lively. And I loved it.

I discovered quickly that, despite Catholic University's adventurous production policy of doing the classics, new plays, and experimental works, the number of students majoring in speech and drama was not as large as I had expected. I remember stamping into Father's office, complaining about the lack of candidates for this great play that I was just about to direct. (Father, for some reason, never did depart for Northwestern.)

"How many did you have show up last night?" he asked me.

"Eight!!!"

"And how many parts in the Saroyan?"

"Eight!"—all the sadness in the world in my response.

"Well, then," came Father's answer, "what are you complaining about?"

Jim Dandy, in spite of or perhaps even because of the limitations of its casting process, turned out to be not too inadequate a production, one that established my directorial credentials and capacity not only at C.U. and in Washington but also in my own opinion. Even now I recall it fondly, remember its bizarre but persuasive theatricality, and think of it as a worthy precursor to *Godot* as well as all those other interestingly imperfect, persistently ambiguous, poetically expressive plays to which I have been drawn so often.

At one rehearsal Walter sat with me in the balcony to point out my staging errors and to suggest improvements, generally in terms of choreography or physical timing. While I appreciated his concern and his discretion, he didn't make me understand the play better, only how to make a piece of comic business more effective. Years later, I found it ironic when Walter became a critic for the *Herald-Tribune;* he seemed to be able to analyze a play's structure and describe its fabric of relationships better than anyone else then writing criticism. Later, especially in those long Sunday articles in the *Times*, I had a great deal more difficulty following his line of thought, much less agreeing with him.

Nevertheless, I was affected by Walter's theatricalist orientation, not so different in premise from what I had been drawn to at Cornell. I never completely accepted that the top figure in a compositional triangle was inevitably dominant, or that left stage was inherently more important than right stage, but the earliest C.U. productions I directed did tend to emphasize concepts of staging more than carefully wrought inner life. I loved levels and platforms, and arranged the patterns of movement on them very deliberately. I planned each movement and position in advance, and marked it exactly in my production script with elaborate notations, arrows, and zigzags, à la Piscator and the young Peter Brook.

Those early productions had strong stage pictures, fluid use of vertical space, a wide range of movement—motivated or not—and carefully structured rhythmical relationships. But the actors were little more than puppets, not always happy about it (especially when I tried to outdo the Boss in sarcasm). I was especially happy with the music and choreography in *Jim Dandy*, the slapstick in Molière's *The Doctor in Spite of Himself*, the formal choral patterns in Racine's *Athaliah*, and the supposedly invisible Chinese prop people in *Lute Song* (adapted from a Chinese classic by Will Irwin/Sidney Howard and later produced on Broadway). Not only Walter but both Meyerhold and Vakhtangov affected me a great deal more than did Mr. Stanislavski, especially since I was dealing mostly with classical and/or nonrealistic plays.

As the most evident non-Catholic on the faculty, I was usually accorded the privilege of directing the annual Lenten production, a religious or semireligious play filled with some kind of cosmic message. I remember vividly my first, *Athaliah*, a somber Biblical tragedy that rarely gets produced on this bank of the Seine. (I was also allowed and even encouraged to conduct, kneeling, the prayer sessions before each class, rehearsal, and performance—a practice akin to a coach's pep talk before the big game, and often producing similar results. Once I even wore a clerical collar to perform an impersonation of Father himself. I may not have been as Catholic as the Pope, but I occasionally gave a reasonably good imitation.)

With his usual skill at diplomacy, Father had procured the services of Florence Reed, a leading character actress of an earlier vintage, to play Athaliah. He often brought in guest stars, the idea being that young actors would benefit through the experience of working with experienced professionals, a practice now adopted by many university theaters. At this time Florence Reed, although in her late fifties, was nearsighted and barely able to remember her lines. Nevertheless we were all impressed with the opportunity of working with her.

For the setting, our talented faculty designer, Ralph Brown, had arranged an impressive pattern of interlocking platforms. "Flossie," as we called her whenever she was not around—arrived a week or so before we were to open. The show had already been staged—her physical movements were sent to her by special delivery letter—and we were only awaiting her presence. I brought her in through the auditorium door of our pleasant small theater to show her the setting as it would look from the audience. She got a few feet down the aisle and then stopped dead. "What are those?" she demanded, clutching my arm in the darkness, in a voice at least an octave lower than her normal bass baritone.

"Those what?" I ventured in a hoarse whisper.

"Those . . . those . . ." she boomed out again, stabbed a bejeweled forefinger in the general direction of the stage.

"Those are platforms, Miss Reed."

"Platforms, hell," she replied, "those are steps!" And, after the proper pause for the meaning to sink in, "If you think I'm going to go up and down on those, you've got another thought coming. Get rid of them!"

Well, obviously, we couldn't get rid of those platforms, or steps; they were too solid and too integrated into the already planned movements of all the characters. Nor had I the nerve to remind her that we had sent her detailed floor plans, as well as complete descriptions of her required positions and movements. We could, and did, eliminate all those elaborate sweeping entrances, those imaginative dramatic exits, so carefully worked out and orchestrated for her. It turned out that our Flossie not only was intensely nearsighted and possessed of the shortest legs of any star actress of any generation before or after, but was also terrified of heights, a "height" being defined as anything an inch off the stage floor. I had to restage almost the entire action of the show, keeping her seated throughout, dead center.

In spite of such an introduction, Florence and I came to be good friends for years to come. I used to visit her in her tiny clutter of an apartment in the Windsor Hotel, and never ceased to be amazed at her vitality and bawdy spirit. When she played the Fortune Teller for me in the first revival of *The Skin of Our Teeth* on Broadway fifteen years later, she didn't look any older; perhaps the ever-present chin strap was a bit tighter, that's all. During her C.U. sojourn, she regaled students and faculty alike with theatrical stories, some of which would definitely have not been rated PG; laughed at our inexperience but tolerated it; and drank us all under the table. I especially remember the story she told about the time she heard that a very famous English actor was going to play Macbeth in New York. "Macbeth!" she remembered crying out—and I can feel the vibrations shaking the floorboards where she stood—"How in hell can he play Macbeth? Why, Macbeth's balls have got to clank, not tinkle!"

Flossie's balls, wherever she is, bless her, are still clanking in my memory, and always will.

WARTIME IN WASHINGTON
1941–1945

My Catholic University year had just started when it threatened to end. On Sunday, December 7, 1941, I was at Griffith Stadium, watching the Washington Redskins' Sammy Baugh throw touchdown passes over and around the Philadelphia Eagles. On the way home I noticed a portion of a headline protruding from a late edition of *The Washington Star:* PEARL HARBOR BOMBED. It took me less than a moment to realize what harbor that was. I've never gone to a football game since.

At the age of fifty-one, my father volunteered and was commissioned a major in the Medical Corps. Eventually, he worked his way up to full colonel. He went off to Georgia for basic training, and then on to Oklahoma, New York, and Berlin. My mother wound up in the heart of the Pentagon, reading X-rays for the War Department. I got classified 1A-L, which meant that neither the Army nor the Navy wanted me; neither did any civilians, because I could still be drafted any time: bad eyes and flat feet. Like Saul Bellow's hero, I was a "dangling man," sending packages and news to my "boy in the service."

After my initial disappointment—and relief—I spent my waking hours wondering what to do. I tried to go back to the American Field Service. I tried the Coast Guard. I pursued the Navy to give me a commission—volunteering for the convoy on the Plymouth-Murmansk run. I thought of just shipping myself abroad somewhere as a reporter, and almost got a job teaching English to the son of Afghanistan's King Abdullah. What I actually did, however, was stay on at Catholic University pretending that the theater was important.

C.U. retooled for wartime service. Nighttime classes for war workers were added to the curriculum. Additional performances of productions were scheduled so that weary civilians would be provided entertainment. And part-time students poured in, adding not only to C.U.'s bank account but to the numbers available for casting. The winter and spring went by very fast, life on the surface not that visibly different, but beneath the snow and saplings there were growing questions. Americans were being driven back and killed in the Pacific, Russians driven back and killed in Europe. How could I just go on teaching "acting," even if it was supposedly for war workers?

By the summer of 1942, I couldn't stomach my lack of direct involvement any longer. Rejected by General "Wild Bill" Donovan's Office of Strategic Services, where I had once more tried out my Russian, failing even with Archibald MacLeish's rather tame Office of Facts and Figures, in the depths of my desperation, I finally hit the right place at the right time, the Office of War Information.

What I was going to be doing there was the usual: writing various kinds of propaganda. Our job was to tell people within our Continental boundaries to grow more wheat or to eat less bread. I wrote to order, on whatever subject and in whatever form: radio spots, leaflets, playlets, dramatic presentations, speeches, letters. Someone pushed a button, and my mimeographed pages popped out. Although what we were all doing so many hours each day didn't seem to be making much difference. We were still getting pushed back on all fronts.

Over the next year, my department, the School and College Services Division—partly aided and abetted by my sterling efforts—managed to become a source and a clearinghouse for all forms of dramatic presentation needed by a great many government agencies engaged in explaining or expounding any aspect of the "war effort."

I got to meet Elia Kazan, whose work as an actor had so impressed me in the Group Theatre's early productions, when the Department of Agriculture hired him to direct a full-length musical revue about rationing. I also became acquainted with Hallie Flanagan Davis, who had headed the Federal Theatre, at whose congressionally induced demise I had snake-danced in Times Square a couple of years before. Hallie was an extraordinary woman, a tiny pebble of Gibraltar. She was always kind and considerate to me, and in later years we stayed in touch for as long as it was possible. My familiarity with the overall university theater helped us at least to get the message, whatever it was, across. The OWI established regular contacts with the American Educational Theatre Association, still a fledgling collection of struggling college and high school theaters, with the National Theatre Conference, and with such educational theater journals as *The Quarterly Journal of Speech*, *Players Magazine*, and *The High School Thespian*.

In the summer of 1943, somebody in Congress decided that propaganda, even propaganda for our side, was not a good thing. Just as our jobs and offices were being ended, I wrote an article for the NTC *Bulletin* entitled "One Theatre," proclaiming and extolling the essential unity of the American theater. If I had learned anything in my year at OWI, it was that we were one theater indivisible, with the liberty to keep it that way after the war was over, and no justice at all in keeping ourselves fragmented and divided. I expounded on the need for an end to the separation between the commercial and the noncommercial, the professional and the nonprofessional theater. The coming of peace, I said, would bring a demand (sic!) for a single, national American theater. More than forty years later, I'm still trying!

Throughout all this, I maintained a part-time perch at Catholic University, continuing to teach the continual stream of "war workers" how to act and how to speak in public. As usual, various fringe benefits evolved from the association. Father Hartke gave my name to the Army War College to coach line officers just returning from various battlefields and eager to communicate their experiences. I accepted the job with verve and alacrity, feeling that at last I was going to make a tangible contribution to the winning of the war. During the next couple of weeks, I did everything I could to see to it that those gentlemen told it like it was. Evidently I was getting results. They kept asking me for more hours. The officers and the War College were pleased. I was pleased and C.U. was pleased. Even the tide of battle seemed to be on its way to turning. It was just too good to last.

It didn't. As soon as my application papers got processed, someone discovered that my birthplace was in Russia. Even though the Russians were supposedly on our side, and even though I was a citizen, my father a major, and my mother a respected civilian employed by the Pentagon, I was abruptly terminated without cause. Those poor inarticulate generals and colonels had to get along without me. One of them, and I am still grateful to him, even rang me up to inquire why his own personal version of the Dale Carnegie Method had disappeared. I was too scared to tell him.

Another time, somewhat later, long after I had left the OWI or it had left me, I was teaching a weekend class for embattled war workers when a Lieutenant (j.g.) Richard Carlson called to find out if Catholic University might have some young actors he could audition for a short film he was directing. Carlson, a former Hollywood semi-hemi-demi star, was part of a Navy film unit in Long Island, along with Robert Montgomery and Gene Kelly. After all our actors had been carefully auditioned, Carlson still hadn't found the type he wanted. That night, he telephoned to ask if I had ever acted myself, and the next day, without benefit of audition, he informed me that if I could get away for three weeks, I was the fellow he wanted. The actors in my class thought the whole thing had been decided in advance.

The next thing I knew, I was sitting in a rubber life raft in the middle of Long Island Sound, just off Old Lyme, Connecticut, squinting at the sun, trying to keep my eyes from tearing up too much. The part was that of a youthful U.S. Navy pilot who had been shot down somewhere in the South Pacific with one of his mates; the two were left floating in a life raft without food or drink, were quarreling, and were dying. Seems to me that I stayed in that raft, with very little more to eat or drink than the character I was playing, for the better part of a sun-scorching two weeks. I got to know a fair amount about the Navy, about Richard Carlson as a director, and about filmmaking—which I found more dull than anything else, even though from time to time I began to conjure up a Hollywood future for myself as the successor to John Garfield.

The entirely Navy crew was fun to be with and never allowed a problem to remain unsolved. We were all staying at the Old Lyme Inn, a splendidly Old World New England hostelry with marvelous food—which we ate together, Navy-style. The three weeks were also not entirely without spirits, playful and otherwise, and I learned to drink and relish my first sweet Manhattan cocktails because they happened to be the Lieutenant's favorite mixed drinks. On the day before shooting was completed, I almost got court-martialed by an irate admiral from New London, who lined us all up and immediately spotted my nonregulation sneakers. Until an aide whispered in his ear that I was only metaphorically part of his Navy, he was contemplating putting me in the brig.

By the time the OWI connection ended, my writing juices were flowing steadily enough for me to turn out a few freelance radio scripts of my own, several of which got done on local stations. One, *This Was Our Town*, about the destruction of the little Czech village of Lidice, achieved network status on NBC's Blue or Red network, I forget which. Although occasionally reviled or actually spat upon as a war shirker or draft evader by middle-aged ladies in buses, I had by now come to accept my noncombatant status and had even come to rationalize my usefulness to the war effort.

When, late in the summer of 1943, Fred Shawn, the tough and Walter Cronkite-like manager of station WRC, the NBC affiliate in Washington, offered me a job as a copywriter, I was inclined to take it. At lunch, I tried to explain to Shawn that I was more interested in and adept at dramatic writing than ordinary day-to-day copy or, perish the thought, commercials; but he managed to convince me, over several Manhattans, that I was qualified to turn out anything. My salary was to be seventy-five dollars a week, a new indoor world's record. The job was without a contract, open-ended; I was to start in ten days. I rode the Congressional up to New York to see a few shows and celebrate my new career as full-fledged staff scriptwriter.

Having breakfast one morning in the coffee shop of the President Hotel, I read a squib in the *Times* saying that Maxwell Anderson's new play *Storm Operation*, a drama about the American landings in North Africa, was being cast. The director happened to be my old prof from the University of Wisconsin, J. Russell Lane, who had been attached to Special Services in London, where his work on an all-soldier production had attracted Maxwell Anderson's attention. Anderson, fresh from his triumph with another war play, *The Eve of St. Mark*, had been in London soaking up local color for his next one. I decided to pay "Rusty," whom I had not seen in five years, a visit.

There he was, sitting with his feet atop a desk in an inner sanctum of the Playwrights Company's rather splendid suite of offices in Radio City, the outer sanctum crowded with all manner of soldier types. For the first, and almost last, time in my life, I got into a producer's office without waiting in line. Rusty was delightfully surprised to have the chance to impress me with his new-found position and power. He introduced me to his girlfriend, Sara Anderson, whom he had fallen in love with when she played Emily for him in *Our Town*. In the ensuing furor, he had left his wife of some twenty-five years, two kids, and whatever academic reputation he had built over the years.

The moment I walked into the office—"just to say hello"—Rusty hoisted his feet off the desk, threw his arms around me, and proceeded to tell me, in detail, the history of his good fortune. He'd always vowed that if he ever got a chance at a Broadway show, he wasn't going to be like all those big-shot New York directors who did their casting in private, didn't answer letters or phone calls, and kept all that undiscovered talent from getting its chance in the big time. On arriving in New York, he had announced in the daily press that he was going to give everyone who got in touch with him an audition or at least an interview. That was five or six weeks ago, and he hadn't yet managed to catch up with each day's incoming mail.

I poured out my own good fortune to Rusty and Sara, explaining that for the first time I felt my own career emerging from the shadows. I was about to bid them farewell so that they might get on with their casting, when Rusty looked at me for a long moment, his head slightly tilted, then said, "Say, you know what! I've got a part for you in *Storm Operation*. Winkle."

"Come on," I said laughing, "I can't. I've just gotten a staff job at NBC."

"It's a good little part," he continued. "And besides . . ." He yelled inside to his general manager, Victor Samrock, "Have we set the assistant stage manager yet, Vic?"

"No!" came back the unseen nasality of Victor's voice.

"Where's Moe?"

"Right in here." Damon Runyon would have loved that voice.

A door opened and a sallow, stubby, stubbly-faced, middle-aged gangster entered the room, his round face topped by a gray fedora and penetrated by a half-smoked cigar glowing in his mouth. Was this Vic or Moe? A gangster or a taxi driver?

"Moe," Rusty enlightened me almost at once, "this is Abe—I mean Al—Schneider; Al this is Moe Hack, the greatest stage manager in the world. What d'ya think, Moe, would Al be okay as your assistant?"

Moe, even though he was a foot shorter than I, managed to look down at me for a minute, then grunted, and went out the door. I was to see a lot of Moe in the next weeks and months, but never without the hat or the cigar. I finally figured out that he took both to bed with him. He was, indeed, the best stage manager in the world, at least my world.

"Well, whaddaya say?"

By this time, my heart was thumping and my mind racing all over the place, trying to reconcile opposites. How to be both scriptwriter and actor? How to get one without losing the other? My heart's desire and my pocket's pride?

"That'd be seventy-five for the part of Winkle," came Rusty's voice, intruding into my philosophical contemplation, "and thirty for being assistant stage manager."

One hundred and five American dollars a week! And I'd get my Equity card. And they were going out of town for three weeks before the

Alan Schneider's parents in Russia, at the time of their wedding.

A. S. at the age of two.

A. S. with his parents at Sabillasville, Maryland, ca. 1926.

A. S. in Glenn Dale, Maryland, ca. 1937.

(above) **Alexander Drummond, head of Cornell's Drama Department—"the Boss," ca. 1940.** *(Barrett Gallagher)*

(left) **Day Tuttle, Director of the Civic Theatre, Washington, D. C., ca. 1939. Without his encouragement, A. S. might not have pursued a career in the theater.**

Piscator's production of *Saint Joan* in Washington, D. C., 1940. Luise Rainer as Joan, kneeling. *(Jordan Studios)*

(opposite) **A. S. in his O.W.I. office, 1942.** *(O.W.I.)*

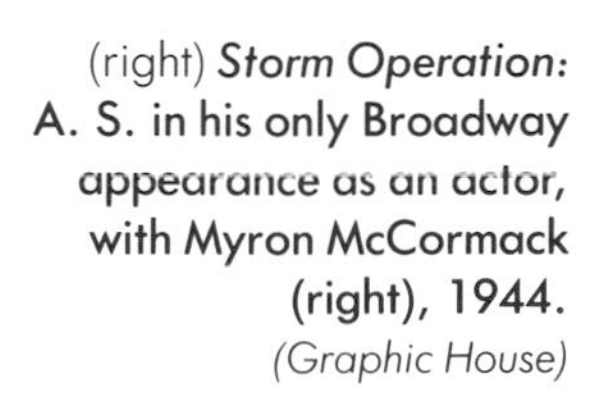

(right) ***Storm Operation:*** **A. S. in his only Broadway appearance as an actor, with Myron McCormack (right), 1944.** *(Graphic House)*

(below) ***Macbeth*** **at Catholic University, 1952.** *(Reverend Gilbert Hartke)*

(top) **A. S., Catholic University speech coach Josephine Callen, visitor John Gielgud, and Father Gilbert Hartke.** *(Reverend Gilbert Hartke)*

(above) ***The Remarkable Mr. Pennypacker:* Martha Scott, standing, and Burgess Meredith surrounded by the family, 1953.** *(John Irwin)*

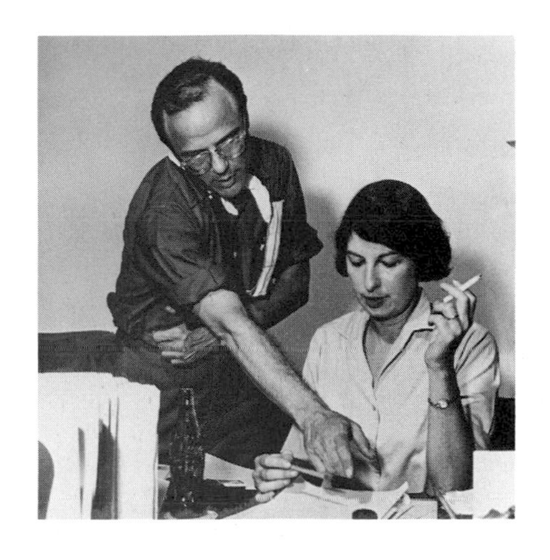

(above) A. S. with Zelda Fichandler, ca. 1952. *(Arena Stage/Vincent A. Finnigan)*

(above, left) Discussing *All Summer Long:* Robert Anderson, Carroll Baker, A. S., Ed Begley, 1954. *(Leo Friedman)*

Anastasia: Viveca Lindfors and Eugenie Leontovich in the "big scene," 1954. *(Impact)*

Summer and Smoke in the round: George Grizzard, Dorothea Jackson, Marian Reardon, Bill Pitts, 1954. *(Arena Stage/Lee Salsbury)*

Off to Paris for *The Skin of Our Teeth*: A. S. with Virginia and Robert Whitehead, 1955. *(Pan American Airlines)*

Broadway opening. So, no matter what happened to the show . . . And besides, it was by Maxwell Anderson, the fellow who'd written *Winterset*, which I loved and in which I had once played Mio, and *High Tor*—whose Van Van Dorn I had just missed getting (because of which I had almost thrown myself into Lake Mendota), and *The Eve of St. Mark*, which had just run a season. I even forgot that I hadn't read the script, or looked to see how many scenes—or lines—Winkle had.

"Don't muff it, Abe!" came Rusty's booming tones. "You remember how we used to talk about how tough it was to break into the New York theater. Well here's your big chance. You may not get another one so easy."

I took a deep breath. "Give me half an hour to make a phone call."

"Okay! But no more. I'll tell Victor to make up the contract, and you'll be back to sign it in half an hour."

The elevator dropped me and my stomach somewhere in the downstairs lobby, and I went over to one of those decrepit phone booths where so much of my theatrical life seems to have been decided. Difficult as it was to locate either nickels or digits, I dialed WRC in Washington and asked for Fred Shawn. "Fred?"

"Yeah?" an impatient voice, not sure of its caller.

"Alan Schneider in New York. I have a real favor to ask you. Could I start the job a few weeks later?"

"Later? Whaddaya mean later? You're supposed to start Monday. What happened?"

Then it all poured out, on my nickel. The theater job. The big chance I just could not turn down. The conflict between responsibility and artistic possibility. The moral dilemma giving way to practicality. Please understand, Fred. A conversation I've had many times since with various versions of Fred. This Fred was more generous than most. He could understand, and did. Not happy about it, or not about to give me his blessing—or another chance. But, at least, he didn't slam the phone down.

I wafted upstairs once more to the Playwrights' office, not even realizing that I had turned down one job without being sure of the other one. I walked straight into Victor Samrock's private corner, Victor sitting there, dark, natty, and slightly sour, as though he had just swallowed a tadpole. Victor collected a handful of printed forms, and held them out for me to sign. The idea that I might want to read anything before signing it did not occur to either of us.

I did manage to see some of the typing he had inserted: "At a combined total salary of $100 weekly." Having added seventy-five and thirty in my mind several hundred times, I started to open my mouth to say something but thought better of it. I was to make my Broadway debut in *Storm Operation* at a hundred per week. Winkle had, as I recall, four lines but lots of silent scenes. Victor Samrock, I discovered over the next thirty years, was one of the toughest and best general managers on Broadway; producers kept hiring him because he never made mistakes accidentally. I had now entered the sacred halls of the American theater. I was going to be on Broadway.

Storm Operation turned out to be a very light drizzle. The script was, at best, tepid, not in any way representative or worthy of Max Anderson's talent as a playwright. The performers—despite the earnestness of Rusty's casting process—were not especially notable. We had some well-known featured players in the cast, among them Myron McCormick, the same Myron McCormick who later distinguished himself by wiggling his stomach in *South Pacific*. The others included Bramwell Fletcher, a lean-faced Millard Mitchell, Gertrude Musgrove, and Cy Howard, a colleague of my Madison days. A much lesser-known actor impressed me most: Joseph Wiseman, who played the small role of an Italian prisoner of war. Joe had an expressive face, long expressive fingers, and an even longer and more expressive body. He was expressive every moment that he was on stage, and he never stopped working on his part offstage. The difference between Joe's inner approach and the outer approach of the rest of the cast was very evident to me. He had gone to the Neighborhood Playhouse and studied with Sanford Meisner, and he was the first Stanislavski actor whose work I was able to watch and admire up close.

Rusty, I'm afraid, didn't help much. A competent director when he dealt with established and tested material, he simply was out of his depth with a new play that had no depth of its own. Max came in from time to time and we made various changes, none of them in any way altering the basic emptiness of the play. The production at best was mediocre, with (in Walter Kerr's much-later phrase) occasional delusions of adequacy.

Even before the notices came in after our Baltimore opening night, the producers fired Rusty. Whenever something is wrong with a show out of town and no one quite knows what to do, the director always gets fired. The idea is that a new director will bring with him something magical, something intangible that will change everything, right all wrongs, pull the rabbit out of the hat. Rusty didn't even come round to say goodbye, he just disappeared. The Wisconsin contingent, including the assistant stage manager, worried a fair amount, but nothing happened. We were promised a magical new director, Elia Kazan or Bobby Lewis. But a few days later we wound up with Michael Gordon, who came from the same Stanislavski–Group Theatre school of directing but not, alas, of the same class. Mike, who had been the Group's lighting man, came in to see the show one night and spoke to the whole company afterward. He gave us a stimulating half-hour lecture on the play, mostly about its political background and historical perspective. It was the most perceptive and penetrating analysis of a play's content and structure that I had ever heard. (This was, of course, prior to meeting and listening to Harold Clurman, Mike's mentor and example.) We were all immensely fired up and encouraged. If he had told us all to stand with our heads in the North African sand, we would have been willing to do so.

All Mike actually did, however, was to reverse the set, flipping it over on its side so that right stage became left stage and vice versa. He kept everything else exactly as it was, spending hours talking with all the leads but changing nothing. The performances remained unaltered in any essential way—as did the script—and our prospects. Audiences came because they had bought subscription tickets, and left as disappointed as they had been on opening night.

My own role, that of a lonely soldier, was small but sympathetic. Armed and helmeted, I crowded nightly in a landing barge, waiting to wade ashore to defend democracy. Meanwhile real soldiers were wading ashore from real landing barges in various theaters of real warfare. It was a strange and not altogether comfortable sensation, this intermingling of art and reality, but I made the most of it. With playwright Anderson's approval, I even got to improvise a few lines, one or two of them managing to find their way into the printed text. By the time we had survived Pittsburgh, and Cleveland, where we spent a lonely rain-swept New Year's Eve, 1943, I had begun to feel that I was part of the war effort. I even managed to send Fred Shawn a Christmas card.

I was no match, however, for my friend Cy Howard, who was by this time in charge of the entire company, including the playwright. Max Anderson was rewriting and improving Cy's lines, feeding him lunch at the best restaurants, and lending him money. Cy loved it. The best acting in that show, I felt, was happening offstage. Cy later became a successful writer and director in TV and film, but never appeared onstage again.

We opened at the Belasco, January 11, 1944, after a couple of previews, certain that we were not going to be around very long. The

Belasco is a beautiful playhouse, now long neglected. David Belasco was said to have had direct access from his office to the stage, so that he could move quickly between his public and his private affairs. We searched in vain daily for the secret doorway. Opening night was very special, my first Broadway show; my parents and a host of friends from Baltimore and Washington came up and were treated to an unheralded bit of excitement. The play was done in a large number of scenes, each one with its own basic setting which had to be put into position and then quickly removed behind a blackout curtain. One scene took place in a tent, with Bramwell Fletcher's desk and field chair set up inside, plus another chair in which Miss Musgrove (never "Gertrude") played most of the scene. As always, I checked the setup from onstage, ran off, signaled to Moe, and turned back to watch. As I turned, I discovered that Miss M's chair, which had just been put in place, had disappeared. There was no time to do anything; the curtain was going up. Bramwell was there all right, sitting at his desk. Miss M, suffering intensely inwardly, had to play the entire scene standing up.

The omission, horrendous as it seemed at that particular moment, didn't make much difference. I seem to remember that Bram somewhere along the way gave his chair to Gertrude and sat on his desk, thus not mauling the staging too much. But Miss Musgrove's rage, already fed by the general sense of our impending demise, knew no bounds. At the act break, she put on her most convincing display of passion to inform me—and the entire world backstage—that she would get me both hanged and fired. Luckily, for me, Moe had actually seen the chair in question properly placed by me, and then had glimpsed it whisked offstage a moment later by a stagehand presumably miffed by Miss Musgrove's anti-proletarian remarks during rehearsals. So I had lesson number one in how to behave on Broadway: Don't antagonize the stagehands; they can kill in more ways than one.

After some eleven unloadings of our landing barge, *Storm Operation* closed, and everyone went his or her separate way, perhaps the saddest thing about the close of any production. People who have lived and worked together in the most intimate, personal way never see each other again. A family is rent asunder. Relationships, habits, friendships are shattered all at once, and the refugees fan out, seeking another place, another set of bonds. Like everyone else, I wandered the streets, waiting for the offers and the agents to pursue me. They didn't. And I had plenty of time to wonder what might have happened if I hadn't walked into Rusty's office that bright morning.

Even when, desperate for something, anything, I returned to the more familiar uncertainties of Washington, I didn't have the nerve to go back to NBC; I could not face Fred Shawn. So, enriched by my great Broadway experience and clutching my Equity card so that all could see it, I went back once more, to Catholic University and those artistically ambitious war workers. Since Father Hartke, helpful as he was, couldn't pay me very much for my part-time efforts, I had to moonlight—or rather sunlight—wherever else I could find something to do.

Always hoping to break through as a freelance writer, I sent articles and short stories off everywhere. *The Washington Post* printed a couple of columns, each netting me five dollars. I even managed to break into the Sunday *New York Times* Drama Section before my Catholic University colleague Walter Kerr, with a piece about veteran showman John Golden, criticizing his too-narrow view of the American theater. "On That Golden Gift," it was called, and brought me a much appreciated fifty bucks.

I managed to get hired for a while by the U.S. Public Health Service, where I puttered around with a variety of interchangeable chores, writing or rewriting speeches for the surgeon general, Thomas Parran, and Mrs. Herbert Lehman, wife of the Senator and one-time governor of New York.

The high point of my mercifully brief sojourn with a variety of inscrutable ladies at the PHS was when I was asked to come up fast with an oath for the newly formed Cadet Nurse Corps, then engaged in increasing the number of available nurses by speeding up their training. I spent every waking hour reading previous oaths of every kind, uttering a few choice ones of my own, and came up with some poetic and properly solemn words for young angels of mercy. The result produced a tear or two every time it was uttered aloud, especially by Mrs. Lehman. Whether or not recruitment was measurably increased, I had no way of knowing.

My next port of call was the U.S. Treasury Department, one of whose public relations specialists, a nervously peppery fellow named Daniel Melcher, had been involved with us at the OWI. Dan hired me to put together a list of dramatic materials related to war bonds; he was going to send them around to schools and colleges across the country. Unfortunately, I had allowed myself to be hired on a fee instead of an hourly basis. I managed to produce a fairly lively (by Treasury standards) booklet, which may even have led someone somewhere to buy a bond; but the fee collected had no relation to my weeks of work. The life of a freelance writer, I decided, was not for me. But I did get to see a lot of the White House—although I have still to set foot inside it.

Somewhere in the course of those last wartime months, I directed a production of Molière's *The Doctor in Spite of Himself,* which was performed by Catholic University students at nearby Fort George G. Meade in Maryland. We were invited by Special Services Captain Robert Fryer, later a successful and distinguished Broadway producer for whom I have never worked since—although, in fact, he turned out to be responsible for my next New York appearance.

The approaching end of the war brought forth various political and idealistic activities. I gave speeches, wrote articles, argued with everybody and anybody who waxed cynical about the Allies' war aims. I was all for the Atlantic Charter and the Four Freedoms. The day Roosevelt died, I walked for miles down Washington's Michigan Avenue, tears streaming down my face all the way.

I was also active in various organizations devoted to our Soviet allies, whose efforts to roll back the tide of Axis advances had aroused our national admiration. I contributed regularly to Russian War Relief, wrote an article on the wartime role of the Soviet theater for *The High School Thespian,* and joined the National Council of American-Soviet Friendship to whose newsletter I also contributed material on the American theater, including an article on the Soviet theater's role in the war.

In the spring of 1945, I met Solomon Mikhoels, the celebrated Russian Jewish actor, when he came to New York on what was, especially later, seen as a carefully orchestrated propaganda visit. Little was I to know—or even imagine—that the same Mikhoels was to be imprisoned and killed by the same people who had sent him over to drum up sympathy—and money. On our side, anyone who happened to become prominently visible during those visits suffered parallel if less bloody punishment. I am certain that despite my clearly expressed enthusiasm for almost everything our Russian allies were accomplishing between 1941 and 1945, Joe McCarthy and company never bothered with me simply because I was too small a potato. Margaret Webster, Howard DaSilva, and a great many others were not, as they were soon to learn—to their great regret and to our theater's great loss. I spent V-J night dancing in Lafayette Park across the street from the presidential residence, celebrating the end of the war, the defeat of fascism, and the continuing liberation of my virginity in the arms of a war widow, whom I shall call Lilian. I had met Lilian at Catholic University, where she played minor roles onstage and major roles in the lives of a succession of male conquests. Lilian was a vivacious brunette, mature and experienced, a far cry from the normal range of C.U. undergraduates. For some reason, she responded at once to my advances; before long we were spending every available hour together, and I was writing letters to my father, with the Army of Occupation in Berlin, telling him about the girl I was going to marry. We once spent an extended weekend together in the Paramount Hotel at Broadway and Forty-third Street, emerging only for an occasional hamburger.

I found myself more and more thinking about marriage, especially since I was worried about my C.U. colleagues finding out that I was sleeping with someone out of wedlock. There were also times when I felt guilty enjoying myself with a Marine's widow. We came close, Lilian and I, all the way through an engagement ring, family visits, and informal announcements all around. At the last minute, some little bird of caution sat on my shoulder to remind me that marriage had mornings as well as evenings, and that our mornings were not that ecstatic. I called the whole thing off. Lilian, in her rage, drove her Chevy straight at me, continuing up across the lawn of my roominghouse, where I was seeking refuge. She also threw the engagement ring into some impenetrable shrubbery. I forgave her the business of the car, but not that forever unfound ring. It had cost me some sixty bucks, a fortune at the time. I never saw Lilian again.

UP FROM THE WARS

1945-1948

The war once over, the Catholic University speech and drama department was besieged by hordes of returning would-be actors and directors, as well as playwrights and designers, all clutching the G.I. Bill. Once more, I was hired full-time, and I soon found myself teaching classes crowded with students most of whom were older than I. I also found myself, once Sergeant Leo Brady returned to the fold to teach, the object of a succession of broken promises and hopes. Instead of benefiting because I had stayed on through the war, I was once more relegated, without consultation or apology, to the kitchen courses: public speaking and radio scriptwriting.

I pleaded with Father Hartke, who explained to me politely that since I was not, after all, a Catholic, I could not expect to be taken care of ahead of those faculty members who were. I sulked a bit in my tent, wondered why I had come back, flirted with a few other offers that drifted in, but stayed on.

Among other chores, I was drafted, during Walter's rehearsals of Philip Barry's *Hotel Universe,* to take his new girlfriend, Jean, out to a movie, where I found her conversation much funnier than the soundtrack's. In May 1946 I got to direct Jean's first musical effort, a revue called *That's Where the Money Goes;* Walter didn't want to jeopardize his romance by tangling artistically with the author, though he often watched rehearsals. There were a few anxious moments when one of us was separating the other two; but in general *Money* went well, and so did Walter and Jean, who were married soon afterward. Some of the material from the show went on to New York (without me, of course) in John Murray Anderson's *Almanac.* Walter and Jean have also had a fairly long run, I'd say. What amuses me is that I was one of the few people at the wedding who thought they had much of a chance; I'd seen them in rehearsal. Sadly, I don't see them much anymore; critics tend to make difficult friends.

By the spring of 1947, I had decided that since Catholic University was becoming a dead end, it might be best for me to move on. No matter how difficult it was to see myself directing without our speech coach Josephine Callan at my side, Ralph Brown or Jimmy Waring doing the set, or Father making the budget turn handsprings.

That summer a very different kind of theatrical environment beckoned. The artistic director of Cleveland's Cain Park Theatre, Dina Rees "Doc" Evans, was a cheerfully feisty, cherubic but iron-willed dynamo of ideas, who had met and liked me in the OWI days and had filed me away for future use. Now she was running Cleveland's municipally funded outdoor enterprise, and out of the blue of those Cleveland Heights skies, she rang me to ask if I would come out to direct Kaufman and Hart's *You Can't Take It With You* and Walter Kerr's own *Sing Out, Sweet Land,* on which I had worked—and whose title I had contributed—back at C.U. Each play was to be done with two weeks' rehearsal. I was not very happy about the choice of shows, one of which I considered a conventional commercial comedy and the other a constant reminder of the place I would be leaving. But these were my two shows, six hundred bucks for the summer, including expenses. I said yes.

On almost the same day, I got a call from my old friend of wartime days, Norris Houghton. I had read and reread and practically memorized his *Moscow Rehearsals,* a classic account of the modern Soviet theater. Norrie was a member of the board of a new "noncommercial" producing outfit, Theatre Incorporated, which had plans for new playwrights, new actors, children's theater, and other elevating contributions to Broadway. It was a young people's Theatre Guild, and some of the young people involved were aspiring actress Beatrice "Biddy" Straight, aspiring playwright Arnold Sundgaard, and aspiring director-designer Norris Houghton. Along with old-time producer Richard Aldrich as a kind of senior adviser, they had launched themselves a year or so earlier with a highly praised production of Shaw's *Pygmalion,* starring Raymond Massey and Gertrude Lawrence, who was Mrs. Aldrich.

They had also brought over London's Old Vic for its triumphant postwar appearance. Laurence Olivier had done *Oedipus* and Sheridan's *The Critic* on the same night; Ralph Richardson, Margaret Leighton, and Joyce Redman had played *Uncle Vanya* to great acclaim; and then Richardson and Olivier had returned as a jovial Falstaff and a cantankerously mischievous Justice Shallow respectively in *Henry IV, Parts I* and *II*. The Old Vic's visit had been an unalloyed celebration, and had restored everyone's faith in the possibility of a postwar renaissance in the American theater, in the virtue of theater companies, and in the art of acting.

Theatre Inc., Norrie informed me, was losing its present casting director, Robert Fryer, to CBS. Would I like to have his job in the fall? Fifty dollars each and every week.

Truthfully, I wasn't exactly sure what a casting director was. And I was still terrified of New York and of the world of the commercial theater. At the same time, I realized that Theatre Inc. was as distinguished an address as I was likely to find for myself. If I was ever to make the break, from Catholic University to the outside world, from Washington to New York, this was the best way to do it—via Cleveland, and the summer of 1947. I bade a quiet, relieved farewell to C.U. and headed west.

The Cain Park Theatre, set in the middle of Cleveland Heights, a fashionable section of Cleveland, boasted a six-thousand-seat amphitheater with a ninety-foot concrete stage. It was an earlier and giant-sized version of Joe Papp's venture in Central Park, although Doc Evans had neither Joe's imagination nor his brand of ruthlessness. She did musicals with large choruses and a few popular comedies. That stage was so immense that you had to have fifty to a hundred actors just to fill the corners. And it seemed easier to cross the stage on roller skates than on foot. In fact, one recent director had done a modern-dress *Macbeth* on it using real tanks.

I loved rehearsing outside in the sunlight, garbed in shorts, sneakers, and a pith helmet—as well as a whistle tied around my neck to summon the multitudes into action. *You Can't Take It With You* was relatively intimate and suffered in its transition to the great outdoors; its setting was as elongated as a subway car. But *Sing Out* turned out to be the kind of visual and vocal extravaganza that filled, and flourished on, that stage. I recall literally hundreds of colonial settlers—in contrast to C.U.'s few huddled souls—frontiersmen, Indians, and, especially, since they were so plentiful and nonunion, children. I added production number after production number, sticking in the few American folk songs Walter had left out.

Audience responses and critics' comments were highly favorable. Everyone loved me. It also never rained on a single night when my productions went on. It was a great summer, and it spoiled me for ordinary summer stock.

By early September, exhilarated and sunburned, I found my way to New York City's Forty-fourth Street, close to Sixth Avenue. I even began to learn about casting directors, or at least about the agents whom casting directors spent their waking hours telephoning. Theatre Inc.'s first show of the 1947–1948 season was Stanley Young's *The Big People,* a smallish though amusing parable about prejudice. Martin Ritt, not yet eminent in films but the possessor of a reasonable stage reputation, was the director. He had already cast most of the roles, selecting Ernest Truex, a very small person but a very fine actor, as the lead. I had little to do on that production except to watch rehearsals and wish Theatre Inc. were not doing it. They were also talking about doing *Macbeth,* to be directed by Norrie, with Michael Redgrave and Flora Robson, first in London and later in New York.

Before I knew where I'd be sleeping, I had the name of every agent in New York, including the ones who wouldn't talk to me. And painful though I found the act of picking up the phone, I called all of them regularly. Another and happier part of my job was conducting the regular auditions, held every Tuesday and Thursday morning. Anyone who sent in a photo and résumé would eventually get an appointment to do a couple of scenes, the idea being that Theatre Inc. was giving new talent a chance to break through. Some had, including Julie Harris and Maureen Stapleton, who had auditioned and then been hired as switchboard operators to keep them from starving to death.

In the files were many other excellent unknown talents, and each week's auditions produced a few more names around which I placed some fervent circles or exclamation points. When *The Big People* went out of town and *Macbeth* got postponed for a while, Theatre Inc.'s producing activity was limited to talk. As a reaction, I became more involved with the audition process—at the same time growing frustrated because I was discovering all this raw talent and had so little chance to make use of it.

The season of 1947–1948 in the New York theater was distinguished not only by Elia Kazan's production of Tennessee Williams' *A Streetcar Named Desire* with Marlon Brando, but by the first stirrings of Kazan's Actors Studio which was setting an artistic pace every other theater group in New York wanted to follow.

My own efforts to get past the Studio's sacred portals as a nonactor were unsuccessful. So, I decided to organize a miniature Actors Studio of my own under the auspices of Theatre, Inc., on the principle that if you can't join 'em, you've got to lick 'em. And I wasn't going to limit myself just to following Stanislavski. Helped along by Norrie's moral support and encouragement, as well as Biddy Straight's cautious approval, I ransacked our casting files and picked out some hundred names. I wrote each of them a letter inviting them to be part of a group that would meet regularly and work on scenes, and invited them to an organizational meeting one midnight. The name of our group-to-be, "Studio 63," picked after long deliberation and discussion, came from Theatre Inc.'s own address, 63 West Forty-fourth Street, next to the Algonquin Hotel, the quintessential theatrical location.

I remember our first meeting vividly. About forty-five people showed up. They included such unknowns as Lee Grant, Darren McGavin, Wynn Handman, Vivian Nathan, Charles Nolte, Will Kuluva, and Lamont Johnson; also Maureen Stapleton, who left us almost immediately to join the "real" Studio.

More nervous than I wanted to admit, I made a passionate semi-impromptu speech about the American theater coming alive again after its wartime doldrums, with the Actors Studio serving as a welcome stimulus. I expressed the fervent hope that we happy unknown few could, with our singleminded efforts, match what Gadge and Bobby and Sandy Meisner were doing over on the other side of Sixth Avenue. At the same time, I felt we should be untrammeled by any specific artistic dogma. We were not going to have classes or work on scenes; we were going to do plays, one-acts, projects, experimental work. And when we were ready, we would invite producers and agents, all of whom would respond to the Theatre Inc. name, to see our work and give us jobs. There was no off-Broadway functioning at the time, or even off-off, nor yet a thriving regional theater. Off-Broadway "showcases" were far from a normal occurrence. What I was offering, therefore, though vague and intangible, was good listening. I got a rousing hand. Everyone said yes, they wanted to be part of whatever Studio 63 was going to be. Even if they had to rehearse after midnight.

The Board, pleased that something was happening, gave me the large upstairs audition room for rehearsals—but no budget. Nor did the room include anything remotely resembling a stage. I had heard about Margo Jones' experiments with "theater in the round" in Texas after her visit to Okhlopkov's "Realistic Theater" in Moscow, and I had read about Gilmore Brown's work in a room in California. Looking at our own room upstairs, I decided that the space had to be used in some such way. I went out and, with my own money, bought half a dozen small "bird's-eye" spotlights, scattered them strategically around the room, and evoked a not uninteresting central playing area with enough room to seat some fifty people.

The problem, of course, was what plays to do. Something that would have good acting parts for everyone, that could be done without a budget, and that would attract a professional audience. I read every one-act play in captivity. Eventually, I chanced on something by Tennessee Williams, *The Long Goodbye*, which had not yet been performed anywhere. *The Long Goodbye* was a moody, poetic character study about a young writer's coming to terms with leaving his past. It had good acting scenes, flashbacks, theatrical juxtapositions, not much scenery, and six good parts.

To accommodate the thirty or so actors who were sticking with me, I decided to attempt four simultaneous productions of the play, using alternate casts. Two of the casts were going to work in the center of the rehearsal room. The other two, assisted by a couple of conventional flats I had dug up and managed to get painted, would try what I euphemistically called "the proscenium version." We were going to work without an opening date, but as regularly and organically as possible; we would show our work when we were ready.

I corralled a smilingly imperturbable Louise Cull from my Cain Park staff as a nonpaid stage manager, together with a couple of assistants—one of whom, Peter Zeisler, had just come up from Washington with a letter of introduction. Peter later became one of the founders of the Guthrie Theater as well as head of the Theatre Communications Group—and also a good personal friend. We worked out an elaborate rehearsal schedule, mostly after eleven o'clock at night, whereby our actors could rehearse in shifts, shuttling back and forth if need be between casts in order to fulfill their professional engagements—or, more likely, to discharge their responsibilities as bartenders and waitresses or waiters. I worked all shifts.

Norrie had, in the meantime, gone off to London to work on the Michael Redgrave *Macbeth*. The remainder of our board of directors, occupied with restoring the fortunes and charisma of Theatre Inc., were having lunch at Sardi's, discussing various grandiose productions that never happened. They had almost forgotten about us. Florence Brown, our efficient and gracious office manager, rented out bits and pieces of space to various people—including a distinguished Russian director, Fyodor or Theodore Komisarjevski, who was working with John Gielgud on a Broadway production of *Crime and Punishment*, and Peter Witt, a struggling agent newly arrived from Europe. I spent a great deal of time chatting with Mr. Komisarjevski, of whose European eminence I had read much during my Cornell days.

As the weeks and months went by, some of our idealism—and membership—began to evaporate. Rehearsal times grew harder and harder to arrange. People grew wearier, and the room upstairs colder. There were numerous times when, after long weeks of endless after-midnight stands, we were all tempted to quit. Often I would go straight from a rehearsal to my casting desk without taking a subway ride downtown to Twenty-first Street to wash up and shave. After living in a smelly furnished room uptown for a few months, I had acquired a one-room apartment in Chelsea, affording me the luxury of a shared hall bathroom. My greatest satisfaction was being able to come home and wash my face with hot water any time I wanted.

Although there was no official "number one" cast for *The Long Goodbye,* I tended to favor the one in which Ray Fry played the writer, Vivian Nathan his mother, Patricia Jenkins the girlfriend, and Whit Vernon—an ex-Catholic University student who had played the title role in *Jim Dandy*—the male companion in distress. Whit's counterpart was Darren McGavin, and Ray Fry's was Lamont Johnson, but neither of these two was, in my youthful estimation, as effective or talented.

Rehearsals, in spite of all the difficulties, were moving us forward to some kind of realization of Tennessee's play. Even with improvised costumes and Salvation Army furniture (which suited the play perfectly) and simple lighting, we felt that the emotional truth and poetic atmosphere were beginning to come through. We set a November date for our "demonstration" and sent out postcards to every agent and producer we knew of. I even succeeded in cajoling Tennessee Williams' home address from his agent, Audrey Wood, and invited him to attend. The morning before the demonstration, not having heard from Mr. Williams, I knocked on the door of his brownstone apartment just north of Washington Square. All I got was a glimpse of a disheveled, mustachioed, and very sleepy figure in a flowered dressing gown, rumpled pajamas, and floppy slippers, who opened the door a crack and mumbled something about how early it was. It was eleven o'clock, a time I felt not entirely unsuitable. He promised to come. He didn't.

At midnight, the night before our "opening," our lead, Ray Fry, called to say that he'd gotten a commercial and couldn't be with us. I pleaded and begged, offering to pay him what he might be getting. Ray very reasonably explained that he just could not afford to turn the offer down. Lamont, the only one of our four original leads left, was out of the city doing something else. It was too late to cancel or postpone; those agents and producers would not come back. Besides, none of the other actors would ever talk to me if we didn't go on.

We decided to go ahead with our assistant stage manager, George Gordon, who had never acted before except in school plays. We rehearsed all night with George, all by himself. The end of the world had arrived, I thought. In the morning the other actors came in, slightly uncertain about what was happening.

That fateful November afternoon, the room upstairs was crammed. Every agent in town. Every board member. Every member of the Theatre Inc. staff, hoping for the best. The occasion turned out to be one of those times, common to the noncommercial non-Broadway theater, where the whole proved much greater than the sum of its parts. All the actors, including George, played it to the hilt. Whit had never had more authority, and Pat had never looked more beautiful. Vivian was transcendently truthful, and even her crying—something she tended to do in every part she ever played—seemed totally necessary. The audience was impressed with the level of the work; various people, board members and agents and producers, congratulated me on having found so many good unknown actors. George Gordon, right, wrong, or indifferent, had saved the day.

Toby Rowland, then just beginning as an agent, and now an established London manager and theater owner, wrote me a kind note about the demonstration and my work—"You have had a great part in developing some fine young actors." He offered to represent me, and to help me in any way he could. I was extremely touched; but the only agent I really wanted was Tennessee's Audrey Wood, and she hadn't shown up—although she had sent her new assistant (also her switchboard operator), "Tiz" Schauffler, who was a close friend of several Theatre Inc. board members.

Several members of the cast, including George, were offered jobs or at least the opportunity to read for jobs, something they hadn't been able to get before. Vivian and Darren both transferred to the Actors Studio because Martin Ritt had seen them. Word of mouth about our work spread. New faces and new names wanted to audition.

Eventually, we scheduled more showings, and, fired with messianic zeal, we embarked on a number of other somewhat larger projects: Arnold Sundgaard's *Mid-passage*, a free-form poetic drama of young people coming to terms with maturity; Vivian Connell's *The Nineteenth Hole of Europe*, a strange and haunting post–World War III play about a group of scary survivors; and Gordon Bottomley's practically unknown *Gruach*—a somewhat overflowery pastiche of Lady Macbeth as a young peasant girl—with Lee Grant playing the Lady in question. Lee was, then and now, extraordinarily beautiful and emotionally riveting, although her New Yorkese inflections did not entirely suit her character's rhythms.

With perspective, it is interesting now to observe what happened to some of Studio 63's talents. Lee, Maureen, and Julie went on, of course, to stardom and acclaim. But they were around only for a while and only on our fringes. Wynn Handman became a director and started the American Place Theatre in New York City. Lamont wound up as a Hollywood actor and later a film director. Ray Fry joined the Actors' Workshop in San Francisco, came with them to New York's Lincoln Center, and then passed into the outer shadows. Vivian Nathan has continued her career quietly but with respect from her colleagues. She now regularly conducts some of Lee Strasberg's former classes at that other Studio. Will Kuluva also worked a great deal on television, and Chuck Nolte, after playing the title role in *Billy Budd* on Broadway, became a playwright and university professor. Surprisingly enough, it was Darren McGavin who went the furthest (?) to what someone has called the belted and epauletted raincoat school of television acting.

On the other hand, Jane Lloyd Jones, whom everyone considered the most talented actress in the group and the one most likely to succeed, never had much of a career and has now left the theater. So has Mimi Norton, who took good care of us in her cuddly little apartment on Cornelia Street. Whit Vernon, the actor who clearly had the most potential, proved unable or unwilling to cope with the theater's agonies, and now tends his uncle's shoe store in Detroit; he does a local commercial now and then, and still sends me a Christmas card every year—something most of the ones who "made it" don't do.

Of the forty-five or so one-time members of Studio 63, about a third went on to some sort of long-term existence in their profession; another third dropped out completely; and the final third, after more than three decades, is about where it was back in 1948. Could someone have known at the time with any real certainty which names would wind up in which third? I doubt it. My casting ability and my perception of acting talent, then as now, were reasonably good. But the vagaries of the theatrical profession—as well as quirks of character—always leave a great deal to the gods. Perhaps that is for the best.

THE MIRACLE ON FORTY-FOURTH STREET

1948

The Long Goodbye's most specific impact on my own future came from the last-minute invitation that George Gordon had sent to a former Yale classmate, a young playwright by the name of Randolph Goodman. At that moment, Randy's adaptation (with Walter Carroll) of Gorki's *Lower Depths,* transposed to a black flophouse in the present-day American South and titled *A Long Way from Home,* was about to go into rehearsal for the American National Theatre and Academy, as part of ANTA's Experimental Theatre series at Maxine Elliott's Theatre. Both writers, by the way, were white.

The Maxine Elliott, as it was commonly known, had opened back in 1908, built and named for one of the star actresses of the period and fabled to have been financed by her friend J. P. Morgan. Miss Elliott wanted to make it truly a woman's theater by introducing such unheard-of conveniences as carpeting, curtained windows, full-length mirrors in all its dressing rooms, and even a bathtub in the star's dressing quarters. It had grown slightly seedier since.

Randy would not have seen *The Long Goodbye* had his friend George not been performing. After the performance, George—flushed with success—introduced me to Randy, and the three of us went across the street to a deli for some coffee. Almost before the waitress had managed to spill some of the coffee into our saucers, Randy was asking me whether I might be interested in directing his play. Looking at George, busy drinking from his saucer, I replied that I thought Sandy Meisner was already doing that. Was the play not at the moment in rehearsal?

Randy explained that Sandy was auditioning some black actors, but nothing had happened except some tedious discussions of what Gorki had had in mind, while his own script of *A Long Way from Home* was being steadily ignored. His director, whom he had not himself selected or approved, would appear daily with stacks of *Lower Depths* translations and volumes of commentary on Gorki. And Randy had already decided he would ask the Experimental Theatre board to get another director, more responsive to his own script. He just could not bring himself to do so unless he had someone else about whom he was enthusiastic—and sure.

Now that, by complete accident, he had seen my work, he felt he had found his man. What impressed him, he told me, was the way in which I had been able to evoke a powerful poetic mood, together with a strong understanding of and sympathy for real people. That was exactly what his play required. If I were seriously interested and available, he would propose to his Experimental Theatre producer, Nat Karson, that I replace Sandy. Oh, yes, I might want to read the play first. I swallowed hard and wondered if I was hearing properly.

That weekend, after all the excitement at Theatre Inc., I planned to visit my parents in Bethesda, near Washington. In my excitement, I managed to remember the phone number there and give it to Randy. Of course I was interested, and of course I would read the script on the train down; I was already sure that I would love it. But there were some practical mechanics of timing that I would have to work out with my bosses at Theatre Inc. And I wanted to make damned sure that ANTA really wanted me—instead of Sandy. There were still a lot of "ifs" between me and fate.

The moment I left town, Randy went to Karson, his producer, and to Robert Breen, who was in charge of running ANTA. The two said they would have to take up the question with Cheryl Crawford, chairman of ANTA's executive committee, who had proposed Sandy in the first place. Randy met with Cheryl; she told him that Meisner was an exceptionally fine director (what had he directed?), a marvelous actor (which he was), and a real pro. I, on the other hand, was unknown, inexperienced, and untested in the Broadway crucible. In other words, a bad risk.

In the face of Randy's continued insistence on making a change, they then proposed another director, David Pressman, who had been functioning as Sandy's assistant, carrying all those Gorki books. David was known personally to Cheryl, was a member of the Actors Studio, and had impressive credits. Randy stuck to his guns, even though they seemed like peashooters.

ANTA was a theater organization chartered by Congress—whatever that meant—and then left without anything to do. Robert Breen had uncovered this mystical charter and had helped to activate the organization to engage in various projects and productions. The American National Theatre and Academy had no academy and was far from national, but it had begun to have a theater of its own. In some mysterious manner Breen, although he had no real professional standing as an actor, had himself played Hamlet in an ANTA-sponsored outdoor production in Elsinore, Denmark. He later organized an ANTA production of *Porgy and Bess* to tour the Soviet Union and Europe.

Cheryl Crawford, of course, had been a cofounder of the celebrated Group Theatre as well as the Actors Studio. She had also been casting director with the original Theatre Guild and successful on her own as an independent producer. She was a power in the theater. Karson had had a relatively distinguished career as a stage designer, ranging all the way from Orson Welles' black *Macbeth* of 1936 through a variety of lavish Broadway musicals to his present job of designing the weekly stage "spectacular" at the Radio City Music Hall. As those three, Breen, Crawford, and Karson saw us, Goodman and Schneider were a couple of dumb amateurs blocking their way to real accomplishment.

Pressure continued on Randy. There was a succession of nastier and nastier phone calls as well as several hastily arranged meetings—wheedling, cajoling, alternating promises and threats ("the show won't go on!"). One day, to Randy's surprise, Karson suggested having Robert Breen himself direct the play, something that had never been mentioned previously. Karson had been delegated to sound out the playwright, whose approval, according to Dramatists Guild regulations, was essential. Randy turned down this new idea, continuing to ask for me as director and increasingly concerned that, far from the scene of the action in Washington, I would decide that I wanted no part of this nest of scorpions.

In Bethesda, meantime, I was about to give up all hope, liking the play more and more each time I read it, afraid to like it too much because I wouldn't get to direct. One evening, the phone rang—a chap who introduced himself as Nat Karson, "call me Nat." His voice, professional and tough, but completely friendly, informed me (as though I didn't know) that he had been talking with playwright Randolph Goodman, whose new play, *A Long Way from Home*, was soon going into rehearsal for a major production in the Experimental Theatre series sponsored by

ANTA. I waited breathlessly. He, Nat Karson, was going to direct it. He would like to have me along as assistant director. Not a squeak about Sandy.

I gulped, thought a moment, wondered what had been happening up there while I was down here. "I don't exactly understand what an assistant director is or does," I informed Mr. Karson, as politely as possible, "but I don't think I want to be one, thank you very much." Then I rang Randy in New York. Randy told me that the triumvirate of Breen, Karson, and Crawford had finally made the decision to replace Sandy. Nat, who had all along wanted the directing responsibility, had evidently decided this was his chance. He had not done any directing before, but this seemed a good project for him to learn on. The offer to have me around not only was a sop to Randy but came from a desire to have someone at his side taking care of the nitty-gritty details. Randy, in shock, told me, "I'm not going to have Nat as my director! The Guild gives me the right of approval! And I'm prepared to withdraw my play if necessary! You can direct it for me somewhere else." He urged me to hang on. I proceeded to hang, with all appropriate symptoms.

Minutes (or hours) passed, and that busy Bethesda phone rang again. This time it was Breen himself. Bob was a saturnine, smooth fellow who could sell plastic ice cubes to Eskimos. "It would be a great honor and privilege," he explained in characteristic low unruffled tones, "for a young director such as yourself to serve as assistant to such a great artist as Nat Karson."

"Look, Bob," I explained back, "I've been waiting for ten years to work in New York. I can wait a bit longer. Besides, doesn't the playwright himself want me and not Nat? What's going on?" The ice cubes got a bit more plastic.

After another half dozen calls, punctuated by conversations with my parents, who were having difficulty understanding the situation, I was beginning to fall apart emotionally. But as the phone calls continued to come, later and later into the night, my inner strength and resistance increased. In one conversation, an increasingly forceful and less pleasant Nat Karson—whom I had never even met—accused me of interfering with ANTA's entire plans for the season. I told him I didn't know what he was talking about.

This was my introduction to the New York syndrome: the maneuvering that goes on along the sidelines, the double-talk, the sparring for every possible advantage, the playing of one person off another. It was everything I hated and yet eventually had to learn to deal with in order to survive. Nat Karson knew that Randy didn't want him, that the playwright had the right to approve the director. He simply figured that Randy was desperate to get his play on, especially after the abortive experience with Meisner, that I was desperate to get a New York credit, and that in time both of us would give in. He was probing as far as he could, with whatever support he could muster, to get his own career as a director launched. And ANTA, having been forced to sacrifice Sandy Meisner to the playwright's will, had decided that his successor would be one of their own, not some unknown and professionally inexperienced director who happened to be a friend of the writer.

I took the train back to New York and Theatre Inc., certain that the entire adventure was over, my golden opportunity vanished. Back to the salt mines. Two days later, a completely friendly phone call came from Robert Breen telling me that ANTA (who *was* ANTA?) had decided that they wanted me to direct *A Long Way from Home*; Nat Karson was going to be the producer; everybody was going to pull together to make this the most splendid event of this season. Oh, yes, John Garfield was doing something called *Skipper Next to God* as the production just before ours, and we'd have to work out an opening date that would fit in with their closing. When could I start to cast? There was no mention of previous phone calls or conversations.

I rang Randy, my phonemate of the week, whose persistence and stubbornness had evidently accomplished this miracle. We shook hands by phone, and I went in to see Dick Aldrich to ask him for a "brief" leave of absence in which to make my New York directing debut. Since Theatre Inc. was evidently already pulling in its producing horns after a fairly tepid season, Aldrich and the board were not unhappy to release me without salary for a few weeks; they wished me well, warning me to look out for all those well-meaning types in the noncommercial theater. Norrie Houghton was especially pleased about my new project, since he was the one who had brought me to New York.

I took off from my steady fifty dollars weekly for the uncertain coastline of my hard-won ANTA beachhead. The total fee involved was two hundred dollars. But, as I kept pinching myself to remember, I'd been in New York for less than six months and here I was going to direct a Broadway play. Sort of Broadway. Since there was no off-Broadway at the time, I didn't know exactly how to describe it. Broadway level, but not exactly on Broadway. Anyhow, I knew that everyone in the Broadway theater would be coming to see my work, even Lee Strasberg.

The casting process we underwent remains, after all these years, simultaneously vague and vivid in my mind. Bob Breen's office—and residence—was in the old Hudson Theatre on Forty-fourth Street. In two weeks' time, we saw dozens of black performers, very few of them suitable for us. There was only a handful of trained or experienced black actors of any description available in those days; the ones who were professionals were generally unable to afford Experimental Theatre salaries.

I went to see the only black plays on display, *Anna Lucasta* and *Our Lan'*. Several times, I journeyed alone up to Harlem and cruised the streets to find likely-looking candidates. Once or twice I pulled people off of stoops to ask them if they had ever acted before, anywhere, and might be interested in auditioning. I spent hours looking for a supposedly excellent actor who I'd heard was working as a handyman or janitor. I didn't find him. We did find an absolutely fascinatingly ugly duckling of a seamstress, Catherine Ayers, and persuaded both her and her employer to spare her for the weeks we needed her to play the role of Four Eyes, the tailor, which we had originally intended to be played by a man.

The choice for our leading male role of Joebuck (Gorki's Vaska Pepel), was between Ossie Davis and Josh White, a well-known singer of spirituals and folk songs, and a smash attraction at Café Society Downtown. I wanted Ossie not only because we had already picked his girlfriend, Ruby Dee, for our younger sister, but because Josh had never acted before. Bob and Nat wanted Josh for his name value. Since I had won my basic battle with the two of them, I was reluctant to tangle again on another issue. Besides, Josh seemed most eager and engaging. I was eventually persuaded to take him and he worked as hard and as capably as he could.

Nat Karson, without consulting either Randy or me, picked Leo Kerz, a refugee from the German theater, to design the set. Leo, who had just done Katharine Cornell's *Antony and Cleopatra* (a bit too heavily), was extremely talented, spoke almost as quietly as Breen, and listened to no one. He went off to his studio by himself to dream up the entire setting, an elaborate version of a North Carolina three-story building, which he finished before I had even met him. Luckily, the design—a copy of which still decorates my office—was most expressive, not only of the environment, but of the play's demands for various playing spaces. I accepted the design, with copious compliments. Costumes were done by Rose Bogdanoff, also from Nat's Federal Theatre days, a determined and most knowledgeable and unflappable lady. They were mostly shopped from Fourteenth Street or pulled from someone's attic. They were fine.

To me, a good producer is not only the person who has the good taste to hire you and never reminds you of this at the wrong time, but also someone who's there when you need him and who stays away when you don't. By that definition, I've had three good ones: Robert Whitehead and Richard Barr in New York, and Zelda Fichandler in Washington. Nat was the exact opposite. He had never wanted to hire me and did so only under great pressure. He was never there when I needed him and always came around when I didn't want him.

Nat did come to our first reading, somewhere in the labyrinthian depths of the Hudson Theatre, where we had held our auditions. Immediately afterward, he took off for his daily stint at the racetrack, informing us all that we could deal with whatever problems arose. We later learned that he left a "spy" in our midst, our stage manager John Effrat (John F. Rat, we referred to him on occasion), who called Nat nightly and let him know everything that was going on. For the moment, Randy and I were not unhappy with Nat's voluntary absence from the scene. And at least I brought Goodman's script, rather than Gorki's, to rehearsal. ANTA remained quietly at a distance, Breen ringing up or dropping in once in a while to see if we were still there. I'm sure that our stage manager also kept him adequately informed.

Surprisingly enough, after all the preliminary agonies, rehearsals were a joy. (Walter Carroll, Randy's coauthor, had to stay down South somewhere working on a newspaper, so I saw nothing of him until near the end of rehearsals.) Randy rewrote whatever we both decided needed changing; he worked steadily and intelligently and without any fuss. The cast, after a day or two of being uncertain about their white director, was not only enthusiastic but as supportive as any I have ever had. They came to rehearsals on the dot, worked hard whether they were center stage or on the edges, tried to do everything I asked of them and then some, and contributed their own special brand of individuality and strength.

Apart from the stage managers and occasional visits from Randy, I was the only white regularly at rehearsals. I had never worked with adult black actors before. Perhaps I deluded myself, but after those first few days of getting acquainted, I lost all sense of black-white distinctions. They were actors, and I was a director. Sometimes they were able to do what I wanted, or demanded; sometimes they did something better. Sometimes I had to lead one of them by the hand, sometimes I grew upset or angry (my standard Achilles heel), sometimes one of the actors let off steam, but the basic working atmosphere was not only warm and creative, it was totally nonracial. I think that the actors involved sensed very quickly my respect for them as individuals, regardless of talent and skill. And although many of them were not, strictly speaking, professionals, not one was without individual spark. They knew that, and they knew I knew it. And they also knew that, Russian though I may have been, I was working with them and not with the Moscow Art Theatre.

From the start of rehearsals, we had been told that if we wanted to use recordings of black spirituals to bridge our numerous scenes, the musician's union required us to pay the salaries of an entire orchestra. ANTA was not going to do that, and I was not about to give up on the artistic necessity of having those spirituals.

Many of the actors, however, had beautiful voices, some professionally trained and experienced. I do not recall ever being as touched musically as I was by those performers, huddled together center stage behind the curtain, changing their costumes and singing "Sometimes I feel like a motherless child . . . a long way from home . . ." while the crew moved furniture and props. They had to sing as loudly as possible to get through the folds of the curtain and effect was better than if we had used the recordings.

Josh White was frightened, especially because he had to play most of his scenes with an experienced stage veteran, Fredi Washington. But no actor ever worked harder on his own inadequacies—or recognized them so openly. He may have lacked technique, internal or external, but he more than made up for this with sincerity and an imposing presence. Sometimes I had to show him, literally, how to move or stand; but once he caught on, he held on to his performance like a rock. We remained firm friends long after the production ended, something that doesn't normally happen on any show, much less one which runs for only six scheduled performances.

For the part of the Actor, we had almost gotten Gordon Heath, fresh from *Deep Are the Roots*, who was about to take off for a career in Paris. William Marshall, whom we did get, was huge, handsome, and slightly menacing. He turned out to be most imposing. Alonzo Bosan, in spite of his advanced age and great frailty, was an elegant and powerful Preacher. Kitty Ayers, as Four Eyes, appealingly androgynous, charmed everyone into hailing her as an "actress," which she may have occasionally suspected she wasn't. I took two days to stage the big fight and chase sequence at the end of the second act, and felt that it was one of the best choreographed scenes I'd ever done. I especially loved watching Earl Sydnor in the small part of a policeman, tying his shoelaces precisely on the same syllables each time. (I used Earl in at least three shows later.) It was a good rehearsal time, and I looked forward to each day of work.

After a couple of weeks of relative calm, reality came back into our lives. Leo Kerz walked in, uninvited, to our runthrough one day to see a piece of business I had given each of the characters entering or exiting the flophouse: opening the garbage can outside the rear entrance and looking inside to see if it might contain a bit of food or something useful. This was a bit of behavior I had observed all my life on New York streets. Leo immediately complained that the actors were destroying his set design. I countered by arguing that the business seemed called for by the characters' impoverished circumstances, but that I would try to get the actors to replace the garbage covers properly.

Another time, there was an argument over a clothesline, heavy with washing, which Leo had strung out at right angles to the front of the stage. The laundry was placed in such a position that the actors had to dodge under it or risk strangulation each time they crossed the stage. It took practically a Supreme Court decision from the ANTA board before Leo allowed me to move his washline a few feet upstage and angle it a bit differently.

Leo quieted down again until a dress rehearsal when he discovered that I had one of the characters, lying in one of the wooden bunks, working with the stub of a pencil on a crossword puzzle of the newspaper that was supposedly insulating the wall on the side of the bunk.

Leo really blew his Germanic top on that one, complaining to everyone who would listen that I was now engaged in a nefarious scheme with my actors to deface his carefully designed wall covering. I thought, as did the actor involved, that I had come up with a particularly revealing and inventive piece of stage business. Otherwise, the character had to lie there for hours without anything to do but cough from time to time and then expire quietly. Eventually, Leo and I reached a compromise on the number of crossword squares to be filled in each day, and Leo instructed the stage manager to see if it might be possible to erase the letters, especially if a *very* soft pencil was used. As the character was supposed to be seriously ill and totally without energy or hope, it was the idea rather than the quantity that mattered. I was appalled at the extent of this talented scene designer's inability to understand the relationship between his setting and what took place within it.

Somewhere in the third week, we decided we could survive a runthrough for the big brass, and announced the time. Nat, made prominent by his continued absence, said he'd be there. Bob Breen said he'd come, but didn't. Nat walked in just as we started and sat, stony-faced and alone, through what the rest of us thought was a very exciting first viewing of the overall play. The actors were excited, the playwright ecstatic. I was pleased. Randy and I turned eagerly to Nat for his reaction.

The reaction was immediate: "I'm taking over."

"What's wrong?" I asked, stunned and bewildered.

The only answer was that the work we had done was "all wrong," and Nat was going to "take over."

When Randy, also horrified, insisted that he very much liked and approved of what he himself had just seen, Nat informed him that his opinion didn't matter, "the producer is taking over." That was my first experience with a phrase I was to hear many times in subsequent years.

Neither Randy nor I quite knew what Nat intended to do. I dismissed the actors, while Randy called both Clarence Derwent and Cheryl Crawford of the ANTA board to inform them that he was quite satisfied with the runthrough and with my work on his play, and that he, as the author, had no intention of sanctioning Nat Karson's threat. Mr. Derwent, also Equity's president and as decent and generous as anyone in the American theater, eloquently expressed both his shock and his sympathy, and reassured Randy that nothing of the sort would happen. Not that Equity could protect me—it was just Derwent's nature to be caring. Cheryl, as I recall, was out of town, or at least could not be reached.

Indeed, nothing did happen. By the time we got back to rehearsal, Nat had disappeared. We went on with the show, Bob Breen telling us not to pay attention to every word Nat uttered. Our concerns shifted to the problem of *Skipper Next to God* having its run extended because of its good notices, thus cutting into the number of our performances as well as into our already inadequate technical rehearsal time. I pleaded passionately for an extension of our opening date, but that, of course, was not possible. In the New York theater, there's never enough time for technical rehearsals. One of the reasons why shows used to go "out of town" was to straighten out the bugs. We were opening "in town" and opening cold.

Toward the end of rehearsals, as tensions increased, we had a few racial incidents. There was a moment in a scene between Josh and Fredi with the line "Go ahead, crow." Suddenly, both actors stopped, turned to us, and complained that the line was a racial slur. I tried in vain to explain that "crow" in this instance was a verb, meaning to boast or exult. They remained skeptical—and uncomfortable. Randy changed the line to "Go ahead, brag." More serious trouble arose one day when coauthor Walter Carroll, a white southerner with a heavy Carolina accent, and a few beers too many, gave a long and rambling and supposedly complimentary speech to the cast, in which he referred to blacks as being like children, all great singers and dancers and natural performers. Coming from him, the message was not exactly palatable. It took a few days and some effort on the part of the more stable members of the company to calm tempers down.

Eventually, when our fingernails had been practically bitten through, *Skipper* went on to a brief Broadway run, and we got into Maxine Elliott's. We had only half a week for what was a technically complicated show. But Leo got our set in, the lighting was done or almost done, the music and sound effects were set. We needed a sound cue each time the upstairs café door opened to suggest that it had a jukebox. And, as sometimes happens in the New York theater, our sound man was a hundred percent deaf. The union had sent him over to us because of his low seniority and because he was the only one they could persuade to work at scale, which was all the Experimental Theatre could afford.

By the time we got into previews in our other half-week, I was alternately frantic, exhausted, numb, just wanting to get it over with. I didn't know it then, but that was about par for the course on any show opening in New York. At our first preview Josh almost froze to the floor with fright, but went on to conquer himself and his audience. The show seemed to work. It had great reality, emotion, intensity—alternately angry and tender, ferocious and gentle, swirling and quiet.

The preview audiences, more and more of them each night, loved it. It was my first New York audience, and I watched like a sentry, seeing where their attention lagged, wondering what they were thinking, trying not to lose my objectivity and ability to see each moment as though I had never seen it before. Randy was walking around biting his fingernails and beaming. Even John Effrat, calm under any kind of fire, managed to smile at me and say, "Kid, I think we got 'em." First time out, and I was already beginning to feel pretty good.

I had to be up at the ANTA offices on the Wednesday before our Sunday opening to correct the final program proofs. They seemed fine: at least my name was spelled correctly. On the title page, though, above the title, there was a line I hadn't known about: "Nat Karson's Production of." No one had told me about this, and I wasn't exactly happy about it. If anything at all had been produced by Nat, it was trouble—and the fourth race at Aqueduct. I persuaded whoever was in charge to change the line to the more customary "Produced by Nat Karson," which was the way the credit had been stated in the two previous programs on the Experimental Theatre Series. I took full responsibility for the change. Nat, of course, was at the track and could not be reached.

The previews Thursday, Friday, and Saturday kept improving, including a tighter rhythm by everybody and stronger individual performances. The applause grew. Nat came back for the weekend and actually saw the show twice in a row. After the final preview on Saturday night, he came backstage to give me a bear hug and a pat on the back. "Kid, you've done a great job. It's going to be a great opening. See you tomorrow." Nothing about his taking over this time. I took the subway home down to Twenty-first Street, picking up a Sunday *New York Times* Drama Section with a nice three-column cartoon of our show (albeit Don Freeman not Al Hirschfeld) on its front page. After less than six months in New York, I was going to have my Big Opening. The American theater was going to discover I existed.

I lived in a top-floor studio at 351 West Twenty-first Street. I couldn't yet afford my own telephone but managed with one belonging to a usually unemployed actress, Denise Flynn, who lived a floor down. After my usual cup of tea, I fell asleep. At about 2:30 A.M., there was a hard knock on my door, and a sleepy Denise said there was an urgent call for me. From someone by the name of Nat Karson.

Apologizing to Denise, I stumbled downstairs wondering what Nat wanted at this hour. What could have happened at the theater since I left him? At the other end of the phone was an angry Nat, unrecognizable as the same fellow who had just embraced me a scant couple of hours before. "You son-of-a-bitch!!"

"What's the matter, Nat?"—the question as much to myself as to him.

"Don't you come around to that theater tomorrow!"

We were having a last rehearsal, just a line-through at two o'clock. Then, and since, I believed in gathering the actors together the day of an opening. Better to be nervous together than separately. "What are you talking about, Nat? You know there's a rehearsal."

"Goddamn it, I mean it, you bastard, you're not coming to that theater tomorrow!"

"Listen, Nat," I pleaded, "take it easy. You just talked to me. What's happened?"

"Just don't show up at the theater tomorrow."

"You know I'll be there at two," I said.

The phone went dead.

Shaken, I wondered if I should alert John Effrat or call Randy. I decided to wait until morning. Maybe Nat would have calmed down by then.

The next morning, February 8, 1948, I rang John Effrat. "What's up?"

"Nat's taking over the production, Alan."

I almost tore the phone out of the wall. "What are you talking about?"

"Listen, Alan, it's opening day. Just take it easy and don't rock the boat."

"What are you talking about? How can Nat do that?"

"He's the producer, he can do anything." John's voice sounded mild, reasonable, patient. "Besides, everyone'll know you really directed it. Just be a good guy and don't bollix things up this afternoon. You'll just disturb the actors—and yourself—and it won't get you anywhere. I have orders not to let you into the theater."

"Orders? From whom?"

"From Nat. And from ANTA."

"What's ANTA? Bob Breen? Cheryl?"

"I can't tell you anything, Alan."

"Okay, I don't care who gave you those orders. I'm the director, and I'm going to be there, John."

"Okay, Alan, I'll have to stop you. You know I don't want to, you know that. But I have to."

I hung up the phone feeling totally lost and helpless. All I knew was that I was going to be at Maxine Elliott's Theatre to take charge of that rehearsal that day at two. I called Randy and cautiously discovered that he knew nothing of Nat's decision. I told him that we might have trouble, but we had had so much trouble already that Randy didn't seem too alarmed at the news. He'd be there at two, with me.

Then I called Bob Breen. No answer.

Cheryl was out of town.

Clarence Derwent, whose number I found in the phone book, was there, knew nothing about any of this, and was outraged. He'd be there at two to see what he could do with Nat, who was, of course, the producer but shouldn't be doing this sort of thing to his director, especially at the last moment.

Finally, I decided to call the only agent I knew who was aware of my existence: Audrey Wood. No answer. In desperation, I called "Tiz"

Schauffler, Audrey's hardworking assistant who had come to see *The Long Goodbye*, and poured out the whole story. Tiz was a recent Radcliffe graduate, as decent as she was tough. She had other plans for the afternoon, but she'd be there with me at two, no matter what. "From now on, I'm your agent!" I was still lost but not entirely without help.

Shortly after one o'clock, I arrived at the alley outside the stage door to find an unsmiling but almost conciliatory John Effrat. "Look, Alan, let's just talk about this. Nat's upset about something, and he's asked me to make sure you don't get into the theater today. He's taking over the afternoon rehearsal."

"But he can't do that, Jack!"

"Yes, he can, Alan, he's the producer." Patiently, quietly. "You've got to learn that."

I didn't learn—and probably never will. "But what did I do since last night? What's Nat so upset about?"

"I don't know, Alan. Look, don't make any trouble, please. It'll be better. The show'll go on tonight, and it'll all blow over."

"Yeah, I know. But I'm the director. I'm still the director!"

"Of course, Alan, just let him take the rehearsal this afternoon. Just this afternoon."

When Randy arrived with George Gordon, he was as happy and excited as I'd ever seen him. I told him what was happening. He was stunned; I remember the blood literally draining from his face. We tried to figure out what was going to happen next, and what to do about it. Had Nat decided the show was going to be a big hit, and was he now making one last attempt to get his directorial credit? Had he possibly just found out about the change in the billing—it had been in the program all through previews—and determined to get even? As the minutes dragged on, Randy's emotions became even more intense and uncontrollable. He ran down to the men's room, off the Maxine Elliott's lower lounge, locked himself into one of the stalls, and burst into tears. Luckily I didn't know then what he was doing or I would have joined him.

Tiz arrived at 1:45, ladylike and formidable in her fur neckpiece and agent hat, the unmistakable aura of Audrey Wood hovering around her. She was just ahead of Clarence Derwent, harried but resplendent in chesterfield and homburg. They both tried to get the facts from Effrat, who kept reassuring them that nothing special was happening. John had not expected these particular reinforcements to show up, and he seemed to be a little less sure of his ground. Clarence eventually headed for the ANTA office to see what he could do. Tiz stayed on, explaining to John in carefully chosen language and tones that in her capacity as agent for Mr. Alan Schneider, representing Miss Audrey Wood, she was not about to see someone else come in at the very last minute to claim credit for directing this show. If necessary, she was even capable of getting up on the stage before the entire audience and telling everyone exactly what had happened. John kept an anxious eye on his wristwatch.

Just before 2:00, the cast started straggling through the alley. "Hi, Alan." "What's the matter, Alan? Aren't you coming inside?" I explained as quietly as I could—John's watchful eye on me—that I was just waiting outside for someone. They looked at Randy, who seemed slightly green. They glanced at Tiz, who had battle in her eye. Gradually, they all went inside, knowing something was up but not entirely sure what. I'd previously asked John to set the chairs up in a semicircle for the line reading on stage, and he reassured me he had. His nervousness was becoming more and more visible.

Nat came down the alley just after two, trying hard not to look at me. There was a lot of effort going on all over the place; as Brecht says in one of his poems, the mask of Evil always shows strain. Tiz tried to stop him, but he brushed right past her and went in. John's face was pleading silently to me not to follow Nat inside. Randy was walking around muttering, "Terrible, terrible," under his breath and shaking his head, almost afraid to look at me. Where was Clarence Derwent? My legs felt weak, and I felt my spastic colon performing "The Rite of Spring" inside me. At the same time, it was as though nothing that was happening was real. The real Alan Schneider was inside the theater, in that semicircle, running that line rehearsal.

Then the stage door opened, and Maurice Ellis came out. "See you at the corner," he said. Then Millie, smiling. Then Ellsworth P. Wright, who winked at me and pointed his thumb in the direction of Broadway. One by one, all of them came out. They had told the assistant stage manager that they weren't feeling well enough to rehearse. Headaches. Stomach cramps. They needed more air. As they passed me, they were all smiling. "See ya down at the corner."

John went inside. I went to the corner drugstore with Josh White and Tiz and Randy and a few others. Nat had sat them down around that semicircle and told them he was taking over the production. That was when they had all discovered, without a word said, that they weren't feeling too well, and had to go to the corner drugstore to have something. When Nat had suggested that the assistant stage manager would get them something, they said it would be better if they all got it themselves. They looked at me, through their various drinks, and nodded. "Just wait." We waited, talking about everything except what was uppermost in our minds.

In about fifteen minutes, John F. Rat showed up, with a small folded note. I looked at everyone before opening it. It was in Nat's handwriting. I swallowed hard before reading it. "Dear Alan," it said, "we're waiting for you. It's going to be a terrific show." Everybody was watching me. They could tell right away by the smile I couldn't hold back that the news was good. I passed the note around, tried to pay the check, but no one would let me. We headed back, trying not to laugh or sing or disrupt traffic on Thirty-ninth Street. Nat was sitting at the back of the auditorium on the other side, but no one said anything to him. The actors all sat down. I said a few things about how much I had loved working on the show with them. They said the lines, more or less casually, as was customary in final rehearsals in those days. Occasionally, one of the actors would throw me a smile that said as much as the lines. Sitting through it all in the front row was Tiz, who had taken off neither her coat nor her on-guard demeanor. Clarence Derwent was at the ANTA office, presumably still on our side. Robert Breen and Cheryl Crawford were still "out of town."

As I recall, neither Bob nor Cheryl showed up at the opening that night; at least I was not aware of them. Clarence Derwent was there, most enthusiastic about the production and especially about Kitty Ayers. So was half of the American theater, including Sandy Meisner, Lee Strasberg, Stella Adler, Robert Whitehead, and the entire Theatre Inc. board. I was so nervous at my first New York directorial appearance—not to mention Nat—that I must have worn several holes in the rug at the back of the orchestra section. Nat did nothing, the actors everything, especially Josh and Fredi, and the show went unerringly well. Except for my deaf sound man, who on the very first cue put the wrong record on his turntable and then consistently remained one cue behind on each of the fourteen times that the cafe door opened and closed. Not that the effects mattered that much to anyone but the director, who had picked each recording with care to fit in with the mood of each scene. For the rest of our run, the union allowed our assistant stage manager to do everything but place the actual needle in the grooves (tape had not yet arrived).

The ten daily critics also came out in full force. And the reviews, though mixed, were basically favorable, ranging, as Randy later put it, from the ecstasy of the *Morning Telegraph*, the racing paper, to the agony of the *Daily Worker*, which pretended to speak for the poor and downtrodden—which is exactly whom our play was about. For some inscrutable reason, their critic—or editor—didn't feel we fitted in ideologically with the current party line. The *Times'* Brooks Atkinson, then as ever paramount among equals, wrote: "Under Alan Schneider's direction, a ragtag performance races through this foul lodging house in many moods—sometimes wild and violent, but sometimes gentle and wondering, with obliquely spiritual overtones. . . . It is vivid and fascinating, and one more Experimental Theatre achievement." Just to keep me from getting carried away, he added that "the play has a finer sympathy for humanity than this racing performance discloses." Many felt that something had been tonally lost in transposing Gorki's story to a black milieu, a transposition we all thought had been accomplished very effectively. One who disagreed strongly with that judgment was the *Telegraph*'s George Freedley, whose double artistic stance—as critic of the leading racing paper in the country and leading literary light and curator of the New York Public Library's Theater Collection—sometimes confused me. George loved everything and everyone, awarding Kitty his vote in the "Clarence Derwent Stakes" and praising my "sensitive direction." He felt that the show was "as exciting theater as I have ever seen all season" and that "the Experimental Theatre had hit its tops for the year" (this after *Galileo* and *Skipper Next to God*!) and was "something of which the whole theatre can be proud."

Later Rosamond Gilder, in her summary of the season in *Theatre Arts* magazine, said that we had "gathered together our finest Negro actors and provided an evening of very unusual interest." The one that pleased me most was in the small-circulation Catholic weekly *Commonweal*, where critic Kappo Phelan started off with the confession that "I've got exactly twenty-two lines in which to assure you that the Experimental Theatre's third production is very good stuff indeed . . . delivered by a number of the best actors it has been my privilege to attend in any season." Phelan ended with: "Whoever the director, Alan Schneider, is—his ought to be the gold star of the evening. However incredible, he does not seem to be interested in promotion, billing, or any kind of large-scale shock technique."

Along with those reviews came some commercial nibbles and a few conversations over lunch, but nothing happened. One nonproducer was interested but informed Randy that he would have to be guaranteed a flop because he needed one for a tax shelter. Unfortunately, with Broadway's uncertainties, we couldn't even guarantee that.

We played out our six scheduled performances, tried unsuccessfully to persuade ANTA to extend our run a bit because business was pretty good, and then disbanded. The actors were disappointed that nothing had happened to extend their employment, but then only a few of them had expected such a possibility. At least they had had a few weeks' regular work, and some special degree of excitement.

Our fate and the strong differences of opinion among our reviewers taught me a lesson early enough in my career to be valuable. That was, not only not to trust the critics in general but not to believe any of their reviews in particular, especially the ones that were favorable. Obviously, it's much better to be praised than blamed, but it's good to know that no verdict is absolute just because it happens to appear in print under a byline. It's just somebody's opinion—the somebody who happens to have that job at the moment, although my Russian-Jewish upbringing, with its inordinate respect for the printed word, taught me to believe otherwise. The morning *Times*' difference of opinion with the morning *Tribune* on my very first New York production prepared me for years of picking up Atkinson's and Kerr's reviews at dawn only to wonder if they had gone to the same play the night before.

As our luck had it, the *Times*' Atkinson liked us very much indeed, but he still couldn't *make* us; he could lead us to the commercial waters, but he couldn't get anyone to drink them, the waters seeming a bit too dark for comfort. Theatre Inc.'s board did tell me how proud they were of me—although, sorry to say, the play was not something they would want to take further. I went back to find a cast for Michael Redgrave's *Macbeth*, newly transplanted from London. *A Long Way from Home*, I had decided, was either a long way ahead of or behind its time.

A few years back, I came across an ANTA brochure on which were listed, year by year, all the productions they have ever produced or sponsored. There was no mention of *A Long Way from Home* in its 1947–1948 season. The brochure also included a list of prizes and awards given to ANTA's productions or performers. There was no word about Catherine Ayers, who received the Clarence Derwent Award that year as the most interesting actress in a nonstarring, nonfeatured role. (In spite of her triumph in Randy's play, Kitty never acted again, and I lost track of her in the increasingly inaccessible outskirts of her Harlem habitat.) Was it revenge, or just plain forgetfulness? I prefer to suspect the latter, and to go on.

AFTER THE DELUSION

1948–1949

My Washington friends, including drama critic Ernie Schier, made much of my having found a big directing opportunity in New York in less than six months. "Miracle on Forty-fourth Street," they called it. But the reality of my continued existence in the big city was completely different. Neither the Redgrave *Macbeth* nor Theatre Inc. itself lasted very long. As is usual with idealistic theatrical enterprises, practical matters—particularly money—always intruded. And no success, no matter how blazing, continues forever—even though, especially early in one's career, one thinks it will. Theatre Inc., born in glory a couple of seasons earlier with the Gertrude Lawrence and Raymond Massey *Pygmalion* and that glorious Old Vic visit, was buffeted on all sides during the spring and summer of 1948, struggled to regain its spirit and verve with Redgrave and Robson, and then quietly faded away.

Studio 63, hoping for lightning to strike twice, continued to meet and work, somewhat haphazardly. I applied to the Rockefeller and Guggenheim Foundations, for a grant to keep Studio 63 alive. Both turned me down. I applied again to the Rockefellers for an extended study of the theater in the U.S.S.R. and, when that was refused, switched to Czechoslovakia, in whose theatrical virtues I had become interested. To my surprise, I was awarded a couple of thousand dollars. I was about to take off for Prague, where the first meeting of the International Theatre Institute was being held, when the 1948 Communist takeover took place. The Rockefeller Foundation withdrew its grant, and I would have been a little nervous about going even if they hadn't.

All through this, I went in and out of Audrey Wood's office searching for Audrey and for plays to direct, occasionally reading a few scripts, and once in a while finding one I liked—which no one ever asked me to direct. For months, I kept bombarding Elia Kazan with reasons to let me into the Actors Studio. Kazan sent me a postcard saying thanks but no thanks. I walked the streets of Broadway and beyond, part of a lonely crowd looking for that nonexistent job. I lived on unemployment insurance and died several times daily. Sunday nights I spent at the home of a friendly television director-producer, Paul Belanger, who had hired me as an actor on Washington radio. Now and then I got a free meal there and watched the beginnings of television drama on a tiny seven-inch Dumont screen. We talked about camera angles and over-the-shoulder shots.

Came the summer, and I still didn't have a job, on stage, screen, or television; by land or by sea. Somewhat dashed by the juxtaposition of success and failure in my life, and beginning to wonder whether I should have even left Catholic University and/or Theatre Inc., I went back to the Cain Park Theatre for three shows this time.

The shows went well. *Lute Song* (which I had done earlier at Catholic University), had to be slightly blown up for Cain Park's ninety-foot proscenium, but was beautiful to watch. I was a bit nervous about *Taming of the Shrew*, my first attempt with the Bard, but I had a lively cast, including Henderson Forsythe and his wife, Dodie Carlson. The third, *The Reluctant Virgin*, which, for some reason that eludes me, had to be changed to *The Reluctant Lady*, was a musical by Maurice Valency, a Columbia professor whose adaptation of Giraudoux's *The Enchanted* had been mildly successful on Broadway the year before. Val and I, though on different intellectual planets, got along reasonably well. I have a fond recollection of him sitting in the last row of our vast auditorium during technical rehearsals, reading some Roman philosopher in Latin. We rehearsed each show for two weeks, a time that proved sufficient if not ample. The weather continued to favor me, opening nights and all. I managed to enjoy myself, occasionally forgetting that I didn't have a job in the fall, as my father's letters never failed to remind me.

During that crowded summer, I somehow found time to write a second article for the Sunday *Times*, this time on directing. Four years earlier, in the heat of anger at John Golden's limited use of the term "the American theater" to refer only to the commercial theater on Broadway, I had dashed off a somewhat facetious response in dialogue that Lewis Funke, editor of what was then called the Sunday Drama Section, had me rewrite as an essay. It was my first publication of a major nature, and absolutely no one paid any attention to it. Except Jean Kerr, Walter's just-acquired wife, who decided that he should write something for the *Times*, too. He did, more regularly.

On this occasion, wanting to make somebody out there more aware of me as a director, I sat down after some of my Cleveland rehearsals and wrote what I considered a serious piece on "The Director's Role." I took for an analogy Winston Churchill's statement that a historian was one who allotted proportion to historical events. I described the stage director as someone who allotted the proper proportions to stage events; someone who established the psychological relationships, the physical and auditory proportions, the fabric of time and space defining a production. It wasn't a bad article, and it helped me sort out my own thinking on the subject, although it still didn't get me any jobs. My byline listed me as the director of last season's *A Long Way from Home*. That's what I still was.

The fall arrived, aptly titled, and found me again loose on New York's streets, never more inhospitable than when one is looking for a job. Nor was there ever anyone less equipped than I to deal productively with those streets—except to manufacture activity. I didn't really know how or where to look—even with Tiz Schauffler, now my official agent, helping me. I had met a few people during the year I'd been in New York, and I kept after them. Tiz was always wonderfully warm, cheery, and compassionate. She kept the scripts coming, the appointments with Herman Shumlin, Harold Clurman, John Houseman, and other magnificos always looming ahead, and my hopes eternally glowing. Personally and professionally, I loved her.

I worked very hard at "making the rounds" but I was too square. Somehow I was never able or willing to "swing" with my contemporaries who went to Walgreen's for gossip, to Sardi's to be seen, or just for a drink at the Algonquin, and who were always at the "right" parties. I rarely went to parties, and recall the disaster one Saturday when I tried to throw a party of my own down on Twenty-first Street. Tiz and Florence Brown, of Theatre Inc., did all the shopping. The place looked great, but very few of the people I had invited showed up.

It's interesting for me now to remember that some of my fellow searchers who clustered around my life and times at Theatre Inc. included Martin Ritt, now a big Hollywood director; Arthur Cantor, a successful publicist and producer in London and New York; and Morton Gottlieb, one of Broadway's leading entrepreneurs. I also shared in the rising hopes of such young playwrights as Ted Apstein, Arnold Sundgaard, and Robert Anderson. I knew them all, had a drink with them once in a while, or went out with them on a double date. Generally, I preferred to go home to Twenty-first Street and read a book; to the Village for a Chinese meal and a movie by myself; or, best of all, go to the films at the Museum of Modern Art, always sure that I would meet a beautiful brunette heiress who would fall for me.

I never found that heiress but always had plenty to do, productive or otherwise, certainly not remunerative. I was on the original Policy Committee of the Equity Library Theatre, intended as a showcase for Equity members, with Aline MacMahon and a few other romantics. (One of whom, stage manager Franklin Heller, has been my friend ever since. Now a literary agent, he persuaded me to write this book.) I never directed anything for Equity Library, but I did "supervise" an unmemorable production of Georg Kaiser's *From Morn to Midnight*.

That season, one hundred relatively established radio and television performers got together to form their own off-Broadway producing company called New Stages. The cofounders were David Heilweil, with whom I had gone to Cornell, and Norman Rose, who had played a leading role in Piscator's production of *Saint Joan* at the Washington Civic Theatre. I wound up contributing one hundred dollars, "lent" by my father, who was assured that it would pay off, and cleaning the women's john in the New Stages' new home, the Amato Opera Theatre on Bleecker Street, where the downtown Circle in the Square now stands.

New Stages' first production, Sartre's *Respectful Prostitute*, was a great success. They never had another because David and Norman immediately started acting like Broadway producers, lunching in style and talking a lot about their plans. The closest I came to directing one of their remaining half dozen off-Broadway attempts was as assistant director to Mary Hunter on Thornton Wilder's adaptation of Sartre's *The Victors*. I kept a detailed account of rehearsals, which Mary conveniently "lost" one day when I lent it to her for her perusal. I even got jilted on the billing, winding up in the classified ads end of the program, in small print, as "Assistant to the Director."

I kept on sending out my penny postcards to everyone I could think of, detailing my virtues and willingness to do almost anything. Everyone kept telling me the postcards were "fabulous," but nothing happened. One especially desperate day, I sat down and typed out letters to fifty producers, offering them my undivided services—directional, administrative, or whatever—in return for a regular job in their office at fifty dollars per week. In addition, I would give them half of everything I would ever earn, in the theater or elsewhere, for the rest of my life. After several weeks, I got back two responses. One said, "No, thanks." The other, from Billy Rose, consisted of a scrawled invitation: "Come to my office at the Ziegfeld Theatre on Sixth Avenue at 2 o'clock on Thursday. I don't have much time."

Aglow with expectations, I ascended the Ziegfeld's steep steps and was ushered into an office, all teak and trophies, that would have made Mussolini jealous. All I could see of Billy perched behind his desk at the far end of the room was his cigar. The voice, a high-pitched New York foghorn, seemed to come right out of the smoke.

"Kid," it said (I was over thirty), "don't you do it!" Do what? I thought. "Don't you go signing your life away. Some day, you might wind up making a lot of money. Remember that!" Billy got up, for the first time letting me see all of his diminutive determined self, and pointed his finger at me: "Don't you do that!"

He also mentioned that he liked my letter, liked me, but had nothing for me. He'd let me know if and when something came up. And that was it at the Ziegfeld that day, as well as with my fifty letters. The something didn't come up for some dozen years. But I never forgot Billy and his moral fervor.

Daunted but not diminished, I kept writing to various producers and directors without mentioning anything about giving them my future millions. They kept right on ignoring me.

I registered with the *Herald-Tribune*'s Lecture Bureau, and gave a few talks on noncommercial theater and its relation to the rest of the country. New York's leading lecture agent, W. Colston Leigh, heard me somewhere and asked me to come in to see him. Leigh thought that I could have a very profitable career as a theater lecturer, and offered to sign me on a period contract. At almost the same moment, Bennington College unexpectedly offered me a job, teaching and directing. I was reluctant to commit myself to either offer because it meant leaving my opportunities in New York. What opportunities? Like prosperity, they were always around the bend—a place toward which I myself was rapidly heading.

I spent two unpaid mornings a week at ANTA, "consulting" and "advising" their Regional Theatre Department, trying to feel useful, and getting more and more depressed. And I kept at least a foot in Theatre Inc., now sinking slowly into the horizon, by directing evening rehearsals with what was left of Studio 63's faithful.

Somehow, we were able to procure from the ANTA's inner sanctum a copy of Vivian Connell's *The Nineteenth Hole of Europe*, at the time practically the hottest script on the unproduced play circuit, and one which Bob Breen called the greatest play of the twentieth century. Several Broadway producers, including Breen, Blevins Davis, and even Michael Myerberg, patron of esoteric masterpieces, were trying to get it on. It graphically detailed the sexual and philosophical adventures of a group of survivors of an atomic holocaust in ornate and lengthy speeches and a variety of four-letter words, and was about as dramatic as a lead balloon. We couldn't tell anyone we were rehearsing it and had to use a code name, *After the Ball*, whenever we talked about it. After *After the Ball* was over—we wound up with a reasonably impressive first act rendering for a selected and surprised audience of producers and friends—the life of *The Nineteenth Hole of Europe* in the American theater came to an end.

My only durable accomplishment of this entire unhappy, confused, and confusing period was, finally, getting into the Actors Studio. The Studio was intended as a "theater place" where professionals could work together and polish their craft between jobs or during long runs. It was Gadge Kazan himself, the most successful director in the commercial theater, who—dissatisfied with the lack of a common vocabulary and approach—joined with Robert Lewis and producer Cheryl Crawford to set up the Studio in 1947. Every young actor in New York, and some not so young, joined him: Marlon Brando, James Dean, David Wayne, Kim Stanley, Montgomery Clift, Julie Harris (she of the Theatre Inc. switchboard and the floor of the Old Vic's *Oedipus*), Eva Marie Saint, Karl Malden, Paul Newman, Eli Wallach, and almost everybody else. I was helping Lou "Gigi" Gilbert, one of Kazan's oldest friends and associates, clean up the place. We were, in effect, the Studio's two stage managers, together and separately getting the room ready for the class sessions each Tuesday and Friday and cleaning up afterward. This was no mean feat after improvisations and scenes that involved an array of physical pieces, furniture, and props, which rarely survived intact. I watched Brando, Clift, Geraldine Page, and a flock of other now well-known actors and actresses tear the place apart every Tuesday and Friday morning. Once, I was drafted into an improvisation that Sandy Meisner cooked up. I played a concentration-camp guard, my "action" being to keep anyone from getting out. Two of the inmates, played by Marlon and David Wayne, were given the "action" to get out. My devotion to the theater or to the Stanislavski Method did not include getting killed. They got out.

For the first time in my creative life, I was able to observe a coherent and workable point of view on the craft of acting—with which the craft of directing is, after all, closely connected. Most of my previous training and experience had emphasized the idea of theatricality and included mainly the technical aspects of a director's work. Now I had a close-up, practical, systematic exposure to the basic concept of stage "reality" and how the actor's own reality contributed to that and made it possible. The blending of these two extreme viewpoints, neither of which I was ever able to accept totally by itself, has formed my own theatrical and directorial point of view ever since. I stayed with it from my thirties into my fifties. Just when I achieved formal membership in the Studio is not clear to me. I seem still to be considered a "lifetime member," though my contacts there in recent years have been minimal.

The Studio kept me going through the years in which I was developing my personal style and strength both while working and not. Every Tuesday and Friday, eleven to one, you went there and felt part of something. The sessions—they were never called classes—usually lasted until one-thirty, especially after Lee Strasberg took over. Afterward, everyone would go to a nearby lunch place and talk about theater, actual and theoretical, with Gadge or Marty Ritt or Daniel Mann or—in later years and locations—Lee. We would sit around eating hamburgers or eggs, talking and dreaming, until two-thirty—and there's your day. That meant no matter what was happening in the outside world, two days of each week were filled up with some kind of artistic stimulation. And if you were rehearsing, that meant more days. We were not getting paid but we were part of something as vital as breathing, and we felt connected, with each other and with the theater.

As I was still unemployed, the Studio remaining my base, I decided to branch out with a ten-week advanced directing course that Lee was giving at the American Theatre Wing, which was then a very active place for new or even experienced professionals. Lee had recently taken over the main sessions at the Studio, and I had been both frightened and fascinated by his Talmudic perception and syntax. Somehow I got together the necessary two hundred dollars, and Lee accepted me, along with nine other "young" directors, all starting or hoping to break into the Broadway scene.

The class was very informal. We would direct a scene and Lee would talk about it. Each of us did two scenes during the ten weeks, and Lee tore us apart equally. For my first scene, I chose Saroyan's *The Hungerers*, a strange and lyrical one-act play that I had always liked. Lee didn't say very much, good or bad, or at least nothing that I can remember now, and I felt somewhat let down.

Near the end of the term, when I was searching around for my second scene, Bob Anderson told me about a new writer, Arnold Shulman, who had written a short piece called *Make a Statue Laugh*. I read the play, thought it was very much like all the other slice-of-life plays of that time, but decided it would be an excellent way for me to show Lee how well I could work with actors.

I was able to cast it especially well, with my old college friend Mason Adams, Ann Hegira, a very fine Studio actress, and an older pro named Henry Lascoe. I got to know and like Arnold, who was a cherubic, quiet, sensitive fellow just beginning to learn about the theater. *Statue* turned out to be fun to work on and very exciting in performance. I began to feel not only that I had another *Long Goodbye* but that *Statue* was a play with potential for the commercial theater.

When he saw the scene, Lee tore it and me apart. The play was no good. The actors were not in any way right. And my direction, whatever there was of it, was nothing. He went on and on, my heart and hopes sinking into the floorboards of the Wing's makeshift classroom, where, as it happens, the Studio now has its permanent home. I was about to leave the directing profession forever when Lee started discussing some directorial problem I had not been able to solve in this particular production. I cannot recall for the life of me what the problem was; I was probably too busy suffering to hear him clearly. He compared me unfavorably with another young director, whose name he had forgotten, who had solved this same problem in much more difficult form in some production Lee had seen the previous season. He went on to describe the other production in great detail. At the end of the session, as we all went up to Lee to bid our farewells, I told him as politely as possible the name of that other director he could not remember. It was Alan Schneider, and the name of the play he was talking about was ANTA's *A Long Way from Home*. Lee gave one of his familiar shrugs but didn't seem in any way surprised. Had it not been for this coincidence, I don't know whether my ego or my willpower would have survived Lee's criticism. Not everyone in the class did.

But one day that spring, I picked up Sam Zolotow's column in the *Times*, the Bible of show business news and gossip, to learn that Lee

Strasberg was going to direct a new play at the Westport (Connecticut) Country Playhouse. The play was called *A Thousand Guys Named Max*, and it was written by Arnold Shulman. I soon discovered that Arnold had finished *Make a Statue Laugh*, changed its title, and given it to Lee, whose comments he had heard that day at the Wing. I was livid. With Lee. With Arnold. With myself. The play, by the way, was not successful that summer, although years later, as *A Hole in the Head*, it ran briefly on Broadway and then made a fairly decent movie for Frank Sinatra. Arnold never quite got there as a playwright, but he works a lot in Hollywood. I see him once in a while and we laugh. In the theater two and two is never four.

Over the years I learned a lot from Lee; at the Wing, that winter of my discontent, and through the centuries at the Studio he made me think differently about the process of putting on a play. As I listened to him telling everybody to dig deeper for individual truth and expressiveness, I loved him and I hated him, often at the same time. He taught me more about acting and, therefore, directing, than anyone else has, before or since—even though I always knew that what he taught me, though it dealt with the truth, was not the whole truth and nothing but the truth.

But, as I've said, he made me think, almost for the first time, about what actors did on the stage and about how actors accomplished what they have to do. "Conscious preparation for an unconscious result," he used to quote his own teacher, Richard Boleslavski. Truth in acting did not mean just naturalism or casualness or underplaying or saying lines sloppily out of the corner of one's mouth. Truth meant actual physical and psychological aliveness, sensory awareness, responsiveness—looking and listening—to the stimuli, real and imaginary, that surround the actor on the stage. It meant using senses, muscles, sensitivity, and imagination to create life on the stage.

Lee also made me think differently about what a director does, as well as about how and why he does it. He made me consider not just the lines of a play but the life of the play, out of which the lines spring. A play, he taught me, is like an iceberg, eight-ninths of which never rises above the surface of the water; but the size and shape of that one-ninth that does rise above the surface are always determined by the eight-ninths that remains below. He convinced me that the director's primary job and responsibility is to stimulate the sensitivity of the actor, not simply to steer him up and down the stage, or from left to right. He caused me never to be satisfied with the conventional, the cliché, the surface of truth—even when it worked, even when it was supposedly "successful."

When I first met Lee, I was still directing more or less from an external base, with emphasis on choreography and stage pictures. It was not until Lee asked me a simple question, "From where has that character come?" that I began to think properly as a director. It seems ridiculous to me now, but I had never consciously asked myself that. And it led to two million other questions: What does the character want? What happens to that character in the scene? What had happened to all the characters in the scenes that were not in the play? And, most important of all, what is "dramatic action"? The answer to that question, by the way, might best be summed up as "a change of relationship." That is the single most valuable discovery I have been able to make as a director, and the single most important lesson I have tried to pass on as a teacher.

Lee himself changed over the years I knew him, growing more flexible while retaining his basic stubbornness. Even more than when I started, I cannot follow his teaching all the way, especially when I work with formal or nonrealistic material, where I feel the need to stress external or technical aspects in a way that much of his teaching denies. A director works with actors, but he also works with a given text and a given stage space. For a long time, I felt that Lee's methodology, which should have been a means to an end, became an end in itself. And I have often said that instead of changing the nature of American theater, Lee and all his disciples, ironically enough, changed the nature of American film. Nor was I always able to like Lee. He was basically a difficult and even abrasive human being. I have a reputation for being difficult myself, although I feel such reputation is somewhat exaggerated. But I respect him and honor his memory. I must credit him fully for bringing me alive as a director at a time when I most needed to have someone do that.

About this time, the Studio—reveling in its new acceptance and fame—was asked to do a television series, "The Actors Studio Presents," a series of hour-long programs that lasted until attrition and McCarthyism ended it. Most of the programs were directed by Marty Ritt or Danny Mann. Naturally, I tried to persuade the powers that be within the Studio and outside to let me direct one little program; but no one was willing to do so. Then, one day, Danny asked me to be assistant stage manager on one of his shows at fifty dollars per week for two weeks. The stage manager was Richard Boone, who later went on to better, and worse, things. The show was some awful melodrama about the sea. But I figured it would be good experience and maybe provide an "in" of some kind afterward. (My father used to say to me, "When are you going to stop getting experience and just get a good job?")

Dick Boone was sympathetic and helpful. Rehearsals, though impossible to watch, were painless to work through, and I learned that whatever Danny was doing in the control booth would not someday be impossible for me. I must have done a pretty good job, because I was immediately asked to take on another one, at seventy-five dollars a week. And there was the unstated promise that if I would do a couple more, I could move on to stage manager. Much as I needed the dough, I said no. That stage managerial trap, either on stage or in television, was not one I was going to fall into. I had seen too many decent directors, unable to find work, go into stage managing, learn to enjoy getting paid regularly and well, and never go back to directing. I'd rather go on unemployment.

Live television, however, I liked. The year 1948 was an exciting time to be breaking into the medium. No one was sure what the boundaries were. The potential for doing live drama, as well as for spreading interest in the theater on a national basis, was very great, and I thought about it a lot, occasionally waxing poetic, as I did once when I wrote a memo to the Theatre Inc. board of directors trying, unsuccessfully, to persuade them to get into television:

> . . . how do you do TV drama for the weekday daytime audience? . . . An answer (not to be confused with *the* answer): Operation Acting, or Rehearsal Two, or Give a Workshop . . . Why? Because the audience loves to criticize actors and acting. It loves to come backstage, because the audience likes to catch personalities off-base. Because the show is simple, direct, varied.

A number of the younger directors I knew were already moving into television, and the idea of following them appealed to me in my darker moments. Sidney Lumet and Alex Segal and Ted Post and George Schaeffer were doing it. If they could, why not I?

As it happened, my big chance came to do exactly that. Alex Segal, with whom I'd gotten friendly when he was directing at the Olney (Maryland) Summer Theatre near Washington, was going to work as staff director for WJZ-TV. He was doing very well, happy to be eating regularly, and enjoying moving the cameras around. Alex called me one day. WJZ-TV was looking for someone else to take on to train as a director—I think at about one hundred dollars per week—and he had persuaded them to consider me. He had given them my credits and *Long*

Way reviews, told them of my interest. They wanted to see me, seriously.

I wrote one of my lengthy and detailed memos to Audrey Wood, still supposedly my agent though I rarely saw her, summarizing the situation:

> As it must to all men, the television bug has bit me. Specifically, WJZ-TV is on the verge of offering me a job as Assistant Director . . . with the idea of training me, if I survive, to graduate to Director. . . . To say that I am torn is to underplay the scene; here's a chance to break into TV, to learn, to make a living, for a change. . . . On the other hand, I will have to give up the Actors Studio almost as soon as I found it . . . and I will have to lift myself out of the theatre completely. It's quite a choice, and I keep tottering back and forth on the precipice.

There was no question in my mind that I was at the Rubicon, and about to cross it and say yes to Alex and WJZ-TV. Then a cable arrived from England that changed everything. It was from Peter Cox, a young fellow I had met several years earlier when he had come to Catholic University from a place in England called Dartington to investigate the arts in America. Father Hartke, busy as usual, had shunted him off to a junior member of the faculty, me. I had liked Peter right away, and we parted friends, with promises on my part to return his visit some time.

In the ensuing years, Peter had become arts administrator for Dartington Hall, a progressive cultural center, nestled in the lovely rambling moors of Devonshire, with a unique blend of rural economics, the seven arts, and various species of progressive social experiments. The Indian philosopher Rabindranath Tagore, who had been responsible for its location there, had thought that spot one of the most beautiful on earth. It had been founded by Mrs. Leonard K. Elmhirst, who was born Dorothy Whitney and later became Mrs. Willard Straight, the mother of Michael Straight (editor of *The New Republic*) and Beatrice Straight. Biddy had told me something of Dartington's work in the arts.

Peter had previously invited me over to codirect a summer workshop in 1949 with Hallie Flanagan Davis of Vassar. Hallie was an immensely attractive and energetic woman, and the prospect of a month in England at her side was very welcome. I agreed, only to learn that Hallie had to bow out. Biddy suggested that I go alone, but I was too busy working on my New York career—especially its television component—to make a long-term commitment. Peter's unexpected cable, with a definite offer of six months' directing and teaching at Dartington, as well as the opportunity to see all the British theater I wanted, forced a quick decision.

"OH, TO BE IN ENGLAND . . .!"

1949

What made me decide in favor of the English, I'm not sure. My mother, as always, supported my art, but my father was unable to understand why I would not take a paying job. Most of my friends, including Alex Segal, thought I was nuts not to go into television. But Tiz encouraged me to try England; Audrey also, I think a bit because it would temporarily end, too, my weekly memos to her.

What I really wanted was to stay in the theater, and WJZ-TV meant I had to commit myself to something else. Besides, I loved being on a ship. And getting ready for trips. I spent eight hectic weeks preparing for this one on the S.S. *America*—whose red, white, and blue smokestacks I could glimpse from the steps of my Twenty-first Street apartment. The sailing date was March 21, 1949.

The Theatre Inc. board gave me messages and presents to transmit to England. Biddy asked me, as a special favor, to take over a trunkful of antique costumes, which, for some reason, her mother needed at Dartington. Dick Aldrich took me out for lunch for the first time, and asked me to go down to Macy's—I don't think he ever ventured that far downtown—and pick up six pairs of the loudest men's shorts I could find for his wife, Gertrude Lawrence, who was playing in Daphne du Maurier's *September Tide* at the Aldwych Theatre. I didn't have the nerve to ask him why.

Once poured aboard by Tiz and various Theatre Inc. staffers, I spent most of the week-long trip discovering the joys of morning bouillon on deck and sampling the greater comforts of cabin class at night. I even managed to work my way past various barriers to first class. No heiresses there either, or at least none I could find. We arrived, all too quickly, past Land's End, where I was somewhat surprised to discover the grass was the same color and texture as in Central Park, and landed in Southampton, whose covered docks looked vaguely familiar.

The trip on the "boat train" to London seemed as long as the ocean voyage. I arrived at Waterloo Station and transferred to a depressingly dark cavern of a hotel most inappropriately called the Great Western Royal. The penchant the British have for dressing up drabness with language has always amused me, but not that particular evening. The Great Western Royal lacked even a kitchen open at that hour. The hotel clerk informed me I could get something to eat in Piccadilly, a bus or tube ride away. Outside there was still, four years after the end of the war, a fairly effective brownout, and the only thing I could find open at midnight was an all-night outdoor stall serving tea and soggy doughnuts.

The next morning, I took the train along the coast to Devon, heading for the old Roman village of Totnes, the closest stop to Dartington Hall. The ride was full of new delights: all those quaint English villages, hedges and lanes, cucumber sandwiches with tea. And lots of Lady Bracknells, though neither Cecily nor Gwendolyn ventured into my compartment.

Rabindranath Tagore was right. Dartington was exquisite, beautifully set in a curve of the gently meandering Dart River, a series of fourteenth-century Gothic buildings nestled together among Devon's lush green hills and dales. If ever there was a Shangri-La west of the Himalayas, this was it. I got the grand tour: a great baronial-ceilinged eating hall with very little to eat, I soon discovered, except rhubarb and cottage pie, potatoes flavored with a drop of meat sauce; a vaulted library with an Inglenook fireplace, usually with neither readers nor a fire; Henry Moores scattered over the Versailles-like formal gardens and terraces; ancient ivy-covered stone buildings housing Dartington's cider mill, wool-weaving, and a progressive school with, it was rumored, nude coed bathing. Finally, there was the new modern theater, designed by William Lescaze, in which my production, as yet unselected, was to play. And all around, clusters of Bauhaus-like stucco buildings where some of the staff lived. No one, however, told me that playwright Sean O'Casey lived in a tiny village cottage a mile down the road, self-exiled years earlier from Dartington's environs.

I stayed that night with Peter Cox in his elegant cottage nearby. There was a gracious and attractive hostess, Cicely Martin (later married to Sir Philip Hendy, director of the National Gallery), whose relationship to Dartington or to Peter was not immediately clear. Dinner produced some delicious lamb, excellent soup, and lots of sherry before and port afterward. Sometime during the blanc-mange, I was asked if I wanted my bottle now or later. Not understanding but trying to be polite, I chose "now." Nothing happened. Half an hour later, however, as I crawled into a very soft bed, I almost yelped with surprise as my right thigh came into contact with something hot and wet, which turned out to be a not so hot-water bottle.

Graham Greene wrote an early novel titled *England Made Me*, which was transformed into a film by my lawyer, accountant, and friend Jerome Z. Cline. I almost got to direct it. Whether my six months in England, from March to October, 1949, "made me" is questionable. They certainly shaped my theatrical tastes and thinking, and helped to determine a great deal of what happened afterward. For Dartington gave me an opportunity not only to practice my directing, but also to journey the length and breadth of England and Scotland, meeting some of the top people in the theater—Tyrone Guthrie, Michel St. Denis, Anthony Quayle, Peter Brook, John Gielgud, Richard Burton, and Sean O'Casey—and reveling in the traditions and craftsmanship of the British theater of the time, a very good time indeed. Like Ina Claire, the English stage entranced me at once with its brilliance, a brilliance not only of performance. It was the amount and variety—and ubiquity—of English theatrical activity, even in what was called a bad season, that seemed staggering to me—and splendid. I also managed to encounter some eminent Britons unconnected to theater—musical luminaries Benjamin Britten and Peter Pears, writer-scientist Julian Huxley, politician Michael Foot, composer Imogen Holst, and art critic-historian Arthur Waley.

It was a feast that more than made up for the still persistent food rationing and the quality of the food not rationed. I have been going back for dessert ever since. Starting out by disliking the British Empire, I fell madly in love with the British in general, their language, their habit of moderation, their small rituals and routines. I also fell in love with a British girl, Eugenie "Jean" Muckle, and subsequently married her. She is a perfect example of the influence the English have had on my life.

My second night at Dartington, we were bused down to Exeter, Devon's county seat, to see the Young Vic's production of *As You Like It*, with Pierre Le Fevre, later of Juilliard, and W. Duncan "Bill" Ross, of the Canadian National Theatre School, the Seattle Repertory, and other places. On our return, the bus left me off at Peter's gate; I could hardly locate the front door because of the fog. A week or so later, on my first trip down to London, I saw Edith Evans in James Bridie's *Daphne Laureola*, a performance as good as Laurette Taylor's in *The Glass Menagerie*. I saw Laurence Olivier and Vivien Leigh, in their New Theatre season of repertory, alternating in *Richard III* and *The School for Scandal*, a contrast as marvelously startling as when I had first seen Olivier do *Oedipus* and *The Critic* in New York two years before; Paul Scofield portraying a blazingly handsome Alexander the Great in Terence Rattigan's *Adventure Story*; and Gertrude Lawrence in *September Tide*, a boulevard drama with no particular distinction save Miss L's presence.

Miss Lawrence, incidentally, was delighted with her six pairs of shorts, which I passed on to her after the performance. She took me out for a tour of London and a black market dinner somewhere in Mayfair, the only steak I had in London. In her chauffeured limousine I summoned up enough courage to ask what the shorts were for. She laughed and explained that her show was closing soon; shorts were still rationed—and expensive. She thought some really loud ones would make suitable closing night presents for the male members of her company.

The next morning, having heard my entire life story over the wine, Miss Lawrence tried to get me an appointment with Hugh Beaumont, better known as "Binkie," god and emperor of the H. M. Tennent organization, which ran the entire British commercial theater. Binkie, sad to say was, that morning, out of town. Nor did he later return my phone calls, and I eventually gave up trying. Miss Lawrence, bless her memory, never forgave me—or Binkie. The shorts, I gather, were a great hit.

That summer and fall, I made several trips to London, and visited the original Stratford, Edinburgh, Nottingham, Bristol, Birmingham, and lots of lesser-known towns. I also encountered the work of the youngest comet in the theatrical sky, a director named Peter Brook, whose productions I saw at Stratford, at Covent Garden, and at the Lyric Theatre in Hammersmith, where he directed an almost-American *Dark of the Moon*. I met Peter in his Covent Garden offices and was amazed to find him, at twenty-six, both so mature and so totally certain of his ultimate destiny.

For some time also, I pursued an older director, Tyrone Guthrie, writing him not my usual postcard but actual letters, offering devotion and assistance if he would only allow me to observe him in rehearsals. I saw several of his productions, including the history-making *The Three Estates*, by Sir David Lindsay, at Edinburgh, which later led to the thrust stages at Stratford, Ontario, in Minneapolis, and throughout the world. But, apart from a glancingly brief meeting at a press conference in Edinburgh, I never got to meet the elusive Guthrie, although I received several profuse and witty letters of apology.

In addition, I saw the work of such directors as Quayle, George Devine, Michael Langham, and John Burrell—then one of the ruling triumvirate at the Old Vic—and others. I spent some time with Michel St. Denis, whose Old Vic Theatre School was just then emerging from the bombed-out interior of the old Old Vic Theatre on Waterloo Road. I watched classes, rehearsals, and a graduation pantomime put together by George Devine, one of the school's three codirectors, along with St. Denis and Glen Byam Shaw. I went off–West End to the Arts, the New Lindsay, the Mercury, where Ashley Dukes held forth, and every other offbeat place I could find. I even managed to see the West of England (traveling) Rep do Roland Pertwee's *Pink String and Sealing Wax* in a town so small I've forgotten its name. Devon was full of little towns barely able to support a pub; they all managed to take in a play once in a while.

At Dartington itself, I wasn't asked to work very hard, which made me feel a bit guilty but allowed me to enjoy its informality and formlessness. There was a resident director in place, Leonard Bennett, neither unprofessional nor unknowledgeable, but somewhat coarse and unsociable, as well as drunk most of the time and usually in need of a bath. I tried to keep on good terms with him, although I soon found that half of everything he told me about anybody or anything at Dartington was fictional.

After a number of other choices were made and discarded, we hit on Saroyan's *My Heart's in the Highlands* for my "big" production. I loved it—though several members of the Dartington staff didn't—and felt its combination of rural simplicity and artistic purity made it an especially suitable choice. The cast, both staff members and local farmers, varied considerably in talent but were eventually united in determination. We rehearsed harder and longer than any previous production, and by the end we managed to put together something I considered respectable. Mrs. Elmhirst smiled approvingly whenever we happened to meet, and would inform me with all of her mysterious elegance that she had "heard good things."

As so often in rehearsals, the dawn is brightest nearest the night. One week before dress rehearsal, our lead, Johnny, turned a perfect yellow. We discovered that he had yellow jaundice and had to be confined to a hospital for an indefinite period. Postponement was out of the question; both our cast and our playing space had other commitments. Getting another Johnny out of the school proved impossible. Friends stopped me on the Dartington "campus" or in a Totnes street corner to commiserate. "I hear Johnny's got yellow jaundice," they'd say. "Dashed embarrassing!" Embarrassing? I was ready to tear my hair out, not to mention shooting myself. Eventually, with Mrs. Elmhirst's blessing and funds, I went to an acting school in London, the famed Italo Conti's, and found another boy, this time a professional, who was not bad.

Then, the night of our first dress rehearsal, I was informed at almost the last possible minute that one of our leading adult actors would not be able to be with us because, as staff chauffeur, he had to pick up Mr. Elmhirst at the railroad station. I raised hell, complained about standards and values being abandoned, suggested that in the interests of art and international cooperation someone else could be found to drive to Totnes to await the train from London. The actor in question was torn in half. On the one hand, he wanted to take part in the rehearsal. On the other, he was afraid that my pleas would cost him his job. They didn't, of course; he was too good a driver, and the Elmhirsts needed drivers as well as art. Mrs. Elmhirst drove the car, Mr. Elmhirst surviving the experience with British chin-up aplomb.

Reviewers were puzzled with *My Heart's in the Highlands* (where are they not?), but audience response was good. I wrote to Biddy, thanking her, and went on to other things. The other things included a two-week summer session with the British Drama League, an association of amateur theater organizations. In light of my accidental presence at Dartington that year, Peter had arranged for the BDL to specialize in American plays. Some twenty-five or thirty "students"—who included Glynne Wickham, newly appointed by Bristol University to run the first university theater drama program in England, and David Jones—later with the BBC, the Royal Shakespeare Company and the Brooklyn Academy of Music—arrived, and for days all of us sat on the lawn listening to the words of Arthur Miller, Tennessee Williams, Eugene O'Neill, and even Thornton Wilder in strenuously British accents. Try as they did, these young people were not very believable as Americans, although I tried, like mad, to be gentle in explaining this. David Jones, as I remember him, did reasonably well with the Gentleman Caller.

Mysteriously present, for part of the session, was John Burrell, then fighting for his artistic life at the Old Vic, though I didn't know that at the time. John's thought was to have all of the BDL students stage the trial scene from Shaw's *Saint Joan* in the Great Hall, a most suitable physical environment. For the second half of the evening, John decided that, in honor of the prevailing American atmosphere, he would direct *Pullman Car Hiawatha,* a one-act play by Thornton Wilder that I did not know. As the only resident American theater person, I was drafted to play the chief role of the Stage Manager, precursor of the Stage Manager in *Our Town.*

I learned plenty from *Pullman Car.* First of all, that it was a near masterpiece; and, second, that it was something I could make use of in various situations. I was introduced to a play with which I have been associated with pleasure and profit ever since, in classroom and theater, situations at the Actors Studio, as the first color television drama on CBS, and at several colleges. I had seen Jed Harris's original production of Wilder's *Our Town,* with Frank Craven and Martha Scott, had enjoyed it but emerged with mixed feelings about its style. Then, during the war, in Washington, I had loved *The Skin of Our Teeth;* while most of the audience were leaving at the first intermission, I was having my faith in the theater restored. Now I reveled in *Pullman Car Hiawatha*'s sentiment and theatricality and humor—even as I struggled not to disappoint my BDL colleagues with my performance.

After BDL's departure, Rudolf von Laban, that grand old man of modern dance, and his daughter, Juanita, arrived. Everyone, including the Elmhirsts, spent early mornings doing exercises out beside the Henry Moores and afternoons discovering the mysteries of Labanotation, a way of recording choreography that Laban had just started to pursue. His agility at the age of seventy gave me hope and inspiration, even though his example never made me into a dancer.

The atmosphere at Dartington, while both pleasant and congenial, could be, on occasion, soporific. I remember Arthur Waley slaving away for weeks arranging a fantastic exhibition of Chinese art, which must have cost a small fortune. In the three weeks it was on display, only eleven people came in to see it. As for Lescaze's theater, no matter how beautiful its proportions or well-equipped its new switchboard, the available audience was tiny. Very few people came from Totnes, and no one from Exeter some twenty miles away. The Elmhirsts' dream of civilized urban comforts in a rural community simply did not apply to the theater.

Sean O'Casey, who lived in a tiny worker's row house in Totnes, was an early victim. When he had first settled in Totnes, Sean had been extolled and regaled by Mrs. Elmhirst. He was obviously the logical choice for playwright-in-residence honors. Promises were made, hopes aroused. His work, unaccepted in London's theaters, was going to find its home at Dartington. Unfortunately, Sean's openly left-wingish social philosophy did not entirely accord with the Dartington Establishment. No sooner had he been set up on his pedestal than he fell out of favor with the Elmhirsts. When he left, by his lights both abandoned and betrayed, he swore never to set foot on Dartington's acres again. Mrs. Elmhirst never acknowledged his nearby presence. When, midway in my stay, I finally met the O'Caseys, it was by sheer accident. Peter inadvertently mentioned that O'Casey lived a couple of miles away. That same Sunday, my way prepared via letter, I trudged down the hill, bearing my mother's weekly shipment of rations—egg-powder and butter—calculated to keep me from starving to death among all the vegetables.

On my way, I encountered a short, slight figure, wearing dark baggy pants, turtleneck, faded tweed jacket, and a workman's cap, sitting cross-legged on a stone wall. When I asked whether he knew where someone named O'Casey might be living, he pointed silently to the house behind him. It was Sean himself.

Subsequently, I met O'Casey's wife, Eileen, and their children, Shivaun, Niall, and Breon, and came down often for Sunday breakfasts, lugging my precious American parcel of goodies. Sean told me of those perfidious Irish, unwilling to produce his plays, and his plans for returning to the London theater. Mrs. Elmhirst and Dartington Hall simply did not exist. The house was always full of warmth and welcome, in contrast to the cool correctness at the top of the hill. Sean was already almost blind but kept up with the world and theatrical news.

In spite of a flock of willing females, Dartington's Elysian Fields grew more and more lonely to this lone ranger from New York. I was just over thirty, my virginity long gone, but still romantic in my tastes and sexual pursuits. I had to be in love with a girl before I jumped into the sack with her. At Dartington, there were plenty of girls to like, but no one to love.

Back in Washington was someone whom I began to think of and pine for more and more, whom I shall refer to as Helen. I had directed her as a dancer in a couple of Catholic University musicals, and I had dated her on numerous occasions, even going up to Bennington, where she was studying dance. Helen was eight or nine years younger than I and possessed a gorgon mother. We were equally rebellious at all restrictions, unsure of ourselves and uncertain of the future and presumably falling in love. Had I stayed in New York, we would have gone on seeing each other, with freedom to consummate our "affair" more comfortably than in Washington. But because we happened to be separated, our "romance," such as it was, bloomed through the mail.

Almost without realizing what I was doing, I decided that I had to have Helen with me, and that one of those little Devonshire towns would make a great place for a honeymoon. Using my last dollar, I sent Helen a steamship ticket. She was more anxious than ever to get away from her mother and responded enthusiastically. Peter and Mrs. Elmhirst offered no objections to Helen joining me, perhaps feeling that, with proper company, I might stay on longer. The thrill lasted until Helen arrived on the grounds; from that moment, I knew that the whole thing would never work. Not only did she seem colder and more distant than before; she refused to involve herself in any way with the life of the Dartington community. After each meal, she sat at the table alone drinking her coffee and smoking her cigarette. While everyone socialized, she remained in the library by herself. We lived together in the staff quarters, argued, fought, wondered, despaired, and decided to get married.

We were married, quietly, in August 1949 in the Registry Office at Totnes, attended only by Peter Cox and one of the cast members of *Highlands*. Mrs. Elmhirst, beaming even more than usual, gave us a most practical wedding gift, fifteen welcome British pounds, worth about sixty dollars. Our chauffeur friend drove us around the Dartington "campus" in an open car, then trundled us off to a brief honeymoon in Widdecombe on the Devon Coast, complete with feather bed from which we rarely stirred, rocky coastal walks, friendly pubs in which they had rarely if ever seen an American, and nothing to do at night except get back into that bed. After a week, Helen joined me in my British theater travels, straining the budget but not Mrs. Elmhirst's continued generosity.

One day in London, having graduated to the Cumberland Hotel near Marble Arch, I was wandering through Grosvenor Square, past Roosevelt's statue. Walking directly toward me was David Stevens, the Rockefeller Foundation's man in the arts, from whom I had been trying to pry money for years. David asked me what I was doing in London. When I told him, in great detail, he inquired whether I would be getting over to the Continent to see any theater. I explained that I didn't have the money, and that Mrs. Elmhirst's fief didn't extend beyond the English Channel. I didn't tell David then that I had played a little hooky that May, taking off for several weeks in Paris, where I had seen Jouvet's *Dr. Knock* and Jean-Louis Barrault-Madeleine Renaud productions of *Intermezzo* and *Hamlet*, and discovered the Left Bank. In fact, I had spent all of my first night there wandering the Champs Elysées, propositioned right and left by the most beautiful young ladies I'd ever seen. David told me to write him a letter asking for a grant to study theater in Europe. He was sure that the National Theatre Conference, which the Rockefeller Foundation was then supporting, would be glad to oblige.

After we said goodbye, I walked into the nearest hotel, put sixpence into a typewriter, and wrote David a letter, asking for five hundred dollars to subsidize a month's tour of the European theater. A copy of the letter, together with a detailed explanation of the circumstances, went to Barclay Leathem, NTC's executive secretary, at Western Reserve University in Cleveland. I had known Barclay during my OWI days; he had at one time even suggested the possibility of luring me away from Catholic University for a job at Western Reserve. Within a week, a check for five hundred dollars arrived at Dartington. Bidding goodbye to all, Helen and I took off for Paris and points south and east.

The theater in England remained with me, even when I was furthest away from it. That theater always seemed to me to have a strength greater than the sum of its individual parts, something not always true in America. What has most affected my thinking is the English theater's functioning as a nationwide habit and not as a local luxury. On all levels. Whatever weaknesses or faults, it was an institution and not a free-for-all, a habitat and not a jungle, a meal rather than a cocktail party. Theatergoer and theater worker alike sensed (I quote Tyrone Guthrie) "the implication that the imaginative stimulus which good theater can supply is a necessity, not merely an amenity, in a healthy community." Or as George Jessel said to me when I bumped into him at Wyndham's Theatre, "Every show has a chance here because they like the theater. We don't have to wait for the reviews."

I have always wanted to be part of a theater, whether in New York or Washington or elsewhere, where we did not "have to wait for the reviews" before we knew whether we were going to eat next week. The closest I've ever come to that happy state has been at the Arena Stage, in some of its later years. Not that I am against the idea of reviews; some of my best friends are drama critics. But I am for continuity of work rather than stop-and-go, hit-and-miss; permanence instead of production-in-transit; a theater that suggests a home rather than a hot-bed motel. I prefer to be judged by my overall track record rather than by last night's notices. And I always hope for a theater operation with a reasonable amount of stability rather than one with an unreasonable amount of chaos—even if I can't make a fortune with it. As I once told a *New York*

Times reporter, "I don't expect to make a million dollars; I just want to work in the theater." A self-fulfilling prophecy, I'm afraid. In Europe, a permanent theater operation with an organic point of view and a reasonable amount of balance is taken for granted. In England, such an operation seems increasingly to be accepted. In the United States, in spite of huge strides in my own lifetime, such an operation—at least in New York City—is still considered the impossible exception.

Perhaps the London theater is changing too, coarsening, becoming not only more expensive but more impersonal and unfriendly. Perhaps I am too romantic about it. But I remember that I have gone to the theater in England hundreds of times, and that only once have I left before the curtain came down. I remember that I have always heard and understood every syllable, no matter where I happened to be sitting. I remember—and I treasure—not only the individual productions and performances, not only what went on onstage, but the comfort and convenience of playgoing, the courtesy and cleanliness I found everywhere, in the box office, the auditorium, and backstage. I remember that the opera glasses I once rented for sixpence had no umbilical cord riveting them to the back of the seat in front of me. The management assumed that I liked the theater. They were willing to trust me.

I remember also the taxi driver who once brought me to the Aldwych directly from Victoria Station to see Alec Guinness in *Mr. Sycamore.* He knew what was playing, he knew what Guinness's performance was like, he cared about what I would think of it—as much as he cared about his tip. I met a cabdriver like that in New York once. He had just emigrated from the Soviet Union.

Helen and I spent a month together in Europe, theatergoing and just going. It should have been terrific—and it was. We didn't have much money, so we stayed in family hotels, traveled by local trains and buses, sometimes by night at lower rates, and eating well but carefully. I remember sitting with her at a café in Paris, drinking *vin ordinaire,* reading a headline in the *Herald-Tribune* that someone was holding at the next table announcing that the Russians had the atomic bomb.

We never knew where we would be going the next day, or cared. One bright morning, we decided to take the train to Innsbruck, hoping to get away from the theater for a while and wander around some mountain scenery. Someone in our compartment was talking about Vienna, the train's final destination. On a whim, over a drink, we asked the conductor how much more it would cost us to continue on to Vienna. "Four dollars." We decided to exchange mountains for museums and bought the tickets. Later, after we had passed Innsbruck, someone asked us if we had our gray cards. We suddenly realized that, in the geography of Europe, Vienna was still under Soviet occupation. We would have to cross their border.

By this time, we were already approaching the border town of Linz, then held by the American army. We were traveling in the same compartment with a sinister-looking Frenchman and an Indian student returning to Bombay from Kentucky, where he'd been learning to make bourbon whiskey. The moment the train stopped on our side of the border, Helen and I, grabbing our two bags, got out and started walking along the tracks to the U.S. command post—while the entire trainload of passengers watched us out of their windows. Presumably the Soviets were watching from the other side of the river.

At the command post, a burly lieutenant with his feet up on the standard GI desk, asked us why we had gotten off. Evidently Linz was not exactly a tourist attraction. I told him we had decided to go back to Innsbruck on the next train because we didn't have a gray card.

"You and her Amurican citizens, bud?"

"Yeah." Not very enthusiastically.

"So, okay, you didn't get your gray cards, huh?"

"Yeah." By this time, I was sure that the Russians were listening by radar to every syllable.

"Okay, so we'll fix that up, right away." Without waiting for my answer, he got on the phone. "Tell the captain there's a couple of Amurican citizens out here got no gray cards."

"Please, we'll go back to Innsbruck, we don't mind." Or to Paris, Or anywhere west.

"No sirree, Bud. We don't let those Russkies do that to no Amurican citizen."

"But . . ."

"Just hold your horses. Captain'll be right up with your own personal gray cards." By that time, I wished I had never heard of gray cards, never taken the train, never met David Stevens in London. All I could see was Russians, looking straight at Helen and me, especially at me, and just waiting to get their hands on us. I explained to the lieutenant about my having been born in Russia. He only laughed harder.

In about two minutes, which seemed like an hour, a motorcycle squad car screeched around a corner and pulled up in front of us, covering us with dust. A cigar-smoking captain and two soldiers, guns at a ready position, climbed out. The lieutenant talked, the captain nodded, Helen and I worried. Then the captain sat down, filled out two gray cards, stamped them three or four times each, had us fill in one or two blanks and sign. Then he tore off again, in a blaze of smoke and dust. Under the same watchful eyes of every train passenger, we walked all the way down the same tracks to the same compartment, trying to restrain the impulse to drop everything and run.

The train started, went about twenty-five feet, then stopped again. Two young, tough, crew-cut Soviet soldiers, their tommy guns held prominently in front of them, got on and started going through the compartments, checking passports—and gray cards. I prayed to all the gods I knew, stuffed two sticks of Wrigley's chewing gum into my mouth, and started reading *The New Yorker* and *Time* magazine simultaneously, wondering what was going to happen to Helen when I got deported to Siberia.

Eventually, the soldiers got to our compartment, slid the door open, and demanded "Pahs*port*!" Our friend from Bombay was sitting closest to the door, and they took his passport first. Although India had gained its independence two years earlier, he had been in Kentucky and still had his old British Empire passport. Suddenly, the Russians started arguing about his passport, forgetting about everyone else in the compartment. I listened to every word, trying not to let them know that I understood their language. One soldier kept insisting that they ought to haul this guy off the train because he didn't have the proper passport; the other soldier kept saying what the hell difference did it make, it was an Indian passport properly assigned. The Indian bourbon-maker, realizing something was up that might get him into trouble, started to explain in a rapid-fire mixture of English and Hindustani. Finally, they accepted the passport.

By this time they must have decided that they'd held the train up long enough. They looked at no other passports in our compartment, grabbed all our gray cards without so much as a glance, and went on, their normal scowls a bit more pronounced. A few minutes later, the train with its blinds drawn down so that we could not discover any military secrets, proceeded to Vienna. I spat out my chewing gum and had a drink.

BACK TO THE DRAWING BOARDS

1949–1950

Like all honeymoons, my European idyll soon came to an end. A cable from Father Hartke at C.U. followed me around a half dozen cities but finally caught up to me in London. Walter Kerr was leaving C.U. to try his hand and mind as a drama critic on *Commonweal*. Would I come back? After the semibitterness of my last year, Father's offer of promotion to assistant professor and a higher salary was sweet to the taste. Sweeter still it was to refuse, and refuse is what I first thought of doing.

Between the pressures of a new marriage, unemployment, and uncertainty of New York's acceptance, I hesitated. Confronted with contradictory desires, I straddled. Would Father let me come back for two days a week? The rest of the time I wanted to spend making the rounds of New York, where Helen would work and study with the Doris Humphrey-Charles Weidman Dance Company. I wasn't sure whether I hoped Father would accept or reject the idea. He hemmed and hawed; I hesitated and kept changing my mind. Eventually he agreed—but made the days Tuesday and Thursday, so that I was effectively in Washington for most of each week, as well as for a month at a time whenever I directed a show.

The apartment on Twenty-first Street was now decorated with my new mate's personal touches and dancing togs, and we started in on the next chapter of my tale of two cities. Every Tuesday morning at six, I took the Congressional down to Washington, taught my first class at eleven, languished all day Wednesday out at my parents' new bungalow in Bethesda or dined with old Washington acquaintances, and took the

Thursday afternoon Congressional back, arriving home usually to find the place empty and nothing in the fridge for supper. The honeymoon was definitely over.

This arrangement endured for a year, more or less. When things were really bad on Twenty-first Street, I would leave Washington on the midnight train, arriving in time to see the sun rise on Friday. Sometimes I would stay in Washington over the weekend. It was during those years of split-city living, married and once more single, that my artistic work as a director specifically and significantly improved, and I was able to take a long step toward what was to become my professional career.

Coming back to C.U. meant that my choice of courses was considerably upgraded, and my influence in the department extended. I now taught directing instead of phonetics. My opinions about realism as a form or on the virtues or limitations of the Stanislavski system were no longer automatically dismissed. And I had a much greater say in choosing the department's annual season of plays, including my own.

My first choice was a new script, John Finch's *The Downstairs Dragon*, which I had latched on to the year before in New York through Tiz Schauffler's stalwart efforts. (Before we opened its title was changed to the less colorful and suitable *The Real McCoy*.) Tiz in her own quiet way had even managed to persuade Jo Mielziner, busiest and most successful scene designer, to consider it for a Broadway production. A converted Catholic highly impressed with Father Hartke's personality and history, Jo had offered to provide the set for C.U.'s production, a real coup for Father.

Dragon—I still think of it under its original title—concerned a real dragon living downstairs in a New York museum, and the way in which the people who inhabited the museum dealt with it. Like so many other and later philosophical whimsies with which I have become involved, this one worked better on the page than on the stage. Jo's set was lovely; the reviews were not. The play died a natural death with us, but the play's theme involved illusion versus reality, a conflict which often engaged me, in more durable dramatic examples, in later years.

In those years at C.U., I was also able to direct *Oedipus Rex*, the first production utilizing Dudley Fitts and Robert Fitzgerald's lean, modern adaptation; *Macbeth*; *Othello*; *The Madwoman of Chaillot*; *The Skin of Our Teeth*; and, best of all, *The Cherry Orchard*—several of which proved to be as theatrically effective as anything I've done since. (It was only after Walter's departure that Chekhov was permitted on a Catholic University stage.) Two of them profoundly affected a young woman named

Zelda Fichandler, who was later to have an enormous importance in my artistic and personal existence. In a much later interview, Zelda confessed that "the biggest influence on me artistically in my early life was Schneider's production of *The Skin of Our Teeth* and *The Cherry Orchard* at Catholic University. . . . These were peaks in my life, and still are. . . ."

Those productions also brought me attention and status in the Washington community; one of them, *Skin,* was to lead directly to my first real Broadway offer. More important, I think, they gave me personal reassurance. I was no longer an unemployed pariah, I was a working messiah, slightly schizophrenic but managing to tread the artistic waters.

In each of the productions, I managed to intertwine a feeling of human reality with theatricality, never satisfied with either of these alone, remembering both Lee Strasberg and Tony Guthrie. *Oedipus* was placed in a barbaric prehistoric society immersed in ritual, with real people but with jagged, kaleidoscopic lighting, sometimes focusing down to catch a detail—Oedipus's fingers scratching at the ground. *Macbeth* had six witches, although the audience was aware of and saw only three at a time. In a flash, the three would disappear and appear somewhere else, high up in the battlements of the castle. People used to come up on the stage after the performance to look for the elevators. In *Othello,* nervous about the artificialities of the soliloquies, I gave Othello a mute servant who always followed him about. And for *The Cherry Orchard,* my scene designer provided gauze walls through which the cherry trees were always present.

But the chief improvement in my work had to do with the way in which I dealt with the actors. I began to veer away from specific ordered "blocking" except in general outline, in a Greek chorus, or in a complex group scene. I concentrated instead on relationships, motivations, meanings, and a carefully thought-out floor plan. The battles of stage movement, I came to discover, may well be won or lost on the drawing board.

Since that time, I have tended more to consider what a character wants or needs, what he or she is doing, thinking, sensing, rather than what he or she happens to be saying or where he or she has to move. I consider the circumstances surrounding the scene, plan basic high points and essentials of position and movement, but encourage the actors to fill in and change things as we go along. This does not, however, mean that my preparation is less extensive or that I necessarily accept the first thing that happens in rehearsal. On the contrary, I spend much more time reading and studying the script to discover the rhythms and subtext.

At various stages of the work, I may try to pursue many different ways of achieving possible results. Very often, I may not know what I want until I see or hear a number of alternate possibilities. I may suggest what is wrong with a specific move, gesture, or manner of interpretation, or I may leave the actor alone to find out for himself. I may ask the actor to try another kind of response in order to justify a stylistic need or a perception of which he may not even be aware. But I rarely tell him or her, for example, to get up or sit down on a certain word or syllable. I simply suggest that by the end of the speech, he or she should be near the window in order to be seen from outside, or that somewhere during the speech he or she ought to find two or three places to examine the letter, or reassure the other character, or reveal something previously unrevealed. I have found that with most of today's actors this approach frees the performers to exercise their own imagination and sensitivity.

When I first began directing, I would normally start to stage a script on the first or second day of rehearsal, partly because there was never enough time, and partly because I thought that was the best way to work. Now, I like to spend the first few days reading the play, talking it over with the actors, answering their questions and clarifying their confusions, exploring the specifics of script and performers.

In the case of that C.U. production of *The Cherry Orchard*, I took more than a week on this stage of rehearsal, including a day or two trying various improvisations with varying floor plans. This was in order to free the actors from specific movements, and was designed to make a heavily Irish-American and youthfully optimistic cast understand and try to behave like Russians. When we finally got on stage, we had progressed to the point where it was possible to work out each act's moves in one evening, something I previously had never been able to accomplish. And the degree of reality—looking, listening, behaving, reacting—was greater than I had been able to achieve with equally competent casts.

The use of improvisation during rehearsals may or may not bring about the desired results. It is worth trying—and trying again—so long as it is not dogma but experiment. That is equally true of every other directorial procedure and device. If it works, fine; if not, go on to something else. I have, for instance, tried playing music to see if that might influence or stimulate the actors. I have experimented with exercises to arouse the actor's imagination and physical responses. Sometimes I have had actors playing a scene at a distance from each other or with their backs turned, to produce a greater urgency of communication. Once I had a cast running up and down the aisles of the auditorium, playing a given scene at full volume, in order to produce the proper vitality in the scene. These devices had a pronounced and immediate effect.

I have also become a great believer in rehearsing privately with groups of two or three actors. Such privacy removes any shyness or inhibition that may exist, even subconsciously, and helps the actor to work freely and spontaneously.

Every play and every performer poses specific problems and suggests specific techniques. Every production must be approached not theoretically but organically and specifically, and with as clear a perception of its problems as possible. Including the problem of rehearsal time.

After I returned to Catholic University, it was almost immediately obvious to all, including myself, that something had happened to my directing. It was not just that I was a better director—I was a different director. My productions were just as full of effective stage pictures, but movement and grouping seemed more clear and connected. The rhythmical relationships were as explicit—I have always considered rhythm to be critical in any scene—but the sense of life was deeper, not necessarily more "realistic" in a photographic sense but clearly more "real." The actors, even in a Greek tragedy, were no longer semipuppets. They were contributing the fullest measure of themselves and were, therefore, more able to grow in their craft as actors. There was no question that something had happened to make me grow in mine.

The Washington critics welcomed my transformation. They greeted *Oedipus* with such words as "magnificent," "shattering," "breathtaking," "electric"—and, in words not always applied to productions of Greek tragedy, "more suspenseful than a Hollywood movie." *Othello* they called "the best show in town." "The entire performance," wrote my friend Ernie Schier, who often leaned backward not to let his public know that he was, "is fast, fluid, and sings with a passion echoed by the beauty of Shakespeare's poetry." Many years later, Lincoln Kirstein, who saw the production by accident, told me it was the best version of *Othello* he had ever seen. About *The Cherry Orchard* they noted its "beauty and depth." And for *Macbeth*, the production was judged "unique and imaginative," rating with *Othello* "in freshness, color, new life." With those reviews, as my father used to say, and ten cents (hah!), I could get on the subway.

My only unpleasant experience came with *Madwoman*, and that had nothing to do with the reviewers. The audacity of Giraudoux's characters and situations, as well as the theatrical richness of his language, appealed to me immensely. We knew that we would need a mature actress as the Countess Aurelia and I was able to persuade Father to let me invite Aline MacMahon, whom I knew to be interested, as guest star. Aline was a well-established and excellent actress. The students and I were all happy with Aline, who was equally delightful onstage and off. Rehearsals were going wonderfully well. Everyone was happy. The show looked better than good.

We had been rehearsing without a proper armchair for Aurelia's big scene, and I wanted to get something that would enhance Aline's presence. None of the chairs dug up by our prop department had yet secured my approval. Finally, more than halfway through rehearsals, what was promised to be *the* chair arrived and was placed in the center of the stage for my inspection. I ran back to the last row of seats to get the proper perspective, turned to look; the chair was gone.

"Goddamn it," I yelled. "Who moved that armchair?"

A small, somewhat frazzled prop girl came out from the wings. "Well, you see, Mr. Schneider . . . ," she started to explain, the tears on the verge of flowing.

"Look!" I thundered back, all the way to the rafters, "when I ask you a question . . . don't answer it!" The remark became a legend. The show didn't.

What had happened earlier that day, and what affected the production much more profoundly than the armchair, was that someone in the local community had phoned up to inform the administration that C.U. was employing a known subversive. The time was 1950, "McCarthyism" just beginning to show itself. Aline's name must have appeared on a list somewhere, and someone remembered. The administration panicked. Father called me in to tell me that Aline had to leave us, and Josephine was taking over her role. It was about two weeks before our opening. When I demanded to know what was going on and why, Father would not come out and tell me. Aline had already been hustled out of town, and I was being presented with a *fait accompli* to accept—or reject by resigning. I called Aline in New York to find out what had happened. She couldn't believe that I didn't know.

All I could do was take a stand. And I was not sure what stand to take. I remember talking to both drama critics with whom I was especially friendly, the *Star*'s Jay Carmody and the *Times-Herald*'s Ernie Schier. Both of them expressed regret, but both, including Ernie, advised me not to jeopardize my career in what could be no more than a quixotic gesture. I wrote out my letter of resignation and prepared to take the train to New York. At the last minute, after talking with Ernie, I made the decision not to resign but to stay on until the end of the year. Aline, gracious as always, forgave me. I never forgave myself.

People have asked me whether I was myself subject to blacklisting for my own activities during this period. Apart from that wartime disappointment at the War College during the war, I was not. And yet, during wartime and after, I had been openly active with the National Council of American-Soviet Friendship, writing an article or two for their publication. I had contributed to Russian War Relief and attended several of their rallies at Madison Square Garden. I had always sought to visit the Soviet Union, applying several times for that purpose to the Rockefeller Foundation, and seeking every possible contact with Soviet citizens in the arts. I had visited the Soviet embassy, had fairly friendly relations with Valentin Bruslov, a cultural attaché during part of the war.

By current standards I was subversive as hell. But no one paid the slightest attention to me, then or later. I was just too small a fish to get the headline. So, whoever it was left me alone, to suffer in my conscience about Aline but lack the guts to put my job on the line. I've often thought of that when I hear people blaming others for not doing what they themselves have not been called upon to do.

Left alone in New York most of the time, Helen had been pursuing her dancing career. She took more and more classes from a variety of teachers, getting an occasional television job. Max Liebman hired her once or twice for television's *Your Show of Shows* and she was clearly on her way. I was pleased but concerned because we were seeing less and less of each other—even on the days I was in New York—and had less and less to say to each other when we were together. I was using my two days a week plus the weekend to make the rounds, go to the Studio (on Friday), read scripts, and let my friends know I was back. And I was both encouraging Helen and very much needing her to encourage me. Tiz had married a lawyer, was about to have kids, and was not too available for my career. Theatre Inc. had faded away for the last time, but Richard Aldrich was still at Cape Cod running the Cape Playhouse at Dennis during the summers and had just taken over a newly renovated Falmouth Playhouse. One day, out of the blue, Aldrich invited me to come up to Falmouth to be resident director alongside Arthur Sircom, who had put on more summer stock shows than anybody alive.

I had never been keen on working in summer stock, even when Day

Tuttle had offered me various intros. Nor was I entirely sure that I would be directing, or how often, especially with Arthur around. But everyone told me it would be good experience and a worthwhile step into the commercial world. Helen and I would get room and board with the actors, and she was offered a hostess job at the local eating place, where the actors always got free hors d'oeuvres—until they got sick of them. I was a little nervous about the entire proceeding, but nothing else interesting had come up. I didn't want to go back for a third summer to Cain Park, which by that time had a different director; he wanted to do *A Midsummer Night's Dream* with live horses. After all those dusty rehearsal studios, Helen liked the idea of being on the Cape for a summer. I liked the idea of working with some New York actors. So, at the end of my first returned year at Catholic University, the summer of 1950, we took a long bus trip north.

Since then, I have been involved in a number of theaters while they were being built or rebuilt. In 1950, I was still unprepared for the chaos at Falmouth. I was also unprepared for what the recent introduction of "packages" meant to summer stock. A "package" meant that the star and perhaps one or two leading players would come in on Sunday, or even Monday, afternoon, check the lights and the acoustics, and then go on. During the week previous, the resident director, "guided" by the star's advance person, would have worked with the other actors, making sure that everything was blocked and timed the way the star wanted it. Floor plans were, of course, rigidly repeated from one production to the next, though the pattern of the wallpaper might alter a shade. Any "creative contributions" by the resident director were out of the question.

As Aldrich and Sircom worked out their season, "my" three shows were *Over 21*, with Eve Arden; *Harvey*, with Stuart Erwin; and *Post Road*, with Zasu Pitts. In addition, I was given the privilege of going over to the Cape Playhouse in Dennis to direct Shelley Winters in *Born Yesterday*. Stu Erwin was doing his show at Olney a couple of weeks before, and Aldrich sent me down to have a look at it. Erwin was actually very funny. I thought we could do even better with the cast I had assembled for him at Falmouth, which included Jean Stapleton and a few other capable if relatively unknown actors. I arrived back in Falmouth just in time for the opening night of our first show, *Caesar and Cleopatra*, with Paulette Goddard, which Arthur was directing. I knew he had been working hard all week moving his actors around the hypothetical Miss Goddard.

The star arrived, about twenty minutes before the curtain was supposed to go up, got into her expensively designed wisp of a costume—which didn't seem to relate to the character, the play, or the other costumes—and climbed into place atop a very rickety Sphinx that the Falmouth scenery department had been struggling with for days. I sat down to watch, hoping to learn how to direct for summer stock. I lasted until her first line, "I'm Cleah—paa-traa, Queeen of Eee-gypttt," delivered in flat Brooklynese, without so much as a glance at the Caesar of the occasion, Francis Compton, who looked vaguely uncomfortable about the whole affair. Then I went next door to the local bar and downed six sweet Manhattans. Manhattans, without the cherry, have been my favorites ever since.

My own experiences later were not much of an improvement. Erwin came in a bit earlier for Mary Chase's *Harvey* and was pleasant to everyone—until he got onstage, whereupon he tried to do all he could to kill Jean Stapleton's laughs as well as everybody else's. Eve Arden was better. She brought her own leading man, and she had all the laughs. She was also not happy to deviate from any of her previous patterns. Ruth Gordon's play had a running gag involving an icebox that made noises every time she opened it. I had cleverly arranged an icebox for our version that made noises with a conga beat, and suggested to Eve that she move in rhythm with the noises. Eve hated the idea. Until one day, at the midweek matinee, the laughs not coming as loud or as fast as usual, she tried doing what I had suggested. The business got a huge laugh, and Eve kept it in the rest of the week. When she left, she asked me if she could take the sound effects recording with her. It was a closing night present from her resident director.

With *Post Road* (by Wilbur Daniel Steele and Norman Mitchell) for which I had been waiting all summer, whatever illusions I had about summer stock vanished completely. The play is a slick, shallow thriller. I had hired practically an all Actors Studio cast, including Vivian Nathan and Ann Hegira, and rehearsed it night and day as though it were Chekhov. Arthur came in once or twice to rehearsal and kept advising me to go fishing instead of digging up all that onstage reality. I kept thinking of what Lee Strasberg would say, and went on digging. Miss Pitts arrived, took one look at our setting and at a special lighting effect I had devised to emphasize her position in the stairwell while she was holding the baby away from its would-be kidnappers—and decided it all had to go. After one rehearsal with our "company," she also wanted to replace all the actors, but it was too late.

I pleaded, begged, explained how the set and the lighting helped the scene—and her. She was adamant. "I was a star before you were born, young man!" Without thinking, I hurled my answer out of the darkened auditorium: "I didn't know you were that old, Miss Pitts." The rest was silence, although the show did go on, in the same set, without the special lighting effect. Arthur was right, I should have gone fishing.

My ultimate test came with Shelley's appearance in the Dennis season. Dennis not only was one of the most beautiful and well-equipped playhouses anywhere but catered to the most fashionable audiences. We rehearsed for two weeks, with Shelley's advance director objecting to almost everything. When Shelley arrived, she objected to whatever was left. She immediately threw a tantrum over the color of her couch on stage, and a larger one over her dressing room wallpaper, three or four more about the actors we had obtained to support her, actors of whom Dick Aldrich had personally approved. She used language not generally heard in public in those days.

Aldrich, still as tall and slim as a matinee idol, was above all a gentleman, mostly concerned with taking care of his wife, Gertrude Lawrence, resplendent and retired for the summer in her attractive lakeside cottage. Aldrich was also an excellent producer. Whatever Shelley's behavior, he knew he had to get the show on. But he didn't have to talk to Shelley afterward, which he never did during her entire run, never threw a party for her—which he had done for every other star that summer—never invited her over to the cottage to see Miss Lawrence, and wasn't there to say goodbye when Shelley left. The show went fine; business was excellent. And a pacified Shelley Winters, having gotten her desired sofa and wallpaper, couldn't understand the cold shoulder. After all, she was only behaving the way she had always behaved.

I completed the season and my transformation to professionalism by being cast in a small role in *Goodbye, My Fancy* with Sylvia Sidney, one of the best and most beautiful actresses alive. My role was that of my usual idealistic young professor. I was terrified, but the experience turned out to be pleasant, and I was glad for a change to be spared the rigors of summer stock directing. I was even mentioned in a notice or two. By the end of the run, I was glad to get back to my New York-Washington axis again, even though some of my actors were amateur, the sofas less ornate, and life more solitary.

By the end of the summer, both Helen and I had more or less decided that it might be better for us to separate. Traumatic as the decision was, both of us knew it was necessary. We went back to New York, talked our way back and forth a few more times, only to realize anew that we were not meant for each other, as the song titles used to say.

Divorce then being much more expensive and complicated than I could manage, I wangled an annulment from a Brooklyn court, establishing "residence" there for the necessary time. The grounds were that when Helen married me she had concealed her unwillingness to have children, that being the ostensible purpose of all marriages. Helen concurred. We bade each other a sad, strained farewell. I have seen her only once since, many years later, when I bumped into her on Sixth Avenue and we had a cup of coffee together. She was, sad to say, working in an office, and no longer dancing.

I spent several anxious days concerned about Catholic University's attitude toward the annulment, worrying that I might be out of a job. I was delighted to learn that a Catholic institution—which happened to need me—was as prepared to rationalize an ethical situation as readily as a non-Catholic one. No one said anything, although Father did express regrets about the marriage not working out. The year turned out well for me in both cities, once I got over the shock of the failed marriage. We had no children. And Helen was most understanding about my not settling anything on her financially. After all, I didn't have much to settle.

INTO THE ARENA
1950–1952

My involvement with "theater-in-the-round" came about largely through accident. I had heard and read about it all of my life, but it was not until I found that our upstairs room at Theatre Inc. was too small and narrow to provide a decent proscenium that I had tried my own hand at it. Once converted, though—and it was hard not to be, with that Texas dynamo Margo Jones beating the drums—I searched everywhere for better spaces and opportunities. For a while I tried to interest the Museum of Modern Art in housing a live in-the-round performing group, matching in theater the "modernism" that hung on their walls. A half-baked "arena" experiment in the basement of the Hotel Edison, sponsored by David Heilweil, my old colleague from Cornell and New Stages, proved more square than round, and successfully delayed the chances for professional central staging in New York City for years to come. I looked elsewhere.

At Fordham, Albert McCleery's scrim-circled ellipse didn't seem a very satisfactory solution to me, although a production I saw there of Saroyan's *Sam Ego's House*, with four actors playing the corners of a movable house, suggested the imaginative potential. The various "Music Circuses" I saw on the Cape that summer were wonderfully theatrical as well as almost Elizabethan in the experience they provided their audiences, but I didn't particularly like the idea of redoing old Broadway musicals even with a new form of audience-performer relationship.

At Dartington, I had taken the Round House greenroom to show the British Drama League some samples of arena technique with a workshop production of Wilder's *Happy Journey*. And later, when I did an

Actors Studio project with *Pullman Car Hiawatha*, I put the actors right in the middle of the audience, even getting Lee to say a few kind words about the sensory experience involved.

But the culmination of all this interest was that a theater called Arena Stage got started in Washington. The idea of the Arena began, I believe, mainly in the mind of Edward P. Mangum, whom I have sometimes termed the Leon Trotsky of this particular artistic revolution because his name and his role have been so forgotten. For years, Ed, a tall, rangy, easygoing Texan, ran the Mount Vernon Players, a small amateur community theater group in Washington. His actors were the ordinary breed of frustrated locals, but his repertory of classics and slightly offbeat modern plays lured me away from my Catholic University cocoon. I spent many evenings watching the Mount Vernon Players in action and having coffee and theater talk with Ed afterward.

At some point in his own dissatisfaction, Ed decided he should get a master's degree in theater at Catholic University and then try for a teaching and directing job with some established university theater. He chose C.U. primarily because it was there and because of Walter Kerr's presence, but Walter left somewhere in the middle of Ed's sojourn. I became his teacher and friend and adviser, eventually advising him specifically to write his master's thesis on Margo Jones, a fellow Texan, who was displaying her talents to the American theater. With her Theatre '47, in Dallas, Margo had embarked on a policy of doing only new plays, and she was doing them only in the round. One day, half in earnest, I suggested to Ed that he should follow Margo's example and start a professional arena theater in Washington.

The nation's capital had had its share of unsuccessful attempts to start a permanent professional theater. Father Hartke had been involved in several of these but never enough to make them work. During the war, while I was still at the OWI, a young Washingtonian by the name of Zelda Diamond approached me with an idea of putting some sort of theater company into the Department of Agriculture auditorium, but she could never persuade the right people.

After the war seemed a more favorable time for something to happen. Washington was growing and becoming more international and cosmopolitan than it had ever been. The National Theatre, Washington's only touring house and one of the best theaters in the country, had just closed its doors rather than accept Actor's Equity's demand that it integrate its audiences. The National "allowed" blacks onstage but not in its audiences. Constitution Hall "allowed" them in its audiences but wouldn't accept any of them, including Marian Anderson, onstage. The new Lisner Auditorium at George Washington University got into a huge imbroglio with its first production, Maxwell Anderson's *Joan of Lorraine* starring Ingrid Bergman, when both the playwright and the star protested, in vain, the theater's ban on blacks in the audience; it almost closed before it opened. Only the Catholic University Theatre was truly integrated, and that was not totally professional, no matter how high its artistic spirits.

When Ed left C.U., his master's degree dangling before him, he got a job heading the new drama department at George Washington, whose Lisner Auditorium had reverted to amateur status following Miss Bergman's brief appearance. As his devoted assistant, Ed acquired a bright and energetic graduate student, Zelda Fichandler, formerly Diamond. Zelda was as indefatigable as she was knowledgeable, ambitious, tough, and a tremendous help to Ed. The George Washington drama department never came anywhere near matching Catholic University's, but the combination of Mangum and Fichandler led to something even more special.

About a year after taking the job, having searched in vain for suitable quarters for a new professional theater in Washington, Ed and Zelda decided to start a theater on a rented houseboat plying its way up and down the Potomac River. It was an ideal summer setting. They would be the directors and would use young professional actors, backed by C.U. and G.W. actors in the smaller roles. They expected to get financial backing easily from their Washington friends and contacts. An option on the boat cost $15,000. They had no trouble at all in raising it, including $100 from me.

Trouble arrived, however, just as they were cleaning up the boat, hiring a company, and about to go into rehearsal. Ed and Zelda discovered that neither of the Potomac's landlords, Maryland and Virginia—nor the District of Columbia—was willing to provide landing facilities. They were too afraid of grass being trampled down by unruly crowds, and Coca-Cola bottles thrown around. The only way our enterprising producers were going to be able to get their audiences on and off their showboat would be by helicopter.

At this point, I believe, Ed might have lost some of his resolution. Zelda did not. She setout on a search for another space. Her family, long resident in the city, knew everyone in Washington, and she went to everyone. When she had almost given up, one of her father's acquaintances, Sidney Lust, offered the Hippodrome, a run-down burlesque house at the edge of D.C.'s skid row. Zelda made Ed grab it, abandoning the boat in midstream, as well as a portion of the money advanced. I remember Ed's excited phone call the day the contract was finally signed. He could hardly believe that he might actually get his theater, their theater.

It was in "their theater" that Arena Stage finally opened in August 1950, while I was still deep in Falmouth: "Edward Mangum and Zelda Fichandler, Managing Directors." Nor was I there when they got rid of the movie screen; scrubbed, rubbed, painted, and carpeted; unscrewed the seats and placed 247 of them on four sides of a 16-by-20-foot rectangle of playing space. No one thought this an historic moment—they were too busy cleaning.

Ed did most of the artistic planning, hiring the actors, selecting the plays. *She Stoops to Conquer* was the fairly unconventional premiere. Zelda scraped the dirt off the marquee and organized the box office. Her husband, Tom, an economist with the Twentieth Century Fund, helped with the accounts. When the D.C. authorities came in a couple of weeks before opening to demand adherence to an absurd rule requiring an asbestos fire curtain between the audience and the performance, Zelda discovered that a "public hall" did not need that asbestos curtain. So, in one of those legal fictions which get so many wheels turned in our society, Arena became not a theater but a "public hall." Arena Stage seems to have survived that particular limitation.

Although I couldn't get to the opening night, I did come to see all the shows that first season. And I always loved the space, even though I occasionally had reservations about some of the performances. I met Zelda, but thought of her as Ed's assistant, although they were actually partners. And almost from the start, Ed invited me to become part of the Arena Stage family. He didn't suggest I should yet leave C.U. because he had no room in his budget for another director, but he did offer me a job as publicity director, promising to let me direct a show as soon and as often as possible. I preferred to wait for the proper time and arrangement. I gave Ed a list of a dozen or so plays I'd like to direct. We talked seriously about my doing Anouilh's *Antigone* or Synge's *Playboy of the Western World*. At one point, I almost agreed to do the Synge, but then decided I didn't have the time. My withdrawal resulted in the launching of Zelda's directorial career.

My first show at Arena in the spring of 1951 turned out to be *The Glass Menagerie*. It was one with which I am still especially happy in memory, one of the most successful—in the sense that it came out almost exactly as intended—and satisfying productions I have ever done. I always say a director is lucky if he gets 51 percent of what he starts out wanting.

In this case, I felt that I got almost everything. Lester Rawlins as Tom, Dorothea Jackson as Laura, Pernell Roberts as the Gentleman Caller. All the right ingredients came together and produced something that was much greater than the sum of its parts. Our Amanda was too young and inexperienced, and no one could have matched Laurette Taylor, but that didn't seem to matter. I had brought Jimmy Waring over from C.U., and his magically detailed set and lighting utilized the space perfectly, and set a special tone. The lights shone through the little glass animals, throwing their colored reflections on the floor where everyone in the audience could see them. And the Bartok music under Tom's opening sequence seemed written for the play; Lester's every move and syllable flowed out of the notes.

I felt completely comfortable in the arena form, my sudden freedom to compose three-dimensional relationships allowing me to use my imagination more freely than ever before. For example, instead of photographs of Tom's father around the room (the obvious way to ensure that the entire audience sees that smiling face), I had a live actor, his head centered in the picture frame he was carrying, appear in an aisle. We lit up his smile on cue with a baby spotlight. The actor in question, Henry Oliver, had a wonderfully cherubic Irish countenance, and I was determined to have a go with the idea, even though during rehearsals, everyone—including Ed and Zelda—begged me not to ruin the production with such an arbitrary and overtheatrical device. After we opened, everyone, including audience and critics, loved it. Some years later, when I told Tennessee Williams about the face in the aisle, he roared with laughter and approval.

The experience taught me not only the range of new values and relationships inherent in the round medium, but the impossibility ever of knowing whether something will work. Over and over again, people have told me that something I asked for could not possibly "work"; and over and over again, it did. And vice versa. The important thing is to try, to search, to venture beyond the conventional and the obvious.

Our opening night, in spite of all the anticipation, almost culminated in disaster from a totally unexpected source. At the end of one scene, Tom, enraged by his mother, throws his jacket at the menagerie table. We had rehearsed this business very carefully so that the jacket would slide along the floor and touch the table, tinkling the glass animals (carefully arranged and fastened to their glass shelves). In preview the night before, Lester had missed the table entirely, thus eliminating a portion of the scene's tension. Little more than an hour before our opening night curtain, I was having a quick next-door bowl of soup—part of what I always call the glamour of the theater. Lester was practicing throwing his jacket at the proper strength and angle. Just as I walked in, he hit the menagerie table smack amidships, shattering and scattering most of the spun-glass figurines and breaking in half two of the glass shelves. White with horror, Lester got on his hands and knees to assess the damage. We all joined him, laboriously trying to piece the animals together. We finished just in time, not one member of the audience seeming to notice the cracks. That night Lester was especially careful, and the tinkle resounded perfectly.

Menagerie was a smash, a new height for the Arena and a new dimension for me. The critics were rhapsodic in their praise. Dick Coe of the *Post* wrote that "Arena Stage had done itself—and T. Williams—proud." Ernie Schier in the *Times-Herald* spoke of my "imagination and insight . . . Alan Schneider . . . demonstrates . . . that he is a sensitive interpreter with a mature grasp of central staging. . . ." The *Star*'s Jay Carmody informed his readers that the "Arena's *Glass Menagerie* is a glowing project. . . ." The show attracted great local attention—though our invitation to Tennessee was not answered—and was revived that summer.

After the production, I thought more and more of resigning from C.U. and committing my fortunes to Arena. My appetite had been whetted. But Arena's finances still could not afford another permanent director, and mine would not allow me to take a chance on becoming a freelance. My father's eternal message about always looking for some kind of security from a job that paid regularly haunted my consciousness.

That summer, as a result of notice about *Menagerie*, I got an offer to direct at Houston's Playhouse Theatre, a slick new rival to Nina Vance's Alley Theatre, which had started up four years earlier as Houston's response to Margo Jones' work in Dallas. The Playhouse wanted me to do *The Primrose Path*, a nothing-much character piece, starring old-time musical actress Ethel Shutta. In effect, I would be doing summer theater in arena form, but I didn't think about that as I drove my old Studebaker sedan, for which I had paid $300 a couple of years before, down to Houston, getting there in two days flat.

Almost from the moment I arrived, I couldn't stand Houston, which was impossibly hot, humid, and filthy, and had strange liquor laws; or the Playhouse, whose round shape drove me and the actors wild; or Joanna Albus and Bill Rozan, the producers, who kept taking pot shots at the Alley and at Nina, with whom Joanna had once worked. I liked

Ethel's openness and humor, loved the ingenue, Pat Brown (who later went on to become the Alley's artistic director), and the young boy, Tommy Shields (who went on to become a television star). The show went surprisingly well, though neither the work nor the results were in the league with *Menagerie*.

To keep myself sane during rehearsals, I snuck over to the Alley, meeting Nina for the first time and seeing her most effective production of John Patrick's *The Hasty Heart*. I also latched on to her gorgeous assistant, Johnny Lee George, and spent as much time as possible with her, having her recount to me in detail the Alley's previous productions and tribulations. I would have spent even more time with Johnny, except that she was married and her husband kept a shotgun in the house. I loved the shape, size, and feeling of the Alley's stage space. It reminded me of the Arena but seemed more congenial. Although I was desperately hoping Nina would ask me to direct something, she didn't. The Playhouse wanted me for another one, but I couldn't go through that again. So I drove back to Washington, at a slightly more leisurely pace, took a few weeks off, and embarked on another year with Father Hartke et al. The arena form was much on my mind, but nothing seemed to be happening to bring it down to my fingertips.

Throughout that season of 1951–1952, Ed Mangum and I kept pursuing possibilities. Ed asked if I would come to Arena Stage for a salary of ten dollars a week, plus one hundred for each play I might direct—a not unusual arrangement with some of the people then contributing their services. I couldn't. Instead, I stayed on at C.U., having my most satisfactory year there, both in teaching and in my directing chores. I introduced a class in Russian theater, and started a graduate seminar in theater, art, and civilization, a rather highfalutin title I dreamed up for students to look at modern art. In November I did a *Cherry Orchard* with which I was especially pleased. In January 1952, I took myself off to New York to the Neighborhood Playhouse to direct another version of *Pullman Car Hiawatha*, with a young student, Joanne Woodward, in one of the minor roles. In March came that C.U. *Macbeth* possessing six witches.

Then, in April or May, Ed Mangum decided unexpectedly to leave Arena Stage. I only found out via a middle-of-the-night phone call from a less calm than usual Zelda. She wanted me to talk to her about coming to the Arena as her partner. As soon as possible.

After all these years, the question of why Ed left is still a matter of conjecture. There are various theories, but all I know is that he went off, to Hawaii, Milwaukee, and eventually a small college in Texas, where he is still teaching and directing. I feel reasonably sure that Ed's departure had nothing to do with his relations with Zelda. And I know that Zelda was shaken and somewhat frightened to be left alone at the helm of a growing enterprise in which she had been, whatever her considerable virtues and contributions, the junior partner. She turned to me not because she wanted me specifically—we had hardly met—but because she realized that she needed someone at her side. I happened to be there, and I happened also to have something to contribute in the area where, for the moment, she was weakest, as a director.

Apart from my surprise, I felt pleased to be asked—and wanted. At the same time, as always, I had reservations. I was happier at C.U. than I had ever expected to be. I was scheduled that fall to direct *The Skin of Our Teeth*, one of my all-time favorites. The British Drama League had offered me another summer session at Dartington. I had saved up enough money for a second European trip, and I looked forward to a summer divided between relaxing Alpine hillsides and nights of pleasant theatergoing in London. Sheila Adams, the wife of my college friend Mason Adams, now on his way from playing radio's Pepper Young to stage and television fame, had told me about a very special female friend of hers to look up in London. Besides, I kept thinking that Ed would probably come back, and then where would I be?

Despite the lateness of the hour, I dressed and went over to a tearful Zelda's apartment. That night, and for days afterward, we talked about what our relationship might be if I did decide to come. Would I be taking Ed's place, which, at the time, seemed artistically senior to Zelda's? On one hand, I felt my experience and position in the community entitled me to that. On the other hand, I did not want to challenge her position in an organization she had cofounded. I was not Ed but Alan. Neither Zelda nor I was able to define exactly what our working relationship might actually be. She was clearly not prepared to "give" the theater over to me, or even to come to some legal agreement about our "sharing" it—although she might have, had I insisted on some such formal contractual terms. I was not prepared or eager to "take command" of Arena. But I didn't want to come if that meant being second to someone whose tastes and temperament I didn't know. Zelda was more sophisticated than I in realizing that, as she once put it, "people can contribute differently and not be subordinate one to the other."

Eventually, after lengthy discussions, we came to several decisions. I decided that I would leave C.U. and come to Arena as its artistic director—but not until the fall of 1952. In the meantime, since Zelda needed a director for the first show of the summer, I would do that one. I suggested and we agreed on *The Hasty Heart*, which I had seen Nina Vance do so well at the Alley the summer before. In the fall, I would assume my full-time responsibilities; and we would let time work out exactly how we might function with each other.

For the moment, we would share in the selection of plays and we would have to agree on whatever actors—or directors—we hired. The small print would have to wait. We would make the announcement as soon as possible, protecting Ed as much as we could, both for Arena's sake and so that Catholic University would know. The die was cast. Zelda was happy, and so was I. And even my colleagues at Catholic University, including Father Hartke, understood and wished me Godspeed. Father even suggested that I still direct *Skin* in the fall.

I went into rehearsal for *The Hasty Heart*, elated with my new situation and still confused as to my actual position with Arena. The show had a fine cast, including George Grizzard and Roy Poole, as well as Stanley "Bill" Pitts (whom I stole from the Alley and who became an Arena regular). Originally supposed to play for two weeks, it lasted for the completely unexpected and unheard-of total of fourteen. My fee, incidentally, was $200. Nor was it increased, affording me my first contact with Zelda's acumen as a producer. The reviews were uniformly excellent—a portent, everyone hoped, of things to come. Carmody wrote that the production was one "to inspire the city to throw its hat in the air in sheer delight. . . . Arena's pinnacle production . . ." Ernie headlined, correctly as it turned out, "Arena's *Hasty Heart* Looks Here to Stay," and suggested that it was "the most professional effort ever to be lighted on the Arena's stage." Dick Coe called it "Arena's finest" and noted that "this skilled production represents a triumph for Director Schneider . . ."

With similar comments from almost every page of print in Washington ringing in my ears, I went off to Europe, leaving Zelda holding both the bag and the reins of power. I felt considerable guilt on both counts, which did not prevent me from having a glorious summer gallivanting around Europe. By gradual stages, a Dutch friend and I worked our way through Paris, Strasbourg, and Zurich to a tiny paradise atop a minor Alp called Lenzerheide. I approached the Matterhorn even though I never tried to climb it, posed heroically at various precipices, and finally found my way down to a valley where I could catch a train that could bring me closer to Leicester Square.

Atop London's Hampstead Heath, I saw and, to some extent, mended my fences with Aline MacMahon, who was spending the summer in England with her architect husband. I also remembered that girl whom Sheila was anxious for me to meet, someone with the musical name of Eugenie Muckle, and not only looked her up but looked her up, down, and sideways. Jean, as she was called, had arranged for me to stay right next to Aline's place in Hampstead, as I had asked her by letter from Switzerland. She thought Aline was my girlfriend. Jean herself lived next to the Heath on the top floor of a small row-house in Golders Green. Apart from being radiantly beautiful in my favorite brunette way, gracious, charming, and unobtrusively aristocratic, she impressed me with her ability to prepare a delicious and charmingly served "high tea" without benefit of a kitchen of her own.

On our first date, Jean and I went to the Haymarket Theatre to see *Waters of the Moon*, by N. C. Hunter, with Sybil Thorndike, Ralph Richardson, and Wendy Hiller. I loved it, and so did Jean. I decided at that moment that this was the girl I had to marry—if I ever got married again. I didn't do very much about that resolution, however, because, in the meantime, after completing my production of *Pullman Car* at Dartington, I traipsed up to Edinburgh and wound up in a roominghouse next door to Claire Bloom, whom I had loved and longed for from afar after her appearance in *Limelight* with Charlie Chaplin. Claire was doing Juliet with the Old Vic at the Edinburgh Festival. I chased her around for a while, getting no closer than a morning cup of tea. Jean listened sympathetically to the story, and seemed more and more attractive to me.

All summer long, Zelda bombarded me with questions, thoughts, ideas, and suggestions. Before I left for England, we had basically decided the season's plays, the season's casts, and the distribution of directing assignments. Things, of course, kept changing. Poor Zel would write to me, needing an immediate answer; but by the time her letter arrived I would have changed mountain peaks, so my answer was rarely forthcoming in time. I remember wiring to get her to hire Joanne Woodward as our resident ingenue. In return, Zelda sent me a postcard saying that she had auditioned Joanne and decided she had no sex appeal. This was the first of many subsequent disagreements about the virtues of various female performers. We've had less trouble, for some reason, deciding on men.

Finally, when I could delay my return no longer, I sailed back to Washington, leaving Jean languishing on the Heath. My first discovery was finding my name listed not as "artistic director," as I thought we had decided, but as "resident director," a change which bothered me though not enough to make a fuss. I started the season by directing O'Neill's *Desire Under the Elms*. The cast was uneven, having been selected largely by letter, although George Grizzard and a newcomer, Marian Reardon, Joanne Woodward's sidekick from my Neighborhood Playhouse *Pullman Car* production, were fine. There were too many doors, and too many mistakes made at every stage of production. With *Desire*, I had my first Arena comeuppance and serious concern about my directorial abilities.

Zelda was remarkably understanding. I went off to C.U. to do *Skin*, as planned, while she directed Noel Coward's *Still Life* (something I had originally thought I was going to do). Actually, I was doing *Skin* at night and in the daytime rehearsing a Chinese play *Lady Precious Stream*, an irrational juxtaposition of effort which I have been wont too many times in my career to embark upon when I could not turn down contradictory and simultaneous opportunities. We were off on our new life together, a bit wary of each other and of what each day might bring, but determined to make things work.

With all its vagaries and vicissitudes, our flareups and estrangements over more than thirty years, the remarkable thing is that there is still a relationship. I consider Zelda one of the truly great statespersons of the American theater, someone who has learned more and grown more in the period of time I have been in contact with her than any other person I know. She is the finest producer I have ever worked with, and her notes to me and to the actors are the most perceptive I've ever seen. She always blames me for not mentioning her work as a director, about which she feels especially proud, and about which I have from time to time had mixed feelings. As a director, she has had to pull herself up by her own bootstraps. And she has pulled herself up to some impressive heights, as several of her Arena productions have demonstrated.

What is immeasurably clear to all of us in the American theater for more than a generation is the breadth and persistence of Zelda's artistic vision, as well as her social conscience; together with her unique ability to articulate with poetic expressiveness the strength of that vision. My hat, baseball or Russian student's, is off to her. And I am most grateful for her original phone call that night, as well as for many later calls, which connected my life and times with Arena Stage's.

THE REMARKABLE *REMARKABLE MR. PENNYPACKER* 1952–1953

Predictably, my first Broadway directing opportunity was totally unexpected—and brought me the wrong play. There had, of course, been a few hopeful glimmers previously, during my sojourn at Arena Stage, and even when I was still at Catholic University. Saroyan's pre-Godot style surrealist *Jim Dandy*, which I had directed as my first show at C.U., was always on the verge of popping up in New York, but when Saroyan rewrote it and set it inside an eggshell, things calmed down. Shortly after the war, I directed *Lute Song*, at C.U., and my production got such a favorable response that another and less gentlemanly producer, Michael Myerberg, kept trying to lure my production script away from me, without fee, by dangling the prospect of my directing it in New York. Myerberg didn't bother to tell me that he had John Houseman already signed. At another point, someone from the office of the Shubert empire called me to say he had heard that I had just done a terrific production of *The History of Tom Thumb*, by Henry Fielding. The review had recently appeared in *Variety*, and it sounded pretty good to him. He wanted to know who Fielding's agent was. I informed him, somewhat sadly, not only that it was Walter Kerr who had directed *Tom Thumb*, but that dear Henry didn't have an agent, having been in (or out of) the public domain for a couple hundred years.

After I transferred to Arena and began to get more professional experience and exposure, various friends kept telling me that I ought to be directing in New York. Jay Carmody, *The Washington Star*'s equivalent of *The New York Times*'s Brooks Atkinson, always wound up telling me, at the end of a long lunch, that my character work with actors was as good as Kazan's, and that my attention to photographic detail made me a natural for the movies. I almost believed him, and waited for my phone to ring with incredible offers of employment.

On one of my irregular visits to New York, I went to see Audrey Wood, who ever since *A Long Way from Home* had occasionally sent me scripts that no one else wanted to do. On her desk was a stack of scripts, two or three of which I confess I transferred to my briefcase while Miss Wood wasn't watching. One of these was *All Summer Long*, a new play by Robert Anderson, about a small boy and his crippled older brother trying desperately to hold back a river threatening to destroy their family home. I fell in love with it at once, borrowed two hundred dollars, and took an option on the script for six months. In my first venture as a would-be producer, I got as far as a backer's audition. A youthful and equally idealistic Ben Gazzara read the part of the older brother, Kim Hunter played his sister, and someone I thought was Christopher Walken was the boy. (Years later, I discovered that it was his look-alike brother, Glenn, no longer an actor.) Giving up on attaining Broadway directly, I decided I had to convince both Bob Anderson and Zelda Fichandler that they should let me do *All Summer Long* at the Arena Stage.

Bob took some persuading. He had written *All Summer Long* (before *Tea and Sympathy*) specifically for a proscenium theater and had already discussed in great detail with his favorite designer, Jo Mielziner, the possibility of flooding the orchestra pit with water and building a real earth-and-tree-trunk river bank up to and over the stage itself. Bob, whom I had first met during the days at Theatre Inc. and through his American Theatre Wing playwriting classes, was convinced that we could not satisfactorily suggest the reality of a river in a small nonproscenium house, but finally he consented (albeit with undiminished skepticism) to let me try it at Arena.

Zelda wasn't so easy to convince either. Arena's only previous venture with a new play, Conrad Aiken's *Mr. Arcularis*, had not worked well. And while Zelda understood the necessity for Arena to occupy itself with scripts more contemporary than *She Stoops to Conquer*, she wasn't sure our audience was yet ready to accept untried material. I pleaded, persuaded, and pushed; eventually Zelda, who liked the script, agreed that *All Summer Long* was worth the gamble. We went into rehearsal just when Elia Kazan's production of *Tea and Sympathy* arrived at Washington's commercial touring house, the National.

I never told Bob but I didn't have a clue as to how we were going to create his river. As always, I figured that in the theater if something had to be accomplished, represented, felt, or achieved, an imaginative director would find a way during rehearsals. I thought that we might properly suggest the river with a loudspeaker hidden in one of the aisles, playing some nice river sounds, fading in and out from time to time in the darkness. I was much more concerned with the problem of getting a portable radio, which one of the characters had to carry all over the stage, to play the proper piece of music at the right time without having any wires showing. Cassette recorders hadn't been invented yet.

Fortunately, however, the director's imagination was—as predicted—functioning at rehearsals. My first hi-fi acquisition after the war had been a General Electric turntable that broadcast a beam that any radio in the vicinity, when properly tuned, could pick up. In effect, the turntable was a sending station for recordings. I donated it to our electrician, Leo Gallenstein, a redoubtable six-foot giant who always seemed able to cope with any technical problem. Leo believed that the Martians were about to land, and kept equipment around to deal with that contingency; but he was quite sane during rehearsal hours. He rigged up my General Electric to broadcast all over the theater. We never told anyone else how he had done it, including Zelda, but to the astonishment of all concerned, except the audience which just took it for granted, the beam always gave us the right music.

My only other problem came when, in order to make one aisle wider in order for the river to seem slightly more credible, I decided to take out four corner seats of Arena's precious 247. Zelda, of course, would have none of it, not even for a new play. I insisted; she held firm. One day, I asked Pernell Roberts, our stage carpenter, to unscrew several seats so I could see what our river might look like. Pernell refused, quoting Zelda's oral and mimeographed decrees to the contrary. Our encounter turned into a historic moment: the first time I ever used in public a now-current but then somewhat private four-letter word. The seats were removed, Zelda ultimately soothed; and people used to go to the aisle in question after the show each night to see where we kept the "water."

In the middle of rehearsals, my English girlfriend, Jean, arrived unexpectedly from London. Our stage manager, Dana Dudley, kept asking me, "You're not gonna get too involved with this English babe?" I assured him I wasn't. I was too convinced that *All Summer Long* was going to be my entree to Broadway. Jean continued to languish in New York, where she was staying with Sheila Adams. Not getting as much attention from me as she had expected, Jean one day informed me she was going back to London. Desperate to hold on to her, and yet unwilling to disrupt my rehearsal schedule to visit her in New York, I sent her a telegram, a fading copy of which still adorns our bedroom: "Hoping produce *Cavalcade* not *Brief Encounter*. Please come down for opening." She came, a few days early.

All Summer Long, with George Grizzard in the part Ben Gazzara had read, and an astonishing young ten-year-old, Clay Hall, playing the boy, finally opened on January 11, 1953, to enthusiastic reviews from the Washington critics. Bob was especially pleased because Richard Coe's initial response to *Tea and Sympathy* had not been very positive; later, after a furious lunch during which Kazan told Coe what he thought of his judgment, Coe published a second, more favorable appraisal.

One particular evening, there were eleven potential producers in the house, as well as Brooks Atkinson. After the performance, as I remember it, seven of them came at me demanding a telephone from which they could call Audrey. Alexander Cohen, starting a producing alliance with designer Ralph Alswang, got to the one available phone first and, in about thirty seconds, concluded his deal with Audrey to do the show in New York, in either the spring or fall. Next morning, Zelda, Bob, and I met in Alex's sumptuous hotel suite, where he and Ralph proceeded to tell us how much they loved the show, loved George and Clay, loved what I had done, loved the Arena production, and then went on to describe the changes that had to be made, mainly to get more sex into the show.

Two days later, Atkinson's review appeared in the *Times*. *All Summer Long*, he wrote, was a lovely small play, extremely well presented in its present context but much too slight for Broadway, both physically and emotionally. At which point, Alex and Ralph remembered that they had several pressing engagements elsewhere, as did the other six potential producers who had fought to get to that phone two nights before. Only the river remained, together with our sold-out houses.

Some weeks later, in Alex's chic New York office, Bob Anderson and I spent four frustrating hours with Alex and Ralph trying to persuade them to reverse their decision. Had they not been moved by the play? Had they not seen the audiences' reactions? After wanting so strongly to produce it, how could they change their minds just because one man had said whatever he had said? Anyhow, what did Atkinson know! Ralph—rangy and large, with a craggy Michelangelo head, slow-speaking but passionate, unstoppable when he got going—paced back and forth in Alex's office, answering my questions. I'd been so long in the hinterlands that I wasn't being realistic. The theater was an economic not an idealistic enterprise. It cost money to produce a dramatic play. Twenty-five thousand dollars! And if a show didn't get the *Times* review, forget it. Luckily, or unluckily, we already knew that we didn't have the *Times* review.

It was my first experience with a system in which audiences go to the theater only because someone tells them to. A play doesn't have a run, it only has a chance. It doesn't have an audience, it has critics. And if the critics, who can be right, wrong, or sideways, don't happen to like it, the play closes. Which has happened to me too many times in too many years.

We argued back to Ralph and Alex that, after all, they had just told us (and were still telling us) they loved the play. They had wanted passionately to produce it in New York. Didn't they have the courage of their convictions? What manner of men were they? Ralph Alswang's response remains imbedded in my mind, the perennial Broadway indictment of my unregenerate non-Broadway-type madness: "You know what your trouble is, Alan? You're too fucking normal!"

My next "almost" came when producer Robert Whitehead, who had been so encouraging about my *Long Way from Home* production five years earlier, showed up at the Arena one evening with playwright George Tabori to see my *Lady Precious Stream*, a charming piece of ersatz Chinoiserie. Bob informed me that he needed a director for Tabori's new play, *The Emperor's Clothes*, starring Lee J. Cobb and Maureen Stapleton. Harold Clurman had been scheduled to direct but had changed his mind. Bob was now considering me, and had come down to Washington, with Tabori, to see my work.

Luckily, *Skin of Our Teeth* at Catholic University was, in my opinion, not bad, and more typical of me than my Chinese play. They decided to see both and shuttled between Washington's downtown and uptown halves, with me watching in both locations and trying to assess their body language and general reactions. George Tabori, whom I had never met before, seemed to be having difficulty getting his long legs into a sittable position in either theater and didn't watch much of either show. I had seen his *Flight into Egypt*, which Kazan directed, a few years before. It was a fascinating, literate expression of a particular type of European mind and temperament that always had a special appeal for me. I had not yet read *The Emperor's Clothes*, but I didn't have to. I already liked it, by association.

Late that night, in one of those hotel suites seen in the movies, I listened to two more inhabitants of never-never land telling me how impressed they had been with my work, especially *Lady Precious Stream,* which was new to both. Tabori was somewhat concerned about how Lee Cobb would respond to a young director but on the basis of two plays, he was ready to say yes to me if I liked the script. Gulping and trying to hide my excitement, I assured him that I would like his play, that I loved *Flight into Egypt,* that I especially admired Lee Cobb, and that I loved Maureen since she'd been a friendly, slightly overweight switchboard operator at Theatre Inc.

"Read the script," said Bob, practical and urbane as always, "and we'll talk tomorrow morning. Who's your agent, by the way?"

I stayed up most of the night desperately anxious to like Tabori's play, and discovering anew with each page that I didn't. It was about an old-time party intellectual in Hungary caught between his orthodoxy and his humanism. The theme was a valid one, but the play seemed intelligent but somewhat forced, a dry diagram of relationships instead of real people. Lee Cobb might be able to make the intellectual's struggle and contradictions credible, but could Maureen—dear, bumbling, and New Yorkish—really convince anyone she was an elegant lady from Budapest? How could I possibly say this to Bob and the author? After all these years, to turn down Lee J. Cobb, Maureen Stapleton, and George Tabori, not to mention my elegant friend and long-time supporter Robert Whitehead, would be madness. I called Bob at dawn to say, "Yes, of course, I love it," and went in to inform Zelda that she was about to grant me a leave of absence from Arena.

Some weeks later, after reading the script a few dozen times and convincing myself that I could do something with it (although I wasn't entirely sure what), I took the train to New York for production and casting conferences at Bob Whitehead's office. I was also going to meet Lee J. Cobb in person, find a nice inexpensive place to stay, work out my contract, and see some Broadway shows. Arena Stage was suddenly far behind me, and my future very close at hand.

I arrived in Bob's office to find him strangely subdued. Harold, hearing of my interest, had decided that he wanted to direct it after all. Both the producer and the playwright felt that since they had asked Harold first, their responsibility was still to him. They also assumed I would understand. They didn't come out and tell me, of course, that Tabori much preferred to have Harold. Why shouldn't he, after all?

I understood everything. Bob, one of the kindest men in the American theater, knew exactly how I felt and wanted to make me feel better.

"Why don't we all go over to Dinty Moore's," Bob suggested, "to have lunch and talk things over?" Then, his arm on my shoulder, "Both George and I—as well as Harold—want you to stay on as Harold's assistant director. It would be excellent experience for you." He didn't forget to add, "And a great help to the production!" I began to feel that I was back at ANTA, together with a much nicer reincarnation of Nat Karson.

"Thanks much, Bob," I managed to say, "but I just can't do that. And, thanks, but no thanks, to Dinty Moore's." I had to head back to Washington right away before I started to cry.

Still, in a confused way I was relieved, saved from my own inability to turn down something that wasn't worth doing. To reverse Beckett's later dichotomy of Vladimir's mental state, I was appalled at Bob Whitehead's cushioned betrayal, but, at the same time, relieved. I took the next train down to Washington, a surprised Zelda, and an understanding Jean. Disappointed, of course, and dashed by the sudden peripeteia, I was determined never to let it happen again. Until next time.

Toward the end of March, right after my production of *Our Town* at the Arena, Jean and I decided to legalize our slightly confusing relationship and emulate that play's George and Emily. Since she was vaguely Episcopalian and I was theoretically still Jewish, we chose an Ethical Culture minister, a friend of my father, to marry us. My parents, surprisingly enough, did not seem to mind my straying from the faith a second time; they were too much in love with their future daughter-in-law. With only a handful of close friends from Washington and Baltimore present, the "English babe" and I had our wedding in the very bourgeois basement of my parents' Bethesda home. Jean was lovely—and nervous—in a magenta taffeta, and I was equally terrified and much less worth looking at in my new blue suit. The minister telephoned to say he'd be late. Tea being the universal balm for both British and Russians, my mother put on the kettle. The minister arrived, hurried and off schedule, anxious to unite us. Just as he was about to utter the magic words—studiously devoid of any reference to Divinity—the kettle upstairs started whistling, everyone pretending that it wasn't. I was sure that God, in some kind of revenge, was sending us a signal, but I didn't have enough nerve to stop the ceremony.

The kettle silenced and the knot tied, Jean and I took off in my three-hundred-dollar Chevrolet convertible for New York City, where I was scheduled to direct Arnold Sundgaard's *Hide and Seek*, a student production at the Neighborhood Playhouse, celebrating its twenty-fifth anniversary. On our way up, we had enough time for a two-day honeymoon at Split Rock Lodge in the Poconos. It rained forty-eight hours straight, and we played lots of Ping-Pong, among other things.

Hide and Seek went swimmingly, but no one immediately hired me to do a Broadway musical. We drove back down to Washington and a summer putting together touring versions of *The Miser* and *Othello* for C.U., and a new season at Arena. Zelda had suggested that Jean could work in the box office, with a subsequent boost in my weekly salary from fifty-five to sixty dollars. It didn't take long for me to figure out that Jean was in effect working twenty hours per week for five dollars, and I prevailed on her to quit. Zelda sure knew how to run a theater.

Things seemed reasonably quiet—and uninteresting—until the ever-resilient Robert Whitehead (trying to make up, perhaps, for *The Emperor's Clothes*) sent me a comedy by Liam O'Brien called *The Family Man*, about a respectable bigamist who kept two wives and two separate but equal families, one in Philadelphia and one in Wilmington, both of which he loved equally but neither of whom he had ever informed about the other. Two acts were completed, and O'Brien was working on the third. Burgess Meredith was going to play the lead, Horace Pennypacker, with Martha Scott as the Wilmington Mrs. Pennypacker. *The Family Man* was a charming comedy, somewhat old-fashioned in its characters, but written with some wit and style, and with a civilized intellectual base. Jean read it in bed one night and laughed a lot. But it was not at all what I wanted to direct in my New York debut. I turned it down.

Bob signed Mel Ferrer to direct, and I continued with my next assignment at Arena, Wilder's *Happy Journey*. I chalked things up to experience, which my father still kept telling me to stop getting so much of and make a decent living instead. Occasionally, on rainy days, I'd get a few twinges of regret.

Came October, and the phone rang again. It was Bob, once more, telling me that Mel had gotten a big film offer and wanted to be released. Would I possibly reconsider? And why in the hell didn't I want to direct this charming, funny, literate, deliciously comic play? What was I waiting for?

"Yes," echoed my Jean, determined to have her say this time. "What are you waiting for, Tennessee Williams?" She was right.

"Would you give me a couple of days, Bob?" I asked, uncertain of Zelda's reaction as well as my own. "I'll read the script again." He would, and I did.

Naturally, while I was reading, the phone rang again. This time it was not Bob but T. Edward Hambleton of Washington's newly organized

Phoenix Theatre. "We're going to open our first season in a new Broadway-sized theater down on Second Avenue, with Sidney Howard's *Madam, Will You Walk?* We've gotten Jessica Tandy and Hume Cronyn. Norris Houghton, who says he brought you to New York, has recommended you highly. Could you read the script right away?"

"Yes, of course!"

Then, as so many times afterward, came the dilemma: Which one should I do? Neither? Both? *Madam, Will You Walk?* was theatrical, interesting, confusing, somewhat unsatisfactory. *The Family Man* was more conventional, funny, interesting, somewhat unsatisfactory. *Madam* was downtown, *The Family Man* uptown. At this point, Hume Cronyn, whom I had not met before, entered my life. Hume, playing at Washington's National Theatre, had heard about my dilemma and his advice was simple: "Jessie and I would love to have you do *Madam*. But if you want my opinion, it would be much better for you to do *The Family Man*. I was offered it myself and almost accepted. In fact, if Buzz Meredith didn't want to play in it, I might have." As an afterthought, he added, very emphatically, "Just make sure you get a third act! That's the only reason that play hasn't gotten off the ground before. It hasn't got a third act!" Neither O'Brien nor Whitehead knew what to do about that other wife in Philadelphia. "If you can fix that," smiled Hume, "you'll be a smash."

Well, I didn't know exactly what to do about that other wife either. But Hume's words tipped the balance in my mind. With Zelda's grudging assent, I rang up Bob Whitehead and said yes, enthusiastically. Jean breathed a sigh of relief. Hume and Jessie went on to open the Phoenix without me. I finished my last show at the Arena and brought Jean to New York, keeping my Washington place—just in case. I don't remember anything about the contract, except that it included Joy Small as my assistant, to take notes. Joy got leave from her British Embassy job, where she was working with a couple of diplomatic types named Burgess and MacLean.

Whitehead's production office spoiled me for everyone else's. Apart from the general splendor of the furnishings and decor, the presence of books, mementos from such luminaries as John Gielgud and Laurence Olivier, and recent copies of the Soviet theater magazine *Teatr,* there were Oscar Olesen and Terry Faye. Oscar, Bob's general manager and associate from wartime days, sported dark shrewd eyes belying a constant half-smile, an incisive probing intellect, and an acerbic sense of humor. He was always especially eager to demonstrate that in the theater two and two could still make four. The incomparable Terry was and is a button of a dynamo, perky, good-natured, tireless, and the best damn casting director in the world. Having started my New York existence in that role, I know how hard and long—and well—she works. Terry is familiar with every actor and actress in and out of captivity, including those who have just made their off-off-Broadway debut the night before; she never forgets a name or a face; and can get anyone five minutes after you've asked her.

Family Man had seventeen children in the cast, and Terry brought in seemingly hundreds into the office, helping me to pick the best ones, including Carol Lynley and Joel Carruthers, who have gone on to various visible careers since. We got Una Merkel for the maiden aunt. For the young lovers we cast Phyllis Love, recently in *Rose Tattoo*, and a young actor named Michael Wager, whom Bob finessed me into using instead of Osgood Perkins' son, Tony, who had not yet acted very much. I tried to get Tony to understudy but he decided to do something else. "Mendy" Wager was the kind of brash, sophisticated New York type whom everybody wanted to have around and who knew everybody, and constantly reminded you of that. He went to all the proper dinners and parties, and could repeat word for word what anyone who was anyone had said the night before.

But, apart from his high-style socializing, Mendy was okay. In a scene in which he and Phyllis played out their virginal affection on their knees, he was quite touching as the young minister.

We had Buzz Meredith and Martha Scott and Una Merkel and all those adorable kids, including a set of twins who occasionally asked Jean how she could stand being married to me. Our only problem was Reverend Fifield, Mr. Pennypacker's chief intellectual opponent. Fifield, a crucial character, was on stage for all the big scenes, but somehow "Bill" O'Brien had not given him many lines. He had what the old actors used to call an eight-side part, that is all his lines and cues could be typed out on eight half-page sheets. ("Sides" were used by old-time actors who had to learn their parts quickly when they were doing a play a week in summer stock.) We tried everyone, from such names and seminames as E. G. Marshall and Kevin McCarthy to unknowns like Rusty Lane, my old drama prof at Wisconsin, who had directed me in *Storm Operation*. Everyone, including Rusty, turned down the part.

Finally, only a day or two before we were to start rehearsals, with all parties slightly hysterical, Terry brought in an older actor, Glenn Anders, who had had a distinguished career but who was now more or less on his uppers. He'd played with the Theatre Guild, starred in plays with the Lunts, and was the only living actor who had been in four Pulitzer Prize plays, going all the way back to Hatcher Hughes' *Hell Bent for Heaven* in 1924. He was perfect, but he insisted on reading for us, an imposition for an actor of his reputation, and he did so brilliantly. Glenn, it turned out, was not only excellent in the part, he made the whole show—and almost stole it from Burgess. Glenn's scenes became the funniest and most believable. He set a standard of hard work and discipline which helped everybody, including those rambunctious kids, and which I've never seen surpassed. From the first day until we closed, almost a year later, Glenn never stopped working, never stopped improving, never stopped demonstrating the actor's craft at its most creative and beguiling. His eight sides (typed by himself) were stuck up beside his dressing room mirror until the day we closed. And I could never walk into that dressing room without his asking me for some notes. I fell in love with Glenn from the first day of rehearsal, and we became firm personal friends for years afterward. He spent his last years in the Actors' Fund home in New Jersey, living into his nineties. One of my most guilty regrets is that I never went out there to visit him before he died. Perhaps I wasn't sure I could bear it.

We were cast. We had Ben Edwards' charming semi-Victorian setting and equally pleasing costumes, with which I'd had very little to do except to praise them. The first rehearsal was tomorrow: my first Broadway show. Then the phone again, the voice of one of my oldest theater friends, Joe Magee, now an agent. Cool and calm, he told me that I should not under any circumstances do the show; Joe had just coproduced Edmund Wilson's *Little Blue Light* with Burgess in a leading role, and, in Joe's considered opinion, Buzz had ruined the entire show and driven everyone quite mad. Unfortunately Joe had been out of town and missed the announcement that I was directing *Family Man*. He'd just returned and was calling to save me from total destruction.

"I know you've been trying to get a Broadway show for fifteen years, Alan. I know how hard and long you've worked for this, and how tough it is to get recognition. You simply must not do this now and let those years go down the drain."

"But, Joe, I'm going into rehearsal tomorrow *morning*."

"Doesn't matter. Get out of it by telling them you're sick. Anything. Get a doctor to give you a certificate. I'll get a doctor to do it for you."

"But Joe . . ."

"Alan, I'm telling you, would I steer you wrong? Meredith is not someone you can work with. I know him and I know you. He'll kill you. Get that certificate!"

I hung up, not sure whether I had heard right. Here was one of the most honest, decent, understanding human beings I had ever met telling me to withdraw from the show. And yet I knew I couldn't. Jean and I went out to dinner, not so much to eat as to think. We walked the streets, even though it was November and cold and I had planned a good night's sleep for tomorrow's rehearsal. I knew I wouldn't be able to sleep at all now, so we wound up at a late movie, Gerard Philippe in *Fanfan la Tulipe*. I laughed a lot and forgot for a while about Joe Magee and Burgess Meredith. I even got a little sleep.

We went into rehearsal the next day with much hoopla as the first production of the Producers Theatre, consisting of Bob Whitehead, Roger L. Stevens, and Robert Dowling (a well-known New York financier and politico). Burgess, "Buzz" as I called him after the first two minutes, turned out to be no trouble at all. He did everything I wanted him to do—only in his own way. He was willing, responsive, friendly, and supportive. The only trouble I ever had with Buzz was the playwright's fault. Throughout rehearsals, which he insisted on attending when he should have been at his hotel working on the third act, Bill kept asking me to tell Burgess (he was the only one in the company who never called him Buzz) not to keep bending his knees so much when he walked. I informed Bill that Buzz had been bending his knees like that all his life. I'd watched him bending his knees in *Winterset* and *High Tor* back in the thirties. I reminded Bill that he had waited almost two years to get Buzz for his play, bended knees and all. Bill said that if I didn't talk to Burgess, he would.

One day, after a particularly good rehearsal when I felt that Buzz would be in a good mood, I asked him out for a drink. My Kazan technique. Over a martini, and as gently as I could, I hinted that Bill was just the tiniest bit concerned about what seemed to be Buzz's slight habit—or rather his unconscious, occasional tendency—to bend at the knees a bit. I added that, of course, I didn't think anything of it but that the playwright would have talked to him if I hadn't.

Buzz's response was immediate and titanic in its fury. "Keep that bastard away from me, I don't want to talk to him. I don't bend my knees when I walk! I have never bent my knees! I don't know what the hell you guys are talking about. You tell that sonofabitch that if he doesn't like what I'm doing, he can get himself another actor. In fact that's exactly what I'm telling you and Whitehead to do right now because I'm sick and tired of his fucking play. . . ."

At which point, he slammed his unfinished martini down on the bar and stalked out into the night, vowing loudly never to return. Bob and I finally got him to come back, but he refused to talk with us for several days, and for several weeks in the case of a stunned Bill O'Brien, who, in terror for his play, was sorry he'd started the whole thing. This was my worst experience to date with the extreme volatility of theater relationships. And it demonstrated the difficulty of steering a safe course between the playwright and the players, the Scylla and Charybdis of the director's journey toward opening night.

Beyond the normal uncertainties and confusions, Buzz gave me no further headaches. My trauma came from another source: my idol, Martha Scott. I had seen Martha do her breathtaking Emily in the original *Our Town* and had fallen in love with her then and there. During the first week's rehearsal, I knocked myself out to please her.

That lasted until the phone rang as I was on my way out one morning, Audrey Wood saying, "What are you doing to Martha Scott?" I didn't know that I was doing anything special to Martha except loving her. "Martha says that so far, you've got Burgess Meredith center stage seven times, and she's center stage only four times."

"I haven't counted," I answered, trying to figure out whether Audrey was actually kidding or not. "Maybe. I just staged it the way it felt right."

"Alan, they're costars. Have you looked at the billing?"

"I know, Audrey, and yes, I have; but you see . . ."

"Alan," Audrey's voice very tight and somewhat condescending now, "you're in the big time now. You've got to understand that you can't just do what you've been doing in Washington. I'm your agent and I'm telling you."

I understood all right. Audrey was my agent and Martha's agent as well. Assuming we ran, I would be getting around $100 or $150 every week. Martha's weekly salary was $750.

"Okay, Audrey," I said quietly, "I'll see what I can do."

That day, I fiddled with the staging a bit, trying hard to serve the play and, at the same time, Martha Scott's equal billing. Martha was as impersonally sweet as ever. I felt I was coping. In the big time.

A couple of days later, Audrey called me again. "Alan . . . I thought you understood what I was trying to tell you."

"What's the matter now?"

"Well, Martha says that Una Merkel gets to hold the kids six times so far, and you've only got her holding them twice."

That's when I knew I'd had it; my proverbial temper was off the leash. "Listen, Audrey," I said, almost crushing the phone receiver in my bare hand, "Una Merkel really loves those kids, and they love her. Martha hates them. All she does is worry about whether they're blocking her, or messing up her dress. And they know it."

"Alan," the voice patient, cold, and low, "she's the star!" Q.E.D. (That's why, I guess, all these years I've preferred to work with actors who are not stars.)

My own voice was neither patient nor low, I'm afraid. "I don't care who she is, Audrey. I'm the director, and I'm going to stage this show the way it ought to be staged and not just to please Martha or to give her equal time center stage with Burgess Meredith. Or equal time with the kids either. Tell her if she doesn't like it, she can talk to the producer."

Which is exactly what Martha proceeded to do, although I got there first. Luckily, Bob Whitehead must have had his own problems with Martha's contractual negotiations and general disposition, so that he wasn't about to be very sympathetic. He told me to go right on directing the play the way I saw fit, and let him deal with Martha. That was Audrey's last call on the subject.

But Martha, after a while, started coming to rehearsals a few minutes late, each day a bit later. Nothing said, no excuses, just late. Enough to make me wait for her before I could start to rehearse. She was just trying to show me she was the star.

I didn't say anything for a long time because I was more concerned about that elusive third act and didn't mind a bit of stalling around on the second. But finally one morning, Martha came in late and I blew my stack in front of the entire cast, including a smiling Buzz and a somewhat lugubrious Glenn Anders watching from a corner. I bawled out Martha as a constant latecomer, in the strongest terms I could call up. I was deliberate and, I suppose, cruel. She was never late again. She also never did anything the way I wanted her to. I had won my battle but lost the war.

Two years later, while having a bit of trouble with one of the leading ladies whom I was directing in *The Skin of Our Teeth*, I told George Abbott, who was also acting in the show, the Martha Scott story. "What should I have done instead of bawling her out?" "Simple," Mr. A. said, not even cracking a smile. "Just start rehearsals with the understudy." Which is what I've done ever since if the occasion arises, without even looking up when the latecomer arrives. It always works.

In the middle of my life with Martha, we discovered that we had to change the title of our play, though we tried every legal, moral, and humanitarian means not to. Someone, it seems, had already used the title *The Family Man* even though his play hadn't gotten on. Temporarily, to meet a press deadline, Bob pulled *The Remarkable Mr. Pennypacker* out of a hat. We all groaned, but were stuck with it. After a year's run, our new name didn't seem so bad. The orange-colored logo with the funny-looking little character with tweed cap and checked plus-fours wasn't so bad. And you could actually read the title, which is more than I can say for most.

The real problem was that elusive third act, in which the offstage second Mrs. Pennypacker had to be gotten rid of pleasantly and, we hoped, comically. In seemingly endless conversations all through rehearsals, Bill had tendered ideas from all of us—the producer and the director of course, but also the stars, Buzz and (given equal time) Martha. As well as the other actors, his girlfriend, his agent, and no doubt the stage hands.

While we were blocking the first act, Bill was holed up in a fairly pleasant suite in the Royalton Hotel, across the street from the Algonquin (where he had most of his meals and all of his drinks), supposedly working on that third act. He rarely stirred outside except to reassure us that he was making definite progress. After a week, pleased with the first act, but not sure what the playwright thought because he had not yet seen it, I started the second. Bob and Ginny seemed pleased, as was Audrey, who had wandered in uninvited and unannounced—to count Martha's center-stage positions, I assumed. The actors, however, were growing increasingly nervous. How could they know what to do with their two acts when they had not yet been told what was going to happen with their characters—and lines—in the third act? And no matter how confident I was—or wasn't—I couldn't tell them.

Finally, one evening after a fairly hilarious runthrough of Act Two, Bob and I decided to track the writer to his lair. We walked into the Royalton, took ourselves upstairs unannounced, knocked on the door, and found Bill, bleary-eyed and haggard, sitting lifelessly before a typewriter into which had been inserted a blank sheet of paper headed ACT THREE. On the floor beside him were scattered dozens of crumpled wads of paper, which when unfolded presented more or less the same appearance. Then the confession poured out. He was totally confused, totally without ideas, totally exhausted, and totally without a third act—which was scheduled to be staged as of the next morning. I wondered why I had ever left the Arena Stage.

Bob and I looked grimly at each other, the celebrated trim Whitehead mustache beginning to tremble on the celebrated classic Whitehead jaw. Something had to be done; and without many preliminary words, we proceeded to do it. We began to improvise a scene. Words. Something. Anything. With Bill pecking away with two fingers, Bob and I wandered around the room, trying to suggest what Pa and Ma Pennypacker might say or do once she had learned of the existence of another separate but equal spouse and family. For five or ten minutes, I would play Pa and Bob, Ma. Then, as our respective wells of inspiration dried up, we switched sides of the room and roles. Bob and I had both had brief careers as actors, and we'd seen enough actors' improvisations to last us a lifetime. We knew the characters and we were quite aware of their given circumstances. We just said and did whatever came into our minds, and Bill typed as much as he could of our dialogue. Evidently we didn't do too badly, because the third act of *The Remarkable Mr. Pennypacker* did not seem appreciably lower in quality than the other acts. It might be a few pages shorter, but then third acts usually are.

My fondest memory of what seemed a harrowing experience in the uncertainties of the Broadway theater, was of a shaken but suddenly revived Bill O'Brien, perched at that typewriter for all of those hours, getting down our immortal and not so immortal lines and imploring us, every now and then, when he just couldn't keep up: "What did you just say?"

I hadn't the slightest idea.

I do remember that we solved the problem of the second Mrs. Pennypacker by suggesting that she had passed away some years earlier. No one ever called us to task for the cop-out, which is what it was.

The play, attractively mounted and graced by robust performances from Buzz, Una, and Tom Chalmers, sweet ones by Phyllis and Mendy, and an acceptable one from Martha, did pretty well in our two tryout weeks at the Walnut Street Theatre in Philadelphia. We were all pleasantly surprised upon our arrival at the St. James Hotel to find that the telephone exchange there was Pennypacker, and took that as a favorable omen. Reviews were uniformly favorable, the subscription audience liking it hugely and spreading the word. They even laughed in the right spots, including that now celebrated first act curtain: "Boy, you belong in Philadelphia!" The actors were as happy as actors can ever be when they're on the road and aren't yet sure what's going to happen to them when they get back to New York. Even all the stage mothers—of whom we seemed to have eternally vigilant hordes backstage—behaved reasonably well. And having all those kids around kept everybody reasonably civil to everybody else even when they weren't meaning it—including Martha, who had a special ability to think daggers and look lilacs.

One of our funniest lines, "No, son. You'll have your chance to vote when we get back to Philadelphia," came to us in an unsigned letter from someone who had seen the play, loved it, and thought we could use another laugh. We used it, and it's still there. Actually we didn't do much rewriting. But I worked on the performances, simplified some of my staging, and smoothed out some of the rhythms.

After Philadelphia, we had just enough previews in New York to get used to our new quarters in the Coronet (formerly the Forrest and now the Eugene O'Neill) on Forty-ninth Street. (Broadway theaters have a curious way of being renamed as well as being torn down.) With Glenn Anders still studying his eight sides of the part, the script stuck up alongside his dressing room mirror, we opened on December 30, 1953. The show looked even better in the Coronet's smaller spaces. The New York audience laughed as heartily as before. The actors were marvelous. I paced back and forth at the back of the orchestra, as I always do, wondering why I was there and whether my stomach would hold out.

The opening night party was in Mendy's apartment. We were dancing or eating or milling around when someone brought in Atkinson's review. Mendy stopped everything to read it out loud: "Uproarious . . . filled the Coronet Theatre with laughter . . . tenderness and charm . . . a lusty show . . . drenched with laughter . . ." and then threw the entire newspaper up in the air with a shout and kissed me on both cheeks. Everybody began to bubble a bit louder after that, the white wine tasted even sweeter, and Jean looked even lovelier than when I had married her some nine months before. Later, Mendy took me aside, and in his familiar impetuously youthful staccato, said, "Congratulations, we'll be here a year." Audrey patted my hand and smiled; enough said. We were just celebrating Christmas five nights late, and New Year's one night early.

Mendy was dead right, as he always was offstage. The other reviews were equally favorable; even those that carped admitted that we were not only funny but fun. We were a "smash"; my very first show on Broadway a "smash." It just didn't seem real. After fifteen years, I had an overnight success.

Next morning, there was a pile of scripts outside my hotel room, including a version of *Jane Eyre* sent by Huntington Hartford, whose office I had been unsuccessful in approaching for years. Almost all of them were comedies, a lot of them just like *Pennypacker* though not as good. In the next days and weeks, I read them all, as I've done with any script sent to me by anybody, ever. I have a constitutional inability to leave a script unfinished, no matter how dreadful. None of them was worth doing. Although I did spend an afternoon with Lawrence Langner and Armina Marshall at the Theatre Guild, talking about *The 49th Cousin*, in which Menasha Skulnick, a Jewish Burgess Meredith, later went on—and fairly rapidly off. Langner had a reputation as a producer who chased attractive performers of both sexes around his desk while he was auditioning them. I wanted to see if his territory included directors. In my case, at least, it didn't, although both he and Miss Marshall did their best to seduce me into following up my Gentile family success with a Jewish one.

Bob Whitehead was delighted and anxious to do anything he could to help me. At Ginny's urging, and against the advice of Oscar Olesen, who was friendly but tended to have a problem for every solution, Bob advanced me as much as he could in the way of royalties so that my tax situation in 1954 would be improved. Obviously, I had no tax situation in 1953. At least twice a day I went out to count the lines in front of our box office, sometimes peeking through the window of the Forrest Hotel.

Joe Magee, forgetting entirely about that desperate attempt he had made to keep me from doing the show with Buzz, called to tell me how much he had enjoyed the first night, and how happy he was for me.

The afternoon after *Pennypacker* opened, Jean and I, flushed with our newly won splendors, as well as emotionally exhausted, took a delayed honeymoon cruise trip to the Bahamas. Jean was so anxious to have me relax for a while that she didn't tell me she wasn't very good on ships. Even before we sailed at midnight from a pier on West Fifty-seventh Street, she was flat on her back with *mal-de-mer*, and she hardly moved until we landed for our two-day stay in the Bahamas sunlight. Returning repeated the process (although we had managed to crowd a fair amount of swimming and tourism into our land days). By the time we got back, we were both in more need of a holiday than when we started.

We came home, almost ready for a divorce, but counting our blessings and our bank account. I sat down to wait for Tennessee Williams.

Tennessee, however, did not arrive that evening. Bob Anderson did.

Incidentally, George Tabori's *The Emperor's Clothes*—Lee J. Cobb, Maureen Stapleton, et al.—closed in about a week. Harold Clurman, with whom I had a friendship for almost thirty years, claimed responsibility for my New York career. He often told me that if he had not decided to direct Tabori's play, I would have started with a failure and might never have gotten another job. I've always been grateful to Harold for not wanting to do *Pennypacker*.

A NOT SO HOT *SUMMER*

1954

Instead of going to work on any new project, I was content to visit *Pennypacker* once or twice a week, mostly to count the customers. The show was doing okay, though not sensationally. Coproducer Roger L. Stevens, convinced that it was going to be selling out and hoping to lift its weekly grosses, had transformed the highly desirable first six rows of seats in the Coronet into elaborate two-seater "divans," sold at much higher prices. These were, however, sold only at the box office, no tickets being assigned to the ticket brokers. The idea was for the extra amount to go to the production. We sold the divans but found that more and more of the tickets assigned to brokers were coming back to us! Some of the jilted brokers not only refused to display our poster, but sometimes responded to ticket requests by saying that we were sold out or were not giving a performance at the time requested.

Producer Whitehead and I tried to fight back. Whitehead threatened retaliation of some kind against the brokers—legal action, withdrawal of all tickets. We soon discovered that even the theater's difficult or temperamental leading ladies or gentlemen were easier to influence than those calm and poker-faced representatives of entrenched chicanery existing behind the scenes of each successful, or unsuccessful, Broadway operation. Roger's "divans" eventually went the way of their Victorian ancestors; the posters got put back. We immediately sold more tickets—with the extra proceeds going to the ticket brokers.

Partly from guilt and partly from desire, I accepted an offer from the Arena Stage to direct a spring production of *Summer and Smoke.*

Everyone in New York, especially Audrey Wood, who happened to be Tennessee Williams' agent as well as mine, had difficulty understanding this choice. After all, I had "made it," with my first Broadway show. I had a "hit" going. What was I doing once more in the hinterlands? Directing, I said. And *Summer and Smoke*, with such then unknown actors as George Grizzard, Frances Sternhagen, Lester Rawlins, Gerald Hiken—and a still unknown today but equally talented Dorothea Jackson playing Alma—turned out beautifully, even though it didn't serve to advance my career, as my New York colleagues kept reminding me. Tennessee, of course, did not come down to see it; in fact, I doubt if he knew it was on. Circle in the Square and José Quintero had recently resurrected *Summer and Smoke* from its Broadway oblivion, and that was enough for him.

I did get a long interview in the Sunday *New York Times*, then as now the hallmark of acceptance; the headline read "Man from Out of Town." The interviewer, Murray Schumach, while sympathetic to my professed intentions, remained uncertain as to how to pigeonhole me. Was I a Broadway director, or was I a regional theater director? I didn't want pigeonholing, I wanted to be accepted as an American director—whatever that might mean.

That spring, I took my weekly royalties and my wife and went off to England once more, Jean somehow managing her seasickness on the Atlantic better than she had done in the Caribbean. We stayed with her mother in a small, square cottage in Hastings, a home from which Jean's "mum," a lovely English lady named Emmy Muckle, had been dispossessed during the war as an "enemy alien." Years before, Emmy had married a German writer and professor, Friedrich Muckle, now deceased, thereby rendering herself suspect. Actually, she had been born and bred in the heart of London, within the sound of Bow Bells—therefore qualifying as an authentic Cockney.

Emmy looked just like Dame May Whitty in *The Lady Vanishes*, and wore hats akin to Queen Mary's. She had a complexion like rose petals and the disposition of a nun well on her way to sainthood. Trying to understand the Russian-style Yank her daughter had chosen to marry was a full-time job. Yet in the ten or so years I knew her, I got very few reproving looks and nary a harsh word. Jean's "Auntie" Rosie was the exact physical opposite, though equally tolerant of my foibles. From youth, her skin had been badly disfigured. Beneath that harsh surface she was gentle, considerate, and extremely sensitive to undercurrents of feeling.

After several trips down to London to sample a fairly uneventful theater season, we rented a slightly broken-down Ford and took off for the Continent. Our basic aim was to wend our way into those portions of Germany where Jean had lived as a girl, visiting some of the relatives and friends she had not seen since she left with her mother for England at the age of eleven. We managed to see the outside of Jean's childhood "castle" in Binau, near Heidelberg, where she had grown up, but we weren't able to get inside. The castle itself was a letdown, being no more than a decaying and graying stone mansion surrounded by mud. This was also my first venture into the German countryside; and I kept wondering, as we went from one muddy or crumbling village to another, what everyone I met had been doing while Hitler was around.

From Heidelberg, where Jean's father had taught at the University—alongside Jaspers, who I understand, regularly visited her mother's kitchen—we meandered into Switzerland, where he had died during the war, chased out of his own country by Hitler and hounded to death in an alien one by the Swiss police. The one person who helped him, a gracious Swiss lady, Elsa Grunder, now lived in Basel. We visited her, and went to a few "off-Broadway" shows in some Basel cellars. Then, without planning to, we wound up in Zurich, where the Schauspielhaus was having a new lease on life.

My casual visit to the Schauspielhaus changed my life. The new dramaturg there was a middle-aged scholar named Hans Curjel, who had visited me during my Catholic University days. I remember Hans telling me, when I informed him there was no regular repertory theater in our nation's capital, that he couldn't relate that information to his friends in Zurich because they would think he was making anti-American propaganda. Hans greeted me with open arms, dinner invitations, and tickets for Jean and myself. The lobby walls were covered with photographs of previous productions, and I happened to take special notice of one showing two tramps doing something interesting—it was not immediately clear what—with their hats. The title of the play in which they were appearing was *Warten Auf Godot*.

Hans explained that "*warten auf*" meant "waiting for," and that Godot was the interesting and mysterious gentleman for whom they were waiting. He also waxed eloquent on the play itself, which he claimed was a masterpiece of the modern theater. The Schauspielhaus production had been magnificent, and it was a pity that it was not still playing. The play sounded very specialized, a semi-Existentialist tract about these two guys waiting somewhere for someone to bring them an answer to the meaning of their lives. Obviously not for Broadway, though certainly intriguing. The author, Hans told me, was Samuel Beckett, an Irishman living in Paris. In fact, the play was at the moment running in a small theater somewhere in Paris, if I happened to be going through there, Hans recommended that I see it. The more Hans talked, the more fearful I got that he was overselling the play. I smiled and listened politely, and then forgot about it.

Actually, Jean and I had thought about going back through Paris in order to see the Berliner Ensemble. The Ensemble, then the rage of postwar European theater, was planning a short Paris season at the Théâtre Sarah Bernhardt, the first time a German company had come since the war. They were doing Kleist's *Broken Jug* and Brecht's *Mother Courage*, with Brecht's wife, Helene Weigel, in the title role. I had been fascinated by Brecht ever since my college days, although what I had read about his work and theories about "alienation" effects had confused more than enlightened me. I had seen a production of *The Private Life of the Master Race*, with Uta Hagen and Albert Basserman, and read Eric Bentley's translations of *Mother Courage* and *The Caucasian Chalk Circle*, but could not visualize how they might actually be performed in a theater. Here was my chance to see the theory in practice.

Off we chugged in our steadily more ailing Ford to Paris. There was no trouble getting tickets; they were obviously not selling out. The afternoon of the opening performance, I was even able to crash a fairly dull press conference at the theatre. A subdued, somewhat colorless, nearly inaudible Bertolt Brecht read for an hour from a prepared German text without once looking up at his audience of, mainly, French journalists, most of whom did not understand a word of what he said. Brecht did answer a few questions afterward, in the same pale tones, through an interpreter, but his audience was as mystified as ever. The general feeling around the room that afternoon was that the evening's performance was going to be even more of a disaster.

It was, instead, a triumph, one of the most exciting evenings of theater I have ever experienced. Even though the simultaneous translation was from German to French, neither of which I know well, I understood every scene. The production was dynamic, clean, and vivid. And what was especially clear was the intensity and truth of the performances: Ekkehard Schall's blazingly sensual Eilif, Ernst Bush's colorfully ruminative cook, the compassionate hulk of Angelika Hurwicz's Kattrin, and—most of all—Helli Weigel's eloquently drawn tapestry of Courage, endlessly determined, endlessly resourceful, endlessly human. Stanislavski plus Kabuki, as I was later to speak of it. At the end of the play, when Weigel hitched herself, animal-like, to her wagon and proceeded to haul it around the stage, faster and ever faster, the entire French audience rose from their seats and shouted "Bravo!" with a fervor I had never seen in a theater, and pounded their hands and feet on any surface in reach. I immediately cabled Roger Stevens and Bob Whitehead that they should read Eric Bentley's English translation, with a view to producing it on Broadway.

In the enthusiasm of finally discovering Brecht, I vaguely remembered Hans Curjel's good words about the fellow named Beckett, somewhere else in Paris. Finding out where, however, was easier said than done. Although Samuel Beckett had supposedly become the rage of the intellectual community in Europe, no one I met in Paris seemed to be aware of where or whether *Godot* was running there. The weekly *Semaine de Paris* had no mention of anything called *Godot*. My absolutely reliable hotel concierge had never heard of it. Even someone who had, the distinguished play agent Ninon Talon, confessed herself unable to pinpoint its location. Inspired by Mother Courage's determination, I tramped the streets of the Left Bank, searching, asking, and poking into every corner. Had it not been for Jean's willingness to tolerate such irrational behavior instead of insisting on pursuits more appropriate to a springtime in Paris, I couldn't have, in Beckett's words, gone on.

Finally, I located my quarry at the Théâtre Babylone on the Boulevard Raspail, like the bluebird, only a short distance from the L'Aiglon Hotel where we were staying. The theater was tiny, the production—especially compared to the recent magnificence and magic of the Berliner Ensemble—primitive. The cyclorama's seams were showing, the tree was obviously papier mâché. I think there were either seven or nine people in the audience the first evening we were there. When we came back the next night, there seemed to be two or three more.

My French is just about good enough to get me safely in and out of American Express. Yet I sat alternately mystified and spellbound, uncertain and sure, knowing something terribly special was taking place on that small, almost bare stage. The performances of the individual actors were credible; they did not, however, especially impress themselves on me as the ones in the Ensemble had, except for Lucky's fantastic physical tremolo. The performance of the play as a whole did with the movements and relationships of the two tramps, whose names kept eluding me even as their personalities took hold. What was the meaning of Lucky's prompt responses to Pozzo's inevitable orders? Was that Capital and Labor? Master and Slave? Britain and Ireland?

At the end of Act One, when that stylized mechanical moon suddenly rose and night fell all at once, I didn't have to "understand" in order to be moved. At the beginning of Act Two, when that once bare, fragile poem of a tree reappeared with bright green ribbons representing leaves, that simple theatrical rendition of rebirth affected me beyond all reason—or expectation. Without knowing exactly what, I knew I had experienced something unique in modern theater—at the other end of the spectrum from Brecht's epic splendor. After those two evenings, *Godot* had me in a grip from which I have never escaped.

The next morning I set about locating the author, to see if the American rights to his remarkable play were possibly still available. After all, he was Irish; his native language was English. Perhaps he had originally written it in English. If not, perhaps he might be interested in translating the play himself. The box office staff was uncooperative, or at least uncommunicative. I left note after note with them, until I finally persuaded someone to tell me Beckett's home address; he had no phone. I took the Metro to 15, rue des Favorites in the Sixth Arrondissement and managed to perch outside the entrance, where I could get a view of his window. I left notes with his concierge; no reply. Was he out of town or dodging me?

When I was about to give up, my friendly Madame Talon informed me she had just heard that the English-language rights to *Godot* had been acquired from Beckett's London representative, Curtis Brown, by British director Peter Glenville, who intended to present the play in the West End during the following season, with Alec Guinness as Vladimir and Ralph Richardson as Estragon.

"Besides," she took the trouble to add, "the play is not really right for the American theater. It's much too intellectual. Unless you could get a couple of top-flight comedians like Bob Hope and Jack Benny to kick it around, preferably with Laurel and Hardy in the other two roles. Would you be interested in something like that?"

I wouldn't.

Under such circumstances, Mr. Beckett seemed as far removed as Mr. Godot himself. Mr. Brecht, though highly inaudible, was at least not invisible. I went back to London and then to New York, deciding that I had better remember *Mother Courage* and forget all about *Warten Auf Godot*.

. . .

Back in New York, instead of finishing out a quiet summer, I came to be reminded of another play I had almost forgotten: Robert Anderson's *All Summer Long*. Bob's success with *Tea and Sympathy* had culminated in his joining the august ranks of the Playwrights Company: Maxwell Anderson, Robert Sherwood, S. N. Behrman, and Elmer Rice (as well as lawyer/financier John F. Wharton), veritable deans of the Establishment. The Playwrights Company had an unwritten rule that if any member wanted a play of his produced, it would be put on regardless of other members' opinions. Bob had decided that *All Summer Long* had languished too long in the outer reaches; he wanted the Playwrights to present it in the fall. Production costs, though high, had not yet become astronomical. And the Playwrights had done rather well over the previous several years; they could take a chance on a play even if the critic for the *Times* had already pronounced his verdict.

Summer was scheduled for the early fall. Jo Mielziner would do the sets and lighting, as Bob had always intended. John Kerr, fresh from his success with *Tea and Sympathy*, would play the leading role of the older brother, Don. George Grizzard had been very good in Arena's production, but this was now the big leagues. For the younger brother, Willie, there was talk about getting Brandon de Wilde, who had been so outstanding in *The Member of the Wedding*. But Brandon, believe it or not, was already too old. So Bob was now willing to consider the Arena's Willie, Clay Hall, who was now two years older but still young enough to be credible. Bob said he wanted me to direct.

It's always reassuring to have a playwright come back to a director after a production's inevitable disagreements and tensions. Pleased as I was with the general prospect, some of the specifics bothered me. In this case, my reservations were certainly not about the script. Nor had Brooks Atkinson's somewhat condescending review scared me off, as it had Alex Cohen and Ralph Alswang, and those other potential producers.

My main reservation was that I wanted George Grizzard, whom I knew, rather than John Kerr, whom I didn't know. I was also concerned about Bob's desire to have June Walker, John's real-life mother (Franchot Tone was his father), play the mother in the play. June was an experienced and more than capable actress; she had just been well greeted in *Ladies of the Corridor*, by Dorothy Parker and Armand d'Usseau. I did not like the idea of having two members of the same family in one production. If you had trouble with one of them, the trouble would spread to the other. And somehow I saw trouble on both ends of the Kerr-Walker axis.

I was also concerned about Jo Mielziner. Not that Jo wasn't brilliantly talented, agreeable, and the leading designer in the American theater. From *Winterset* to *Streetcar* and *Salesman*, his work and artistry had always been admirable. The trouble, then and now, was that Jo was always too busy. He was always involved in at least a half dozen projects, including a couple of musicals. In the case of *McCoy* at Catholic University, he had never been available for discussions beforehand. With *All Summer Long*, I knew that he and Bob had already been working out specific ideas long before I came into the picture. The ideas centered upon having that naturalistic river bank set directly into the orchestra pit. This was, of course, the exact opposite of what we had tried to achieve in our much less elaborate Arena production. But, as Bob kept reminding me, we were doing the show not only in a much larger theater this time but in a proscenium theater as well. And, most important, using that other phrase seemingly in everyone's vocabulary, we were doing it in the "big time." The kind of small, suggestive, evocative setting we had used at the Arena simply was not "good enough" for Broadway. I accepted Bob's choice of Jo Mielziner.

Without much help from me, Jo designed a suitably poetic setting, slightly reminiscent, in its silhouette, of *Salesman*. I had absolutely nothing to do with his design except to explain that the kitchen space was too small and the door opened the wrong way for the action I foresaw taking place. With a couple of strokes of his drawing pencil, Jo fixed both the kitchen and the door. I never got used to the river placed in the orchestra pit with its realistic detail, nor did I feel it was nearly as effective as our imaginary "river" at the Arena, although I tried very hard not to let anyone know my feelings on the subject.

Bob and I agreed about the rest of the casting. We were lucky enough to get Ed Begley, at the height of his considerable physical and vocal powers, for the father. For the brother-in-law we corralled John Randolph, who was able to extract every bit of humor and truth from his role. Bob agreed to let George Grizzard understudy, although he and I were somewhat worried about the effect of George's presence on John Kerr, who knew he had played the role of Don very well at the Arena. The real problem came in casting Ruth, our ingenue/leading woman. We must have seen every attractive young actress in New York for the role, holding off our decision as long as possible. The final selection was between Georgianne Johnson and Carroll Baker. Georgianne was more mature and experienced, and clearly the better actress. Carroll, who had only recently come into the theater, was sexier and more vulnerable.

Both Bob and I found something in her physical presence that appealed very strongly to us. The rest of the Playwrights Company looked at Carroll with a jaundiced eye and urged us to cast Georgianne. Usually, when faced with a decision between a better actress and one who "looks the part," the director tends to favor the former, the playwright the latter. In this particular case, both Bob and I were obviously so smitten with Carroll Baker's physical attractiveness that we let our senses overrule our intelligence. Carroll was overjoyed; the stalwarts at the Playwrights Company were not.

Rehearsals started early in August. Everyone was uncertain and insecure. Having done the show before, I was probably impatient and expecting results long before the actors were ready to produce them. John Kerr, who had been so beautifully effective in *Tea and Sympathy*, turned out to be basically inflexible as an actor. Bob Anderson kept apologizing for John, perhaps feeling I might be hoping to justify a takeover by my friend George Grizzard.

Almost every day, John and I would argue about something, important or not. As I anticipated, June Walker got into the act—always in favor of her son. In the meantime, she developed her own problems which neither she nor I were able to solve. George sat it all out, sulking and waiting and hoping, and yet not daring to hope because he knew how Bob felt about him. Rehearsals were not exactly joyous.

Carroll, who had started off impressively with her performance as the self-obsessed narcissistic Ruth, soon receded into uncertainty and shallowness. A play which had seemed so well constructed and tightly knit in Washington came to feel very unclear in New York. I felt Bob's confidence in me evaporating day by day. There was pressure on us to fire Carroll; both Bob and I refused, growing less and less sure we were right. I felt the production getting away from my control.

One afternoon, I dismissed everyone from the rehearsal but Carroll. I set myself a single objective: to break through Carroll's façade of shellac and glamour and reach her interior emotional self. In the play, Ruth had to throw herself on an electrified fence in order to kill her unwanted unborn child. I tried every trick in the acting manual in order to get Carroll to play the scene believably. I pleaded with her, cajoled her, mocked her, shouted at her—anything to make her actually feel something, and show it. Finally, just when I was about to give up, she broke out in an absolute torrent of sobbing and emotion, the tears flowing, her body heaving violently and spontaneously. Simultaneously exultant and terrified, I ran to her and put my arms around her, comforting her and begging her forgiveness. She calmed down, though whether her forgiveness was ever genuine I do not know. I do know that, although she played the scene with tremendous reality that one time, she was never able to come through with more than a suggestion of that ever again. Which is one reason, perhaps, why I don't trust improvisations as much as I should. We never replaced Carroll, or anyone (including the director). She eventually opened to a set of notices as favorable as everyone else's. Gadge Kazan saw her in the show and took her for his film *Baby Doll*, where he had the same kind of trouble as I had getting her to break out of her personal shell.

For reasons clear only to producers and company managers, the Playwrights Company chose to ignore *All Summer Long*'s Arena ancestry and picked Washington as our tryout town. We were scheduled for two weeks at the National Theatre. I welcomed the idea of familiar backgrounds and faces—the hero returning home—but I dreaded the responses of critics and audiences to a play they had previously admired locally. Especially when we weren't exactly reveling in this particular version.

Technical rehearsals, always impossible, were a shambles. There's never enough time for technicals. In the European theater they take weeks. In America, we take days—or hours. Washington has a very strong stagehands union, and they are usually good workers, but the rules under which they operate are ridiculous. That we happened to be opening on Labor Day did not help. We needed a thunder sheet for our big storm scene when the river overflows and defeats all our young hero's efforts. We had been assured the National possessed one. Upon arrival, we discovered they didn't. Since all sources capable of providing a proper thunder sheet were closed until Tuesday, I called a friend at Catholic University to ask if they had one. They did, of course, and he suggested that we send someone to pick it up. The stage crew said they were all too busy, so our assistant stage manager went. Ten minutes after he returned, glowing, with a serviceable thunder sheet, our crew walked off the set. C.U., it seems, was considered a nonunion house.

We finally got the crew back, and we even managed to use the thunder sheet; but not before I personally apologized to everyone for my antiunion behavior. That incident affected my relationship with National Theatre crews for the next ten years. In fact, Scott Kirkpatrick, the National manager and an old C.U. student of mine, told me that the union at one time seriously considered not permitting me to work there again. As someone said, one of the ironies of the twentieth century is that the dictatorship of the proletariat took place not in the Soviet Union but in the stagehands' union.

I also learned, after driving stage manager Peter Zeisler ragged, that synchronizing technical elements—lights, music, and scene changes—on Broadway-bound shows was infinitely more difficult than at the Arena. All our scene changes involved a scrim on which one of Jo's especially designed "blips" was projected to musical accompaniment; as the music faded, the projection went off, the scrim rose, and we moved into the next scene. "Music—scrim—blip—blip off—scrim up—music out"—that was the way it was supposed to be. Coordinating that sequence of confusions proved almost impossible; eventually I gave up, determined never again to do any Broadway play with more than one scene, one light, or one music cue, or any piece of scenery that had to be touched by a stagehand.

I wasn't getting along with my actors; I wasn't getting along with the playwright or the producers (all of whom seemed to sit grim-faced in their hotel rooms at night); I wasn't getting along with myself. Everyone was growing more and more certain of disaster, and I kept wondering how we had gotten to this point.

The worst came the day before opening when John decided to wear his green basketball jacket inside out. I wanted him to wear it the regular way. He wouldn't; I did. He insisted; I insisted harder. Besides, I was the director, wasn't I? Finally, in exasperation, I grabbed the jacket away from him, and threw it into the wings. He'd wear it the way I wanted him to or not at all. To this day, I don't remember how—or if—he wore it. By this time, the basketball jacket was largely irrelevant, a symptom of the chaos in which we labored. Had it not been for good old Ed Begley's stolid plugging along, Clay Hall's youthful cheerfulness, and—yes—everybody's patience and professionalism, that chaos would have swallowed us up.

Miraculously, the show turned out better than anyone expected. Even the Washington reviews were favorable, with only occasional references to the greater simplicity at Arena. By the time we opened in New York on September 23, 1954, we had recovered some sense of each other's worth; Zeisler had achieved a portion of that mysterious combination of "blip—scrim—blip" between each scene; even Johnny Kerr was beginning to seem real. We opened at the Coronet Theatre (where *Pennypacker* had played and where the stagehands and house staff were especially friendly to me) on what is called an interim booking. That meant we'd get another theater if the response was good. On paper, it was, and we moved to the Booth. The best review came from our favorite critic, Brooks Atkinson, who wrote that "*All Summer Long* is a poignant and beautiful play. . . . Some excellent actors under the sensitive direction of Alan Schneider are . . . putting on the finest performance of the new season . . . a remarkable piece of work . . . the first piece of art this season." Atkinson thought the New York production was much more effective than the one he had seen at the Arena Stage. Some of the other critics, none of whom had seen it in Washington, loved it: "Stimulating drama," "a play of substance, humor and integrity," "a fine event in one's life."

Unfortunately, the public kept thinking of us as a bickering family show, with little humor—and no stars. They stayed away, in large numbers. I remember waiting outside of the Booth's box office one afternoon to see how we were doing. There were two little white-haired obviously-not-from-New York ladies in front reading the blowup of our Sunday *New York Times* ad, with all its superlatives. One of them stepped up gingerly to the box office to ask: "Is this a hit?" The box office manager, torn between his seeing me and his wanting to get our weekly box office receipts below a certain figure so that the theater could legally evict us, replied, "Well, it's a sort of a hit."

The ladies looked at each other and said: "Well . . . we don't want to see a sort of a hit, we want to see a hit," summing up the whole attitude of the Broadway audience.

We lasted a few weeks, getting respectful attention as a sort of a hit, but never breaking through. Bob was crushed, I remained just plain numb. Carroll stayed friendly for years until she went off to become a sort of movie star. Ed Begley kept in touch until his death. I still see John Randolph once in a while. Clay Hall is no longer acting. I never saw either John Kerr or June Walker again. The production of a play is like a shipboard cruise; the passengers get very close to their fellow passengers, then once the ship comes back to shore they never see each other again. As I've said before, that's one of the saddest aspects of working in the theater.

Years later, Bob confessed to me in a letter that at various times during the *All Summer Long* imbroglio the producers wanted to fire me, but that he resisted—in spite of my bad behavior—because he felt I had been too devoted to his play for too long a time to be tossed aside, for whatever reason. In the copy of the published version which he signed for me, he wrote: "Thanks for all you did for this play. If it hadn't been for you, it would never have seen the light of Broadway. It was tough;

it was rugged—but I think we came out with something we could be proud of."

Yes, I was proud of *All Summer Long,* as well as sad that it hadn't worked, sadder still that I hadn't worked well on it. But I was a lot tougher and stronger and wiser when it ended than when it began. I needed that toughness and strength and wisdom to get me through the next one.

RUSSIAN MAURETTE
1954

Guy Bolton was a commercial playwright whom I'd heard of for years but never thought I'd meet. Guy had written hit musicals with P. G. Wodehouse and was an intimate of Noel Coward and Ivor Novello. He lived on the south shore of Long Island and played a good game of backgammon. I was a Russian peasant transplanted to the good old U.S.A. But Guy Bolton had just adapted a play on a Russian subject, by French playwright Marcelle Maurette, originally titled *Tatiana* and then changed to *Anastasia*. The play dealt with a group of White Russian émigrés in Berlin who were trying to palm off a German impostor as Anastasia, one of the daughters of Czar Nicholas II of Russia.

The producer of *Anastasia* was Elaine Perry, daughter of director Antoinette Perry, for whom the "Tony" Awards are named. I had met Elaine in that summer of 1939 when I had briefly worked at the Braddock Heights (Maryland) Theatre where she was resident director, though I'm sure she didn't remember me. Elaine wanted George Abbott to direct, but he was either not available or not interested. For some reason, he told Elaine to get me. I think Walter Kerr, who had directed Elaine's previous production of Jean Kerr's *King of Hearts*, had also recommended me, explaining that I was Russian and had the right flavor.

Elaine, knowing only my work on *The Remarkable Mr. Pennypacker*, responded with, "But he only does comedy," but was ultimately persuaded by the combined efforts of George Abbott and Walter and reluctantly offered me the play. Suspicious of the play's subject matter and literary quality, I reluctantly agreed to read the script. It turned out to be an old-fashioned melodrama, with stock situations and cardboard characters—but with one terrific blockbuster of a recognition scene. I read it twice, thought about it, then decided that it was not a play I wanted to direct.

Meeting Guy Bolton, however, was not an experience I wanted to turn down, so off I went to have lunch with Guy at the Blue Ribbon Restaurant on Forty-fourth Street, a sort of poor man's Lüchow's and, sadly, now no longer in existence. My intention was to inform Guy as diplomatically as possible that I was an "artistic type" director who felt that his play was "too commercial" for my tastes. (The subtext of that comment was that I didn't think for a moment that it had a chance.) To this day, I don't know exactly what happened during the lunch except that when we got to the coffee, instead of saying no to Guy, I said yes, and we were making plans to work on the script and round up a cast. Was Guy's charm so persuasive? Was my previous determination to say no just a pose? Guy was about seventy; was I afraid that he'd have a heart attack if I turned him down?

I remember coming back after lunch to tell my disbelieving wife that I was going to direct the play after all. She gulped. And then we both decided the only way *Anastasia* could possibly work would be to cast it with Actors Studio actors, who would locate subtext where none existed, give it resonances undreamed of even in its author's subconscious, and create reality where there was only the phoniest kind of theatricality. I went over to Elaine Perry's office on Fifth Avenue to tell her I'd decided to do the play—but only if she'd let me have control of the casting. I never mentioned the Actors Studio, about which she previously had dropped some unsympathetic hints.

Elaine already had Viveca Lindfors lined up for the false Anastasia and Eugenie Leontovich as the real grandmother, the Empress. Both ladies had strong—and differing—accents. We decided that the rest of the cast shouldn't have any. I'd heard that Leontovich was both ham and prima donna; there were also rumors that she was strongly anti-Semitic. (In my second thoughts about having said yes, I often thought of that as a way out.) On the other hand, next to Greta Garbo—and, of course, my wife—Viveca Lindfors seemed the most gorgeous and glamorous woman I had ever seen. I had seen her only in films though. What was she like on a stage? Could she act? My answer came a lot faster than I wanted, in the form of a phone call from director Margaret Webster, who had just directed Viveca in a John van Druten comedy. I knew Ms. Webster casually, had read her book on Shakespeare, and admired her tremendously. Peggy, as she was called, proceeded to inform me that

Viveca Lindfors was absolutely impossible on stage, unreliable, unpredictable, crazy, and a few other things. I must not, under any circumstances, use her in my production of *Anastasia*—or anything else. Shades of Joe Magee and Burgess Meredith!

I thanked Peggy profusely, than mumbled a few choice Russian expletives to myself. Elaine had already signed Eugenie and Viveca, and had complete confidence in them. I had already insisted on determining the remainder of the cast. How far could I push without increasing an already growing reputation for being difficult with producers as well as actors? By this time also I had been reassured that Eugenie was far from being anti-Semitic; in fact, she made very good matzoh ball soup. George Tabori kept calling me up to tell me that his new wife, Viveca, was going to be great, and that she was eagerly looking forward to working with me. Perhaps Peggy Webster, I kept telling myself before going to sleep each night, had been thinking of someone else.

We plunged into the casting. Elaine and Guy responded well to most of the Studio people I brought in—among them Boris Tumarin, David J. Stewart, Vivian Nathan, and, especially, Michael Strong. I had more trouble getting these "left-wing" actors to suspend their prejudice against what they thought might be a "right-wing" enterprise than I did the other way around. Mike Strong, especially, was concerned about appearing as a doctor in love with a princess, until I was able to convince him that the doctor was, after all, intent on restoring her to being a commoner. I also persuaded Hurd Hatfield, of *Dorian Gray* fame, to take what was for him a small role. All these actors turned out to be perfectly cast though some of them did not always think so. Even Viveca wavered in her feelings about whether the play—and her role—was progressive or reactionary.

Our chief problem lay in casting the role of Prince Bounine, in charge of the gang of plotters who were trying to pass Anna off as the Czar's daughter, enriching themselves in the process. Bounine was what we called "the John Barrymore part"; it needed someone who could be both bravura and real. I was delighted to get Joseph Anthony, who was known for his character work but not as a leading man, but a bit nervous about his reputed temperament. I also knew that he was an established director, as were three other members of the cast. Replacements were handy in case I didn't come through.

For designers, I had no trouble persuading Elaine to take Ben Edwards, who had worked so well on *Pennypacker*, and who at least had time to talk to me before designing the scenery. Ben came up with a simple but graceful and functional design, with lots of room for all the scenes. Guy Bolton loved it. Guy, dapper and completely informal, loved everything and everybody and only asked that the actors said all his lines exactly the way they were written. When they didn't, he wrote me a note about it.

My third Broadway production was rehearsed quite differently from the way I had done the other two. For a few days we sat down and read the play together, talked about it, and worked out the actions and objectives and adjustments in great detail. The few non-Studio actors smirked a bit in the background, but even they had to join the ritual. Elaine immediately realized what she had gotten herself into, but the results were so interesting that she decided to wait and see. Guy kept wondering when we were going to get on our feet, but so long as his lines were said, he wasn't too worried. The first act seemed almost to stage itself. I blocked each scene in outline; and those imaginative, sensitive, and determined Studio actors filled it in. Viveca, as it turned out, loved not knowing where anyone was going to be onstage. She herself was rarely in the same place twice.

Viveca, whose personal sympathies were definitely anti-Czarist, was afraid at first of making the character too sympathetic. Within days, she had rationalized the play into a defense of the poor against the hypocrisies of the rich. Eugenie remained cool and objective, totally oblivious to social meanings; all she cared about was how to make the play work. And yet through some mysterious stage chemistry, she and Viveca—divided as they were by temperament, training, and political orientation—were getting along.

We were doing so well that, one day, I dropped my guard and made a bad mistake with Joe Anthony. At the end of the act where Prince Bounine tries to get the phony Anastasia to reenact the ceremony of reviewing her regiment, I felt that Joe was not getting enough "build" in the speech.

"It's the end of the act," I pleaded with him. "Couldn't you play it just a bit faster and with more momentum so that it really hits a climax!"

Joe pulled himself up to his full six feet, drew in his breath sharply, and barked back at me: "Don't you dare give me results. I'm an ac-tor!"

Everything stopped. Then I recovered some measure of equilibrium to ask him, "What do you want me to say?"

His answer, which baffled me then and amuses me now, was: "Tell me . . . tell me, I have to catch a train!!"

I wanted to tell him was that I could not understand why a director couldn't ask an actor to find a way of building a speech in a climactic manner. If the actor needed an inner reason, he should tell himself he had to catch that train. Under the circumstances, however, I couldn't say that to Joe. Instead, I apologized. Joe did the speech again, more slowly and unclimactically this time. We went on to something else. Eventually, he caught the train.

I always remember George Grizzard's story about John Gielgud in Hugh Wheeler's *Big Fish, Little Fish.* George had a number of similar entrances, on each of which he had to come in, breathless, as though he had just climbed five flights of stairs. He was concerned that all the entrances seemed the same. "How do I make them different?" he asked John, who was directing. John looked at him a moment, then said offhandedly, "Oh, I don't know. Just go home and do one of those little Stanislavski things. Then come in as if you were out of breath differently each time."

I plunged ahead with the second and third acts, although I kept skipping the big scene, much to everyone's surprise and Eugenie and Viveca's consternation. The two of them were raring to get into it, but it was really a love scene and love scenes should be played only when the lovers knew each other better. We were rehearsing in an upstairs studio at the New York City Center on Fifty-fifth Street—cold, bare, filled with crummy rehearsal furniture—a typical rehearsal environment. For our big love scene, I wanted something more suitable.

Even in that room, though, there were lots of laughs along the way. I remember with special fondness the first time I heard Eugenie saying to Hurd Hatfield, who was playing her nephew, "So you are in love with this sleeping beauty?" In Eugenie's rich lavender-flavored Russian dialect, the line always came out: "Saw, you arrh in lawv wid dees slipping byuhty?"

"Sleeping," I would repeat to Eugenie. "Not slipping . . . sleeeeping."

"Dot's wat I'm saying," Eugenie would answer, "slipping byuhty!"

Eugenie's troubles with the King's English reminded me about how the mystical word "beat" had entered our acting language, to represent a unit of text, a piece of the dramatic action. That word had come neither from music nor from the beat generation. It had arrived back in the late twenties simply because another Russian actress, Maria Ouspenskaya, formerly of the Moscow Art Theatre and then teaching at Richard Boleslavski's American Laboratory Theatre, was trying to find an English word approximating Stanislavski's fundamental idea of a piece of the text (the Russian word "*kussok*"). The closest Madame could come instead of "piece," which she didn't find quite right, was "bit." But with Maria, as with Eugenie, "bit" always emerged as "beat." So it became a "leetle beat." And that's why American actors and American directors break up their pages of script into little "beats."

I delayed work on the recognition scene as long as possible because it was not only the core of the play but the key to the play's success. If we started off on the wrong foot with it, that would have been like taking a wrong turn from which we could never get back. Nor did I want to lead or force Viveca and Eugenie into any definite patterns until they were ready to form the patterns themselves. I wanted them to feel their own way—and then pull out all the stops.

One evening, after every other scene in the play had at least been outlined, I invited the two of them to dinner at my fairly spacious and old high-ceilinged apartment up on Central Park West, into which we had recently moved from our Greenwich Village cubbyhole. My two stars had been getting along reasonably well, if a bit formally. As usual, when a show has two equally matched star roles, there was a certain amount of rivalry, jockeying for position, and inner insecurity. Viveca, of course, respected Eugenie, while worrying whether she might be too much of an "external" actress, even a bit old-fashioned. Eugenie, a keen old warhorse, had immediately taken the measure of Viveca and was concerned with how she might stack up against the younger actress's throbbing virtuosity. I think that I got them together outside of regular rehearsals at just about the right time.

After a lengthy dinner, which was as Russian/Swedish as my German/English spouse could manage, I played some of my old 78 r.p.m. Russian recordings of schmaltzy folk music, which brought tears to everyone's eyes. Then, without any urging on my part, Eugenie began to tell us about her life in Russia. Viveca listened, rapt, literally curled up on the rug at her feet.

Emotion and cognac (as well as tea) were both flowing when I suggested that we read the big scene, something we hadn't done since early in rehearsal, when the approach to it had been fairly tentative. They sat next to each other on the couch and started saying the words. Soon Viveca began to move around, arranging her moves perfectly to suit the situation and lines. Jean, sensing what was happening, withdrew gracefully. The scene went on. If anyone had come into that living room, he or she would have felt the presence not of artifice, or of a play by Guy Bolton, but of real human beings directly involved with one another—

which, I suppose, is what Viveca's and my mutual teacher and guide, Lee Strasberg, always taught us acting should be.

I could only hope the scene would seem as powerful once we got it up on stage. Back in our rehearsal room the next day. It was still too pure and intimate, and I didn't want either Viveca or Eugenie to feel self-conscious or inhibited. Rehearsals are always private sessions, which is a fact of theatrical life that people who are not in the theater rarely recognize when they ask to sit in on them. This one was even more private than any I'd ever encountered, and I was determined to keep it that way. I staged it over a period of two or three days, simply and organically. Mainly, I tried to get my two actresses to work out their own direction and form, and then allow me to select from and shape their responses.

"There's nothing in the scene you *have* to do," I told them right at the start. "Just listen and react."

What I wanted was for each actor to start from something within and then build off the other's reactions. Occasionally I prevailed on Guy to trim a line or two where the sentiment got too thick. I believe we cut several minutes from the original text, ending up with seventeen taut minutes of truth.

Things kept happening every time we rehearsed it, deepening and extending that truth. There was a moment in the scene, for example, where I had Viveca tugging childlike at Eugenie's skirts as the older woman tried to tear herself away from accepting her as her granddaughter. We tried this simple piece of business in a dozen ways. Then one day, Viveca's emotion was so strong that as she was tugging, she just wouldn't let go when she was supposed to. Eugenie started laughing, and Viveca began to laugh, too. That proved to be marvelous because, at that moment, it was clear that crying wasn't enough; Viveca had to laugh with her tears, as did Eugenie. It was a rare and very precious moment.

When we had our first runthrough of the scene for Guy and Elaine, they were enthralled. So were all the other members of the cast when they finally were allowed, almost on tiptoe, to enter the sacred precincts. In that bare room, those two actresses, from different backgrounds and traditions, with only the most rudimentary of props and none of the beautifully eloquent costumes Ben Edwards was soon to provide, were both absolutely truthful and absolutely riveting. The cast could hardly talk afterward. We all knew we had something—if only we could hold on to it.

For those inevitable out-of-town tryout weeks, we went again to Philadelphia, exactly retracing my *Pennypacker* routine. We played the Walnut Street Theatre, stayed at the St. James Hotel, made phone calls on the Pennypacker-5 exchange. Joy Small took my notes, on a clipboard to which one of the electricians had attached a small bulb so that she could write more easily in the dark.

It was too good to last, and it didn't. A day or two before the opening, Joe and David Stewart, longtime close friends, began to bicker publicly. David had always felt he should be playing Bounine instead of understudying him. Another problem arose when we made some cuts at almost the last moment; our Studio-trained actors were happy neither with our timing nor with their cuts, which interfered, they said, with their characters' inner lives.

More important, I had my first disagreement with Eugenie on the staging of her final exit from the scene. I had imposed the image of a mother putting her small daughter to bed, turning out the light, and tiptoeing out of the room backward, making sure that all was well with the girl she was leaving behind. When Eugenie realized that I was asking her to make her exit backing out, she drew all four feet ten inches of herself up into a tight exclamation point.

"You are esking me, en actriss from de Moscow Art Teatre, to *back* out of de room! On my beeg exit! Neverrrr!!!!"

I explained in detail the image I wanted. I begged her to try it once with a matinee audience. One day, I literally got down on my hands and knees. Finally, she tried it at one preview, to such an ovation that she realized I might be right. From then on, all hell's angels wouldn't have stopped her from backing out, very slowly. In fact, she soon discovered that she could back almost to the door, move forward a few steps to comfort Anastasia, then have more room to back up again. I began to think that the exit was taking a half hour, and was almost sorry I'd started the whole thing.

My most intense Philadelphia trauma was caused, however, by my best and closest friend in the cast, Vivian Nathan, playing the Charwoman who is first to identify the peasant girl, Anna, as the "real" Anastasia. I had known Vivian at Theatre Inc., Studio 63, and the Actors Studio. We had shared our lives, inner and outer, for years. The afternoon of our Philadelphia opening, while I was working out the curtain calls, I was thunderstruck to find Vivian furious and finally walking offstage in anger. Having been assigned the sixth curtain call instead of the fifth, and the sixth dressing room rather than the fifth, she felt betrayed. She intended to withdraw from the show, and was giving us two weeks' notice as of that moment.

Even this early in my Broadway career, I knew something about the importance of hierarchy in the theater, but to be honest, I had paid no attention to the allocation of dressing rooms—or the subtleties of fifth versus sixth curtain call. I tried to explain all this to Vivian, as well as to persuade the actor taking call number five to switch with her, but she refused to leave the dressing room in question to talk to me. I could hardly believe it, especially a few hours before opening. I guess I didn't realize the role of ego in an actor's existence, and the absolute need for status. In the years and productions that came afterward, I was to learn that harsh lesson over and over again.

Vivian stayed with the show, but she didn't speak to me for weeks.

Our opening in Philadelphia produced the most encouraging response to any of my three Broadway-bound shows: "Superbly acted and staged" . . . "One of the real hits of the season" . . . "Not to be missed" . . . "Stirring entertainment" . . . "Skill that is seldom seen in the theater." The reviews were so good that we got nervous. The Philadelphia reviews made sure that we had a home in New York: the Lyceum, an attractive old theater that had once been prominent but hadn't had a hit in years.

We put in a few more of Guy's daily suggestions and cuts, smoothed out some rough spots, and roughed up some of the overly smooth ones. A number of the deepest cuts turned out to occur in Eugenie's long speeches; she fought like a tiger against them, but once overruled she worked like a trouper to learn them. In the meantime, Elaine was beginning to worry that Joe Anthony wasn't colorful enough; maybe we should replace him. "Over my dead body," I said. Elaine was also worried that David J. Stewart was getting too colorful—which he was—Boris Tumarin too fussy, Michael Strong too dull, and even "the" scene slack. Guy continued radiant, waking up early each morning to slip his line changes scrawled semilegibly on little pieces of paper, under my hotel room door. About a week before the New York opening, after an ultimatum from our Studio actors, we "froze" the show. No more changes. We were impatient to get to New York, to move into the Lyceum, and to embrace our future.

The Lyceum, beautiful and tradition-flavored, lies slightly east of Broadway, and remains, therefore, reasonably far down in the pecking order of New York theaters. In this particular order, Forty-fourth and

Forty-fifth Streets west of Broadway are at the top, the other streets trailing off in direct proportion to their distance from Shubert Alley, which joins Forty-fourth and Forty-fifth, equidistant from Broadway and Eighth Avenue. Anything on the east side of Broadway is practically in Sheboygan. In my first two Broadway ventures, I had been in a theater four long blocks from Shubert Alley's Holy Grail (except for those precious few weeks at the Booth, whose limited seating capacity makes it a special case). Now I was actually going to make Forty-fifth Street—but, of course, on the wrong side of the track.

Once we got to New York, I felt my job was to keep everyone as calm as possible and not to fool around with the chemistry. "The" scene would do the rest. We had a couple of previews, and suddenly people were standing in line at the box office. At the final preview, however, someone in the balcony laughed at a first-act line of Bounine's that was not supposed to get such a response. Guy panicked, fearing that something fundamental was wrong. I told him the laugh probably came from some personal quirk that would never show up again. (It never did, by the way.) Besides, we were opening the next day. The actors had warned me, and I was not about to make any additional changes. At three that morning, Guy rang me to say that he had discovered the trouble with the line in question, and was rewriting it to guarantee no laugh on opening night. I told him I didn't think this was a good idea, and to please go back to sleep.

The afternoon of our premiere, just in time for our usual pre-opening line rehearsal, a highly distraught Guy Bolton met me at the Lyceum stage door with that ever-present piece of paper in his hand. I told Guy we shouldn't make any last-minute changes, especially if they involved Joe Anthony. Guy explained that the change in the line was insignificant, just a word order reversed, and that Joe could learn it in a minute. Then why make it? Because it was his play, his line, his right as the playwright. Guy's voice rose; and, as with our first meeting at the Blue Ribbon, I was sure he would have a heart attack. Okay, okay, I'd tell Joe. Which I did, a few minutes later, as quietly and as casually as possible, waiting until I could take him aside for a moment when he came in, cheerful and natty, ready for another opening, another show. I explained that Guy had prevailed on me to ask Joe to make a slight change in one line, a very slight change, nothing at all. I wouldn't have asked him to do it, but Guy was an old man, a very old man. I was sure Joe would understand.

Joe did. Right in the long corridor connecting the Lyceum's stage to its dressing rooms, he grew pale, his face a mask of pain, his voice reduced to an explosion of breath: "Don't you *ever* do that to an actor!" and stalked off to his dressing room, which was one level up the circular staircase downstage right. He slammed the door so hard I thought the set would fall down. Later, a hand-lettered sign appeared on the door. It said: "Mr. Anthony does not choose to speak to Mr. Bolton, Miss Perry, Mr. Schneider." I didn't worry about the billing.

Our line rehearsal, a half-hour later, was solid ice. None of the actors knew what had happened but they did know something had. Joe wouldn't look at anyone—though the point of the rehearsal was to recapture our spontaneous looking and listening—and snapped out his lines in a determined monotone. Viveca and Eugenie kept looking at me, and I kept looking back, pretending that whatever was happening had to do with nerves. Elaine came over fourteen times to ask me something. I kept listening to the line rehearsal and avoiding her. Guy sat in a corner looking very small and old.

In the Lyceum lobby before the performance that night—December 29, 1954—there was a kind of excitement always present when the audience already knows that it's going to see something good. In every other square foot of the theater there was gloom so thick you could eat it with a fork. I went around to everybody—except Joe—for my final good-luck wishes. It was like wishing the Christians good luck with the lions. Everybody looked at me as though I had just committed mass murder. I went out to the balcony steps to join my wife and witness the debacle.

Once the curtain went up, no debacle became readily apparent. David and Boris and Joe, the conspirators, had never played more fully or truthfully. I watched Joe through a microscope, but could detect no molecule of disturbance. Viveca, however, was consciously or unconsciously giving a performance different from anything any one of us had ever seen. Anna had become a mad, neurotic, inchoate creature from whom all sympathy and warmth had vanished. Elaine came running up to me at the back of the auditorium and whispered, "What the hell is she doing?!" I shook my head, wonderingly, and cautioned her to silence. I was afraid the audience would hear her better than they could hear Viveca. Soundlessly, I kept repeating to myself, "Well, this is it . . . ," and kept looking at Jean, sitting silently on the balcony steps beside me.

At the first intermission, the applause was polite but far from thunderous. Elaine told me she was going backstage immediately to "kill that girl."

I grabbed her arm, not too gently, and said, "Absolutely not! I'll go. It's that second act that'll make us or break us."

"What are you going to say to her?" Elaine practically sobbed.

"I don't know," I said, "but *you* stay here!"

I went backstage, through the most elegant pass door on Broadway, to Viveca's dressing room. She was getting into her second-act costume and hairdo, George Tabori standing next to her calmly drinking a glass of champagne. (Visitors between acts on opening night are even less to be tolerated than irate directors, but who could say no to a royal Russian princess, or to the author of *The Emperor's Clothes*? Certainly not the peasant who was directing.) "How did it go?" asked Viveca, looking breathtakingly beautiful and completely serene, between strokes of her eyebrow pencil. I embraced her gently—otherwise I might have strangled her—kissed her celestial cheek, said, "Terrific! Now . . . *this* is the act," and went out. My performance, I thought, was among the better acting jobs of the evening.

I knew that if I had torn into Viveca at that point we were finished. She would not only have gone right off the rails, she would have taken the rails with her. The first act didn't matter. The third act didn't matter. What mattered was that scene.

And, as the theatrical gods would have it, I turned out to be right. In Act Two Viveca was another person, resplendent, radiant, alive, and doing what she had done at rehearsal. Only more beautiful. Eugenie's first entrance didn't come until that second act, and she knew nothing about what had happened. "The" scene uncoiled and uncoiled like a giant spring, releasing circles of emotion further and further into the auditorium. That audience didn't know what had hit it. At the halfway point, the sniffles started coming; by the time the scene was over—seventeen minutes later—practically everyone was weeping, men as well as women. The applause at the end, after Eugenie had finally backed off, was a sustained thunderclap.

Elaine came over to hug me. "What did you say to her?" she managed to get out through her own tears. I smiled enigmatically. I could even see the back of Guy's head in the center of the orchestra right next to his wife's, both of them clearly sobbing away. I wanted to sob, too, with relief, but couldn't. I was too drained.

I don't remember the third act at all. I think there was one.

The critics, for once susceptible to emotion, were unanimous in their hosannas, especially to the performers, the adjectives flowing: "enthralling" . . . "superb" . . . "profoundly moving" . . . "grand" . . . "gripping" . . . "transcendent" . . . and a few lesser ones, like "marvelous." Special praise, of course, was lavished on the recognition scene, those "seventeen memorable minutes" as the *Times* later called it. "No single scene has been so widely admired," wrote my friend Brooks Atkinson. "The best single dramatic scene in town," proclaimed the *Daily News*. *Life* called it "one of the best scenes ever acted on Broadway." Arthur Gelb, in a *Times* follow-up article, said it somewhat differently: "Not since *Death of a Salesman* made even strong men weep . . . has a Broadway play yielded so many soggy handkerchiefs." And Guy confessed to a reporter, "I didn't realize how effectively it [the scene] would come off. I didn't know it had so many possibilities. . . . Suddenly I found my own lines making me cry." In his inscription on a copy of the play that he later gave me, Guy wrote, "With great affection and gratitude for his work in bringing the play alive."

That scene stayed with me a long time. Through a year on Broadway and another on the road. Through a variety of performances and actresses. Through a series of scripts with similar—but not nearly as effective—scenes that kept being sent to me. It stayed with me through endless amateur productions and countless auditions. It was particularly with me, a couple of years later, when I took Viveca to the Radio City Music Hall to see Ingrid Bergman and Helen Hayes do that same scene on film. I'll leave judgment to those who saw both versions. What I remember most vividly is Viveca, as she sat down, starting to take off her brown leather jacket, starting to lean back—then sitting motionless and silent during the entire film. If there were any tears in my eyes, they were not for what was taking place on the Music Hall screen.

We settled in for a year's run and, ultimately, a variety of voyages elsewhere. Vivian resumed talking to me, and Joe finally emerged from his dressing room, although he would sometimes hole up there, reading—or at least looking at—old Russian newspapers. I guess that was his way of recapturing some of his original freshness and reality. Viveca and Eugenie became firm friends, as well as the toasts of the town's theatrical and social circles, winning many acting awards, including the *Variety* critics poll but, interestingly enough, not the Tony. That injustice was perhaps more bearable than having one of them win it and the other not. Viveca became so interested in the story of Anastasia that she read everything she could about the several "real" Anastasias who were cropping up especially after we had opened. One, Anna Anderson, came to see the performance, and Viveca almost collapsed.

As with my other hit and my "sort of hit," I came to see the show at least once a week, as unexpectedly as possible, so the actors could not "adjust" their performances. Sometimes I found matters wonderful to behold, and would go to the Blue Ribbon or one of my favorite Chinese restaurants in the area, glowing all the way. Sometimes I found the show so sloppy and slow that I could hardly sit through it. I would call a rehearsal. Then I'd come again, a day or two prior to the scheduled rehearsal, and everything would be fine again. No rational excuse existed for the change—except that actors were human. Rehearsal cancelled.

Once David had taken to standing on the table in performance, and had resisted all stage-managerial attempts to remind him that this was not the original pattern for the scene. I took David out for a drink and explained to him patiently that standing on the table didn't seem to me to suit either his character or the scene—and besides, that wasn't the way I had staged it. Why did he insist on standing on the table? David explained that he'd simply had an impulse and had followed it. Lee Strasberg, with whom he was currently studying at the Actors Studio, had told him always to honor his impulses (which perhaps also explained why Viveca, who was also at the Studio, varied her performance nightly). What was so terrible or wrong with honoring an impulse?

What was indeed wrong was that the stage manager was upset, the director disturbed, and the producer livid. Some of the other actors—including members of the Studio—were openly questioning whether this was exactly what Lee had meant. For the first time in my life, I journeyed to Lee's home on Central Park West to ask for his advice. Lee listened to my whole story without saying a word. Finally, he turned to me and said, "The trouble with you, Alan, is that you are too concerned with staging." I thanked him and went back to the theater, determined never to seek artistic advice from that particular mountain again.

"David," I said, "if you stand on that table again, I'm not going to argue any more with Elaine Perry about firing you."

"Oh," replied David, "if that's the way you feel about it." He never again got up on the table. I'm not sure whether the impulse remained; if so, it was successfully smothered—with no evident side effects.

That ended the problem with David. Others remained. Viveca continued never to give the same performance twice. As a result, her relationship to the rest of the cast steadily deteriorated. Now, at periods during the run, she and Joe weren't even on speaking terms, Joe announcing publicly that he didn't want Viveca near him. "The" scene remained as consistent in its nuances as was humanly possible, even after Cathleen Nesbitt replaced Eugenie.

In spite of all the problems and headaches, it was great to have a real hit running, not just for the director's royalties (relatively modest compared to today's), but mostly for the accompanying sense of solid accomplishment and acceptance. After fifteen years in the hinterlands, five less than the usual twenty, I was now a real Broadway director. The profession was becoming aware of me. It respected me, even though my picture was not yet on the wall at Sardi's. I didn't really want to become part of the Establishment, although some part of me did hanker for that. "Success" actually bothered me a little; accomplishment—however that might be defined—didn't. And I now felt that I had "made it" with something approaching quality material. I knew that *Anastasia*, with all due respect to Guy and the actors, wasn't in the same class as something like *Streetcar* or *Salesman*. But at least it had some class; it was in the "grand tradition," and theatrical as hell. Maybe it would lead to something even better. After all, both of my Bobs, Whitehead and Anderson, were expressing their respects and pleasure at my latest success. Audrey was pleased enough to say two words in a row to me. She was the best and most influential agent in the business; she was bound to come up with something for me. My bank account was growing. I even had to get an accountant to do my income tax.

On the personal side, there were many good things as well. I had just turned thirty-eight, was in good health, and possessed more than enough energy to drive actors to good performances, as well as desperation. I was happily married to someone whose own ego was fulfilled through helping to satisfy mine. We had a new apartment, friends, a life together. Scripts were coming in; nothing special, but there was always hope. On a scale of one to ten, my prospects seemed to be about eleven.

NO HITS, NO RUNS, TWO ERRORS
1955

Pride, as they say, goeth before a flop. Or, a series of flops. Not that "flop" is a word I like to use very much in talking about the theater. Let me rather say "error of judgment." Or errors of judgment.

Pennypacker and *Anastasia* and *All Summer Long* had—as Brooks Atkinson put it—shown that this "new director [had] as much artistic authority as the old reliables." Those old reliables were, of course, Elia Kazan and Joshua Logan, who between them had directed practically every serious dramatic show on Broadway for more than a decade. I was now getting to be an established and active New York director. But here I was, having always thought of myself—in my secret soul—as the artistic successor to Kazan, being transformed, through my play choices and the nearsightedness of the critics, into another commercial Josh Logan.

Proud of my new-found professional standing, I decided, therefore, to wait before plunging ahead with another project. Audrey was getting scripts for me. The Theatre Guild, for some unclear reason, liked me. Warner Brothers, impressed with my ability with actresses in big scenes, dangled a seven-year contract in front of me—provided I would do a couple of movies with Doris Day. I waited for something more suitably artistic to come along.

I should have waited longer.

In January 1955, a few weeks after *Anastasia*'s opening, a couple of youthful producers, Bruce Becker and Robert Ellis Miller, asked me to come to their rescue. The show was *Tonight in Samarkand*, a psychological thriller with poetic overtones, written by French boulevard playwright Jacques Deval, and adapted by Lorenzo Semple, Jr., now a successful screenwriter. *Samarkand* was under the artistic control of Herman Shumlin, a producer of distinction as well as a fine director, with whom the producers were very unhappy. The play had been a big hit in Paris, but their production in Princeton was languishing, even with film star Louis Jourdan in the lead. The idea of being "called in" to help appealed to me, though I was not keen on antagonizing someone as eminent as Shumlin (also represented by Audrey Wood). I liked the idea of not having to go through the entire process of casting and rehearsals. I agreed to come down, incognito, to render an opinion. The production seemed rough and the performances uneven, but the show was salvageable. I suggested that the producers hang on to Herman Shumlin, since I had no desire to replace him. Miller and Becker informed me that Shumlin had become so difficult that the actors would no longer work with him. I finally gave in—provided that Shumlin still receive billing as the director. I was to be credited only as "production supervisor," whatever that was.

I saw the show again, proposed some cast changes that were accepted enthusiastically, and started to rehearse with the new people—while the ones being replaced continued to play at night, a process I do not recommend. I soon discovered that the actors who stay don't like replacements, even when the replacements are clear improvement; they worry about who might be next to go. The situation reminded me of a print my father used to keep in his medical office. It juxtaposed the faces of an angel, God, and the Devil. When you first came in, my father explained, you saw the physician as an angel; when he cured you, he became God; when he sent you the bill . . . ! That was exactly the sequence confronting me with *Samarkand*, even though the producers and I kept reassuring the company there would be no more changes.

Through a good portion of the Washington tryout, I lay exhausted in bed at the Willard Hotel, trying to work on rewrites with Lorenzo, arbitrating among a cast of unhappy actors, and coping with two producers who constantly changed their minds about everything except their determination to make *Tonight in Samarkand* the biggest hit of the season. I suspected, even then, that whenever someone thinks only of making a show a hit, instead of dealing with the nitty-gritty, the show isn't going to make it. A brandy alexander at my side, I studied the Willard's overfancy wallpaper, and kept wishing I were somewhere else. My mother and father beamed radiantly from a distance, enjoying my nearby eminence.

Several dozen brandy alexanders later, I made it on foot to *Samarkand*'s New York opening, February 16, 1955. Apart from script and cast problems, we had had lots of technical difficulties with our combination of turntable and sliding stages. On opening night, every transition from the fortune teller's tent in and out of the scenes in his crystal ball moved like magic. The effects were startling, mesmerizing, breathtaking. The circus music was captivating.

The critics, however, were not swayed. Most of them disliked either the play or the production, or both—mostly both. Some of my personal notices weren't bad—"Alan Schneider has directed a very good company with intelligence and imagination"—but that didn't make anyone, including me, feel any better. In spite of all the traumas, *Tonight in Samarkand* was a theatrical challenge I enjoyed, and a production of which I was proud. It was fun while it lasted, but it didn't last long. The show, those turntables and crystal globes and lions and all, closed almost immediately.

Herman Shumlin, who had not been there, had won. Alan Schneider, who had been there every moment, had lost. First error of judgment.

My favorite producer, Robert Whitehead, ever a knight errant, came almost immediately to my emotional rescue. Ever since *Pennypacker*, Bob had been looking for another project we could do together. At one point he was going to have me direct a play with the poetic title of *Stars in a Person's Backyard*, written by Jay Presson and starring Chris Cronyn, the young son of Hume and Jessica. At the last minute something happened: no show. This time, Bob was planning a "revival"—another theater word I resist—of Thornton Wilder's *The Skin of Our Teeth* for the "Salute to France" production, to be put on in Paris that summer by ANTA. *Skin* was going to be part of the annual Théâtre des Nations Festival at the Théâtre Sarah Bernhardt.

Bob had already persuaded Mary Martin to take on the role of Sabina, which Tallulah Bankhead had made famous. Florence Reed was going to play the Fortune Teller, as she had in the first production; Helen Hayes had agreed to play Mrs. Antrobus; and Bob was working on George Abbott, who hadn't been onstage as an actor in years, to play Wilder's Mr. A. Helen, incidentally, had been sought by Thornton to play his original Sabina, but, because she was doing something else at the time, she had suggested Tallulah as an alternative. Bob had seen my *Skin* at Catholic University and wanted me to direct.

I jumped at the opportunity, although I knew even back then that "revivals" rarely helped a director's career. But I had always loved the play and relished this opportunity to work with those three great ladies and one gentleman of the theater. Besides, after all those hotel rooms in Philadelphia and Washington and Boston, Paris seemed very inviting. Helen and Mary couldn't have been more charming and gracious. Helen just asked that I not show her what to do, make whatever suggestions I like, and serve as her editor when she did too much. Mary told me she was terrified and would need me to work with her every minute. George Abbott, somewhat reluctant to take on an acting chore, finally agreed to our entreaties on two conditions: he wouldn't rehearse after six o'clock, especially in Paris, as that would interfere with his social life, and he wanted "none of that motivation business" to confuse him. All he wanted from me were the moves and stage business.

We cast the production in about two hours and went into rehearsal at the Belasco Theatre at just about the moment my new pink-cheeked daughter, chose to be born—on April 5, 1955—at St. Luke's Hospital, the first member of the Schneider family to be born in this country. Naturally, I had to spend more time in the rehearsal room than with Jean at St. Luke's maternity ward. At least now I could afford to have a child. *Anastasia* was still going strong; we named our daughter after Viveca Lindfors. I aleady had a Eugenie in my family, this being Jean's legal name. So I now had a Viveca/Eugenie combination to deal with at home as well as at the theater. That made for a fair amount of conversation and column items. We called our home-grown Viveca "Vickie." The other one was much too beautiful and formidable to have a nickname.

For some reason which I've forgotten, Bob chose to go with designer Lester Polakov instead of our usual Ben Edwards. Lester is a brilliant designer, who had done Bob's production of *The Member of the Wedding*. (His later decision to leave the theater for a teaching career because he was no longer willing to work under Broadway conditions and rules is a sad one, and suggests how much talent is lost to our theater by such defections.) A lovely Russian lady named Helene Pons, who left the theater and the country for more personal reasons, designed the witty and handsome costumes. And I was able to get Frances Sternhagen, who had played Sabina for me at Catholic University, to understudy the ladies. It was all going to be lots of fun.

Helen was totally wonderful right from the start, and she knew it. Mary, who was less experienced with nonmusical material, had some trouble finding her way; she asked for extra time with me and came to rehearsals hours ahead of everyone else to work on her scenes. I soon discovered that while all I needed to do with Helen was "edit" her richness in detail, with Mary I had to propose specifics, which she would then embroider and make her own. One day, for instance, I suggested that Sabina dust everything. Not only did Mary find a dozen laughs in dusting various odd places like the floor; she even got a few out of dusting herself. Florence, of course, was like the Rock of Gibraltar, imposing and immovable. While George Abbott, slower than everyone else and not blessed with too strong a voice, never had an untruthful moment—in spite of his disdain for the Stanislavski version of how onstage truth ought to be attained. Don Murray, who had just made a success as the young sailor in *The Rose Tattoo*, won out over a host of talented juveniles for the coveted role of Henry, created by Montgomery Clift. Mary's son, Larry Hagman, joined us later in Paris for a bit role. He also seems subsequently to have done rather well elsewhere.

My production was basically straightforward, with nice movement and strongly vivid act endings. I also introduced the idea that whenever the characters broke out of the play to talk to the audience and among themselves, they use their own names (a convention I had tried in my Catholic University production). Helen and Mary were ambivalent about doing this until Thornton approved enthusiastically. He loved the idea of Mary referring to *Peter Pan* and other plays she had been in; the real names contributed to the sense of actuality he had always wanted in these interruptions. Thornton came to a few rehearsals with his sister, Isobel, and was as delighted as a child with what he saw. Basically he left me alone, although he made a few line changes and suggestions, and wrote me a few notes. He particularly liked my groupings and fluid movement. "I'm a very happy fella," he wrote me after our first runthrough. "I love the whole production and am crazy about it. . . . I mention no names." I felt pretty good about life, Thornton Wilder, and the pursuit of theater.

Word was getting around that "we had something," and everybody in the theater tried to get in to see us at the Belasco before we left for Paris. At our final runthrough, we were packed with professionals, all of whom expressed regret that only the French would see us. Couldn't we do the show over here? There was a sudden flurry of activity embracing ANTA, Bob Whitehead, and Roger Stevens; then Bob announced that upon our return we would play a short tour—Washington and Chicago—and then, perhaps, a few weeks at the ANTA Theatre in New York. Having gotten into all this as a lark, with a free trip to Paris thrown in, our stars were not too sure they wanted the additional exposure, although they finally succumbed to Bob's blandishments. Every day seemed to bring a new and pleasant vista for the future. And I had never gone through a smoother rehearsal period. The actors seemed content with everything. The script was, of course, sacred territory. It wasn't until we were practically on our way to the plane that I had my first disagreement with anyone—in this case, Bob. I felt the nonstarring members of our troupe were discriminated against in our seating arrangements and protocol on the plane, and said so. I was upset, Bob was upset; the seating arrangements remained unchanged, as did the protocol.

I left behind both my Eugenies and both my Vivecas, and flew off to Paris with a light heart. Our only concern was that we soon discovered the Festival schedule had us sandwiched in between the Berliner Ensemble, which had five years of rehearsal, and the Peking Opera, which had five hundred. We barely had five weeks, but were expected to be as good. Suddenly, our mission became more political than artistic: competing for glory with these two Marxist-oriented giants. That seemed a step beyond worrying about a notice in *Variety*. All our faces began to get serious in the Paris sunshine.

Rehearsing in Paris proved more difficult than in New York. Everyone was always a bit late coming in from sightseeing, shopping, eating, or drinking. Rehearsal hours available to us at the Sarah Bernhardt were highly irregular, working conditions even more so. French stagehands, mostly Socialists or even Communists, were determined to help the American "imperialists" no more than they had to. They worked according to rule, managed not to understand a word of English when they felt like it, and rarely said "hello," "goodbye," or "thank you" in any language.

One evening, Bob and I went to see the Ensemble's *Caucasian Chalk Circle*. The production was so exquisitely beautiful, so polished, and so extraordinary in its technical achievements that all we could think of was how inadequate and ill-prepared our pickup artistic team seemed in comparison. The Germans had even brought along an extra turntable in case the one onstage failed; we were scrimping on hand props. Their premiere was as triumphant as the opening night of *Mother Courage* the year before. The entire audience stood and cheered for endless minutes. Bob and I walked back to our hotel in silence.

Our own opening night atmosphere on June 28 was like Election Eve at Republican headquarters in Mayor Daley's Chicago; no matter how hard we ran, we knew we were going to come in second. But on the surface, our spirits remained unshaken. Thanks to Helen's generosity, her senior claim to Sarah Bernhardt's ornately furnished dressing room had been relinquished to Mary. When I went inside its historic environs just before curtain time to wish my Sabina well for the last time, Mary kissed me warmly, gave me a gold tie clasp with "Love, always, Mary" inscribed on it. She and Richard Halliday, her husband/manager, told me that she had never worked with a director who had helped her more, and that she hoped she would never do another show without me. This is one opening night sentiment, by the way, which I have found, over the years, never survives unfavorable reviews.

I walked out into the auditorium feeling on top of the world, with the exception of East Germany and China. I was at the Divine Sarah's former working place, my producer respected me, my playwright supported me, and both my leading ladies loved me. I sat down in the back row to read my name in the elaborate Théâtre des Nations program. The celebrated red velvet curtain went up, and I remembered the story of Ellen Terry, prevailed upon to come to one of Bernhardt's performances. She waited until that same curtain had gone up about a foot, and then, in a stage whisper heard around Europe, said, "Dreadful, isn't she?"

Mary came out, in Sabina's wispily sexy maid's uniform, and went into Thornton's opening monologue, explaining the play and describing the characters. The audience laughed politely, not quite sure what was happening. Then Helen walked in, the archetypical housewife and mother—and comedienne—flourishing her watering can, with the water steaming, to revive her frozen flowers. The audience roared. Whatever Helen did from then on, they kept roaring. Whatever Mary did brought only chuckles. Mary's was familiar territory. Helen's was peculiarly apple-pie American, and new.

Suddenly I felt a hand clutching my left shoulder, a voice spitting into my ear, "What have you done to my wife?" I turned directly into the pained countenance of Richard Halliday, whom I had just left smiling benignly at me in Sarah's and Mary's dressing room. At first, I thought Dick must be drunk; then I decided he must have mixed me up with someone else. I put my finger to my lips and turned away, my heart beating loudly enough to be heard in the Sarah Bernhardt's fifth tier.

It was only after the show that I was able, with Bob's help, to understand what I had done to Richard Halliday's wife. I had neglected to tell her that Helen Hayes might get as many laughs as she would. Or more. In the original production of *Skin*, a dozen years earlier, with a very noncomedic Florence Eldridge as Mrs. Antrobus, Tallulah had had the laughs practically for herself. Here, it was fifty-fifty, or less, for poor hardworking, unwitting Mary. And I hadn't told her. Worse still, I had "made it happen." At our celebration party in her dressing room after the show, Mary hardly looked at me, and she never spoke to me again except in passing. So much for the gold tie clasps.

To make the evening complete, I left the party early because I was scheduled to take off for Switzerland at dawn, on the trail of Jean's father's manuscripts. My taxi had hardly gone one block when a car sped out of a darkened side street and plowed into the side of the taxi at the precise spot against which my back was resting. I tried to get out of the taxi and fainted. The next thing I knew I was flat on my back in the street, looking up at a tight ring of black-kepi'd French policemen. I remember my only concern was that my jacket would get dirty. A policeman picked me up as tenderly as though I were a baby and drove me in his car to the City Hospital, the Hôtel de Ville. Eventually, after what seemed to be hours of explanation and confusion in my very bad French, someone got the idea that I had something to do with the Théâtre Sarah Bernhardt. A few minutes later, a white-faced Bob Whitehead showed up.

I begged Bob to have me transferred to Paris's legendary American Hospital. The French authorities were afraid my back would not survive the ambulance trip; I said I didn't care. The ambulance was, indeed, bone-clanking, but the American Hospital was like Shangri-La, complete with both Margo and Dr. Ronald Colman. I remained on my back, uncertain whether I would walk again, receiving get-well cards from the cast and visits from Helen, Bob, and Isobel Wilder. Mary sent a card. After hundreds of X-rays, they still didn't diagnose the culprit: liver, kidneys, spleen, nerve endings. The French critics, in the meantime, didn't diagnose our production too favorably. They couldn't even understand the title.

The good news was that one week later I walked off a plane at Idlewild Airport, straight into the arms and amazement of my wife, whom I had not informed of my Paris misadventures. My back ultimately got better, and I've been walking, more or less, ever since. When I tried to sue the driver of the guilty car, he turned out to be a physician whose main concern was not my recovery but the problem of keeping secret the fact that on that fateful night he had been escorting home a passenger, quite clearly his mistress. Suing a French citizen proved impossible, especially where mistresses were involved. I had to settle for workman's compensation, which almost paid for the Band-Aids. I didn't care. I was walking again. And I was out of the Hôtel de Ville. By the skin of my teeth.

Mary Martin was now threatening to quit the show. Bob suggested that he would be happy to replace her with Kim Stanley, who was waiting in the wings. Mary decided to go on—with her own director. This enterprising fellow was Vincent Donehue, director of *The Sound of Music* and an old friend of mine from early Washington days. Vinnie, albeit slightly embarrassed, worked with Mary while I went on with the rest of the cast, including an astounded Helen Hayes. This arrangement persisted all the way through two weeks in Washington, another fortnight in Chicago—where Vinnie and I often had a room-service late supper together at the Blackstone Hotel—and our sold-out, month's engagement in New York, which could have gone on forever but, luckily, didn't.

In Washington, incidentally, my romance with the National's stagehands went into a new phase. Each afternoon, for example, we rehearsed the scene where Sabina has to deal with the scenery flying and sliding off in various directions. Every evening the scenery proved temperamental—putting poor, confused Mary into a tizzy. We thought the stagehands were doing it on purpose. The fact of the matter was that the stagehand who rehearsed with Mary during the day worked elsewhere at night. After rehearsal, he simply wrote a note of instruction to someone else, who came in for the show each evening. Not having been properly rehearsed, the unknown someone got things a tiny bit off. Naturally, Mary decided I was behind it all. Nor was the situation improved when Dick Coe, one of my favorite Washington critics, wrote that Mary's performance wasn't up to what her present understudy, Frannie Sternhagen, had done at Catholic University three years before.

Getting to New York was a relief. Even though the New York critics were rhapsodic—"A brave, intelligent and provocative play, and an honor to the American theatre" (Watts, *Post*); "A gem!" (*Variety*); "Gay and colorful and fast . . . a warm and winning show" (Kerr, *Herald-Tribune*); "It is perfect" (Atkinson, *Times*)—even though we never had an empty seat or less than a standing ovation at the end, it was with a collective sigh of thanks that all of us departed *The Skin of Our Teeth* for less cosmic matters. Some weeks later, Bob recouped his investment with an NBC live television special, directed by Vincent Donehue—although I was occasionally allowed in the control room. George Abbott, his vocal powers strengthened by both camera and microphone, stole the show out from under both the ladies. I'm not sure whether Mary and Helen ever spoke to each other again.

I went back to holding the small Viveca in my arms, less and less certain of more and more. *Skin* had promised so much and started so well. It had ended with ashes in my mouth. And I kept wondering why I had ever decided to do it. Little did I know, then, that its special blend of happy and unhappy experience was soon to have a most significant effect on my later life and career. It was to bring me together with Samuel Beckett.

Third Acts

WAITING FOR BECKETT
1955–1956

That fall, while giving a talk on the American theater at my Alma Mater, the University of Wisconsin, I received an urgent long-distance phone call from a producer unknown to me, Michael Myerberg, asking if I might be interested in doing a Broadway-bound production of a play called *Waiting for Godot*, with—long pause for emphasis—Bert Lahr and Tom Ewell. A year or so before, Bob Whitehead had asked me what I thought of the play's New York chances, and I had responded only halfheartedly. Intrigued as I had been by the play, I could not imagine a production in Broadway terms. Myerberg had produced the original *Skin of Our Teeth* in 1943 for Thornton, almost going bankrupt in the process. For *Godot*, he had wanted Garson Kanin, but "Gar" suddenly became either unavailable or uncertain about the project's prospects. On the basis of my work on *Skin*, Thornton Wilder had strongly recommended me. Did I know the play?

I explained to Myerberg that I had seen *Godot* in Paris, but was a bit worried about doing it with stars. I asked for time to read and think about the play again. On the way home, I stopped in Chicago to pick up a copy at Brentano's and stayed up all night with it in my cramped train compartment. It seemed as cold and as abstract as it had on my first reading for Bob, but somehow I couldn't say no to it. Even warned by Walter Kerr about the risks of Myerberg as a producer—as a director Walter once emerged barely unscathed from a Myerberg-sponsored production of an ex-C.U. play called *Art and Prudence*—I made the decision to go ahead. Rehearsals were to start in a few weeks, and we were scheduled to go to Philadelphia and Washington before getting to New York's Music Box Theatre shortly after Christmas.

Two roles remained to be cast, and I was determined to find a couple of understanding performers who could strengthen me against Lahr and Ewell, both of whom had confessed varying degrees of bewilderment with the play. I suggested a great unrecognized comic from Catholic University days, John McGiver, for Pozzo, and a recently arrived young American from Israel, Alvin Epstein, as a possible Lucky. Myerberg insisted that I go to Paris to consult with the author and to London to see Peter Hall's production of *Godot*, which had recently opened at the Arts Theatre. After repeated requests, or rather demands, from Myerberg to Beckett's agent in London, the playwright had reluctantly agreed to meet with "the New York director"—I don't think Beckett knew my name—for half an hour. After my previous attempt to penetrate his privacy, I wasn't eager, but agreed for two reasons: I wanted to ask the elusive Samuel Beckett a bookful of questions about his play, and I thought it might be helpful to see an English-language production of *Godot*.

One week later, I found myself in a first-class cabin of the S.S. *Independence* bound for Cannes—and then by train to Paris and London. By a startling coincidence, arranged by Myerberg, I also found myself the captain's-table companion of Thornton Wilder, who was on his way to Rome and other places. Wilder had evidently informed Myerberg that he could clear up whatever difficulties I might have had in interpreting the script of *Godot*; in fact, he might be able to improve on Mr. Beckett's translation, which Mr. Wilder did not particularly admire, although he considered *Godot* one of the two greatest modern plays. (The other was, I believe, Cocteau's *Orphée*.) He had seen the French and German productions and understood perfectly what *Godot* was about.

Crossing the Atlantic with Thornton would have been a treat on any occasion; he was an extraordinary conversationalist on a practically inexhaustible range of subjects, with a peppery wit that flavored every sentence. Crossing with him determined to improve on Beckett's script was a double-sided experience. The first thing Thornton did was to make sure that I understood the play. *Godot*, he explained, was an existentialist work about "the nullity of experience in relation to the search for an absolute." The audience had to understand that Godot himself represented the absolute, and all of Estragon's and Vladimir's gyrations represented the nullity. If that wasn't entirely clear, a brief dip into Heidegger or Jaspers would clear it all up for me. "Dread," "the leap of faith," "the absurd," things like that.

We met regularly to go over the lines. Thornton started with suggestions for changing a few of them; by the time we got to Cannes, he had changed almost every single one, including the whole of Lucky's speech. I listened religiously on each occasion, trying to keep my mouth from falling open. It seemed to me that, whatever Thornton's knowledge and insight, he was removing all of Beckett's simplicity and poetry. I vowed to have none of it, although I took copious notes.

So detailed and regular were our daily meetings that a rumor later circulated that Wilder had rewritten the play. Thornton may have been amused by that thought; Beckett was not. What did happen was that I became very familiar with the script, both in French and English, discovered its inner structure, and found out what I needed to ask Beckett in the limited time we were scheduled to have together. I was also indebted to Thornton for his suggestion that I bring Beckett a bottle of Lacrima Cristi champagne. We parted in Cannes, I on the Blue Train for Paris, Thornton for the Italian Alps.

At the time, Beckett had no telephone—in fact, the only change I've noticed in him since his worldwide success is the acquisition of one—so I sent him a message via *pneumatique*. Within an hour, Beckett rang up saying he'd meet me in the lobby at six o'clock—at the same time reminding me that he had only a half hour to spare, and making it very clear that even that amount of time was accorded me out of duress. He wasn't exactly cordial.

Determined not to be put off, I stationed myself in the Lancaster's excessively gilt-and-plaster lobby—a secretarial memo pad with all my questions in it under one arm, and a large bottle of Lacrima Cristi under the other, waiting for Mr. Beckett to appear. Appear he did, promptly on the stroke of six, his tall athletic figure ensconced in a worn suede lamb-collared shortcoat; his face—as long and sensitive as a greyhound's—bespectacled in old-fashioned steel rims, and already familiar to me from the photograph on the dust jacket of his books.

Greetings somewhat stiffly exchanged, the biggest question became where we might drink our Lacrima Cristi. My hotel room didn't seem to have the proper ambiance. We decided to walk a bit to see if we could come up with a solution. Walk we did, as we have done so many times since, and talked about a variety of matters, including, occasionally, his play. When I asked Beckett my first question, "Who or what is Godot?"

wondering if he might echo Wilder's nullity and existence, Beckett stared off into space for a while and then answered, "If I knew, I would have said so in the play." I almost threw away the memo pad; certainly, I didn't open it again in his presence.

Eventually, we took a taxi to his very sparsely furnished skylight apartment, on the rue des Favorites in the Sixth Arrondissement, and wound up finishing most of the bottle. I plied him with some of my studiously prepared questions as well as all the ones that came to me at the moment. He tried to answer as directly and as honestly as he could. I discovered that Beckett was perfectly willing to answer any question that was specific, a specific meaning or reference. He would not—and would never—go into larger or symbolic meanings, preferring his work to speak for itself and letting the supposed "meanings" fall where they might.

According to him, Godot had "no meaning" and "no symbolism." There was no "general point of view involved," but it was certainly "not existentialist." Nothing in it meant anything other than what it was on the surface. "It's just about two people who are like that." That was all he would say.

About three hours later, Beckett had to leave for a dinner appointment but suggested that we meet around midnight at Fouquet's. I did not know what or where Fouquet's was, and Beckett explained patiently that it was the restaurant on the Champs Elysées where he had regularly met with Joyce; perhaps I might find that interesting. I did, and he came, and we talked for hours—my early life in Russia seemed particularly to intrigue him. The next evening we had a leisurely meal at one of his favorite restaurants in Montparnasse, after which I persuaded him to come with me to a performance of *Anastasia* at the Théâtre Antoine. The production, including that recognition scene, turned out to be artificial and old-fashioned, and Sam's suffering was acute. (Luckily, I didn't know at the time that he had suffered through my production of *Skin of Our Teeth* the previous summer; I don't think Beckett had yet identified me with that experience.) Immediately after *Anastasia*'s final curtain, we escaped back to Fouquet's for solace and nourishment. Shortly before dawn—since I had a plane to catch for London—we again separated. As I was about to take off, Sam asked me almost shyly, "Would it be ahny help at ahll if I came to London to see *Godot* with you?" He had not been to London in some years, had never liked it since his early days of poverty and struggle there, but he would be willing to come if I thought it would be helpful. I could hardly believe what I heard. Helpful!

Two days later, Sam came over incognito, though some of the

Thornton Wilder and A. S., on the S.S. *Independence:* A. S. on the way to his first meeting with Samuel Beckett, 1956.

Waiting for Godot: Tom Ewell, Jack Smart, Bert Lahr in Miami, 1956. *(Stan Wayman, Ratho-Guillumette)*

Krapp's Last Tape: Donald Davis, 1960. *(Sherwin Greenberg/ McGranahan & May, Inc.)*

Endgame: Nydia Westman, P. J. Kelly, Lester Rawlins, Alvin Epstein, 1958. *(© Alix Jeffry, 1958, Harvard Theatre Collection)*

The American Dream: Sudie Bond, Nancy Cushman, Ben Piazza, John C. Becher, Jane Hoffman, 1961. *(© Alix Jeffry, 1961, Harvard Theatre Collection)*

Happy Days: a conference as seen by Al Hirschfeld. A. S., John C. Becher, Ruth White, Richard Barr, 1961. *(© Al Hirschfeld, 1961. Drawing reproduced by special arrangement with Al Hirschfeld's exclusive representative, the Margo Feiden Galleries, New York.)*

A. S. Rehearsing *The Caucasian Chalk Circle*
for the opening of Arena Stage, 1961. *(George de Vincent)*

Happy Days: John C. Becher and Ruth White, 1961.
(© Alix Jeffry, 1962, Harvard Theatre Collection)

Who's Afraid of Virginia Woolf?: Uta Hagen, Arthur Hill, George Grizzard, 1962.
(Friedmann-Abeles)

Who's Afraid of Virginia Woolf?: Uta Hagen, Arthur Hill, Melinda Dillon, George Grizzard.
(© Alix Jeffry, 1962, Harvard Theatre Collection)

After the opening of *Who's Afraid*: Clinton Wilder, A. S., Richard Barr, Uta Hagen, Edward Albee.
(© Alix Jeffry, 1962, Harvard Theatre Collection)

London newspapers, hearing vague reports of his presence, began searching for him. To this day he strongly dislikes interviews, cocktail parties, celebrity socializing, and all the other public concomitants of the literary life. He stayed at the very non-posh Strand Palace in Piccadilly, very near the Criterion Theatre where *Godot* was playing, having transferred from the Arts. That night, and each night for the next five days, Beckett and I went to see his play, an experience that proved extremely painful to its author, distracting to its performers, disturbing to the director, Peter Hall—who took years to get over his resentment at my being there with Beckett—and extremely enlightening to me. The production was interesting and effective, though scenically overcluttered, and missing many of the points that Sam had been clearing up for me.

My fondest memories are of Beckett's clutching my arm from time to time and, in a clearly heard stage whisper, saying, "It's ahl wrahng! He's doing it ahl wrahng!" about a particular bit of stage business or the interpretation of a certain line. He particularly erupted when the Boy at the end of the second act pointed to the heavens when he was asked by Vladimir where Mr. Godot lived. On several occasions, Sam wanted to give notes to the actors about what they were doing or not doing, and I had some difficulty persuading him that notes should be given only through the director. Once or twice we ventured backstage, although Sam found it increasingly impossible to hide his disapproval of the proceedings.

Every night after the performance, we would retire to a pub to compare what we had seen and heard with what he had intended, try to analyze why or how certain points were being lost. Every night, also, we would carefully watch the audience, a portion of which always left during the show, sometimes expressing their disapproval loudly. I always felt that Sam would have been disappointed if at least a few hadn't.

Through the week, I discovered not only how clear and logical *Godot* was in its essentials, but how human, friendly, and warm Sam really was underneath his basic shyness. When I met Sam, I wanted primarily to latch on to anything that might help make *Godot* a success on Broadway. When I left him, I wanted nothing more than to please him. I came with respect and trepidation; I left with a greater measure of devotion than I have ever felt for a writer whose work I was translating to the stage.

Myerberg had urged me to convince Sam that we needed him in New York. Sam, on his side, confessed to being unable to face the trials of our rehearsal and tryout periods; he promised, however, that he would try to come once we had opened—making his first trip to the United

States. He had evidently had a series of unhappy relationships with various American publishers, agents, and literary hangers-on, and was somewhat leery of our habits and rhythms.

I wasn't entirely convinced that the shy, thoughtful, intensely serious writer I had gradually gotten to know would be particularly helpful in steering two Broadway comedians through the shoals of his strange and unusual script. I wrote Myerberg that I already had the answers to my many questions, and that his absence in New York would not necessarily be to our disadvantage. I suggested that Beckett's particular blend of purity and intellect was not exactly suited to sitting in a hotel room in Philadelphia rewriting the second act. Myerberg, in the meantime, remained uncommunicative about anything other than my immediate return to New York, which he repeatedly demanded. Our original plans were that I should return via the *Queen Elizabeth*, spending my shipboard days absorbing Beckett's insights and working on the script. Myerberg wanted me to fly back at once. He even signed Bert and Tommy's name to a couple of cables urging me to do so; they later told me they knew nothing of this.

Before going to Paris, I had met with Myerberg's scene designer, the very talented though inarticulate Albert Johnson, who had done the original production of *The Skin of Our Teeth*. Though he kept coming up with all sorts of beautifully wrong abstract designs, we finally agreed on a basic, carefully wrought tree and a relatively simple rock surrounded by a cyclorama. Johnson had sworn to get a detailed floor plan to me in time for my return voyage, but nothing ever arrived. I sent a series of frantic letters and cables; no floor plan. Nor did I hear from Myerberg about the casting of the other two roles, which was presumably going on without me. The only hard news came in a telegram informing me that rehearsals had been moved up three days to give us more time.

When the *Elizabeth* docked in New York, I discovered what Myerberg had been doing while I was abroad. That included changing the set and preventing Johnson from sending the revised floor plan on to me. Myerberg and I almost immediately came to blows over his amended setting, which was much too complicated and symbolic for my tastes—as well as for my knowledge of Sam's comments on the overelaborate and cluttered London design. He had also, in direct contradiction to his promise, committed himself to the casting of both Pozzo and Lucky. Instead of John McGiver, he had signed Jack Smart, a radio actor who had built a minor career in films and television, for the former; and Charles Weidman, a fine dancer and a great choreographer who had never acted before, for the latter. Myerberg had ignored my suggestions for casting the Boy, and had hired someone who looked good but was too old and inexperienced.

I felt like quitting on the spot. Myerberg had already lived up to his reputation for being devious and unreliable. I was terrified that we were starting off on this difficult play with all the wrong ingredients. The setting was wrong. We had two stars who were probably more concerned with themselves than with the play, and two other actors who were almost certainly miscast. And we had a producer who not only did not understand but did not want to understand the problems and confusions I already saw looming. Only my memories of that great gaunt figure of Samuel Barclay Beckett kept me going. I couldn't bear the thought of walking out on him.

Bert and especially Tommy were actually highly supportive during these early days. They knew I had spent a great deal of time with the author and must have picked up something that might help them during rehearsals. They were not about to start off again with another director. And, although I could do nothing about replacing Smart with McGiver, or persuading Myerberg not to give a role whose climax consisted of one long and difficult speech to a performer who had never spoken on stage, I did manage—with Bert and Tommy's help—to restore most of my original simpler setting. I cannot say that much of my original faith or enthusiasm remained.

We plunged into rehearsal, with a Bert terrified, Tommy nervous, Charles Weidman silent, Jack Smart almost catatonic, and the director whistling as he walked by the graveyard. Myerberg had furnished us with an unheated room in an old music studio he owned somewhere downtown. Bert's teeth kept chattering, not only because of his basic fear but because the room was freezing cold. The actors, unable to object to the script, objected to our rehearsal conditions. On the second day, our stage manager, John Paul—who was also Myerberg's general office factotum—informed us that we would be moving uptown to a hotel ballroom near Myerberg's office. The ballroom proved considerably warmer, even though its huge expanse further contributed to our feelings of abandonment and isolation.

The first week's proceedings went reasonably well. We read the play several times, trying to catch its rhythms and tones. Bert soon discovered that what I called "Ping-Pong games" between Estragon and Vladimir were very much like vaudeville routines, and began to have a little fun. With both Wilder and Beckett behind me, I managed to come up with enough illuminating comments daily to keep everybody satisfied—at least on the surface. Every two minutes, Bert would smile and say, "It's all opening up, kid. It's opening up!" I would feel good for a couple of minutes, until Bert would come up with the idea of replacing the end of the "Let's go. / We can't. / Why not? / We're waiting for Godot" sequence with his old vaudeville "Ohnnnnggggg" instead of Beckett's "Ah." Or ask me to cut the Lucky speech because no one understood it. And, anyhow, the audience was coming to see him and not the guy playing Lucky, wasn't it?

There was a lot to "open up." And four actors who had entirely different ideas of the best way to do the opening up. Bert kept saying he was the "top banana," and that the "second banana," Tommy, was really the straight man who should be feeding Bert his laughs. Tommy (and I) kept trying to explain to Bert that this show had two bananas. (I was afraid to tell him that perhaps the character of Vladimir was slightly more central to the play's thematic core than the character of Estragon. "Thematic core" was not an expression calculated to win Bert's heart.) Jack Smart kept struggling with Pozzo's complicated stage business, finding himself almost unable to coordinate whip, pipe, atomizer, watch, et cetera, with his lines. Charles stood still and moved beautifully but kept delaying the moment of his speech. I was getting encouraged and discouraged simultaneously.

Somewhere during those early rehearsals, which he occasionally attended, sitting silent and saturnine away from us, Myerberg sprang his big surprise. We had originally been booked in Washington and Philadelphia prior to opening at the Music Box Theatre (partly owned by Irving Berlin, one of Bert's good friends). Our advance sale at both locations had not been going well. Myerberg had canceled both and was instead taking us for two weeks to open a new playhouse, the Coconut Grove in, of all places, Coral Gables, Florida, near Miami. His only explanation was that it was a fine new theater with very comfortable accommodations next door for all of the actors and the director. We also discovered that he had been offered a generous two-week guarantee.

It was only years later that I got the whole story from Tommy Ewell. The owner of the Coconut Grove, a Miami businessman named George Engel, had been hoping to open his newly furbished and enlarged playhouse with some kind of Broadway splash. Engel had approached Tommy, whom he knew and who was then at the top of his commercial career, having recently played *The Seven Year Itch* both on Broadway and, with Marilyn Monroe, on the screen. Would Tommy come down to Miami to open his new theater with that same play—and Marilyn? As inducement, Tommy told me, Engel was offering an oil well apiece to both him and Marilyn. Tommy approached Marilyn, who agreed to come for two weeks; but at the last minute either she or her studio got scared of her appearing on a stage, and she pulled out. Tommy then suggested to Myerberg that Engel might be persuaded to take Ewell and Lahr as a substitute for Ewell and Monroe. Engel, desperate for "name" stars, grabbed on to the idea.

I don't know if Engel ever offered Myerberg an oil well in addition to his two-week guarantee. Tommy says he never got his. Perhaps there were no oil wells to begin with. Whatever the details, we did go to Miami, with most of us—from Thornton Wilder on down—fighting and kicking to get Myerberg to change his mind. He didn't.

After two weeks of rehearsal in our hotel ballroom, the play very roughly on its feet, we took a train down to Miami—or was it Samarkand? The theory was that we would at least rehearse the lines on the way down, but Bert's wife, and especially his about-to-be-teenage son, John, kept him occupied. Any hour of the day or night, their voices could be heard through the walls of their compartment. And at one point, I recall preventing Bert from tossing his son off the train—a humanitarian action I have had some occasion to regret in recent years since John became a theater critic. I have no memories whatsoever of the rest of our cast on that train except that Charles was hidden away somewhere trying to learn Lucky's speech—which he still had not come close to delivering—and Jack was somewhere else trying to learn Pozzo's business—which he had never gotten right.

Arriving at the Coconut Grove Playhouse complex—architecturally best described by my wife as "Miami Beach ungepotched"—we found our apartments to be indeed comfortable and convenient, right next to the theater. There was also a fancy restaurant, a fancy foyer with a fountain which eventually contained real live goldfish, a fairly conventional eight-hundred-seat auditorium fronting on to a Broadway-sized stage—and no dressing rooms. Tommy and Bert et al. had to dress in a couple of trailers set up in an alley off the stage door. The Miami audience was being informed, in large type, that Bert Lahr, "Star of *Harvey* and *Burlesque*," and Tom Ewell, "Star of *The Seven Year Itch*," were about to appear in their midst in "the Laugh *Sensation* of Two Continents," *Waiting for Godot*. The name of the author appeared only in very small print. My name, luckily, hardly appeared at all.

Rehearsals went like a snowstorm in an orange grove. We never seemed to be able to get through a single day's rehearsal as planned. The closer we got to opening, the more Bert insisted on his "top banana" prerogatives. My telling him that Tommy was also supposed to get laughs made me the enemy. Tommy, who had persuaded Bert to do the show in the first place, was well acquainted with his colleague's insecurities and idiosyncrasies; he kept reassuring me (and himself) that he could deal with them.

Every day we came closer to our January 3rd opening, and every day Bert got more and more away from the play, from himself, from all of us. Like all good comedians in vaudeville or revue, Bert was an inveterate worrier offstage, the saddest of all men. With us he gradually got himself into such a state that he could not remember a line or a move. Nor could he rehearse for as much as an hour at a time without some kind of physical complaint requiring medical attention. The action of the play required Bert as Estragon constantly to return to his mound to go to sleep or just to sit down. Bert never came back to the same location twice, even though the stage manager had marked the location of the mound with a taped X on the floor. (Years later, critic John Lahr accused me of tying down his father's freedom of movement to a mark on the floor.) When Bert finally had to accept the fact that I would not consent to cutting Lucky's long speech in its entirety, he insisted on going offstage during the speech so that he would not have to listen to it. And he kept ad-libbing lines and sounds which had worked for him in the past.

Our Pozzo kept getting weaker rather than more secure in his role, never did anything the same way twice, and refused to pay any attention to my comments. At the same time, Jack had a strong voice and presence; if I could keep him from falling down, he might get away with his performance. Poor Charles understood Lucky's speech perfectly but could not learn it, could not speak it even after he learned it, and was absolutely riveting in his silent moments. Each day, he would manage to go a sentence or two further into the speech and then—literally shaking—run off stage to hide in the wings. For years one of America's most accomplished dancers, a pioneer in the transition from ballet to modern dance, Charles knew exactly what he had to do in the part of Lucky, but his fundamental shyness and his own inner demons made it impossible for him to speak on stage.

Tom Ewell went on searching for the reality of the play and the truth of his own character. Like Bert, he was a natural comic, but he cared about the play and understood it as something larger than himself.

As Vladimir, he suggested a modern Malvolio; I told him more than once that he should be playing Shakespearean clowns. We worked well together, talked about the play and about Bert, solved some of our problems together, and at least were sometimes able to share some of our frustrations. Bert tended to feel that I always took Tommy's side against him. I felt I wasn't on anyone's side—except the play's.

During those first days, Tommy still felt that he could evolve a way to work with Bert. By the end of a week, he realized that it was hopeless. Bert had to dominate, and Bert had to get the laughs. We might have been able occasionally to fool the audience into thinking they were working together, but Bert could not fool Tommy. Bert would just not look at Tommy or listen to him. He was never concerned with the scene or the situation; he just wanted Tommy to feed him the line so that he could get a laugh out of his response. If Tommy's line seemed to be getting the laugh, he would find a way of topping it. Tommy tried to explain to Bert that this play was different, that it was vaudeville all right but a different kind of vaudeville, in which the laughs were to be shared. I'm sure that Bert tried to understand—even though he couldn't. Nor could I really get to him, even when he managed to get to rehearsal. Maybe Jed Harris—or Garson Kanin—could have pulled things together. I couldn't. All I could do was provide the doctors and nurses and dentists who kept getting in the way of our rehearsals. Every morning, in rumpled gray pajamas, Bert came over to our kitchen, to drink Jean's coffee and tell me, "It's opening up, kid!" His wonderful rubber face was sadder than ever, and my own face trying hard not to let him know that I felt it was all impossible.

Three or four days before our opening, we had what was called a runthrough, although stumblethrough would have been a more accurate description. Myerberg's eyes were more cavernous than ever, but I don't remember that he had much to say. My most severe critic, Jean, thought that the production had possibilities—if only Bert would realize that his serious moments were as important as his laughs. Tennessee Williams, who happened to be staying down at his Key West residence, thought the second act was wonderful. The first "needed work."

Soothed by some friendly comments, Bert began to feel his oats. He even enjoyed the play a little. Tommy, on the other hand, realizing that Bert was taking everything away from him, making Estragon instead of Vladimir the center of everything, grew more worried daily about the play's future and his own part in it. He must have decided then that he would not go on with Bert and the production beyond Miami if Bert did.

I kept trying to hold on to both of them, but in my heart I knew that going on with Bert would be impossible for me. Those last days before our opening, with the constant shiftings and maneuverings going on between Bert and Tommy, as well as among Myerberg, Bert, Tommy, Lester Shurr (who happened to be both men's agent and who was not happy that either one of them was in the play), and myself were positively Byzantine in their proportions. I despaired of ever making it through our opening night.

I was almost right.

Nine o'clock of January 3, 1956, arrived on time in Miami. The audience didn't. Everyone who owned a Cadillac or who could wear a mink coat descended on the Coconut Grove Playhouse at dusk and paraded through its goldfish-infested foyer to eat and drink at length in its ultra-posh dining room, all done up in special decorations for the occasion—although the dressing rooms were still not ready. In fact, the play and production seemed secondary to the rest of the evening's performance. Everyone knew everyone, and everyone kept talking to everyone else through all the wining and dining—and, eventually, the seating, which didn't take place until almost ten o'clock, more than an hour after it was scheduled. When they all got seated, they still would not stop talking, even though the house lights went off and stayed off for about five minutes.

Up went the plush gold curtain, and instead of *The Seven Year Itch* or *Harvey*, that audience got *Waiting for Godot*, not the "laugh sensation of two continents" but a very strange sensation indeed. At first they laughed—at Bert trying to take off his shoe, at Tommy realizing his fly was unbuttoned; but as soon as they realized that the actors were on to more serious matters, they stopped. By the time they got to the Bible and the thieves, they were laughless. As they realized what they were in for, a few of them started to whisper, a few to groan, more and more of them more and more audibly. Somebody walked up the aisle, muttering, to get another drink. Someone else joined him. Whole groups started to sneak out. Then droves, driving right up the aisle to the goldfish. Onstage, Tommy and Bert, aware and not exactly aware that something was happening, tried to continue. Familiar with the activities of audiences in burlesque houses, Bert tried to stem the tide by broadening his stage business. He got a few laughs and stepped on a few of Tommy's. I remember having to hold on to Tommy's wife to keep her from charging forcibly onto the stage to hit Bert. I couldn't stop her from doing some forceful muttering of her own.

By the intermission, at least a third of the house had left. Another third didn't come back afterward; they were too busy drowning their resentment in the theater bar, where the dialogue was more familiar. I slunk into our trailer camp in the alley. Tommy was tight-lipped and grim, Bert no different than he had ever been. Jack Smart, as usual, was a tower of whipped cream. Our Lucky, played that night by understudy Arthur Malet because by that time everyone, including Charles himself, had realized that it was impossible for him to deliver, had done reasonably well—being rewarded with stunned silence during his long speech, and a small round of faint applause afterward.

How they ever got through Act Two, I have no idea. Presumably only the diehards or those whom the steak dinner and whiskey had rendered immobile stayed on, awake or not. We wound up with three mild curtain calls, and both Tennessee and William Saroyan standing up in different sections of the audience shouting "Bravo!" Afterward, we wended our way home next door for a cup of tea and lots of sympathy from Jean.

The next morning, there was a straggle of a line at the ticket booth, which lifted our spirits immensely until we realized that they were waiting to get their money back. More people cancelled their tickets, and many just didn't pick them up. The reviews for the audience and the building were excellent—and extremely unfavorable for anything that took place on the stage. The goldfish got raves. Walter Winchell, who covered the evening, accused us of being both indecent and immoral, and suggested we should all be tarred and feathered and ridden out of town on a rail. A local critic by the name of Jack Anderson complained that we had "disappointed" and actually "sandbagged" our audience; I've always wondered if that was the same Jack Anderson who later became the noted investigative reporter.

Myerberg was shocked by the reception, although he tried hard not to let us know. The actors had never experienced anything remotely similar, and were blaming everything and everyone; at the same time, they somehow pulled together in their ultimate distress and shame. Our second-night audience, similarly loaded (in all respects), proved equally ambulatory. But from then on, though our audiences remained relatively small during our two-week run, they grew in interest and staying power. Our nightly reception became almost enthusiastic—especially from the ushers, most of them students from the University of Miami, who cried and held our hands and told us that they, at least, "loved it." A few days into the run, Tommy came into the theater smiling for the first time in whenever, holding an absolutely ecstatic mimeographed review from one of the hotel news sheets. The review called our show "astonishing . . . It is a play so enormous in scope, so compelling as to require complete attention and in a sense devotion." Not exactly a "money review," but it cheered us up. I wrote critic-hotelier Charles Cinnemon a heartfelt thank you note, and took him out for a drink. Tommy personally paid to have the entire review reprinted in one of the local papers. It looked even better in newsprint.

Entirely unsure of our individual and collective futures, we kept talking about rehearsing, changing, trying things, based on audience reactions. But Bert, who seemed most anxious to rehearse and make changes, proved as unstable and unreliable as ever. He always found some reason for not rehearsing. One day he got a letter from someone, which he insisted on reading to me. "How can you, Bert Lahr," it said, "who has charmed the youth of America as the Cowardly Lion in *The Wizard of Oz*, appear in this Communistic, Atheistic, and Existentialist play?" There were tears in Bert's eyes as he begged me to explain to him what "Existentialist" meant.

Somehow, we managed to play out our run, although without any further rehearsals. I got to see a bit of Florida and a fair amount of my nine-month-old daughter, Vickie, whom I had been neglecting. Strangely enough, the more performances we played, the more our obvious lack of success seemed to bring us together as much as it separated us. The show even got a bit better, although I could hardly bear to watch it, even on occasion preferring the theater's bar. Once or twice, Tommy and Bert relaxed and came together onstage to share the same script; and there was a hint of what might have been. (Offstage, I don't believe they ever again exchanged one word.) Jack Smart continued to fall apart nightly without the audience being any the wiser, and eventually required hospitalization. With encouragement from all, Charles went on for a couple of performances before taking a train back to New York, but could never complete the speech. It was sad to watch him, and I couldn't.

The future of the production remained as enigmatic as Godot himself, though we kept on waiting. Myerberg would inform us one day that we were going on to Philadelphia or some other city; another day, he would say that we were going straight to New York—or closing in Miami. Bert would decide that he was staying with the show—then would change his mind. Tommy told me he would not continue—but he didn't send in his notice. The rumor was around that Myerberg was talking to other stars—but to replace whom? To directors also—but he still had a contract and a commitment with me. I was almost sure I'd go on with Tommy but not with Bert, but Tommy kept saying he wasn't going on in any case. Eventually, Myerberg told us he was closing the show in Miami.

Painful as it was, that decision brought a certain kind of relief. I suppose that if Bert had gone and Tommy had decided to stay, and if we had gotten another star in whom I could believe—and if Myerberg kept me on as director—I would have wanted to stay. That was a lot of "ifs." I would not have gone on with Bert and without Tommy—even though Bert was, in many ways, wonderfully effective and good casting. But I knew that it was not Estragon's show. To make it his and destroy the balance Beckett had created—as Bert wanted me to do—was impossible for me.

In all this mess, there was no one obvious or even hidden villain—not even Bert Lahr. We were all the villains, and we were all the victims; and sometimes the twain do meet. All the ingredients were wrong from the start. And we should never have gone to Miami. As Bert put it, it was exactly like "bringing *Giselle* to Roseland." Everyone of us knew that and felt that and had always known that, but still we came. Now it was just too late. Perhaps *Godot* could have played as Bert wanted it to, just for the laughs. Perhaps it might have worked in a normal, more sophisticated setting in Washington or Philadelphia, with plenty of laughs, together with some real moments of Beckett's poetic texture and meaning—as Tommy and I wanted. It couldn't be both ways simultaneously. It could certainly be done with four good actors playing in the same way even if they were not quite sure of what they were playing. It could not be done by four actors, no matter how good they were, in four different ways. At least I learned that lesson for the five productions of *Godot* I was to direct in later years.

Myerberg wound up taking the play to New York and Broadway that spring, without my services, with Bert Lahr back in business as Estragon and E. G. Marshall very clearly playing Vladimir as a "second banana." Herbert Berghof, who knew the play very well and had done a workshop production of it in his school even before Miami, directed it and was highly praised. He had a most effective Pozzo in Kurt Kasznar and an excellent Lucky in Alvin Epstein, whose long speech became a real tour de force. The production and the play got respectful if divided reviews.

I never saw Herbert's production, nor he mine. He took some potshots at mine anyhow, saying that I had directed it "for style and crucifixion," whatever that meant. I've listened to the recording of the Broadway version a number of times, and have yet to find anything at all different in Bert's performance from what he did in Miami. What I missed was Tommy.

I wrote to Sam in Paris, taking full responsibility for the failure in Miami, and hoping he would understand something of what had happened. I didn't go too much into detail. His almost immediate answer was so startling that I have never fully recovered from it. Nor has any other playwright ever had his generosity under the circumstances, although one or two have come close. Sam told me that the failure was all his fault; he had, after all, written the play. Besides, he didn't mind failure. He had breathed deeply of its vivifying air throughout his life. He was concerned about the failure in Miami only because it caused me pain.

I experienced a somewhat more specific pain when I got back to New York to discover that Myerberg had no intention of remitting my Miami royalties, inconsiderable as they were. I determined to submit my case to arbitration, which my contract entitled me to do, against Audrey Wood's strong advice. Audrey told me no producer would hire me again. I didn't care; I just wanted what my contract said I was supposed to get. Eventually, I got it, the arbitration being messy and unpleasant. And various producers have hired me again, even Michael Myerberg who lived long enough to offer me another play, which I was happy to turn down. The "debacle" turned out to be exactly the opposite for my career. I had met Sam Beckett, and he had met me. For that, I have never stopped being grateful to Michael Myerberg, Thornton Wilder, Garson Kanin, and even Herbert Berghof.

The shambles at the Coconut Grove Playhouse is recorded in history. My anguish over the *Godot*-in-Miami is unrecordable. I not only wanted to shoot myself and blow up the Coconut Grove, I wanted to leave the theater forever. In spite of Sam's attempts to reassure me, I considered myself a total failure, commercially and artistically, without prospects or possibility of redemption.

Even mathematically speaking, I was losing ground. During 1953 I had directed ten productions, starting with the Arena's *All Summer Long* and culminating with my first Broadway venture, *The Remarkable Mr. Pennypacker*. In 1954 I wound up with three, the Arena *Summer and Smoke*, and *All Summer Long* as well as *Anastasia* on Broadway. The year 1955 had witnessed only two, *Samarkand* and *Skin*, neither one exactly pleasant; I had actually started on *Godot* in December. Here I was in early February 1956, my most disastrous failure just behind me, without a show on the horizon. And, for the first time since I had "arrived" in New York, no one was offering me anything.

One month later, in spite, or because, of the *Godot* fiasco, producer Henry Myers, now associated with Richard Aldrich, decided that I was just the right director for *The Little Glass Clock*. *Clock* was a zany, ersatz French farce, written by a British drawing-room-comedy writer, Hugh Mills. Aldrich and Myers had, in their time, done a number of literate and successful plays together. This combination gave me the illusion that *Little Glass Clock* might have a chance. In my heart, I knew it didn't. *Clock* made *Anastasia* seem like *Hamlet*. Furthermore, I could not have been more unsuitable as its director; I was both inexperienced and uninterested in directing comedy of style or manners. But I had to get over *Godot*, and here was my chance, in crystal!

Only the topnotch cast gave us any kind of chance. They included Reginald Gardiner, one of the movies' best stiff-upper-lip comedians; Bramwell Fletcher, who was a kind of poor man's Maurice Evans; John McGiver; and a wonderfully elegant English actor almost unknown in this country, George Curzon. A surprisingly spry and agreeable Eva Gabor was also in the cast, and she tried very hard to match the others, at rare moments succeeding. She did throw delicious parties at her mother's residence, where I was delighted to find a bed in every room, including the kitchen.

The elaborate setting and costumes were contributed by Cecil Beaton, a friend of both Myers and Aldrich, whose taste was superb. Indeed, I suspected that he always knew we didn't have a silk thread of a chance even while his designs were helping us to keep kidding ourselves that we did. We were consistently buffeted by every possible wind of ill fortune, starting with an absentee playwright who was charming but incapable of rewrites, a cast whose abilities were less than met the eye, and concluding with our almost fatal opening in Princeton, where the little glass clock on stage almost got swept off its resting place by the swirl of someone's cloak.

I had the royal honor of sharing an adjoining bathroom with Mr. Beaton at the Princeton Inn, and was somewhat surprised that he actually needed one. Our week in Baltimore brought more gloom than box office business, together with a flock of my old high school chums, all of whom smiled bravely and pressed my hand. Then came the Broadway opening on March 26, after which, thank heaven, the *Clock* stopped ticking. It was, as one critic put it in an understatement, a "sorry evening."

Why did I choose to do it? Not only did I have to recover from my *Godot* experience, I wanted to go to Europe that summer, and I was sure *The Little Glass Clock* would help to pay the bills. What happened was a great and useful lesson. That was the first—and last—time I ever did a show for *that* reason.

The only development that kept my faith, as well as the rest of me, alive that summer was the receipt of a Guggenheim Fellowship to explore the "open stage" in Europe. I had applied a half-dozen times for a Guggenheim, for everything from running an acting school in New York to visiting the theaters of Moscow and Leningrad, with notable lack of response. This time I not only had excellent references—Tyrone Guthrie, Thornton Wilder, and Margaret Webster among them—I hit the right button at the right time. Interest in "open" stages, "thrust" stages, "flexible" stages was in the air, and Europe was the place to find them. Europe was also a good place to forget my two "flops." I bundled the whole family off to London. With the help of play agent Margaret Ramsay (whom I'd met previously as a result of our mutual admiration for Beckett's novel *Watt*), we moved into a charming mews flat in Knightsbridge, and Peggy got me an assignment to direct an American play at the Arts Theatre Club, then in the throes of trying to live up to its reputation as a tryout theater. It was at the Arts, after all, that Peter Hall's reputation and production of *Godot* had been launched. Its restaurant also served terrific whitebait.

After scratching about for an American play acceptable to the Arts' fairly informal management, and having been turned down on such obvious choices as *The Glass Menagerie* and Paul Osborn's *Morning's at Seven*, we finally hit on Horton Foote's *A Trip to Bountiful*, which Kim Stanley had played with distinction in New York. As usual, I cast the show fairly well. My leading lady was Margaret Vines, whom critic James Agate had once labeled the most talented actress of her generation. John Glen, a veteran of Peter Brook and Stratford-upon-Avon, played the male lead as though he had been born in Texas. Mavis Villiers, a marvelously funny American tragedienne, and several other resident aliens, too, provided just the right flavor.

Bountiful was appreciated by my friends, but did not lead to bigger and better things. The Sunday critics, Kenneth Tynan and Harold Hobson, each gave us a flattering paragraph; the dailies were merely polite. Straight American drama rarely succeeded in London. All I really got from the experience was a short tour of the British Isles: Liverpool—where I was in on the beginnings of the Beatles—Manchester, and Dublin, where the *Irish Times* compared us favorably with the good old days at the Abbey.

In June I went over to Paris, to face Samuel Beckett for the first time since *Godot*. Sam was compassionate, understanding, supportive, and again told me to forget about my great failure. In some ways, I think we came closer than if *Godot* had been a success. We talked about the New York production—which neither one of us had seen and in which Bert Lahr had made a great impact, evidently at the expense of the play. He never criticized that version, but he made me feel that what I had tried to accomplish in Miami was, perhaps, closer to what he had wanted. Through a succession of Montparnasse meals and long walks in the Luxembourg Gardens he made me understand most of all that he appreciated my concern for his work, that the actual results in Miami didn't matter to him. I took Sam to see the Berliner Ensemble's visiting production of Brecht's *Galileo*, and he actually liked it! I came back from Paris feeling much better about my relationship with Sam, and about the world in general.

My most satisfying memories from that whole summer remain the sensory delights of London, mixed in with the torment of once more being unrecognized and forlorn; those endless English cups of tea-and-talk while nothing tangible was happening to my career; my wife's urging me onward in spite of everything; and my daughter's delighted chases after pigeons in Trafalgar Square.

I remember too the rough, chill, all-night cross–Irish Channel trip from Liverpool to Holyhead. And opening night at Dublin's Olympia Theatre, home of so many Irish theater triumphs, where there wasn't a soul in the place, including stagehands, until almost an hour after our scheduled curtain time, when everyone on both sides of the curtain came streaming, quite happily, from the pub across the street. I was staying at the Moira Hotel, which, again without my knowing it, had been one of Samuel Beckett's haunts. I picked up a copy, "under the table," of *Ulysses*. And I crossed over the Liffey every day, wondering where the tides of my life were taking me.

In spite of everything, it was a summer to remember. But, although I didn't know it then, it was the year that I would long remember: the year Samuel Beckett came into my life.

OFF AND ON—AND OTHER PLACES

1956–1959

My next five years were destined to keep me rattling around from one corner of the American theater to another, in New York, Washington and San Francisco, commercial and noncommercial, on Broadway and off, with lots of help from Audrey Wood, Samuel Beckett, the Ford Foundation, and—most of all—Zelda Fichandler.

Zelda got me back home, offering me a production of Arthur Miller's rewritten *A View From the Bridge* to open the new Arena Stage at the "Old Vat," a remodeled brewery located near where the Watergate complex stands today. While in London, I talked with Miller, who was temporarily in town with his new wife, Marilyn somebody, and saw Peter Brook's production of Miller's play, with Anthony Quayle (not too well done, as it turned out).

Zelda had abandoned the Hippodrome, casting about in the wilderness for several years before finding a suitable new place, overlooking the Potomac. Little were any of us to know that, years later, the Kennedy Center would arise almost on the ashes of the "Old Vat." With a larger playing space, to which I responded immediately, and an excellent cast, which included off-Broadway mainstay Michael Higgins as Eddie Carbone, *View* proved itself most strongly, giving the Arena a big boost in its new life and location. Zelda decided that I should do *Tartuffe*, the season's third show. Having done Molière before only at Catholic University with student casts, I was eager to find out if I would fare as well with young professionals. We also started talking about a new work by Sam Robins called *Answered the Flute*, which I had brought to her some time before. Ever since *All Summer Long*'s success, I had tried to persuade Zelda to do more new scripts, but she was too concerned with establishing Arena's stability to take any chances with untried works.

Boosted by *View*'s success, I got a nice letter from Miller apologizing for not being able to see my production, as well as an offer, via Audrey, to direct two weeks of *The Glass Menagerie* at New York's City Center of Drama and Music. The star was to be Helen Hayes, who had asked for me. Finally, my first crack at a Tennessee Williams in New York! The only trouble was that all this was supposed to be happening at the same time as Zelda's *Tartuffe*.

I wrestled with myself for about ten minutes, and then decided to ask Zelda for a release from my contract, putting my request in such a way that she knew if she didn't release me, I would go anyway. This was highly unethical behavior on my part and it took Zelda a couple of years to forgive me—but she did let me go. To make up for my precipitous unfairness, I offered to do two shows for her sometime instead of one. Later that season, as punishment, she made me pay for my tickets to *Answered the Flute*, which went on without me.

My experience with Helen Hayes in *Menagerie* proved the direct opposite of our work together in *Skin*. Helen had known and idolized Laurette Taylor, the original Amanda, and she was torn between wanting and not wanting to better Laurette's performance. As a result, she would constantly ask me what Laurette had done—as if I knew—and then try to do either the precise opposite or, on occasion, the exact same thing. One day, I tossed everybody out of our rehearsal room and, on bended knee, begged Helen to please forget about Laurette and just play her own instincts and truth, which she proceeded to do, beautifully.

Helen was and is a remarkable actress, with an extraordinary capacity for detailed truthfulness. In *Skin*, her second-act Atlantic City speech revealing various domestic discoveries, including the announcement that "the tomato is edible," was a gem. Her basic problem, if I may presume to such boldness, has been that she tends to cover up the truth, to hide from it. Perhaps this stems from her personal tragedies—her husband's drinking himself to death and the loss of her daughter. Whatever the reason, she has sometimes sought refuge in character tricks and physical artifice—despite her very special ability to sense and create truth on stage.

The City Center's producer, Jean Dalrymple, got us James Daly for Tom, and Jim was okay, if somewhat inflexible. Lois Smith was an absolutely lovely and heartbreaking Laura, perhaps the best one ever; and her breezy and engaging Gentleman Caller, Lonny Chapman, was almost equally effective. Both were from the Actors Studio and their scene together was without flaw. One critic later said, "It is difficult to imagine the encounter more superbly played." The *Tribune*'s Walter Kerr called the evening "a beautiful production of a beautiful play, and what are you waiting for?" in spite of a complete mess-up of light cues at our opening performance, which resulted in all the night scenes being played in perfect daylight, and vice versa.

No matter how successful, however, revivals don't do much for a director. Despite the glowing response to the first major revival of his play in years, Tennessee didn't even come to see us—or communicate with me in any way. Evidently no producers came either, because I didn't get to do another stage play in New York for almost a year.

Walter Kerr's attention did give me a shove in another direction. In addition to his critical duties, Walter was then a consultant to Robert Saudek's Sunday afternoon Ford Foundation–supported *Omnibus* TV program, on which Alistair Cooke introduced various literary masterpieces. Walter had himself written an adaptation of Sophocles' *Oedipus Rex* for Saudek and suggested me as director. In my first few years in New York, Walter—a longtime close friend—seemed studiously to avoid giving me a good notice for fear that someone might accuse him of favoritism. After *Skin*, he relaxed and said a few nice things both in print and in person.

After pursuing Michael Redgrave, Judith Anderson, and Peggy Ashcroft, we got a very young (twenty-seven) Christopher Plummer and a cast made up largely of Canadians, including William Shatner and Donald Davis, whom I practically had to smuggle across the border. Chris was nothing short of magnificent, and more than made up for the greater conventionality of Jocasta, played by Carol Goodner. As the Messenger Michael Strong, fresh out of *Anastasia*, held up the cause of American actors doing the classics. Our Chorus, made up mainly of ex-C.U. students, was coached by C.U.'s Dr. Josephine Callan. It always helps to have people around who are familiar—and friendly.

Critical response to that December 1956 broadcast was—beyond belief—favorable. "One of the most powerful and memorable dramatic events in television's brief history." "A distinguished achievement." "Powerful and magnificent." "Television made history and history returned the compliment with the presentation of *Oedipus Rex* on *Omnibus* last night." Chris received raves. I have always considered him the finest classical actor in the Western Hemisphere, and thought that he would prove to be Olivier's successor, a peak he has never, for some reason, reached. Many years later, Walter Kerr called his Iago "the best Shakespearean performance of our time."

Despite all this acclaim, including the impressive full-page photo spread in *Life* magazine, I wasn't exactly swamped with more offers to do TV. In a mass medium, *Omnibus* was just too small potatoes. Had *Oedipus* been produced on *Playhouse 90* or *Producer's Showcase*, I might have gone to Hollywood instead of writing this book.

Undaunted, and perhaps smitten with a new desire to approach the classics, in May 1957 I went off to do a Giraudoux play, *The Enchanted*, at Boston University, where I soon discovered that college actors had even more problems dealing with nonrealistic material than I did. Two months later, I also directed a much too short-lived dramatization by Nathaniel Benchley, Robert's son, of Charles Finney's fantasy classic *The Circus of Dr. Lao*, in a new theater just outside of Chicago. Buzz Meredith played the old doctor with both humor and verve. Despite some interesting scenes and imaginative performers—including ever-reliable John McGiver and a young actor from Catholic University named Louis Camuti, who must have been triple-jointed and who played a serpent that would have done credit to the Garden of Eden—the material proved too unwieldy for the stage. *Lao* was, years later, made into a very unfilmic film starring Tony Randall. It continues to intrigue people with its theatrical possibilities; maybe someday someone will find a way to make it credible as a stage piece. We tried and failed.

My return to Broadway, such as it was, came with another dramatization, Nathanael West's *Miss Lonelyhearts*, adapted by Howard Teichmann. Audrey Wood got me the job, with old-timer Roger Stevens and a newcomer named Lester Osterman as producers. For the role of William Spain we had bluff, hearty Pat O'Brien. The cast also included Fritz Weaver, Ruth Warwick, and Henderson Forsythe. But the show just didn't work. Again a dramatic script and live actors couldn't make believable what a narrative only had to suggest. The show pleased some of the audience but none of the critics, and closed almost as soon as it opened. I did get Pat over to dinner one night, and during the evening he fell in love with our two-year-old Vickie, winding up on the floor recording her favorite song, "Catch a Falling Star," with her. Pat was the most good-natured falling star I'd ever worked with.

The year ended as it had begun, with another television show on *Omnibus*. This time it was James Lee's adaptation of Boswell's *The Life of Samuel Johnson*, with Peter Ustinov wearing several pounds of makeup, giving a gargantuan performance as Johnson. I understood that a dozen directors had turned down the sprawling script, and I almost did the same. But the idea of working with Ustinov finally swayed me, and I plunged in, with my camera director from *Oedipus*, Seymour Robbie, at my side, and a vast cast, including Ellis Rabb, Clarence Derwent, and every actor in New York who could speak reasonably proper English. Cecil B. DeSchneider had to rehearse everybody in Manhattan's East Side right in the middle of a New York City transport strike and one of the heaviest snowstorms in years. Somehow everybody managed to get there, and we had a great time together.

Rehearsals were both a jumble and a joy—with dozens of different locales involving alehouses, madhouses, prisons, theater auditoriums, and streets. Ustinov, with or without his makeup, was one of the funniest persons alive. He craved attention at all times, and got it—with jokes, witticisms, and twitches galore. He had a way of injecting levity into a tense atmosphere more successfully than anyone I have ever known, before or since. His pigeon-Russian is, I venture, on a par with Danny Kaye's. And Peter's makeup, the contribution of prize-winning makeup man Bob O'Bradovich, was matched only by Peter's comments on the number of hours it took him to get into it each morning. Peter's own "Johnson's dictionary" definition of television, which he scribbled out one day during a camera rehearsal, is worth quoting: "A medium for the confusion of fools and the edification of none." His words on directors are perhaps even more apt: "Those so deficient in imagination and so hardened in the way of cruelty that they must needs think aloud with the assistance of living beings." He was only kidding. (I hope.)

In our cast was an excellent character actor, Will Geer, who had been blacklisted during the McCarthy period and had been unable to get work on television. His scene was short—and uproarious; Will got every speck of the laughs that were there. I had hired Will without any knowledge of his "tarnished" background and by the time the network executives discovered we had him and began to object, we were all devoted to him. The criticism persisted and increased, but Bob Saudek, to his eternal credit, refused to kowtow to demands from above that we replace Will immediately. The networks did not fall, nor did the nation. And Will Geer, from that point on, kept on working in television. Before he died, he even became a celebrity, in *The Waltons*. Later I worked with his daughter, Ellen, at the Guthrie Theatre; she told me that he still remembered what our show had done for him.

Achieving the proper bawdy, rowdy realism for the period once brought us, on camera—television was all live then—to the brink of disaster. A scene at Highgate Prison, called for a prisoner to be "hanged." The "prisoner" in question was Ted Tenley, who had played the Dauphin with me in the Luise Rainer/Piscator *Saint Joan*. On the air, Ted's body suddenly went limp quite differently from the way we had planned it in rehearsal; in fact, quite unrealistically for a man being hanged. I cursed the actor and switched to another camera focused on the crowd. Afterward, it turned out that the slipknot in Ted's rope had not been properly released and he had actually blacked out. I was told that Ted, once revived, absolved any of us from blame, saying he so appreciated Ustinov's performance "I'd be glad to be hanged again." A doctor associated with the studio said that Ted's blackout might have been psychologically caused by "overrealistic" acting. I wonder what Ted's reaction was to that.

The performance was greeted with almost apocalyptic enthusiasm all over the country. One leading critic wrote, "*Omnibus*, still the leader among television cultural or experimental shows, offered its prize programs of the season in Boswell's *Life of Samuel Johnson*. James Lee's vivid dramatization . . . was one of the best entertainments ever to come before the TV camera." Jack O'Brian's nationally syndicated column said: "Peter Ustinov yesterday gave TV one of the amazingly masterful performances of all its history." Others were equally rhapsodic: "One of the landmarks in television history," "an acting masterpiece," "artfully directed, beautifully produced," "the best program of the year."

This time, our efforts did not entirely fade out with the credits. Ustinov received an Emmy for his performance. Seymour Robbie and I collectively took a Sylvania Award for "Distinguished Achievement in Creative Television Technique." Suddenly, there was talk about a stage adaptation for Broadway, with Peter repeating his television role. Cheryl Crawford and Joel Schenker, both respectable names, took an option on the material. I waited. Nothing happened. Jimmy Lee, who had gone to Hollywood directly after writing *Career* for off-Broadway, seemed too busy out there to get around to writing *Johnson*'s stage version. Peter went off to do *Spartacus* with Kirk Douglas, and have a lot of fun with a lot of other people. I was left with only the reviews, and my father contributing his usual message: "With that and fifteen cents [which I think it was at the time] you can get on a subway."

During my Guggenheim summer in London, when I had gone over to Paris to face Sam Beckett and relate the full story of the Miami *Godot*, Sam had spoken about the new play on which he was currently working (with difficulty) in French, which he had barely mentioned when we first met, and about whose progress or lack of it he had written to me even before *Godot* opened. Since some of his letters to me on that subject have already appeared in print—with his permission if not exactly his approval—I include them here: ". . . I have retired to my hole in the Marne mud [his country place near Ussy which he has had since *Godot*] and am struggling with a play." Later on, he confessed, "Afraid no plays to show you. I did finish another but don't like it. It has turned out a three-legged giraffe, to mention only the architectonics, and leaves me in doubt whether to take a leg off or add one." Finally, he wrote to me in London, "Have at last written another, one act, longish, hour and a quarter [later amended to "over an hour and a half"], I fancy. Rather difficult and elliptic, mostly depending on the power of the text to claw, more inhuman than *Godot*. My feeling, at the moment, is to leave it in French for a year, at least."

The play in question was called *Fin de Partie*, and the New York press, already intrigued and baffled by *Godot*, had started to publish tidbits about how "weird" it was, even more so than his previous play. According to one report, it dealt with two men buried up to their necks in sand. The Sunday *New York Times Book Review*'s main columnist, a well-known literary critic and scholar, proceeded to translate the title as *The End of the Game* or *The Game Is Up*.

By the spring of 1957, *Fin de Partie* was taking shape, and was scheduled for presentation in Paris in a production by Roger Blin, *Godot*'s original director. At almost the last minute, the play cast and ready to go, the French management lost its nerve, and the production lost its promised theater. George Devine and London's Royal Court Theatre came to the rescue, offering their premises for the French-language premiere, a gesture which persuaded another French management to take it over and run it in Paris through the fall.

Sometime during that spring, Sam sent me a copy of the French text, which I tried, without much success, to have translated. What small glimmers I got from my own reading were enough. Here was another Beckett play and a chance to atone for *Godot*. But this time I had somehow to make sure that no producer would get in the way of a proper presentation. I borrowed $500 from my father, who didn't really understand what had happened with *Godot* but knew that I had suffered a lot; called up Barney Rosset of Grove Press, Sam's publisher, whom I had not yet met, to tell him exactly what I planned to do; and sent off a cable to

Sam asking for the rights to present *Fin de Partie* off-Broadway, which was where *Godot* should have been done.

This was the second time I had taken an option on a play, the first time being Bob Anderson's *All Summer Long.* This time I was more uncertain about what I was doing and yet more determined. The entire proceedings were impetuous, naive, and without any real plan for production. But Sam, bless him, agreed. "I have finished translation," he wrote almost at once, "and am sending it to Barney today. . . . Now it's up to Barney and you—if your interest survives a reading of the script. Whatever the two of you decide is, in advance, okay with me." The two of us, over the phone, decided that my five hundred bucks could give me an option on the play for at least six months, maybe longer.

In the meantime, I was exploring the off-Broadway situation, which was burgeoning. My first choice was the Cherry Lane Theatre in the Village, one of the most attractive and intimate (it seated just under 199 people). After a number of conversations with Noel Behn, the Cherry Lane's manager—I never met the mysterious and reclusive owner—Noel agreed to present *Endgame* (which he also had not yet read in English) as soon as the Cherry Lane's current occupant, Sean O'Casey's *Purple Dust*, had concluded its run; that would be around the first of the new year (1958). Noel and his producing partners, lawyer Jerome Friedman, publicist Barry Hyams, and actor David Brooks—who were establishing themselves as interesting and successful off-Broadway entrepreneurs—would have preferred acquiring the rights directly from Sam, but since I had already optioned the play, they had to deal through me. I was not really interested in functioning as producer, but I did want to maintain the necessary amount of artistic control over all the elements of production, including casting, publicity, and going to Miami. Not that I didn't trust Noel, who was always extremely affable and easygoing; I just didn't trust producers as a species. Fate was knocking at my door for the second time—and this time I was going to be more careful about answering.

Sam, I think, was not entirely sure of what I was doing, but he was kind enough to let me do it. "It seems funny," he wrote, "to be making plans for a text which does not yet exist and which, when it does, will inevitably be a poor substitute for the original (the loss will be much greater than from the French to the English *Godot*) . . ." Eventually, though, after weeks of patient and not so patient waiting, the English script did come into existence, and into my mailbox as well. One hot night in July, I closed the doors to my study, took the phone off the hook, and sat down to read "the ashcan play," as it had generally become known by this time. It was only with the greatest of difficulty all during rehearsals and afterward that we could get either the press or the public to understand that the two chief characters were not in the ashcans.

Although I came to *Endgame* via the text rather than—as with *Godot*—via the theater, the first impact was even more powerful. I was prepared this time: two years of contact with Sam, a reading and rereading of several of his novels, and everything I could find that had by this time been written about his work. I was no longer limited to Wilder's existentialism. Whatever the reasons, I found myself bowled over by the power and intensity of the new play. I did not immediately understand everything, but I found myself carried away with the theatrical possibilities of this terrifying and funny, horrible and beautiful, tone poem of a play.

The two gentle old people in the ashcans were immensely human and marvelous; I still think of their scene as being one of the greatest love scenes in dramatic literature. Equally fascinating were the two central figures: a blind, majestic, and yet pitifully human tyrant, and his shambling automaton attendant and confidant. I didn't spend much time trying to figure out what this particular collection of characters "meant" or "was about"—whether they represented the last four people left on earth after an atomic explosion; or the older generation being tossed on the ashheap by the younger; or, as someone suggested, Pozzo and Lucky in the third act of *Godot*. What I understood or felt immediately was that just as *Godot* dealt with a promised and expected arrival which never took place, so *Endgame* seemed to be dealing with a promised but unfulfilled departure. In the words of the play itself, "something was taking its course," and I knew that that something had been well worth waiting for.

More than anything else, *Endgame* seemed to be a kind of tragic vision, a prayer to a God who might or might not exist. Far from depressing me, the play lifted me right out of myself, exhilarated me, providing a dramatic tension as strong and all-embracing as the one I had felt all those years ago when I had first discovered *Oedipus* or *Lear*. And what most impressed and delighted me was that the play demonstrated Sam's special gifts of language and rhythm, for making the sublime ridiculous and ridiculous sublime.

I told Barney that the part of Hamm needed a combination Oedipus, Lear, and Hamlet—a neat trick of casting even at Broadway rates, much less off-Broadway. Nevertheless, I was all set to try. And, more important, Sam was willing to let me try.

Sam wanted me to fly over to see the Paris version before it closed at the end of October. I had a fund of practical questions which could best be answered by Sam in person. Luckily I was able to persuade Noel Behn and his triumvirate that this trip was necessary; a transatlantic voyage is a sizeable item in an off-Broadway budget. One night in October, I took off in a rainstorm on my second pre-production pilgrimage to Samuel Beckett. I was sure the plane would crash and that I would never see my wife and daughter again. There were a couple of moments when I wondered whether any play, even one by Sam, was worth all this.

Once I had safely landed at Le Bourget, my spirits rapidly revived. As it happened, Sam and I missed each other at the Gare des Invalides, where he had come, unannounced, to greet my arrival. We met at my hotel, this time a modest one, much more suited to off-Broadway than the Lancaster. For four days, we met for lunch and later took long walks through Montparnasse, along the Seine, and through the Latin Quarter. We had dinner together too, talking about *Endgame* until all hours. One lovely sunny afternoon we polished off a pound of grapes while looking for a place in which we could play a game of Ping-Pong. Another time, I found a bookstore along the river that specialized in books on chess and presented Sam with one titled: "Five Hundred Endgames." I even got to meet Sam's "wife" Suzanne, and Barney Rosset showed up unexpectedly at a performance.

Nor did I forget my questions, although I was often tempted to. After a run of almost a hundred performances, the French production of *Fin de Partie* was in its last week when I arrived in Paris. I think I went to see it three times, twice with Sam, and once while following my English translation with a flashlight provided by a helpful usher until another usher politely told me I was bothering the actors. I spoke, as well as he and I could, with director Roger Blin, who also played Hamm, with the members of the cast and crew—who enlightened me about some of the technical problems and details of their production. The Paris production seemed to be basically what Sam had wanted; although, like all practicing playwrights, he was gradually discovering that all actors have imaginations and get ideas that might seriously affect or even distort the intentions of the author.

Sam tried to respond to my specific questions no matter how obvious or stupid they seemed to him. "What were Clov's visions?" "Who was that mysterious Mother Pegg who kept cropping up?" "Was Hamm really bleeding through that handkerchief over his face at the beginning of the play?" (Obviously, that was a metaphor.) Each time I read the script or saw the play in performance, I came up with a flock of new questions.

Sam was always patient and tolerant of my ignorance, and he helped me more than I can ever say or know. When I left for home, as I told Noel Behn later, I knew *Endgame* a hundred times more clearly than when I had arrived. I knew what Hamm should look like and sound like, knew how the ashcans should be placed and why, knew how carefully and exactly I would have to work on the play's rhythms and its tones. The mosaic of larger meanings was gradually falling into place, its total design still shadowy but at least perceivable.

Sam, on his side, catching me fresh from my Samuel Johnson enterprise, told me of his own interest in Johnson and of a play about Johnson and Mrs. Thrale that he had started to write and then abandoned. He asked me how playwright James Lee had handled that relationship, how the scenes had been played, what Ustinov was like as Johnson. At one point, I suggested that Ustinov would be great as Hamm but that I was sure we could not get him.

That was, of course, the main question: Who was there in New York who could and would want to play Hamm in an off-Broadway production at the Cherry Lane? In Paris, Blin had given a bravura performance in the grand manner, as only the French theater could offer. George Devine was scheduled to play Hamm in London the following year; he was excellent casting. And the Royal Court was his own theater. What we needed was a large-scale actor like Peter Ustinov, who wouldn't do it, or Paul Muni—who was seriously ill—or Charles Laughton, or Orson Welles, or . . . ?

On my departure day, Sam endeared himself to me more than ever. I had decided to return via London, and for some reason was taking the boat train. We had said our goodbyes the night before. I found myself at the Gare du Nord searching for the right platform when I unexpectedly ran into Sam. He wasn't sure which train I was taking, but had come to the station and searched through all the trains that were going to London around noon.

I left Paris slightly depressed about the casting problem, but not about Sam. His last word of advice especially cheered me. "Do it the way you like, Alan, do it ahny way you like!" Somewhere there was bound to be an American Hamm.

For two months actors streamed in and out of the Cherry Lane offices, telephones rang all over New York City. Our first choices for the parents were P. J. Kelly and Nydia Westman—and we were fortunate in getting both. To this day, I have difficulty seeing anything other than their sweet smiling faces in those ashcans. We had several strong choices for Clov, but waited for our final selection until we had found our Hamm. My choice was Gerald Hiken, who was in a Saroyan play on Broadway and not available.

Hamm himself remained elusive. We couldn't even find Orson. Donald Davis, who had once played Teiresias for me and who was later to make a fine Krapp, was unavailable. Morris Carnovsky was available but nervous. Jacob Ben-Ami wanted to play it, but I was nervous about him. Muni was indeed not to be had. Laughton wrote us a letter saying that he was fascinated by the play but would rather have had Ilse Koch make him into a lampshade than play Hamm. Other actors were interested but not available, or available but not interested; still others were interested but somehow not suited. We despaired, postponed, kept looking.

Eventually, I cast Boris Tumarin, a very fine Russian-trained actor with whom I had worked before, and who I felt had both presence and intelligence. We then took Alvin Epstein for Clov. Among the actors we rejected were Peter Falk, Gene Saks, Shelley Berman, Ron Leibman, and Jack Klugman.

The day after New Year's, 1958, we went into rehearsal. First rehearsals of a new play are always a kind of adventure into the unknown, and this is especially true of a Beckett play, where so many of the conventions are changed or ignored—a plot with a beginning, middle, and end, clear-cut character progression, dramatic mobility and color—and yet so many new ones laid down—tones, rhythms, and cross-currents of relationship, which the author has built into the very fiber of his material. No other playwright I know of writes stage directions which are so essential and organic—as we discovered on each occasion when we ventured to disregard or to oppose them. I soon found myself not only hewing more and more faithfully to his printed demands, but demanding equal allegiance from the actors when they tended to go off on their own tangents—as actors are wont to do sometimes.

Designers also. Our setting for *Endgame* was being designed by a talented young newcomer to the New York scene, David Hays, whose reputation was largely based on his designs for O'Neill's *Long Day's Journey into Night* on Broadway and *The Iceman Cometh* off-Broadway. David was bright, eager to please, and very quick. Noel had suggested him, and I accepted. I made the initial mistake of showing David several photographs of the Paris design; his response was to try for the exact opposite. We talked about simplicity; he kept complicating things—shades of Albert Johnson! Finally, in desperation, I happened to look at the stone-and-brick walls of the Cherry Lane and decided that they were marvelously suitable for Hamm and Clov's "shelter"—even to the doorway in exactly the proper location for Clov's ten-by-ten-foot "kitchen." David, who was not happy with the idea of using actual walls rather than his painted visions, brought up the problem of the two windows required at the back. With Sam's wholehearted approval, we painted them, complete with hinged window frames, boldly and theatrically on the brick wall. No one minded although some found additional philosophical overtones in two obviously painted windows on a bare brick wall. I'm not sure that David Hays has quite forgiven me for not letting him design more of our setting, but he did light the bare stage beautifully.

We didn't shy away from all meaning, but I have discovered that the director's function is not so much to explain the author's "meaning" to his actors—whose need to express that meaning clearly to the audience is not necessarily assisted by their understanding it intellectually—but rather to lead the actors, by some theatrical and dramatic means, to *do* those things which will *result* in transmitting the author's meaning. No actor can act out the *meaning* of *Endgame*—or any other play. They can and do act the characters in the situations and relationships that the playwright's text provides. In this case they did act as actual people in an actual situation—and with imagination, intelligence, variety, and a sense of form.

Beckett himself has always stressed that he is writing about what he calls "the local situation"; i.e., Hamm and Clov (as well as Nagg and Nell) are individuals operating in a given set of circumstances. They are never to be considered as abstractions or symbols (which no actor can act), or as representing anything other than themselves. After that, if anyone wants to look for significance of some kind, let them do so at their initiative and peril. As Beckett himself wrote to me during rehearsals, "My work is a matter of fundamental sounds (no joke intended) made as fully as possible, and I accept responsibility for nothing else. If people want to have headaches among the overtones, let them. And provide their own aspirin."

Early in rehearsals it became convenient for me to suggest to the actors that the relation of Hamm and Clov (like that of Vladimir and Estragon) could be likened to that of the mind and the body, the intellectual and the physical faculties, inseparable and yet always in conflict. But I never thought they *were* literally the mind and the body, or that that was what Sam had intended. It was simply a theatrical language, leading the actors, I hoped, into certain areas of creativity. Certainly it was more helpful than trying to figure out whether the names of Hamm and Clov meant ham and cloves, or the Biblical Ham and the cloven foot, and a dozen other such secret codes—all of which are irrelevant.

A couple of days into rehearsal, I discovered that I had made a serious mistake in casting Boris as our Hamm. He was an excellent actor, extremely intelligent and sensitive. He probably "understood" the play as well as or better than any of us. But vocally and physically, he was just too weak. He also had a slight Russian accent. Hamm seemed to be becoming a petty tyrant rather than a gargantuan one. One day after I could no longer dodge the issue, I told Boris he was an eagle on that throne; while what I wanted was a lion. I tried again to find a lion, and this time came up with a young and relatively unknown performer, Lester Rawlins, who had played my Tom in the Arena Stage *Glass Menagerie*. Replacing Boris was not easy—he had been in several previous productions of mine, and we were personal friends—but I had to do it, for the play's sake and Sam's. Lester may not have been a lion, but his deep, strong voice and his solid physical presence made a real difference.

Rehearsals started to go extremely well, and for the first time I relaxed and dealt with the normal problems of each day's work. Alvin perked up when Lester entered the cast, and the two of them provided a believable and provocative combination. When Lester didn't look formidable in the toque that our playwright had called for, I asked Sam if he would mind using a Beckett-style derby instead. Sam agreed, I'm not sure how enthusiastically. The derby allowed Lester to be serious and comic at the same time. As Nell, Nydia Westman was often baffled by her physical circumstances or her lines, but strove valiantly and with evident goodwill to do whatever I or the playwright asked her. P. J. Kelly, at that time the oldest living member of American Actor's Equity, told me that he had had many similar experiences in his seventy-eight years, especially, as he confessed, with Irish playwrights. He had first played love scenes as a juvenile at the Abbey Theatre more than a half-century earlier, and he was quite content to play an older lover in another Irishman's play now. Both Nydia and P.J. coped good-naturedly with the numerous practical problems of making entrances and exits from below the stage, and spending the entire evening in two non-custom-made ashcans. On one occasion, P.J. accidentally got banged by one of the lids, and I thought he might be seriously hurt. He never mentioned the incident.

By the time we were well into rehearsals, our "producers" had no illusions about my responsibility to the author. A number of times during this period, one or the other would get worried that I was making the play too serious, and bring up the question of whether it was funny enough. I felt that the production was already awash with legitimate laughter. Had I not retained that much coveted artistic control by the terms of my contract with the Cherry Lane, I might have been forced to make fundamental changes—with which I was partially or completely in disagreement—or risked being fired. As it was, I was able to resist all attempts to change or distort what Sam had written, or the intentions he had personally confided to me.

One thing that bothered everyone, especially the actors, was Sam's instruction that Hamm and Clov's faces should be red, and Nagg and Nell's faces should be white. As we approached our opening, the need to have that question answered overruled my attempts not to answer it. Eventually, I was persuaded to write to Sam for the answer. "Why is Werther's coat green?" he asked. In other words, because the author chose to see it that way.

The closer we got to opening, the more I felt that this time, perhaps, my production of a Beckett play was going the way I wanted it to go. The texture of Sam's writing was gradually emerging, rich in both its serious and its comic elements. Cast morale was high, and every cast member was as faultless as I could possibly expect him or her to be. Their dedication to the enterprise was remarkable, especially in view of the nominal salaries they were getting, and off-Broadway's general lack of glamour. The electrician, a member of a more powerful union, was getting more per week than any of us, including the playwright. Interest on the part of the public was considerable, but we were not getting as much publicity as we wanted. I even forgave the producers for coming up with a logo and a poster that featured two cartoon-like ashcans with heads peering out from them, instead of something more dignified. Besides, Sam liked it. Throughout, I kept constantly in touch with Sam, letting him in on all our ups and downs and continuing to question him in detail about various practical matters—his answers always opening up new vistas and new possibilities.

About three weeks after rehearsals had begun, we held the first of five previews with audiences. Apart from our producers and ourselves, the only other person who had seen any rehearsals was the critic of the *Village Voice*, Jerry Tallmer, who had been so perceptive about *Godot* that my natural caution about critics faded away when he asked to be allowed to observe rehearsals. Jerry came a few times and made some suggestions, which I rejected. It was obvious that he hadn't liked all of what he had seen, and his later review—which questioned my ability to direct Beckett at all—made that attitude abundantly clear. Our preview audiences felt exactly the opposite. They laughed and cried in all the proper places, never seemed to be bored even if they might, on occasion, be puzzled. Not only did they survive sitting through the hour-and-a-half without intermission (I had refused to add one) but they stayed in their seats at the end, clapping wildly. Miracle of miracles, we started to sell out, an unheard-of event at off-Broadway previews. Advance sales began to hum; the general feeling and word were that we had a great play. We crossed our fingers and hoped for a good performance on opening night.

We opened on January 28, 1958, on one of the coldest days of a very cold winter, at the start of one of the heaviest snowstorms. The actors gave the most sustained performance they had yet played—at least the parts of it I saw. When I went backstage beforehand, P.J. asked me if I wanted him "to put on his old-age makeup." I looked at him for a moment, and then said "Sure." My agent, Lucy Kroll (she had succeeded Audrey Wood when I directed *A Trip to Bountiful* in London), had finally consented to come off-Broadway. And even though about half of the Cherry Lane's 189 actual seats were occupied by members of the working press, there seemed to be a special air of excitement.

We had rigged a special curtain that resembled the sheets covering the ashcans and Hamm's chair. It opened sideways. Just as it did so, the radiators on the Cherry Lane's stage began to clank. Normally our building superintendent, Robert Earl Jones—whose son, James Earl Jones, was just then beginning his theatrical career—shut the radiators off several hours earlier, so that by the time the audience got in they had stopped clanking. This particular evening, because the weather had turned to freezing and because Noel Behn wanted the opening-night audience to be comfortable, he had left instructions with Robert Earl not to turn off the radiators until around 7:30. As a result, they started to clank practically from the moment the curtain opened, choosing Hamm and Clov's best lines to make the loudest noise.

For the first time in my theatrical life, I thought seriously of stopping the performance and starting again; I almost ran down the center aisle to do so. What stopped me was the realization that they were going to go on clanking for the better part of an hour, and I could not ask the audience simply to sit there and wait for them to stop. Nor could I sit there and listen to those radiators clanking through Samuel Beckett's best lines, not to mention some of his best pauses. I went next door to the Blue Mill Restaurant to drink a succession of double Manhattans and ruminate on how another Beckett play was going to be destroyed.

Between each drink, I would venture back into the Cherry Lane, more and more sodden, to listen to those damned radiator pipes continuing their grisly staccato accompaniment. Although the sound must have been lessening, I kept hearing it louder and louder, with not a single one of Beckett's lines coming through. The actors seemed more or less unaffected. The audience clearly was not. Whether because of the performance, the pipes, or the presence of so much press, they seemed respectful but cool. Lines that had brought roars to our previews produced faint smiles; those that had resulted in smiles produced nothing. Instead of those tense, wonderfully quiet silences we had previously earned for the more emotional moments of the play, I heard seats creaking, programs rattling, and throats clearing. Opening night was the only night when I could not hear our onstage alarm clock ticking from my perch at the back of the theatre. As Adlai Stevenson said in a completely different context, it hurt too much to laugh and I was too old to cry. I cried anyway.

The radiators finally stopped, somewhere in the second half. The curtain finally closed. The applause, strangely enough, was not bad. I started upstairs to the dressing rooms, only to be stopped by Lucy, enveloped in the huge fur coat that all lady agents seem to wear, who grabbed me and kissed me and told me how wonderful the show was. "Those radiators!" she exclaimed, her eyes rolling up toward the heavens. "What a touch! . . . Of course, you'll tone them down a bit. But . . . what a touch!" I dashed upstairs to avoid putting my hands around her neck.

The actors were fine, tired but elated. Oh, yes, they had heard the radiators, but after all, what could they do? Even the producers were still talking to me; Noel was still smiling and saying, "Well, we pulled it off, didn't we?"

Did we? The interval between the curtain and the first reviews in the morning papers is a period of purgatory than which nothing in the various hells of the theater is worse. Somehow, most of us at the Blue Mill drowned our thoughts in more Manhattans or other versions of solace, and made small talk as though it mattered, and managed to survive that special purgatory that night, almost as though we were characters in a Beckett play ourselves.

At midnight some TV commentator said he had hated everything, but we really didn't expect anything from television. A half hour later, a spy we had planted behind one of the presses at the *Herald-Tribune* rang up to say he could read us Walter Kerr's notes directly from the galley sheets. Walter hadn't liked *Godot*, calling it a "plastic carrot of a play." Did we want to listen to him? We did. His review was not exactly glowing, but somewhat provocative and certainly respectful—there were even two or three possible quotes. Our spirits, imprisoned behind those clanking pipes, began to stir. Another Manhattan!

Just after one o'clock, unable to bear the waiting any longer, I rang up the press room of the *Times* myself, getting a bored voice on the other end which, after a bit of gentle prodding, promised to locate a "bulldog" edition containing Brooks Atkinson's column. The *Times*, of course, was crucial for us. A few interminable minutes later, the voice came through once more: "It's pretty stiff." Then, having thrown the bomb, proceeded to read verbatim and in complete monotone an absolutely beautiful notice from Brooks, clearly understanding the author's intention and point of view, and highly appreciative of its rendition on that stage. Not a word about radiators.

Three weeks later, in the middle of another snowstorm, Mr. Atkinson added further to our laurels and our run with an excellent and perceptive Sunday column. But the jubilation that night was so intense that we couldn't resist letting Sam know. Though it was just dawn in Paris, I telephoned him and informed his sleepy self that the two chief critics in New York had liked his play—and its production. The "debacle" in Miami had been redeemed. As usual, Sam's concern was with the performers and the management, though he expressed his gratitude and relief at the favorable reception. Win, lose, or draw in the notices, Sam's opinion of the entire venture and of me would have been no different. The important thing for him was not the winning or losing of the race but the running of it. I went home, aslosh with Manhattans but with the weight of that Miami *Godot* off my shoulders for the first time in two years.

Kerr and Atkinson, of course, weren't the whole story. As was usually the case, the afternoon popular papers were more baffled and less perceptive. Several of them mentioned the radiators—favorably. *Endgame* ran for three months and more than one hundred performances. It was generally regarded as one of the highlights of the season on or off-Broadway, and even Jerry Tallmer could not prevent its receiving a *Village Voice* "Obie" for the best foreign play of the season. The weekly press, most of whom came on the second night—sans radiators—was for the most part favorable. We had a bad break when an extremely favorable review in *Time* got crowded out for lack of space. Our audiences grew more receptive and even enthusiastic as the run progressed; hardly anyone ever walked out; the performances got fuller and more relaxed. Even the publicity improved.

Best of all, we had not failed Sam. Though he would not come to New York to see the production, news and comment about it continued to reach him regularly. He seemed to like the production photographs; eventually he was to hear the recording we made—with Gerald Hiken playing Clov. By then, he must have been able to visualize at least some portion of our production, and I continued to write him in copious detail about all of it. For the next three months, all of us at the Cherry Lane continued to look forward to hearing from him, and cherishing his occasional "greetings to the players."

Endgame was the beginning of the rest of my life with Sam.

Early that spring, I was immensely pleased to hear Zelda's voice once more. My defection from *Tartuffe* forgiven, she wanted me to come down to do an Australian play with a poetic-sounding name, *The Summer of the Seventeenth Doll.* By coincidence, through the suggestion of my Aussie-born secretary/assistant, Joy Small, I had seen the play a year or so earlier on Broadway. Laurence Olivier had seen *Doll* on one of his Australian tours and had brought the entire company to London, where it had a very successful stay. He had also sponsored it in New York, where it lasted only one week. I had seen the show on its last night and had decided that there was something there, but I wasn't getting it because I couldn't understand the company's thick Australian dialect. More out of a desire to make things up with Zelda than out of a strong desire to direct this particular play, I went back to Arena again.

The moment I got to working on *Doll*, however, I was surprised to find that the play was a knockout—an Australian combination of Tennessee Williams and Arthur Miller. It was funny and extremely truthful, and it packed a tremendous emotional wallop. The cast seemed among the best I'd ever worked with at the Arena, especially two newcomers, Dana Elcar and Louise Latham, both of whom are now extremely busy in film and television. Their big reversal scene at the end of the second act, when he proposes marriage as a way of hanging on to her, and she responds by almost killing him—marriage, in her eyes, spelling the end of both their youth and their relationship—was as powerful as any scene I'd ever directed.

The play was hailed by all the Washington critics, most of them agreeing that it was the best show of the Arena season and one of the finest productions Arena had ever done: "the biggest smash Arena has ever had," "a beaut of a play," "corkingly presented," "thoroughly engrossing," "vastly funny . . . searingly melodramatic." Richard Coe, alternately everyone's friend and foe, even got in some personal comments that, favorable or not, hit close to the bone: "Alan Schneider comes back to us as a director with a robustness his work previously had lacked. Here is a physical awareness of actors and their bodies, of audiences and their grittier senses I find immensely welcome in this developing director. I had begun to wonder if he would ever burst out of the subconscious, for that is something his very special directorial style must do. . . ." And since *Doll* had been a failure on Broadway—without anyone interested enough to ask why—Dick also made the point that Arena had now discovered it could go far and fruitfully "in defying the dictates of Manhattan," something that Zelda has done more and more, up to and including a time when there is hardly any viable Manhattan—or at least Broadway—theater left.

In the summer of 1958, Jean and I and our Viveca, now three and growing as beautiful as her namesake, went off to England, where I was supposed to direct an American play called *The Deserters*, by a fellow with the unusual name of N. Thaddeus Vane, not a chap out of Dickens but a real live New Yorker who had settled in England to live.

I had met Norman Vane somewhere in my Broadway gyrations a few years back when he was working on an earlier play about alligators lurking in toilet bowls. The play was terrible, but Norman had a lively cheerfulness that, added to his unusually free spirit, made him irresistible. He went after a new "bird" every five minutes. Sometimes he'd be squiring one around in his open MG and actually make a U-turn in the middle of the block to pick up another one. When Norman rang me from London that playwright Wolf Mankowitz and Oscar Lewenstein of the Royal Court directorate were planning to do Mankowitz's *The Deserters*, I could barely believe him. It had no distinction whatsoever, on any level, except that in the big scene a nun kissed a soldier on the lips. In 1958, yet!

At that time, my love affair with the English was still so dominant that anything which could get me to London for the summer was impossible to resist. Although *The Deserters* deserted us before it got to London, it did manage to rack up a sizeable tour. But the important result of the enterprise was, as usual, an accident. During rehearsals, an agent by the name of Emmanuel Wax (somehow known as "Jimmy"), called me to say he had a starving young actor-playwright out in Chiswick by the name of David Baron, who could do American accents very well. Would I see him as a possible understudy? Understudies were the farthest thing from my mind at that moment, but as a favor to Jimmy, I suggested that David Baron come along to our palatial rehearsal quarters in the YMCA at Tottenham Court Road some afternoon. A few days later, a dark-haired serious young man, wearing the biggest horn-rimmed glasses since Harold Lloyd, came in accompanied by a baby carriage containing a small boy, and his dark-haired and quietly shy wife, Vivien. Evidently they didn't have enough money for a babysitter. David read a scene or two very well, and with a most convincing American accent. Vivien wanted to read too until I explained that we were plentifully supplied with female understudies. I hired David on the spot, delaying the actual date of signing until we came to London, which of course we never did. In spite of the disappointment, David Baron and I hit it off. Later, after our play had closed, he confessed to me over a pub drink that he had himself had a bad experience that very spring with a play he had written. David's play had opened at the Lyric in Hammersmith, been blasted by all the critics except Harold Hobson, and had come off at once. Would I like to read it? I came through with my usual response to almost any playwright I meet, "Yes, I would." David's play was called *The Birthday Party* and the name on the cover was David's real one, Harold Pinter. I believe that David, I mean Harold, had a framed copy of the Lyric's box office receipts for the week: one pound, six and something. Not enough for him and Vivien Merchant to pay for a babysitter.

The rest of that lovely summer I spent being drawn in a vaiety of directions, none of which got me anywhere except geographically. I went off to walk in the streets of such places as Paris (with Sam) and Rome, and contemplate a measure of sanity.

Back home that fall, I peddled *Birthday* around to everyone I knew, with no results. Zelda said it wasn't a play at all and wondered why I'd asked her to waste her time reading it. The Arena wouldn't last a season doing such plays, she said. Yale, Boston, off-Broadway, even some Broadway producers, including Richard Barr, felt pretty much the same. I also had some badly typed manuscripts that Peggy Ramsay had given me, by a fellow named Ionesco, which she liked but nobody wanted to do. They were titled *The Lesson*, *The Bald Soprano*, and *The Chairs*. I wanted to work on them at the Studio, but all the actors I approached couldn't make heads or tails of them. It's nice to know now that one's taste is ahead of the pack, but I didn't know it then. I went into deep despair, relieved for a while when the Ford Foundation chose me as one of ten American directors for a grant. They awarded me the beneficent sum of $10,000 to direct a series of plays in the regional theater. In sympathy, Jean became pregnant with our second child.

My despair was somewhat relieved, and my roller-coaster career took another lurch that winter when I was suddenly offered a two-character play called *Kataki (The Enemy)* written by a young television writer, Shimon Wincelberg. Two-character plays are tough enough—over the years I've directed around a dozen of them—but this two-character play was unique in that one of the characters spoke only in Japanese; it was, therefore, practically a monologue for the other character, talking English. *Kataki* was actually an extension of a television show about a wartime incident in which an American and a Japanese soldier, stranded together on a desert island, are transformed from enemies to friends—and then back to enemies once the war returns to their island. It had something to say about our individual humanity, and it said so in a highly unusual and theatrical manner. Whether it was "for Broadway" was another story.

Sessue Hayakawa, newly rediscovered and acclaimed for his role as the tyrannical officer in *The Bridge on the River Kwai,* was playing the Japanese soldier. As the American I cast Ben Piazza, a young actor whom I had seen and admired in Joe Anthony's production of *Winesburg, Ohio.* George Grizzard, always my first choice, was doing something else. A designer named Peter Dohanos, whom I hadn't known before, did a beautifully naturalistic reproduction of a desert island, making the stage wider by subtly sliding the scenery back and forth.

Sessue, who didn't speak much offstage either, was extraordinary at communicating meaning without one understandable word of dialogue. As a critic said afterward, he made thought interesting. Ben was fine, but he was a Studio actor who required constant nourishment from his partner. Sessue, a completely instinctive, untrained, external performer, wouldn't do any more than he had to. He had some difficulty even in understanding why I wanted him at every rehearsal since, after all, Ben had all the lines. In spite of this artistic dichotomy, the two went well together; and the play got more and more clearly shaped, and exciting.

We had started without having a New York theater. In Philadelphia, still my favorite place to go before the storm, the critics were much better than anyone expected: "The problem of the two-character play *without* a telephone has been met and, we believe, conquered . . . ," said one. "Written and played with charm . . . masterful portrayal." *Variety* trumpeted: "Here is a show that could conceivably go a lot of places . . . one of the best directed jobs of the season." And our word of mouth was equally good. Suddenly everybody, including the Shuberts, began to think about us. We got the Ambassador Theatre on Forty-ninth Street, which hadn't had a hit for an even longer time than the Lyceum but was better than no theater at all.

Sessue continued to amaze us. He must have been over seventy but looked fifty, with coal-black hair, good skin, and fantastic energy. He went out every evening with a different companion, usually a waitress whom he had spotted during his evening meal. On opening night our production stage manager told me that Sessue had a young woman—evidently French—in his dressing room. When I sent the assistant up with instructions to get her the hell out of there, Sessue sent back a curt message: "Tell Mr. Schneider he only has me on the stage. This is a private matter." The French connection stayed.

As it happened, there were two openings that memorable night, April 9, 1959: one onstage at the Ambassador, and the other at St. Luke's Hospital further uptown, where my wife was giving birth—a juxtaposition we had always kidded about but never expected. After a brief visit with Jean that afternoon, I was, of course, downtown. I wasn't present at the birth, and Jean never got to see the show.

The stage crew, with whom I was on excellent terms, had a "pool" going on the exact time the baby would arrive. I also had worked out a special signaling system with the stage doorman by means of which he would let me know at once whether it was a boy or girl. At 9:35 that evening, as the second act was half over, the doorman came out into the house, his hand held up in the signal, "It's a boy!" I almost let out a whoop right in the middle of the play. Joe Monaco, our electrician, won seventy-five bucks. Everyone wanted me to call the new arrival Sessue Schneider, but I balked. "Viveca" was fine; "Sessue" wasn't. When I finally rushed up to the hospital after the curtain, David Alan looked like a miniature Chinese prize fighter, but I didn't care. Even the *Times* didn't matter that night. I had a real live son.

The *Times* would matter soon, however. Most of the reviewers were ecstatic: the *Post* called *Kataki* "dramatic," "touching," and "memorable"; the *News* cheered its "powerful suspense"; and Walter Kerr in the *Tribune* lauded the "stunning play" and its "virile, resourceful direction." All of the reviews except one made it sound like a hit, but that one was Brooks Atkinson's in the *Times*. And *Kataki* was not a hit, all because one man happened not to like it. Mr. Atkinson did not like to accept that fact nor has any *Times* critic. Nonetheless, the rest of us in the theater know it and have to go on.

After *Kataki* opened I went back to Arena once more to do John Osborne's *Epitaph for George Dillon,* which though not as linguistically dazzling as *Look Back in Anger* seems to me a more solid play. Arena had selected Michael Lipton, a handsome and intense young leading man, as George. I didn't know Mike then, but I did know Philip Bosco, who was doing the Producer, and a young character actress named Esther Benson, who was to play George's unrequited love interest. They all turned out to be wonderful, especially Mike.

I loved the work and enjoyed going to every rehearsal as well as all the discussions after. Mike, scared and uncertain as always, was fun to work with. It was the first of our many shows, in which I have cast him in every conceivable way, and a lifelong friendship. The reviews, especially Mike's, were enthusiastic all around. We were even asked to come to the Boston Arts Festival after the run and season ended, and we played there mostly in the rain to clustering room only. Elliot Norton and Elinor Hughes liked us a lot, in spite of the raindrops, which they reviewed together with the performance: "The rain was persistent but the performance was absorbing," and "The drama was dampened, doused and deluged at the Boston Arts Festival on Wednesday night but it was not drowned out. Nor was its lustre dimmed. . . . *Epitaph* is strong enough for a rainy day."

The day after I finished *Epitaph* and got dried out, I was asked by NBC's Robert Graff to direct *The Secret of Freedom,* an hour-long TV film written by Archibald MacLeish, who had just won the Pulitzer for his *J.B.* I had always loved MacLeish's poetry, and had liked his radio play *The Fall of the City,* which the Washington Civic Theatre had staged during my time there. Bob had seen the *Variety* review on *Kataki* and had decided on the basis of something the critic said about the way I dealt with realistic details of behavior that I would make a decent film director. The reviewer was quite right; Bob quite wrong.

Bob and I gathered together a topnotch cast of stars: Tony Randall, Thomas Mitchell—who, when people asked him whether they had seen him somewhere before would answer "Yes, Buffalo"—and Kim Hunter; along with Lonny Chapman and John McGiver, whom I seemed to carry around everywhere with me. The script was literary and philosophical rather than dramatic, and took place in a small New Jersey town where the citizens finally caught on to the true meaning of democracy. We spent several weeks on location in an idyllic little New Jersey town by the name of Mount Holly, where I have never felt so un-idyllic in my life.

On our first day of filming, for some technical reason, we started off by shooting a climactic scene from the middle of the script. The character played by Tony Randall had just had a fight with his wife, played by Kim Hunter. In the shot, he was to come hurtling through the front door, bolt down the steps of his neat suburban lawn, and round the corner of his neat suburban property. We rehearsed the scene several times, at about six o'clock in the morning before anyone in that part of New Jersey was up. I had carefully and, I thought, cleverly placed a child's tricycle in such a position that Tony would have to hit it in his furious travels. And I had asked him to cut across the corner of his lawn to demonstrate his impatience and his deviation from normal routine. The scene had no dialogue.

After the rehearsals with the actors, I gathered our crew together and made a little speech about how much I depended on them and appreciated them. They, in turn, expressed their complete faith in my film directing debut. I wore my usual baseball hat, a new pair of chinos, and a plastic smile to hide my fears. The first shot of my first film was about to happen. "Lights . . . Camera . . . Action!" Tony came out of the door perfectly; a worried Kim, holding a cup of coffee, hovered in the background. He hit the tricycle perfectly, sending it off perfectly at the right angle. He started perfectly up the sidewalk. Wanting him to cut across the lawn at just the right spot, I yelled, "Cut." Tony started to cut across the lawn. To my surprise everything came to a halt. I looked around to see what was the matter. Our camera operator came over to me and slapped me on the back. "Great going, kid!" he said. "You saw that cloud coming! You're going to make a great director. You don't miss a thing."

It was like that all the way, with me missing everything there was to miss. The script was too literary and dull. My shooting was unliterary, unfilmic, and duller. The final blow came toward the end, when I had John McGiver, playing a grocer, holding up an egg in his hand and making an important cosmic-political speech about the nature of the universe, moral and otherwise. We spent what seemed like hours lining up the shot, to make sure that the egg was in the exact left-hand bottom corner of the frame. The camera director, who was more experienced and even more temperamental than I, assured me that the egg was exactly where it had to be, although every time I looked in the camera I couldn't see it. I deferred to his greater experience. Next day, the rushes showed that I was right; our egg was nowhere to be seen. John, in the meantime, had already flown off to California, where he was shooting another picture. In our film, John gave a speech about an egg that wasn't there.

I wasn't there much either. Although when the film was shown on television the next spring, in spite of its pontifical dullness, it received mildly respectable notices. Archie got blamed for pontificating. The actors got praised. And no one noticed the missing egg—except the director.

I came back from New Jersey to find that a New York producer, Sidney Bernstein, had finally raised the money for an off-Broadway production of *Summer of the Seventeenth Doll.* I was terrified it would suffer as badly as *All Summer Long,* the only other play I had moved from the Arena to New York. Luckily, it didn't and in fact, it was one of my few Arena transfers that improved behind a proscenium.

Almost all of the New York critics, including one from the Communist paper, *The Daily Worker,* who specially appreciated seeing a play in which he was told how the hero and heroine made their living, seemed to like it. Norman Rosten, not usually given to hyperbole, said, "a magnificent performance of a lovely play." But Brooks Atkinson, from whom I had expected the best response, gave us only grudging acceptance: "Although *Summer of the Seventeenth Doll* has some of the flatness of a documentary and is lacking in literary distinction, there is more inside than the original production revealed. It is interesting to see how much Mr. Schneider and his actors have drawn out of it." Knowing how important a review in the *Times* is to a serious play, I gritted my teeth and barely dared to hope. If *Doll* didn't make it, there was no way I could continue to work in the New York theater. I would move out into the suburbs, go to Columbia, get a degree in Russian Studies, and forget about the theater entirely.

Doll ran more than a year, and produced a fan letter from Laurence Olivier himself, who thanked me for sharing his faith in the play. I put it away somewhere for safe-keeping, and have been looking for it ever since. I remained in the theater.

I did not, however, remain in New York. Directly after the New York opening of *Doll* in October, my domestic life changed appreciably. With a four-year-old daughter and a new son, I found New York harder and harder to deal with. Within a six-month period we had eleven murders in our neighborhood. Reluctantly, we took off for the suburbs, my father lending me enough money for a down payment on a lovely old house in Hastings-on-Hudson. Jean and I, remembering her home town of Hastings, England, originally went out there on a lark; we fell under its spell and wound up living there for twenty years.

Equally reluctantly, I took off for the first of my Ford Foundation assignments into the hinterlands, intended to make it possible for me to afford a "normal" married life. I went to the Alley Theatre in Houston to do *Godot*, fearing its reception might be as unfavorable as the earlier one in Florida. Artistic Director Nina Vance gave me every support. The production, without stars, and somewhat more relaxed in its comedy, was greeted favorably by the Houston critics, and proved highly successful.

Zelda also kept me away from home. At the start of the 1959–1960 season, she asked me back to direct a new play this time, Josh Greenfeld's *Clandestine on the Morning Line*, which had won a Ford Foundation playwriting award. Its title relating to horse racing, *Clandestine* was a slight, Saroyanesque piece, that was a bit confused but I liked it and had a good time working with Josh. Everything was going along reasonably well until one morning, in the middle of rehearsals, our leading lady, Susan Steell, who happened to weigh close to three hundred pounds and who was as jolly as she was large, didn't show up at the theater. We called her at her apartment and got no answer. Investigation showed that Susan had had a big steak dinner the night before, with lots of wine; she had had a fatal heart attack. Both Josh and I had to go down to the city morgue to identify her body. It was a terrible experience. That was the only time that I have been through the experience of an actor dying in the middle of rehearsals. It is bad enough when their deaths come afterward, as they have in increasing numbers through recent years.

The actors rallied round with great understanding. Susan's replacement, hastily flown in from Denver, came through nobly. Josh rewrote like mad, and never lost his equilibrium. He had an amazing capacity for dealing with his personal problems, which later stood him well when he needed to face the problem of an autistic son. The play, being a new script, got special attention from the critics, who split fairly evenly. Coe liked the central character but not the play. Carmody, on the other hand, called it "hilarious," "haunting," and "splendidly daffy," adding that "joy continues to abound at Arena Stage." Even the *Times*'s Atkinson came down to see why the Ford people had given money to a play with such a strange name. Atkinson's final impression was that "Mr. Greenfeld's general decency and fresh humor outweigh the theatrical deficiencies of his script." The play eventually went on to New York, with a mixed black and white cast, James Earl Jones playing the role of the racetrack man originated at the Arena by Alan Oppenheimer. I wasn't available, unfortunately, to direct it. I was too busy meeting a new fellow named Edward Albee, and going on with an older fellow named Samuel Beckett.

CATCHING ON OFF-BROADWAY
1959–1960

From 1954 on, I had been constantly offered commercial Broadway comedies that were far from "commercial," and, except for the case of *The Little Glass Clock*, I constantly turned them down. I didn't want to continue as the poor man's Josh Logan. Off-Broadway, then just beginning to materialize as the place where foreign and literary and avant-garde plays could be done, was what appealed to me. Even with a second child, I hadn't worried too much about its dubious economic rewards. Nor had I yet been touched by that dictum from British essayist and critic Cyril Connolly: "The pram in the hallway is the enemy of art." After all, I'd never expected to make a living in the theater. Hadn't I started my New York career "off-Broadway," at Maxine Elliott's? I chose to do Beckett's *Endgame* instead of something called *Fig Leaf in Her Bonnet*, driving my poor hard-working agent, Lucy Kroll, mad with frustration.

"You've already done that, Alan," she pleaded with me when I insisted on preferring Beckett to whoever it was. "You're past that!"

Lucy and I parted contractual company shortly thereafter, but we have continued to see each other over the years, professionally and personally; and she now admits that my decision, at least vis-à-vis *Endgame* and a very short-lived *Fig Leaf*, was correct. I still collect yearly royalties from *Endgame*, not huge but steady.

After *Summer of the Seventeenth Doll*, I realized that I could work off-Broadway with better quality material than I was being offered for Broadway, and under more conducive, not to mention creative, conditions. The economic rewards were slim. Twenty-five to fifty dollars a week was not exactly a fortune even then. But, of course, there was always the chance, and sometimes the hope, that one thing might lead to something else.

It was entirely through off-Broadway that I came to meet playwright Edward Albee and to direct seven of his plays on Broadway. And, like everything else that's happened to me in the theater, getting to meet Edward came about only through a series of accidents.

The first and most important accident was Samuel Beckett's interest in radio, his concern with the sound of the human voice and its power to evoke an entire world. Shortly after *Godot,* he wrote a radio play, *All That Fall,* which created the daily life of an entire Irish village amid a comic kaleidoscope of life and death. I am certain that Sam did not possess a tape recorder, but, having once listened to actor Patrick Magee's voice on BBC reading from *Malone Dies,* he had written a play for that voice, a piece for one actor and a tape recorder, titled *Krapp's Last Tape.* Those two plays were his first original writing in English since the war and demonstrated a warmth of feeling as well as a type of robust humor not as evident in the plays he had originated in French.

Shortly after my production of *Endgame,* Sam sent me a copy of *Krapp,* and I found it, as I had his first two plays, both touching and highly comic, with the additional virtue of being much more immediately comprehensible. Toward the end of 1958, Pat did the play in a very well-received production at London's Royal Court. Through most of 1959, without much encouragement, I tried to drum up an off-Broadway presentation. Everyone was interested—Beckett was already known to the cognoscenti—but there didn't seem to be any theater people who understood his newest play, or wanted to put it on.

Krapp's Last Tape was, so to speak, a portrait of the young artist as an old man. It was about what was important and what was unimportant at various stages of one's life. It was about the role of memory, and the value of love—seen through Beckett's special language and imagination. I don't believe that any other writer has ever expressed the feelings of the struggling unknown artist more truthfully or more succinctly than in Sam's few, but oh so revealing, lines: "Seventeen copies sold, of which eleven at trade price to free circulating libraries beyond the seas. Getting known. (Pause.) One pound six and something, eight I have little doubt."

The main trouble with *Krapp* was that it was a one-acter, without another equally special one-acter to go with it. I persuaded Barney Rosset to let me take it to the off-Broadway coffee-house theaters then springing up, Caffè Cino and La Mama and others. But somehow the conditions or the circumstances—or the deals—were not right. The closest we came was with a well-known jazz club downtown on Third Avenue, the Five Spot Café, where Thelonious Monk, I believe, had first attracted attention. Barney thought that *Krapp* would work well performed several times a night in the Five Spot's friendly, if not too large, back room. The manager liked the idea because it provided him with inexpensive entertainment. Barney liked the idea of blending the worlds of theater and jazz. Even Sam was interested, in theory. I held out, wanting the play to be done but nervous about subjecting such an intimate and delicate dramatic mood to the vicissitudes of assorted bar sounds. *Krapp* needed something other than a smoke-filled room, with beer drinkers staggering in and out on their way to the john. Actors' Equity wasn't too happy either about allowing one of their actors to play three or four shows a night.

Without consulting me, Barney one day sold the option on *Krapp* to a young man, Harry Joe Brown, Jr., recently arrived from Hollywood, where his father was a relatively successful film producer, who wanted to establish his own credentials off-Broadway. Harry Joe was a seductively attractive postadolescent, with curly hair, a disarming smile, and—presumably—money. He knew very little about the theater but was anxious to learn. He was quite happy to have me as his director. Barney went off on another publishing adventure, leaving Harry Joe and myself to sort out matters. I went to see him off and on, but nothing much was happening to *Krapp's Last Tape*. Evidently, his money was more of a mirage than a reality.

Into our lives came a second and much more experienced gentleman. This was Richard Barr, who had recently decided to put a stop to his Broadway career and try his hand in a more congenial corner. Barr had had a long association with Charles Bowden, and the Barr-Bowden combine had a reputation commensurate with those other two Richards of my past, Aldrich and Myers, gentlemen producers looking for what was basically conventional and, hopefully, commercial material. I had known Richard Barr casually over the years—he happened also to hail from the Washington area—but I had not been particularly attracted by his taste in plays. I did hear, however, that Barr had just acquired the rights to a short play, *The Zoo Story*, written by a mysterious and reclusive young American named Edward Albee, said to be connected to the founder of the Keith-Albee circuit of vaudeville palaces. Albee, who had just retired from a job as a Western Union messenger, had through some strange series of circumstances just had his play produced—in German—

at the Schiller Theater's "Werkstatt" or Workshop in Berlin. The European critics had gone wild over it, and somehow it had found its way to the William Morris Agency in New York, where a young agent, Edward Parone, had brought it to Richard's attention with the idea of his, Parone's, serving as director. Richard wanted to launch his off-Broadway career with a production of *Zoo Story*, but couldn't find another one-act to go with it.

In the meantime, Richard had heard something about *Krapp's Last Tape* also missing a companion piece. He knew me, he knew all about Beckett, and he had seen both *Godot* and *Endgame*. He knew nothing whatsoever about Harry Joe Brown, Jr., and when he found out was not exactly happy. Richard was, and still is, good-natured and agreeable even under difficult circumstances, but he was determined to make his own mark in the new and exciting off-Broadway world. He had left Charles Bowden and teamed up with a coproducer, H. B. Lutz, who was providing most of his financing. He needed a play to go with the one he had, and he was willing to acquire another director, me. He didn't need Harry Joe Brown, Jr. or Sr.

Harry Joe, on his side, really needed a Richard Barr but couldn't admit that to anyone, including himself. He was holding back, and yet he wasn't moving us anywhere. Ready to shoot Barney for not having waited a bit longer, I manipulated and negotiated to bring Richard and Harry Joe into the same room, and frame of mind. By this time, I had read the script of *Zoo Story* and decided that it was the most original and powerful American work I'd come across in years. I had also met Edward, in his modest semi-Spartan apartment in the West Village.

Though friendly enough—through the good offices of both Richard Barr and composer William Flanagan, his closest friend—Edward was both taciturn and shy, emitting only a handful of words in our few brief meetings. Even then I sensed below his surface calm a tremendous inner intensity, like molten lava, waiting to break out. Silent as he tended to be, Edward did agree to Beckett's play being done in conjunction with his. On his end, Sam, largely on my and Barney's say-so, approved of *Zoo Story*. Somewhere in my inner soul, I dared to assume that since I was directing *Krapp*, Richard and Edward would surely want me to do the other one. But I was so concerned about getting Richard and Harry Joe together on some kind of contractual arrangement that I was too afraid to ask.

Reality soon obtruded on my dreaming. I knew that Ed Parone wanted to direct *Zoo Story*, and I knew that Edward for some reason was passing him by. I also discovered that John Stix was doing a work-in-progress version of *Zoo Story* at the Actors Studio, with Lou Antonio as Jerry and Shepperd Strudwick as Peter. I made sure that I got to a showing. The actors were very well cast, the production exciting. Edward was there and evidently liked it. I began to worry in the opposite direction: would Edward (and Richard) expect Johnny to direct *Krapp's Last Tape* as well? Two separate directors for two one-act plays seemed a bit much.

Uncertainty on all fronts continued for some time, blending eventually into totally unprepared-for certainty. Richard—his partnership with Lutz newly minted and coined as Theatre 1960—finally worked out a legal arrangement with Harry Joe, the two of them disagreeing then and ever since as to what it actually was. I was signed to direct *Krapp's Last Tape*, on a double bill with *The Zoo Story*, for a fee of $500 plus a weekly royalty of $25 for as long as it would run. The director for *Zoo Story* was going to be Milton Katselas, whom Edward had known for some time. I never learned why Edward Parone, John Stix and his two actors, and everyone else had receded into the distance.

Buttressed by Richard's moral support, and Harry Joe's perennial smile, I offered the *Krapp* role to Eli Wallach—who turned it down. We then proceeded to suggest it to at least a dozen other character actors, including Michael Strong, Keenan Wynn, Martin Balsam, and Gerry Hiken. Those realistically trained actors had difficulty grasping the virtues of one of the most expressive dramatic monologues in the English language. Perhaps they thought the role wasn't big enough. Or they didn't want to work with me. Eli, I'm happy to acknowledge, soon played opposite Joan Plowright in an even more esoteric play, Ionesco's *The Chairs*. I like to believe that his having turned down *Krapp* and then watching it move into universal acceptance influenced his choice.

Almost in desperation, Richard brought up the name of a youthful Canadian actor, Donald Davis. Donald was a friend, and had played Teiresias in my television *Oedipus the King*. I liked him as a classical actor, but thought he might be too mannered or too "grand" as Krapp the derelict. Richard differed and eventually, under the circumstances, convinced me that I should take Donald, who could not have been happier or more amenable. Richard and I traipsed all over the Village searching for a possible—and available—theater. At least we wouldn't have to dodge the customers in the back room of the Five Spot Café. I wrote to Sam to express my delight and my anticipation of the outcome.

In the interim, my other life—such as it was—also went on. Zelda, encouraged by my prowess with *Doll* and *Dillon*, had offered me a chance to direct my favorite play, *The Cherry Orchard*, which, as I've mentioned, I had done once before with student actors back at Catholic University. My cast included Michael Lipton, from *George Dillon*, playing the eternal student; a radiantly beautiful and Russian-looking young actress named Gwyda Donhowe as the spinster sister; and Philip Bosco, who gave a performance as the landowner more honest and powerful than Albert Finney's or James Earl Jones's or Raul Julia's in later and better-known productions in London and New York. As my good mother was to say, a year or two before she died, when I took her to see the all-black version of which Joe Papp and his cohorts at the Public were so proud, "They don't seem very Russian to me."

Naturally, according to Murphy's Law, just as I was happily and enthusiastically plunging into *Orchard* rehearsals, Richard and Harry Joe settled on a theater, the Provincetown on MacDougal Street, and an opening date. The theater was a perfect choice—small, congenial, and loaded with tradition from its Eugene O'Neill days; the opening date was not. It was two days after my *Cherry Orchard* opening on January 12, 1960, a date as fixed and immutable as Zelda herself. I would have to give up *Krapp* or give up *Orchard*—or rehearse both shows simultaneously, one in each city.

Edward took for granted that I would simply walk away from the commitment in Washington. Harry Joe wasn't sure how to deal with the problem, but didn't stop smiling. Richard, with his usual practicality, looked at the cast and the calendar, and came up with an interesting solution. He wanted me, and he was willing to put up with a few logistical problems. Since *Krapp*, after all, consisted of a relatively small cast, one actor and a portable tape recorder, why not bring the cast down to the director instead of bringing the director to the actors? His mother, a dowager lady of some social standing, had an elegant apartment in the Embassy section of Washington. Donald could stay with her quite comfortably, and we could have plenty of room to rehearse. Without, needless to say, any additional expense, Donald's train fare to Washington being the same as my train fare to New York.

As luck would have it, the Christmas and New Year's vacations for the Arena Stage company coincided perfectly with the first previews of *Krapp's Last Tape*, thus affording me the opportunity to be present in New York a few extra days. About a year earlier, I had commuted daily and nightly between *The Summer of the Seventeenth Doll* in Washington and a bill of Thornton Wilder one-acters in Brooklyn, but the stakes hadn't seemed so large. I was extremely grateful for Richard's vision and statesmanship as a producer, as I have been many times since.

Zelda was not entirely happy about my split-focus enterprise. Each day I rehearsed *The Cherry Orchard* for five hours at the Arena, persuading the actors to start a half-hour earlier so I could finish up by four-thirty. Usually I'd meet Donald for dinner somewhere; then, by six-thirty or seven, we'd drive to Richard's mother's apartment where the trusty ancient tape recorder we'd picked up for a few bucks in a Sixth Avenue pawnshop was resting, its single red eye waiting to be ignited. *Krapp* ran about fifty minutes, eventually tightening up a few, with Donald "on" all the time; by about ten o'clock, we were both ready for a beer.

All the show's props, except for the rented swivel chair, fitted easily into a suitcase. On my weekly Arena days off on Mondays, we journeyed to New York to check out the Provincetown stage with Mark Wright, our redoubtable stage manager, see something of the *Zoo Story* rehearsal, and have sound man Gary Harris—whose studio made the top of W. C. Fields' desk look like a vision of order but who was an electronic genius—make us a proper tape for the younger Krapp. That tape was the armature for the entire performance, and Davis's voice, rich and resonant, ultimately made a startling contrast with his wavering crotchety older self.

Donald had insisted that he control the tape recorder himself rather than have the stage manager feeding a control-room tape into the speaker. In the hundreds of performances he eventually played, off-Broadway and on tour, he never had a moment's trouble with his cuing, though every other actor who followed him did, on occasion. The night I watched one of his successors, Herbert Berghof, do the show, the curtain had to be pulled because Herbert got the tape so tangled that he could not go on. Herbert and I have always tangled on Beckett.

After several weeks of this double-shift schedule, I began to enjoy it. Donald came to the final runthroughs of *Orchard*. And the Arena cast grew more and more fascinated by my after-hours goings-on. Neither Richard nor Harry Joe came down to Washington, presumably trusting my regular telephone calls reporting daily progress. As my two opening-night dates converged, however, the pit of my stomach moved closer to my throat. *The Cherry Orchard*'s problems of tone and rhythm are considerable; since it was also my favorite play—I have directed it five times—I was determined to make the Arena version special.

Donald and I worried increasingly about what would be happening in previews to his carefully structured performance once he found himself behind Krapp's real library table, in Krapp's real and squeaking swivel chair, out of my hands and into Richard's and Harry Joe's. Also, I had come up with the idea of a kind of "pool hall" type swinging lamp over Krapp's desk, something not mentioned in the script; and I was concerned about Sam's reaction. When a letter came back saying he liked the idea, I felt it a good omen for the transition to New York, even though I knew that the baby would now have to walk without me for a while.

Once the *Krapp* previews began, I was commuting as often as possible between Washington and New York. I had still to deal with the final runthroughs of *Cherry Orchard* and managed to see all of them, dealing with whatever artistic and technical problems required my attention. Donald was doing very well, and the audience response was excellent. If occasionally his makeup and size made him appear more Italian than Irish, and if his gestures seemed occasionally a shade overtheatrical, his voice was so nuanced and mellifluous as to be almost mesmerizing, his stage business impeccably detailed and true. No wonder that tape never got him into trouble.

I was more worried about what was happening to *Zoo*, which had, in the meantime, changed directors. Milton Katselas, Edward's original choice, had been "let go," and Richard and Edward were somehow sharing the direction between them; Katselas's name remained on the program. I thought William Daniels as Peter was just right, George Maharis as Jerry somewhat unsteady but still compelling; but the production as a whole seemed to lack both form and intensity. Although I had never worked on a bill of one-acts before, I knew that for our evening to succeed, both plays had to work.

Cherry Orchard, with strong performances from Phil Bosco and Mike Lipton, with whom I was staying and sharing midnight hot chocolates, finally opened to an excellent reception. I had demonstrated that I could do Chekhov, which no one in the New York theater ever offered to me. My tale of two cities was half over. That same night I drove back to Westchester, appearing early the next morning at the Provincetown for technical rehearsals. We had only a few light cues, all expertly handled by Mark, who was able to conceal his slim form behind one of our black velours in a cramped corner offstage left. Much against my instincts and desires, the producers had scheduled *Krapp* first on the bill. That didn't help my growing unease. One night I had some words with George Maharis, whose voice I would inevitably hear coming up from the downstairs dressing room while Donald was struggling onstage with his tape recorder and silences. I felt that George enjoyed continuing his characterization as Jerry beyond the proscenium. (As I once told Edward, I considered myself a combination of Jerry and Peter, although I never went on in either role.)

Krapp and Zoo, which was what the evening came to be called, opened at the Provincetown on Thursday, January 14, 1960 and, of course, made off-Broadway and American theater history. Although the reviews were not uniformly ecstatic for both plays—most critics favored one over the other—they were positive enough to keep us going a season or more, moving on to two other theaters, a road tour, and acceptance as major works in the modern theater. The Provincetown had a requirement that any production it housed had to leave for a limited number of weeks each year so that its lessee could put on a show of his own. Otherwise we might be playing there yet.

"After the banalities of Broadway," wrote critic Atkinson, "it tones the muscles and strengthens the system to examine the squalor of off-Broadway . . . one of the few stimulating theater evenings of the season." Other critics had even less trouble finding proper words. "Such an evening doesn't come along very often on or off-Broadway," wrote the *News*. "Genuine and tantalizing," said Walter Kerr in the *Tribune*. The *Post*'s Richard Watts, who became an Albee fan for life (even though John Simon never forgave him for it) added, "Off-Broadway theatre lives up to its highest adventurous principles. An absorbing evening." The *Village Voice*'s Nat Hentoff, slumming from his chores as social commentator, said, "*Krapp's Last Tape* for what it intends, is closer to being perfect than anything else in films or theatre this season except *Wild Strawberries*." And a fellow of whom I had never heard, Tom F. Driver, writing in the *Christian Century*, of all places, said that "*Krapp's Last Tape* is the best theatre now visible in New York." Harold Clurman, the one critic I really respected, even when he didn't like me, never said much about the Beckett play or even mentioned my name, although he thought that Albee's play was "the introduction to what could prove an important talent on the American stage."

Highlight for me of all our fine notices was a paragraph tucked away near the end of Jerry Tallmer's piece in the *Voice*. Jerry made up for the pain he had caused me earlier. "The performance by Donald Davis as Krapp and the staging in every minute particular by Alan Schneider—not least the phenomenal synchronization of living actor and dead voice—is inspired, inspirited, perfect: *the first full realization in America* [italics mine] of a work by Samuel Beckett. Since *Endgame*, I have had strong private reservations about Mr. Schneider's fitness to direct Beckett. I now publicly abandon them." Sam hadn't seemed to be affected by Jerry's apparently dismal view of my work on *Endgame*; he obviously wasn't going to consider me resurrected here. Inspirited, I decided to send him Tallmer's review anyway. If Sam ever read it, he didn't tell me.

With such a response, it was not difficult for the Messrs. Barr, Lutz, and Brown to parlay the production into a big off-Broadway success. We took a flock of prizes and broke *The Iceman Cometh*'s record as the longest running off-Broadway play—*The Fantasticks* hadn't yet started its streak. Richard Barr did something for me no other producer, off-Broadway, on Broadway, or anywhere in the universe, has ever done: he voluntarily doubled my weekly royalty. I was now going to get $50 a week. And I got my first mention ever in *Vogue*'s "People Are Talking About" column. People were talking about "the extraordinarily astute collaboration between Samuel Beckett, who wrote *Krapp's Last Tape*, Alan Schneider who directed it, and Donald Davis who plays the solo role."

What pleased me even more was the announcement, almost simultaneously with our opening, of the closing after five performances of a Broadway venture called *A Distant Bell*, a new play starring Martha Scott. I had nothing against the play, and I had forgotten my old tangle with Miss Scott. It was just that I had told Lucy to turn it down so that I could direct *Krapp*. For the first time in a very long while, I had actually done something right

BECKETT TO ALBEE TO CHANCE

1960–1961

The success of *Krapp and Zoo* gave me a new lift and a new image; I was "an off-Broadway director." Suddenly I realized that I liked the shape and scale that this description represented. I liked working in this less frenzied, more intellectually and emotionally stimulating, and at the same time more intimate theater. I had not been at home on Broadway, even though I knew that the large rewards still rested there. But I did not know how to survive in that rather rancid jungle, though I had managed to hack out a path for myself. On the other side, I had been very happy at the Arena, but neither the level of the work nor the recognition possible there satisfied me often enough. After my three efforts off-Broadway, *Endgame, Doll,* and *Krapp,* I regretted not having come upon the scene earlier, envying those of my peers and colleagues who had put out more or less permanent roots, such as José Quintero at his Circle in the Square, Joe Papp and his Shakespeare in the Park, even David Ross and his attempts at Chekhov, which I felt were in no way superior to what I was able to do. Now I felt, at least partially, at home. The only sad fact was that it was not possible to make a living directing off-Broadway. I had to support two kids and a wife; we had outgrown the pram but that hallway was still there.

Things weren't too bad that year. I managed to stay in New York—by leaving it once in a while. With both *Summer of the Seventeenth Doll* and *Krapp's Last Tape* running, I at least seemed to be relatively solvent, highly in demand, and able to pick and choose from a few alternatives. I went to Boston University to direct Sidney Kingsley's *Detective Story.*

I went to Florida again, this time to the Royal Poinciana in Palm Beach to direct *Two for the Seesaw* with Kim Stanley (who evidently needed some money fast) and Kevin McCarthy—an engagement arranged by Lucy Kroll, with whom I still had a sort of informal relationship. I had never worked with Kim but I knew her from the Studio and from seeing a lot of her in London in 1958 while she was there playing *Cat on a Hot Tin Roof*. Kim was totally miscast as Gittel, but managed to be wonderful anyhow. We were getting along beautifully, and I was amazed at how effective she was. Three days before we were to open, Kim walked out, saying that she just could not bring herself to play something for which she knew in her heart she was not right. I wanted to kill her, but underneath I couldn't bring myself entirely to blame her. We had to go on with Kim's understudy, a talented youngster named Mary Tahmin, who was plucky but nowhere near as good, and an unexpectedly stalwart performance from Kevin. But Florida still jinxed me, and I was glad to get home. I did *Twelve Angry Men* at the Bucks County Playhouse with a wonderful cast. Reginald Rose, its author, said it had never been done better. There were lots of meetings with Reggie and various producers' talk about "bringing it in," but nothing happened. The actors played it very well for two weeks and then went back to New York to look for other jobs.

That summer, Joe Papp, who had once wanted me to direct George C. Scott and Colleen Dewhurst in *Antony and Cleopatra*, only to be preempted by my command-performance field trip for "Mac" Lowry and the Ford Foundation, came back to me. For his summer in Central Park he asked me to do *Measure for Measure*, not my favorite Shakespeare but a good opportunity to demonstrate my classical strengths in New York. Gerald Freedman was directing *The Taming of the Shrew*, which I would have preferred. But I felt that I could not turn down either Shakespeare or Joe twice in a row, and said yes.

I cast the production with Joe sitting beside me and guiding every choice, but I did manage to get in a few of my own. Most of the actors and even the scene designer, Eldon Elder, came with the territory; but I did contribute Theoni Aldredge, who had never worked with Joe before. Theoni got herself a lifetime job; as it turned out, I didn't, although the show came off well on all counts, including the most spectacular curtain call I've ever choreographed. I was then in my Stratford (Ontario) phase and determined to outdo both Tyrone Guthrie and Michael Langham, at least in my curtain call.

I respected Joe immensely, but we didn't always agree. My biggest disagreement with him, as I remember, came over the hiring of Phil Bosco—my grand Lopahin of the previous season—whom I wanted for Angelo. I lured a very reluctant Phil up from Washington, where he was quite content to stay forever, to audition, and he seemed heaven-sent. Joe kept objecting and suggesting other actors. I could not understand why until years later. Although offstage Phil talked like a New Jersey truck driver, which was much closer to his real personality, onstage he sounded just like John Gielgud. Joe was trying to develop an American approach to speaking Shakespeare, and didn't want someone who spoke too well. Determined to get Phil, I stuck to my vowel sounds, and Joe eventually gave in, forcing me, in return, to take Mariette Hartley as Isabella and then blaming me for what he came to consider an inadequate performance.

My second basic difference of opinion with Joe had to do with the casting of Lucio, the fop. From the start, Joe had wanted Roscoe Lee Browne. I thought Frederic Warriner was better suited. I got Warriner, but I should have taken Roscoe Lee, whom I couldn't quite see fitting because he happened to be black. It was a great lesson. I did manage to round up a cast of enterprising comics, especially Christine Pickles, Tom Wheatley, and John Call, as well as two attractive and sexy subplot ladies, Kathleen Widdoes and Lori March. And I was glad to give the part of the Executioner to a young actor I had once taught in an acting class at the American Theatre Wing back when I was unemployed. It was his first association with the New York Shakespeare Festival. He also happened to be black; his name was James Earl Jones.

We opened on July 25, 1960. The critics, on the whole, were more than favorable. *The New York Times* for some reason sent its Sunday columnist, Lewis Funke, who said that it was "An absorbing and riveting play . . . pierced by the lightning." The *Post* termed us a "handsome and exciting production. This is as good a *Measure* as you are likely to see. Don't miss it." The production had its good moments even though it didn't lead to much. It was my first Shakespeare in many years, and I tried to give it both vitality and a measure of humanity. Theoni's costumes were among her best ever. I enjoyed working outside again, all those years after Cain Park—although I didn't resurrect my whistle and pith helmet. But it was, ultimately, a somewhat frustrating experience. Joe and I were both too strong-willed to get along. I never worked for him again, although we maintain an intermittent acquaintanceship. He once asked me to do *Hamlet* with Frank Langella, but Frank, who was wary of the venture, withdrew when Joe made too preliminary an announcement. Years later, Joe provided a place where the Juilliard Theatre Center, which I then headed, could extend Liviu Ciulei's highly acclaimed production of Wedekind's *Spring Awakening* when Juilliard's reigning monarch, Peter Mennin, refused.

I have always found Joe easier to deal with at a distance than in closeup. He has always kept his word to me, even without a written contract. He gave me my entire fee for the *Hamlet* that didn't happen. For *Spring Awakening*, he raised part of the production budget and gave Juilliard every dollar of its unexpected profits. When our plans to do Beckett's *Rockaby* and *Ohio Impromptu* with Billie Whitelaw and David Warrilow were aborted by Equity's refusal to accept Billie's international credentials, Joe handled himself with dignity and eloquence, especially at the arbitration proceedings. I believe he has both taste and vision, and I have the highest respect for him as a man of the theater.

No sooner done with Mr. Shakespeare than I was called back to Mr. Beckett, this time to do a television version of *Waiting for Godot* for Public Television's Play-of-the-Week. This was a new step in television programming, the idea being to do the same dramatic program at the same time each evening for a week. My fee was $750. Joining the Directors' Guild of America, which I had to in order to direct, cost me $2000. I didn't entirely mind, once I figured out how I could raise that much, because membership would enable me to continue in both film and television work. What I minded was that I didn't get paid all of my $750 by producers David Susskind and Ely Landau of Talent Associates until DGA went to arbitration. Even then, I wound up with dribs and drabs for years afterward.

I'm not sure that Sam Beckett really wanted a television *Godot* done at all, although Barney Rosset saw it as a possible source of high revenue and talked him into permitting the presentation. Sam has consistently turned down all sorts of film offers for his work. He insists that he writes for the stage and does not feel that his material translates into any other medium. I am certain that he did not approve of the producers' original idea to use Rayburn and Finch, two early-morning radio personalities, as Vladimir and Estragon. Eventually, after trying for Bob Hope and Jack Benny, Laurel and Hardy, Sid Caesar, Milton Berle, and a few other reliables, they agreed to my somewhat more prosaic but possible choices: Burgess Meredith and Zero Mostel. Kurt Kasznar and Alvin Epstein repeated their original Broadway roles. I don't think the television people were too happy having me as director, but Beckett and Rosset gave them no choice.

For the first time in my television career, I decided to do the camerawork myself, with a solid and experienced associate director, Eddie Waglin, helping me to keep the cables unclogged. We worked for three weeks down at the Second Avenue Studios, always packed with incoming productions. Burgess was well cast as Didi, the thoughtful, constantly confused but striving professor. And Zero, except when he was cutting up, made Gogo a great sympathetic struggling blob of humanity; as a comic actor he was in the Bert Lahr league—but he understood the play and knew exactly what he was doing. Together, they were uproarious and moving. Everything was going well until the day we got into the studio for our two days of technical rehearsal and shooting. The show was, as then customary, done live, with just enough time for a full camera rehearsal and one dress rehearsal before the broadcast. There was no time for experiment—or error.

Our five-hour camera rehearsal proved more difficult and uncertain than anyone had anticipated. My inexperience didn't help, although it was not the only factor. The second day, we had another five hours, just enough for a "dress" and then "on the air." Burgess, who had slowed things down considerably the day before by not knowing either his lines or his moves, didn't show up at the time scheduled. We milled around and waited, finally telephoning him and discovering that he was not exactly in shape. By the time he arrived in the studio, we were frantic. Whether he had had a bit too much, was tired or just plain scared, I don't know; normally somewhere in the clouds, he was now way off in outer space. He insisted that he could not go on without cue cards. We said that was impossible. He got cue cards, hastily made up by someone who hadn't read the play. We staggered through our "dress," Burgess always about to collapse and Zero grown gravely serious. I have always been capable—too capable—of hot anger. That technical crew—its hopes for something special and poetic smashed by Burgess' sudden erratic behavior—was collective ice; they could have disemboweled him with pleasure.

Having no alternative, I proceeded with the show, trying to compose the shots as planned and pretending that Burgess was not looking at the cue cards. Even now I am amazed that any portion of it came off at all. The production was reasonably well reviewed, the performances praised even when the play was termed (as usual) "baffling." Barney bought a kinescope, transposed it into film, and has carried on a fairly lucrative business sending it around the colleges. He advertises it as "a film by Alan Schneider," driving me into quiet hysteria. I've heard of feature-length films being shot in weeks, perhaps even days, but never in hours. Especially with cue cards.

Life went from bad to worse on the next one, my almost-return to Broadway. Somewhere in my academic past, probably at Cornell, I had formed a strong attachment to Benn Levy's popular comedy *Springtime for Henry*, in which comedian Edward Everett Horton had made more summertime farewell tours than Sarah Bernhardt. Out of the blue came an offer for me to direct on Broadway Benn Levy's recent London hit, *The Rape of the Belt*. His wife, Constance Cummings, a classically beautiful American actress with whom I had fallen in love years earlier when I saw her in films, was to play the lead. The play itself, akin to an earlier piece called *The Warrior's Husband*, was a lightweight comedy about Amazons. It was possible in London—where Miss Cummings, Kay Hammond, and John Clements had pulled it off—but had no real chance in New York's harsher climate. Much against everyone's opinions and my own conscience and common sense, I agreed to do it. Benn Levy and Constance Cummings were too much of a combination to turn down.

Playwright Levy being bedridden at the time, I went to London to spend some time with him and Connie, get some rewriting done, and talk about the New York cast. Benn was one of the gentlest and most generous persons I'd ever met; we hit it off very well, and soon developed what I considered a close relationship. Connie had never had a hit in New York, and Benn wanted her to have it with *Belt*. His physical condition was worsening and he had to enter a hospital; he was afraid that this would stop her from going. Torn between my professional desire for Connie and my human feeling that she should be with her husband, I urged a postponement of the show. The producers were either unable or unwilling. Shuttling between the Levy home and his room in the hospital, I found myself emotionally ground to pieces by a dilemma neither could resolve. Benn grew more and more haggard, Connie more strained in her indecision.

After a week of this, she decided, heeding his last appeal, to do the show. I flew back to New York to complete our casting. Unfortunately, Kay Hammond was also ill, with the beginnings of the disease that eventually killed her. We were able to get Joyce Redman, a pert, delightful redhead both onstage and off. In addition, we got accomplished American performers Peggy Wood and John Emery as Hera and Zeus, and my now constant Phil Bosco as a brash and highly contemporary Herakles. Again, apart from the occasional thoughts of poor Benn languishing in a London hospital, rehearsals were a delight. Never have I been more enamored of my leading ladies. Joyce was always aglow and ready with a barroom tale; Connie, having played her role in London, was of course way ahead of everyone else. Offstage she looked as though she had stepped out of a cologne bottle; onstage she was equally delectable. I tried not to tinker with her performance too much because she was obviously doing what Benn wanted her to do; but would, occasionally, make suggestions, to all of which she responded enthusiastically. She never failed to tell me how much better the show was looking here than it had been in London, and how helpful I was being to her and to everyone else. The heartfelt and encouraging letters from Benn, slowly weakening though he was, reinforced my determination to go all out for him. He was already, he said, writing another play for Connie and me to do together.

Our premiere at the Boston tryout was a nightmare. During a final preview, Phil—who had been impressing both ladies with his performance but who had perhaps gotten a bit carried away with his athletic prowess—misjudged his jump off a fairly high wall and seriously injured one leg. For our opening, we had the choice of a hopelessly effeminate understudy or a Herakles on crutches. Always going with the actor, I chose the latter, and I made an explanatory pre-curtain speech that was as painful to me as Phil's leg must have been to him. Compared to my performance, Knute Rockne between halves was stone. How anyone survived that night, I don't know.

I do know that I didn't survive the morning. Our reviews were ambivalent, the wrong way. They liked parts of the show, especially those involving Joyce Redman; they didn't like others, especially those involving Constance Cummings. Less ambivalent was an early morning phone call from the producer's suite: Connie had been up since dawn trying to find another director. She wanted to get rid of me at once. To this day, I'm not sure that Benn concurred or whether she ever told him. The producers, on the other hand, had no intention of letting me go. They just wanted me to know what was going on—and to get back to work.

Of all the times I have felt like getting out of the theater or never again having anything to do with theater people, this was probably the worst. Mary Martin had done the same thing, but my relationship to Mary had been a superficial one. During the *Godot* fiasco in Miami, Bert Lahr had given me all the trouble, but then I had not been too easy for him either. Connie was not only an actress whose work I admired and whose person I adored; she was supposedly a friend, someone who had confided in me. She and I had shared in her husband's anguish and deepest hopes. To be tossed aside by her without even a word, because a critic or two had not appreciated her performance, loomed as a betrayal I could neither understand nor survive. To continue as director with her no longer wanting me was impossible.

I was on the next train to New York, and no amount of persuasion from the producers was sufficient to get me back. They signed up Albert Marre. Phil's leg got better, but the show evidently didn't. It closed almost as soon as it opened. I never saw Connie again until years later when she was suggested as (and became) a replacement for Uta Hagen in the London *Virginia Woolf.* Neither of us ever mentioned our previous acquaintance.

My life and sanity were saved by a telephone call from Edward Albee. Would I like to direct his new one-act, *The American Dream,* which Richard Barr (with a new partner, Clinton Wilder) was doing on a double bill, alongside Edward's adaptation of a Melville story, *Bartleby the Scrivener,* off-Broadway, at the York Theatre? I had a hard time holding back my shout. Why me? Because Edward had watched me during the *Krapp* rehearsals and liked the way I had seemed to respect the author's words and intentions. He was sure I'd do the same with his play. Who was directing *Bartleby?* It was actually an opera, with music by his close friend, composer Bill Flanagan. Bill had been the one responsible for getting *Zoo Story* on; he'd sent it to David Diamond, who had sent it to someone in Berlin who arranged a production at the Schiller Theatre; Bill Flanagan had a director friend, William Penn. Enough said.

I was delighted and touched by Edward's offer, and looked forward to working with him, Richard, and Clinton, a very pleasant gentleman also. The only conflict was that I was scheduled to do another one of my Ford Foundation productions at the enterprising Actors' Workshop in San Francisco. This time there was no conflict with dates, so long as Edward thought that two weeks of rehearsal plus whatever previews would be enough. He did. We shook hands, metaphorically, over the phone; and I went off to talk about the set with Bill Ritman, from *Krapp and Zoo.*

Before I left for San Francisco in early December, we were able to cast *Dream,* using people either Edward or I knew well. Sudie Bond, a young actress who could look eighty, had already played Grandma in an off-off-Broadway workshop of *Sandbox.* John C. Becher would be Daddy, an "avocado blob," in Edward's words, and Gladys Hurlbut, a fine character actress whom I did not know, was to be Mommy. Jane Hoffman from the Actors Studio was Mrs. Barker, née Stern, but soon changed to Barker to remove any "ethnic" connotation. Tom Hunter, a young friend of Edward's, was to be The Young Man.

With the *Dream* script close at hand, I took off for San Francisco's Actors' Workshop to direct *Twinkling of an Eye*, a new play by Hamilton Wright and Guy Andros, about a crazy family in the tropics preparing for a nuclear holocaust. The script had come to me from Audrey Wood, and I had been able to talk the Workshop's directors, Jules Irving and Herbert Blau, into letting me do it, although they were not entirely enthusiastic about its virtues. Having heard so much about the Workshop's experimental work, I wanted to see what they were all about.

Herb met me at the airport, sorry that I'd just missed his production of *Endgame*, which he had not previously mentioned to me. It had run, he proudly explained, three hours, the implication being that it would have been even better if it had run four. He was about to embark on a contemporary *King Lear*, which at the same pace, I figured, should run about three days. I began to worry what I'd gotten myself into. Would *Twinkling* seem too short?

The Workshop, highly touted on the West Coast and now beginning to carry weight with the more "intellectual" critics in the East, although many of them had not seen its work, seemed to me to be almost totally disorganized. Compared to Zelda's tight ship at Arena, it was a derelict. My stage manager, who Jules had told me was "the best in the world," was a nice-guy amateur at best. The entire technical staff was idiosyncratic, to put it mildly. Productions—and *Twinkling* was a complicated one—were more or less slapped together. No wonder *Endgame* had run three hours. On top of which, the acting roster was rigidly split between their regular company, most of whom had daytime jobs in San Francisco, and a recent New York contingent brought in at $200 per week by the Ford Foundation's largesse. The two sides were literally not speaking to each other.

Obviously a metaphor of something or other, probably the decline of the West, *Twinkling* remained elusive to both groups, as well as to its director. The rehearsal period this time around was far from happy. I seemed to be spending more time listening to actors' complaints about the script and each other than rehearsing. I did manage to give the resident ingenue some advice about getting into films, in which I thought she might do better than she was doing in the theater. Her name was and still is Katharine Ross. And I met a very interesting young character actress, Ruth Maleczech, who played a small role in *Twinkling*, as well as her husband, Lee Breuer, whom I was able sincerely to encourage. Lee, without much help, attention, or budget from either Jules or Herb, did an imaginative laboratory staging of Brecht's *Chalk Circle*. Both Christmas and New Year's, spent in one of those tiny drab residential hotels in downtown San Francisco, were lonely and blue. So were most of the days in between. Jules was friendly but not really there when I needed him. Herb was very serious.

As I recall, Ham Wright came out and changed a few lines. But the play's riddle proved unsolvable by us, and its reception was as unfortunate as everyone had been predicting. I think Jules and Herb were not entirely unhappy that this intrusion from New York had not come off. Both of them had read *The American Dream* and didn't think much of that either. I could hardly wait to get on the plane for New York.

As luck would have it, the day that I was coming—just in time for *Dream*'s first rehearsal—San Francisco was fogged in. I rang Edward from the airport, suggesting that he run things, just reading the play once or twice, saying something nice to the actors afterward, and letting them go home.

"Please," I told him, "just let the actors read the play and, for heaven's sake, don't discuss it or say anything profound. Whatever you do, don't *explain* anything! Just tell them they are great and send them home. I promise you I'll be there tomorrow."

Nervous and excited, this being his first new venture since *The Zoo Story*—and not entirely sure the fog wasn't my fault—Edward agreed to do exactly as I had asked.

That afternoon, I flew off, happily, to New York. At the airport, both Edward and Richard were waiting for me in a hired car. Considering the expression on their faces, it could have been a hearse. I inquired about the long looks. They waited until we were on the freeway, then explained that Gladys Hurlbut had just quit as Mommy.

"What do you mean, quit?" I asked. "She just started. What happened? Did she get a better job?"

"No, I don't think so," Edward said quietly. "No, she didn't. She just said she didn't want to be in the play. After the reading . . . which went very well," he added.

"What did you do today?" I finally asked, as we sped closer and closer to ground zero.

Edward, as though speaking to a child, told me. "We read the play, and I told them how great they were." Then, looking straight at me, "Exactly as you told me."

I gulped.

"Then they asked some questions."

My head came up. "Questions?"

"Yes. And I didn't answer them."

Aha, I thought. "Did you say anything at all to Mommy?"

That did it. "Well, no . . . All I said was that Mommy was a tumescent monster." Edward seemed immensely pleased with that description.

I knew exactly what had happened. Gladys Hurlbut had gone home after the rehearsal and looked up "tumescent" in Webster's. Discovering, no doubt, that it meant "bloated," "glowing with sexual desire in the dark," something repellent to her sensitive nature, she had decided to withdraw. She didn't want to play anything tumescent, monster or otherwise. She wouldn't even answer her phone when I called her.

The incident, laughable as it now seems, is a perfect example of a playwright's tendency to be too logical, exact, and unsubtly graphic with actors, the results not always accomplishing his noble intention: to explain exactly what he meant. I would never have told any actress that Mommy was a "tumescent monster"; that is a phrase for the critics to use later. I would simply have suggested (as I later did) that Edward's Mommy should treat everyone else as though he or she did not exist, that she should always talk louder than anyone else, that she should never listen to the other characters, that she should have contempt for them all, that she should, perhaps, want them all to disappear. In effect, I would hope, this would be telling her something which might help to make her a most "tumescent monster" indeed. Especially if we had cast her well.

Failing to "detumesce" Gladys, we reshuffled the cast we had. Jane Hoffman became Mommy, much to her satisfaction and ultimately ours. Another very capable actress, Nancy Cushman, who was understudying, was thrust into the role of Mrs. Barker and subsequently gave a definitive performance. After a day or two in which we developed a growing uncertainty about Tom Hunter's ability to play the Young Man, I was able to persuade Edward to accept Ben Piazza, who had been so good in *Kataki*. In fact, we came out of the woods much stronger than we had gone in. Thank you, Gladys; thank you, Edward; but, please, don't do it again.

Bill Ritman's setting, a simple formal arrangement of arches and some heavy gilt and brocade furniture, proved most amenable to my staging, the actors to my directions. I got the idea of hanging up some empty picture frames, a bit symbolic but funny. After only eleven days of rehearsal, I think, including previews, we were in shape to open. The show was funny with a bite, and ended with some strong emotion. Our reviews, in sharp contrast to *Bartleby*'s, were uniformly good. "Caustic and hilarious," quoth the *Times*. "Should be seen by all," said the *Journal-American*. Richard Watts, now firmly behind Edward, wrote that the play was "packed with untamed imagination, wild humor, gleefully sardonic satirical implications and overtones of strangely touching sadness, and I thought it was entirely delightful." Walter Kerr, a trifle more cautious, said, "Those who are following the young playwright's finger-poking progress will want to incorporate this one into their travels."

There were lots of others like that, all beautiful to behold at that moment, no matter how faded the clippings may have grown. I often wonder, though, whether Edward might have been better off not to have wowed all those critics so violently and so early in his career. Harold Clurman, that combination of showman and wise man, put the matter very well in his *Nation* article: "It is dangerous to make 'stars' of playwrights while they are in the process of growth; nor should our attention consist of slaughtering the playwright's second or third play on behalf of the hallowed first one." Tennessee Williams and William Inge as well as a flock of other not-so-young playwrights would, I think, agree. Perhaps even an older Edward Albee.

From my own directorial point of view, I found *American Dream* a charming and well crafted "cartoon" detailing the decay of American virtues and values, and amazingly prophetic in certain of its insights. Where it failed for me—or I for it—was in Edward's inability to blend the more somber stylization of the Young Man with the other highly colored comic-strip characters. Grandma exists on yet another level, but as narrator and author's *raisonneur* and favorite she generally gets away with most of it. I could never say this to Edward directly. Nor did those feelings affect my own desire or ability to direct his play, which I liked and admired. If I had spoken out, my feelings might have affected his. That's why I kept silent at the time, perhaps to the play's and his own detriment. He now has my apology.

WAITING FOR ALBEE
1961–1962

The American Dream opened in January 1961. I was not to direct another play by Edward until almost two years later, October 1962. In between, came what was probably the most continuously active period of my directing career, highly productive if not always highly remunerative, a stormy calm before that very calm storm that was *Virginia Woolf.* I put on more than twenty plays in about as many months, not only shuttling between my two fixed points of New York and Washington but working in Chicago, Long Island, Wisconsin, and California. If I had come to New York as the poor man's Logan, I was now rapidly developing into the poor man's Tyrone Guthrie.

Included in all this activity were two world premieres—one by Samuel Beckett—my first Pinter production, and an assortment of American and European classics. The problems and crises with which I was confronted were considerable, far beyond financial reward or career advancement. Yet I must admit to feeling more in control, more secure of my inner self as well as of my craft, more "on the way" than I had ever been before—or since. Without knowing it, I was waiting for something big to happen, and filling in the time in between.

The period started with a complete debacle. After the success of *Dream*, not only the Beckett imitators but almost all of the Albee followers began to send me their scripts. Jack Richardson, whose *The Prodigal* had attracted considerable attention, came to me with his *Gallows Humor*, which Richard Barr was going to produce; and for a while it seemed that I would be directing it. Jack Gelber offered me *The Connection*, which

I had seen in its original Living Theatre version, to direct in London, largely with the original cast. As I indiscreetly proclaimed to my wife one day, I now had the ruling off-Broadway playwriting trio, Albee, Gelber, and Richardson, all coming to me with plays. Pride, as always, comes before the fall.

Having appreciated the Living's *Connection* even when I hated it, I chose Gelber and London. This kind of "théâtre vérité" appealed to me after the stylization with which I had most recently been involved. But no sooner had I started to rehearse at the St. Martin's Theatre—an environment, by the way, that could not have been more wrong—than I began to realize that Gelber did not want me to direct his play at all. Everything we had talked about in one Village bar after another, the changes I wanted to make from what had been done in New York, he dismissed with contempt. All he wanted was an exact copy of before, which I would not and could not give him.

The first weekend of our rehearsals, I was confined to bed with the flu (caused, no doubt, by the lack of central heating). I had sneaked out to see Peter Coe's production of *Oliver* at the New Theatre nearby, and was especially enraptured with Sean Kenny's huge architectural settings. When I got back to my hotel there was a note from producer Seymour Hacker, saying that my assistant, Nicholas Garland, was "taking over." No reason given. No word from Jack.

I always felt, though I could never prove it in a court of law, that the whole scabby scheme had been a setup. Jack had wanted to direct his own show in the first place. British Equity wouldn't give him permission because he had no standing as a director. I did, so they let me in. Once we were there, Jack took over, using Garland as his front. No matter what I did during rehearsals, I wasn't going to be kept on. My philosophical friend and bubblingly informal agent, Margaret Ramsay—who knows more about scripts and, perhaps, theater people than anybody alive, even Audrey Wood—kept reassuring me that it didn't matter, I'd get another one. I got on the next plane for New York, regretting only that the refund on my ticket had to go to the producer, who had bought the original.

What compounded my disappointment was the realization that my London fiasco had in addition cost me the opportunity of directing *The Death of Bessie Smith*, which had been chosen by Edward and Richard to replace *Bartleby* on Theatre 1961's double bill at the York. They got Lawrence Arrick to direct it instead. This was the first of many times during the ensuing association when I was expected to keep myself available for something from them—as "most favored director," Richard used to call me. And the first of many times when, no matter how hard I tried, I wasn't.

Dream and *Bessie* continued at the York, gaining momentum and strength and new kudos. No new plays were offered to me that I cared about, either for off-Broadway or Broadway. I went off into the hinterlands.

The hinterlands, that spring and summer, included almost simultaneous productions of *Krapp's Last Tape* at the Arena—Sam Beckett remaining unable to understand how it was possible to do his play without a proscenium arch framing it—and my first *Uncle Vanya*, at Chicago's Goodman Theatre, then under the artistic leadership of John, née Johann, Reich, who had studied with Max Reinhardt in Vienna and had tramped New York's streets with me in those good old 1948–49 days when we couldn't get anyone to hire us. I had seen an especially beautiful production of *Vanya* done by the Moscow Art Theatre in its London visit back in 1958, and had since then found my interest in the play increasing steadily.

My *Vanya* production was, I suppose, reasonably standard college level. Goodman then employed the guest-star system, and we had Walter Abel—whose "starving artist" role I had once played in the Washington Civic Theatre's *Merrily We Roll Along*—but Walter wasn't that much better than several of the kids. What distinguished and made the whole attempt worthwhile for me was casting the role of Sonya with a young actress named Linda Dillon, who was a senior acting student at Goodman as well as an understudy and hanger-on with a Second City troupe that included two young performers named Barbara Harris and Alan Arkin.

During our tryouts, John had seriously tried to discourage me from using Linda. He admitted her talent but warned me that she was highly volatile and completely unpredictable as an actress. He had another actress whom he found much more suitable for Sonya. I insisted on using Linda, no matter the consequences. I was fascinated by the combination of her fragility and sensuality, intrigued with the unconventional way in which she was able to make a line seem utterly spontaneous, and impressed with her emotional range and richness. During our four weeks of rehearsal, interrupted by flying visits to Washington to cope with Donald Davis in the round, I wound up alternately adoring and hating Linda. She always did too much and yet not enough. She was never the same twice in a given scene, even when she had found something wonderful last time. She was always wanting to quit the cast or leave school or kill herself. And yet, at the same time, I felt she was extraordinary, the most talented young American actress I'd ever worked with, the potential peer of Geraldine Page and perhaps even Kim Stanley. I was sure she'd be a big star one day, and I wanted to be with her when that happened.

Two other university theater productions followed, Ionesco's *Bald Soprano* and my perennial favorite, Thornton Wilder's *Pullman Car Hiawatha*, at Hofstra College; and another Ionesco, *The Chairs*, a dramatization of Shirley Jackson's *The Lottery*, and John Mortimer's *Dock Brief* at the University of Wisconson–Milwaukee. All the short plays seemed to come off well though not world-shakingly. A very shy Paul Shenar, later to distinguish himself at William Ball's American Conservatory Theatre as Julian in *Tiny Alice* among other roles, played a tiny part rather well, in *The Lottery*. The hinterlands were fun but ultimately not satisfying enough. I came back to New York convinced that the best work I could do had to be done there, off-Broadway.

As fate would have it, Sam Beckett had just informed me that he had written another new play in English. It was called either *Many Mercies* or *Tender Mercies*, he wasn't sure which. Would I be interested in directing it—for the first time anywhere? Would I? I went immediately to Richard and Clinton. They were willing, sight unseen, to present its world premiere at the Cherry Lane. I flew off to Paris for my usual preproduction talks with the playwright, thanking Sam for his many and tender mercies to me.

When I got there, Sam invited me to his apartment to read the new play; presumably he did not want to let the manuscript out of the house. Excited by the honor of that rare invitation, I must confess that I was less excited by my first reading. Somehow the script did not satisfy my expectations of what Sam's next play would be. Like *Krapp* it had been first written in English instead of French; unlike *Krapp* its leading character was female. What I was surprised to find and did not feel happy about was a leading character delivering what was practically a monologue while at the same time being confined to one place on the stage. After *Krapp's Last Tape*, with its realistic tone and copious possibilities for stage movement and business, that seemed to be going too far in the other direction.

Not that I ever expressed any of this reservation to Sam, or even completely to myself. By this time, I knew that any Beckett play would be unusual, unexpected, surprising, and stretching the fabric of drama even more tautly in some direction. With the author quietly and presumably nervously reading something in another room, I sat in Sam's modest study, surrounded by his books and a few small prints on his walls, turning the pages of his manuscript, letting the words and rhythms flow over me. I cannot say that the script had the same immediate impact on me that *Endgame* had. But about the third time through I realized that there might be a great deal more on each page—of poetry, of truth, even of laughs—than I was yet able to perceive.

This was the first time I had been present this early in the gestation period of one of his scripts, and Sam asked for my opinion on two questions he had not yet settled. For Winnie's music box tune at the end, he had not yet decided between two alternatives: "When Irish Eyes Are Smiling" and "The Merry Widow Waltz." Which one did I prefer? I tossed that one around for a while before telling Sam that I thought the "Irish Eyes" lyrics were a bit too much on the nose. I liked the schmaltz of "The Merry Widow." Perhaps it was overly sentimental. But in the context of Winnie's unusual circumstances, perhaps the sentiment would seem justified or, at least, suitably ironic. Sam agreed. "The Merry Widow Waltz" it would be, for eternity.

He also was not sure about which title to give it: *Many Mercies* or *Tender Mercies*, or (a new thought he had had recently) *Happy Days*. I could answer that at once. Again, it was the ironic significance of the latter title, its double or even triple overtones, that made me tell Sam he had to call the new play *Happy Days*. I think he felt that might be a little pat, but he did take my suggestion. *Happy Days* it was to be, as long as the English language existed. Luckily, I wasn't thinking about that at the time. When, years later, Robert Duvall made a film called *Tender Mercies*, I wondered if he knew that Samuel Beckett had preceded him.

In between my several readings and lunch with Sam and Suzanne (whom he had not yet married but with whom he had been living for years), we talked about the production as well, especially the size, location, and construction of the mound of earth and Winnie's various positions in it. Also, Willie's position. Also, the backdrop. Sam was most anxious that the color and design of the background would suggest the ultimate in blazing light. He also wanted a trompe l'oeil effect to represent that expanse of unbroken plain and sky surrounding Winnie and receding to infinity. He even drew me a number of very charming pen-and-ink sketches detailing exactly where and how the actress playing Winnie would be positioned during each of her two acts.

I realized that Sam was continuing to explore the possibilities of the actor's art—to see how much could be done, not only while the performer's mobility was denied but even with a diminishing presence. I also knew that most good actresses, especially those capable of playing Winnie, would be terrified of having to perform a monologue as long as Hamlet's entire role, while stuck up to their waist and then to their neck in a pile of stage earth. Willie was another matter. I could think of a large number of actors who could accept a part with only a few lines and the audience seeing only the back of their head most of the evening. But Winnie . . . ? Maximal pause.

Again, I kept all these thoughts at the edge of my mind, preferring to continue my exploration of the script's virtues, finding new layers on each page. Somehow, I felt that Sam had a special affection for this play. And I kept remembering, even though he never mentioned the fact, that for the first time in our relationship as author and director he had entrusted me with a world premiere. I asked him all the questions that occurred to me at the moment, but I knew it was going to be very special and very difficult.

Sam drove me back to Invalides in his "*deux chevaux*" Citroën to catch my bus for the plane. A few more questions along the way. We were both nervous, and we both knew it. I asked him once more if he might possibly come over for rehearsals. Richard and Clinton, I was sure, would pay his way and put him up. (I wasn't sure.) There were the usual farewells and handclasps, Sam's final by now ritualistic "Do it ahny way you like, Alan." The last sight of him, his great gray shock of hair bobbing from side to side as he walked away. Would he ever talk to me again after I had directed *Happy Days* for the first time in the world?

Upon my return to New York with a copy of the script, I got together with Richard and Clinton to make plans for the production. The two, collectively known as Theatre 1962, were riding high as off-Broadway impresarios, with *Krapp's Last Tape* and *Zoo Story* running now at the East End Theatre and a planned repertory of *The American Dream* and *The Death of Bessie Smith* at the Cherry Lane. *Happy Days* was slated to join that repertory. *Happy Days*, I soon discovered, did not have as many performances scheduled at the Cherry Lane as its other two inhabitants, but I did not believe myself to be in any position to object. Besides, I figured that once we had opened, the number would soon change.

William Ritman, of *Krapp* and *Dream*, was again going to be our designer. I talked to him about what Sam wanted, showed him the sketches, and decided with him about the exact shape and dimensions of the mound. The setting was, as usual with a Beckett play, simple but loaded with booby traps: a parasol that had to burst into fire at the right moment; a music box that played "The Merry Widow Waltz" loud enough to be heard; a mound that was big enough and high enough to hide Willie but still let us see his shoulders. We built a beautifully shaped and textured mound; our public relations department, of course, had us shoot photographs before the mound was painted and tufted with grass—which eventually appeared on the cover of the published play. For years people asked me why our mound looked like that. It didn't.

We found our Willie without any problem. He was John C. Becher, *American Dream*'s Daddy, and perfect. Winnie was another story. We thought about a number of actresses, from Helen Hayes—who wasn't interested—to Jane Hoffman and Nancy Cushman of the *Dream* cast—but I wanted someone with greater individuality and a larger flair. At some point we hit upon Ruth White, a wonderful actress who was known to all of us for her special combination of pathos and humor, who was available, and who might be interested if we could explain the play to her in the proper way.

I gave Ruth the script, assuring her that I didn't entirely understand it either, but that with Beckett one always figured things out along the way. The thing to do was trust the material and try not to worry too much about what it "meant." Ruth was interested but scared. At the time, a play like *Happy Days*—even coming after *Godot* and *Endgame* and *Krapp*—was uncharted territory inhabited by a tribe of demons. Those demons almost made her turn down our offer. But her basic curiosity and acting instincts, as well as the combined persuasiveness of Messrs. Barr, Wilder, and Schneider—not to mention Edward Albee lurking on the sidelines—prevailed. When I told Ruth that I would be happy to rehearse part of the time alone with her at home, she consented. After all, we didn't need a lot of space in which to move around.

Rehearse alone we did, with dear Ruthie plying me with good English tea and even more delicious Irish good nature. She remained as terrified as ever at the task before her, but at least there was no one but me observing her terror. We talked, questioned, experimented. We went over her lines again and again, explaining them, organizing them, relating them to each other. We spent endless time with the placement and movement of every prop; the toothbrush, the mirror, the gun, all the objects that came out of and went back into the bag—or didn't. We searched religiously not only for the exact nuance and meaning of each line but for colors and rhythms that brought meaning of their own. More than once, Ruth despaired and felt she could not go on. More than once, she was certain that she was failing me—and Mr. Beckett. She would start to cry, tell me that she couldn't find a way, that I had to get someone else, and then cry harder. Over and over again, I would talk to her, kiss her, comfort her, encourage her, and bring her back to Sam's play.

It was almost as though she herself were Winnie, unable to go on and yet going on. I had said to Ruth from the beginning that Winnie's overall objective, her through-line while she was sinking deeper and deeper into the scorched earth was: To Live. Ruth's through-line, wavering as it did as we sank deeper and deeper into the script, was: To Go On. She somehow managed.

When after a few weeks she came together on stage with Johnny Becher, the two of them were astonishingly effective; sad and funny and truthful all at once. Ruth's round smiling Irish pudding face, topped by that funny little hat we found for her at some Salvation Army outlet, and John's slightly droopy, good-natured openness made a perfect combination. Bill's finished setting was stark and properly functional, exactly what Sam had asked for. The parasol, after numerous attempts and arrangements, finally worked; the music box tinkled with the proper tune and volume. Everyone seemed pleased, even Ruth. The producers—and Edward—came to one of our occasional runthroughs and loved it. So did our audiences for the five previews we were allotted. Our producers were economy-minded, as usual; they had announced at the start of rehearsals that they were bringing in our production for $2200, and they stuck to their budget. This was at a time when off-Broadway productions cost around $10,000 at least.

Another good omen: the *Times*' cartoonist, Al Hirschfeld, had been coming to rehearsals of my productions for years, covering his notebook with preliminary drawings ostensibly for next Sunday's paper. Over the years, only one or two had actually appeared—never, of course, with me in it. On the first Sunday of our rehearsal period, a beautiful cartoon practically covered the first page of the Drama Section—complete with Ruth's mop of hair, John's eyebrows, Richard's horn-rimmed glasses, and my bald spot. I've never been fonder of the latter.

We opened on a Sunday night, September 17. The show went better than ever, even with the Cherry Lane packed with members of the press. The actors were funny and moving, the play crystal-clear, a rare piece of theater music. Nobody left during the second act. No radiator pipes clanked. Oh, yes, the parasol didn't ignite with as much force as usual, and I had a moment's agony. But Ruth went right on, and no one noticed.

Ruth White, lovely, sweet, gentle, laughing Ruthie, was uniquely human, unforgettable, a rare lark of a Winnie. Plain and beautiful at the same time. Compassionate and wise. An endless delight. I could have gone on hearing the echoes of her words in my mind's ear, seeing the endlessly shifting nuances of her face in my mind's eye forever.

"Was I lovable once, Willie?" she would ask. "Was I ever lovable?" That night, she was indeed, and every night of the all too short run that followed. Every night of her all too short life. I loved her then and still do. In any other theatrical society, Ruth White would not have been dismissed simply as a character actress of some ability. She would not have had to struggle so long and so hard to be recognized—or even to get roles. She would have been appreciated as an actress of the first rank. "Rich with the quiver of life," as one critic once described her work, she was in my opinion equal in talent and capacity to such world-renowned "stars" as Madeleine Renaud, or Helen Hayes, or Peggy Ashcroft. And she was never more lovable than those nights she played Winnie.

John Becher too, with his slanted eyebrows, his dry wit, and his marvelous timing, came through as a very effective Willie. "Them? Or it? . . . Willie, what would you say, speaking of the hair on your head, them or it, Willie?" Ruth would plead, desperately trying to look over her shoulder to catch a glimpse of him. Then a pause, a tilt of his head upward, followed by Johnny's still, small kazoo of a voice: "It." That was not something I could have possibly imagined, sitting on Sam's couch that first day reading the script for the first time.

Minutes later, laughing and crying in Ruth's dressing room upstairs at the Cherry Lane, I could hardly believe that the plain, almost raucous woman in the faded silk wrapper was the same magical Ruth White I had just seen on stage. Everyone else was there too, telling everybody how happy they were, how proud to have been part of the adventure. Almost for the first time in my off-Broadway experience, it seemed almost as though no one really cared what the reviews would say. We had our own opinion about what we had done, and that was what mattered. After a while, all of us went over to the Blue Mill for the usual, the usual this time being mostly beer. Some time after midnight, we scattered to our various residences, not yet knowing and presumably not really caring what the morning papers might be saying about us.

Presumably. My recently acquired abode in Hastings-on-Hudson was one half-hour up the West Side Highway. Once I got into my Volkswagen, I headed unerringly uptown to Times Square, getting there just before one o'clock and dashing to the nearest newsstand to pick up a *Times*. I couldn't wait. The *Times* critic was new, Howard Taubman, and had been brought over from the music department to cover the theater. What would he say, I thought, turning frantically to find the right page. Taubman's first sentence was as far as I needed to read. I read it, reread it, and wended my way back to the car, leaving the rest to come later. "With *Happy Days*, Samuel Beckett has composed a song of rue that will haunt the inner ear long after you have heard it." As an afterthought, I picked up the *Herald-Tribune*, where I knew that critic Walter Kerr would be continuing his running battle with Beckett. When I read it, I could even laugh: "Well, happy days are gone again." Luckily, I had read the *Times* first. Mr. Taubman, whoever he was, went on to say that "Mr. Beckett's threnody is grim, but in its muted, tremulous way it shimmers with beauty. For he has refined his theater into something that parallels the elusiveness and overtones of music." He even found a moment to praise my nonmovement direction: "Alan Schneider has directed the play with a memorable combination of delicacy and strength." And he loved Ruth, John, Bill, and—most of all—Samuel Beckett.

The other reviews, which we read the next day, were almost evenly split, not always along predictable lines. Some of the lowbrow critics really liked it for varied reasons, while the so-called highbrows—Jerry Tallmer, Robert Brustein, Richard Gilman et al.—felt it was below the Master's standard. It was pretty much the usual pattern with Sam and the critics. *Godot* was well clobbered the first time around. Then when *Endgame* opened, it was clobbered also—with a number of the critics saying it wasn't nearly as powerful or rich or true or something as *Godot*, which they had previously clobbered. Then came *Krapp* or *Happy Days* or the next one, and the same process was repeated.

With the split in the notices, and even with the *Times* review, we soon discovered that business was only fair. Richard and Clinton, after cutting down on the number of performances each week—instead of increasing them, as I had originally hoped—decided to put up the closing notice. We ran five or six weeks but only twenty-eight performances. We did get out to Princeton for a special performance in January, followed by one at the YWHA uptown. But neither the stage nor the auditorium at either location had the imtimacy and ambiance of the Cherry Lane. It was a disappointing conclusion to a project which had promised much more, and I was both sad and disappointed for all who had been involved. I wrote to Sam, who reassured me. People who had seen Ruth's performance continued to talk about it. Unfortunately no film or tape exists, an indication of how little we treasure what we do in the theater.

Four years later, in September 1965, we managed a bit of an afterglow. Theatre 1965, now composed of Richard Barr, Clinton Wilder, and Edward Albee, brought *Happy Days* back for another limited run at our same old Cherry Lane. It was preceded by two weeks of Madeleine Renaud and Jean-Louis Barrault (followed after two nights by Wyman Pendleton) doing the play in French, prior to a nationwide tour of schools and colleges. Madeleine's performance, which I watched several times, was more relentless and harsher than Ruth's, which gave the play more humor and humanity, as well as variety. Nor will I ever forget Barrault's beautifully undulating fingers as he asked for that French postcard. But I've not forgotten John either, who was also less stylized and more human.

What pleased me most of all later and assuaged my general disappointment was an article by Peter Brook in the British theater magazine *Encore*. It was entitled "*Happy Days* and *Marienbad*," and dealt with the relationship between the play and the Alain Resnais film in some depth. Brook, whom I have always considered the most imaginative and gifted director working in the English-language theater, had seen my original production of *Happy Days*. He seemed to appreciate the play in a way no one else had. "Beckett at his finest," he wrote, "seems to have the power of casting a stage picture, a stage relationship, a stage machine from his most intense experiences that in a flash, inspired, *exists*, stands there complete in itself, not *telling* not *dictating*, symbolic without symbolism. For Beckett's symbols are powerful just because we cannot quite grasp them; they are not signposts, they are not textbooks nor blueprints—they are literally creations." No one has ever explained the importance of Samuel Beckett's work more simply or powerfully.

Peter, I might add, also managed to say "There was a beautiful performance by Ruth White, and a quite perfect production by Alan Schneider." That made up for the number of performances of what remained for years my favorite Beckett play.

Earlier that same year, 1961, Zelda asked me to open the new Arena Stage, which she had finally seen through to completion, the Arena's third home and the first specifically designed for that purpose. I had opened its previous space, the "Old Vat" with *A View From the Bridge* in 1956, and I suppose that Zelda felt that had been a good omen, and I a logical choice. We had kept in touch over the years and months, Zelda tending to call more often when she had a problem than when things were going well; but that's standard operating truth in most theater—or human—relationships.

I particularly remember one of her late-night calls when an about-to-be-tearful Zelda (not at all her normal self) asked me what I thought of her choosing some sort of three-sided audience seating, akin to the original Circle-in-the-Square, instead of another four-sided arena. She was under increasing pressure from her architect, Harry Weese, as well as from her board. Besides, that would give her more seats. I liked the Circle's stage, and especially its advantage of having a proper back wall to use as a façade or background. But "arena" to me always meant four sides, an audience enclosing and surrounding the actors; it was that particular form that gave the Arena Stage its own individuality and special flavor.

I thought back to the Alley's *Hasty Heart* and *Gentle People*, to Arena's *Menagerie*, performed so eloquently in the midst of that tiny space. And I urged Zelda not to give in, to keep her own vision intact. The Arena, by accident or design, had started a certain way and had established itself in that way. Don't give up that fourth tier, I told her. "And, for crissakes, don't make it too big!" I was even afraid of the 36-by-30-foot size stage she eventually got; over the years and productions, I've grown used to it and find it the most comfortable stage I've ever worked on. Zelda kept the arena form, compromising a bit because that fourth section is, in theory, removable. I believe it was removed once.

Wanting to open her new home with a new American play, Zelda wrote to Williams and Miller and Hellman and a few other native playwrights to ask if they had something. After all, Washington was the nation's capital, and that capital was getting a new playhouse, which, she hoped, would rank with those of any other international capital. Whether she ever even had a response from any of these playwrights I do not know. She certainly did not get a play.

Undaunted and enterprising as always, Zelda asked me one day what I thought of Brecht's *Caucasian Chalk Circle*. I told her that ever since first seeing that play in its Berliner Ensemble production, I had been wanting to direct it. She had decided on *Chalk Circle*—in spite of strong opposition and pressure from certain members of the board about choosing a non-American—*and* Communist!—author. In the meantime, we had gotten the rights for Eric Bentley's translation and started selecting our company of actors. In August the Berlin Wall went up, and with the Wall came the wailing, on all sides. How could Arena possibly make such a choice now? What would that be saying to the world of theater and to the world outside? Zelda stuck to her guns, at the clear risk of losing the big ones on her board, including the World Bank's Eugene Black. *Chalk Circle* it was to be, and I was going to direct it, as well as four other plays out of the eight-play season.

For Azdak (as well as Vanya and a range of other leading roles), we got my specialist in confidence men, David Hurst, whose work Zelda knew and liked. After all, Azdak was the prize con man of them all. For Grusche (and Sonya!) I wanted my Linda Dillon, whom Zelda did not know. Over the years, Zelda has usually been willing to listen to me about all sort of subjects and people; when the time came to make a real decision, she never would take my word, preferring to judge for herself. Linda would have to audition. Linda, on her end, having been assured by me over and over again that I loved her, that Zelda wanted her, that Arena Stage was the perfect stepping stone for her career, didn't understand why she now had to audition. She didn't want to audition. She didn't audition well. At the Goodman she had auditioned very badly, and I had almost not taken her. She would not, repeat *not*, audition. If that didn't suit Zelda, she—Linda—had another offer in Chicago. That was that. Linda hung up the phone in tears, real tears, not indicated ones.

As is usual with such impasses—which I've many times had to face, along with all directors, playwrights, actors, producers, and everyone else connected with the theater—the solution lies somewhere in what I would call the Gordian Knot method. As scene designer Boris Aronson used to say, in a marvelously thick accent, "In de teatr dere are awnly two rools. De first rool is: For each production dere is alvays a wictim. De second rool is: Dawn be de wictim." I told Zelda that I swore by Linda, who in my opinion was more talented than anyone I knew or didn't know. Besides that, if she wouldn't hire Linda—without an audition—I was not going to direct those five shows, including and especially *Chalk Circle*. Contract or no contract. Q.E.D.

Not entirely without qualms or resentment at my ungentlemanly behavior, Zelda hired Linda, for some astrological reason now transformed into "Melinda." Within three minutes of Melinda's arrival at Arena, Zelda was as devoted to and enamored of her as was everyone else around—including those whose hearts she managed to break. There was just something utterly vulnerable in Melinda's eyes and cheekbones.

Melinda was the most affecting Grusche and Sonya I've ever seen; when she stumbled while crossing the diagonal strip of light on the Arena stage floor which represented the broken mountain bridge, over which she was escaping from the cruel soldiers, the audience literally gasped. Her Sonya, matured by a year's personal growth and a few more severed romances, was stunning. She also managed a lovely mournful Caroline in John Mortimer's *What Shall We Tell Caroline?*, a sexy leper in a new play, *The Burning of the Lepers*, and a radiant Kitty in Saroyan's *The Time of Your Life*. Her much later *Close Encounters of the Third Kind* wasn't even in the ball park, though it got her more attention.

Almost at once, we had trouble with Eric Bentley. A few weeks before rehearsals of *Chalk Circle* were to start, Eric sent me one of his usual pin-scratched postcards casually informing us that since he had just gotten an offer for an off-Broadway production, he was now withholding our rights. Here we were with a new theater, a specially selected group of actors, and no first play. I was ready to fight, kill, even sue Eric. Zelda had a calmer and more statespersonlike answer. She had heard of another adaptation done in London by a new writer named John Holmstrom, represented by my own agent, the ebullient Peggy Ramsay. Why didn't I call Peggy to get a copy of Holmstrom's version and see if the rights were available. I did, and they were. In addition, the adaptation seemed more playable than Eric's. We went ahead with the Holmstrom, not really caring about telling Eric too much. When, a few weeks later, he found out, he sent me another postcard, saying that if we didn't use his version, he'd sue us. Scout's honor.

Working on that first show in the new Arena was alternately dusty and exhilarating. Nothing was impossible and nothing worked. Designer Peter Wexler came up with simple but extremely effective set-pieces, and some wonderfully exotic costumes; the production was spectacular and yet starkly theatrical. It swirled through the new theater like a species of Oriental dance, hypnotizing almost everyone who saw it. Our one-man orchestra, Teiji Ito, added a musical beat that filled the entire space.

From the first time that we performed it in front of an audience, *Chalk Circle* was clearly going to be an event. The combination of the beautifully designed new theater in Washington and a show that equaled any of the Stratfords in magnificence and excitement proved irresistible. Even banker Black liked it, grabbing my arm one day and asking me where this fellow Brecht came from. President Kennedy was scheduled to come to our opening on October 30, 1961, and the Secret Service checked everything out; at the last minute, the West German embassy made such a fuss that Kennedy decided to be diplomatic and stay away. Jackie did come.

The press was uniformly favorable, local, national, and international. The *Post*'s Richard L. Coe, a staunch supporter of Arena during its entire life—although occasionally he would surprise everyone by being overly sour—said it "offered striking theatricality" and was "witty, ringingly vibrant and deftly touching." John Beaufort of the *Christian Science Monitor* called us "a theatrical event of potent significance." *The New York Times*' Taubman came down and glowed. "Pounding drums and brass fanfares would not have been out of order to proclaim the official opening . . . of the Arena Stage's impressive new home. . . . The production staged by Alan Schneider is well worth a trip not only to the Arena Stage but to Washington . . . New York . . . has no permanent company to compare with the Arena Stage. And how long has it been since New York had *The Chalk Circle* in so illuminating and enchanting a performance?" The *London Times*, not usually interested in American cultural currents, praised us sedately and concluded that "Alan Schneider's colorful fluid production . . . has got Arena off to a brilliant start in its new home." I suspect that even the French and the Italians could not avoid mentioning us. Maybe even the Russians.

Brecht's New York agent, Bertha Case, with whom I had become especially friendly, told me that it was the best Brecht production ever done in America. She told everyone, from the people at the Berliner Ensemble to the playwright's son Stefan, who had inherited the Emperor's Western Hemisphere domain, that she had finally found the right director to do his father's plays. She swore to me that she would never allow a New York production of *Circle* unless I was the director. I even believed her, sort of.

Certain that some kind of lucky lightning was going to strike, I was never out of one rehearsal room or another during the next twelve months, deep into 1962. No sooner was *Circle* on than I was rehearsing Arena's next show, a double bill of *American Dream* and Mortimer's little-known but sweetly perceptive play about the generation gap, *What Shall We Tell Caroline?* The evenings were going well, but the afternoons tended to be tense. I must have been tired, and so were the actors. I quarreled too often and needlessly with too many of them, including David and Melinda, with whose Grusche I had not a moment's tension.

I went home for Christmas and, to identify myself to my son and daughter, installed new productions of *Endgame* and *Happy Days* and *American Dream* (again!) into Theatre 1962's repertory season at the Cherry Lane, and came back to Washington to direct three more plays in a row for Arena—an impossible chore for everybody concerned. First I did Wallace Hamilton's new play about the contagion of prejudice,

The Burning of the Lepers, which contained a few orgiastic moments but not much else. Then came *Uncle Vanya*, better cast but somehow not as unified as my Goodman production. I ended the season (and my madness) with Saroyan's *Time of Your Life*, which came off better than anyone, especially its director, expected.

Taking a deep breath, in July 1962 I drove out with my family to Milwaukee's University of Wisconsin once more, this time for a triple-bill—in the Fred Miller Theatre, later to become the Milwaukee Repertory Theatre—of Beckett's *Act Without Words, II*, my reliable *Pullman Car Hiawatha*, and the American premiere of Harold Pinter's *The Dumbwaiter*, which almost everyone, including Harold's publisher, insisted on calling The Dumb Waiter.

The University surprised me—and Harold—by flying him over for the opening, and he seemed pleased enough with what he saw through his jet lag. I was already scheduled to direct both *Dumbwaiter* and *The Collection* off-Broadway in the fall. Harold had to "pay" for his trip over by giving a local ladies' club talk, whose opening words I have never forgotten: "My name is . . . Harold Pinter. I am a playwright. I've written two plays. In my first play I used dots; in my second play, I used dashes. My first play ran one week; my second play ran one year—thereby proving conclusively the superiority of dashes over dots." It sounds even better in the kind of clipped brittle staccato that Harold uses so well.

From Milwaukee, I hauled Vickie, age seven, David, age three, and Jean, aging rapidly, across the country at breakneck speed to get to Palo Alto, California, where I was scheduled in August to do a combined student-professional production of another Brecht play, *A Man's a Man*, at Stanford University. In what all four of us always refer to as the Medicine Bow Incident, the transmission of our ancient Chevy wagon, which I had bought from one of the Arena actors, melted in the Wyoming heat and fell out. I had to wire my father in Bethesda for enough cash to purchase the only available car in Medicine Bow.

We eventually made it to Stanford, where *A Man's a Man*, performed to my chagrin in a vast auditorium instead of the promised small theater, turned out reasonably well. Faculty members Wendell Cole and Douglas Russell, both excellent designers of more than professional caliber, contributed the sets and costumes respectively. My Galy Gay was Stan Weese, one of the San Francisco Actors' Workshop's best comedians. Bloody Five and his quartet of machine-gunners were properly huge and macho; and the Widow Begbick was played by a youthful and suitably sexy Joanna Akalaitis, who was later to surprise me by becoming a pillar of the avant-garde of the seventies. Bertha Case contributed a fond opening-night telegram. She also, without my knowledge, was completing plans to have the Lincoln Center put on *The Chalk Circle* during the following season, with Jules Irving, recently transposed from San Francisco, directing.

A parenthesis: That kind of artistic "betrayal," no matter how often manifested or how inevitable, has always been hard for me to forgive. Betrayal in any form—ever since that Polish kid in Sabillasville, whom I had befriended, got beaten up by a gang and then blamed me—is something I don't get over easily.

Early on, before I was in any way established, Jean and I had taken in a struggling young actor who had played a small part in one of my productions. Jean fed him, and I held his hand, encouraging him in his writing ambitions. I even arranged for him to get the dramatic rights to a novel I had just read, *The Cut of the Axe.* For a year or two, I worked with him on his adaptation, which turned out to be produceable. I was helping him show it around to various producers, when I discovered, accidentally, that it was already in someone's hands, and John O'Shaughnessy was slated to direct it. "Producer's choice" was the way I had it explained to me. *Cut of the Axe* went on and soon off; it was the unkindest cut of all.

More seriously, after I saw the Berliner Ensemble do its original production of Brecht's *Arturo Ui,* in which Ekkehard Schall gave such a fantastic performance, I decided it would be perfect for America. I brought the German text back and gave it to George Tabori, then still married to Viveca Lindfors, both of whom I was seeing a fair amount of at the time. I felt he was just the right person to adapt the play for Broadway production. George loved the script, as well as all the production photographs and material I brought him, got the rights from Bertha, and worked on it—with my sideline assistance—for a year. At the end of that time, he managed to inform me quietly that Anthony Quinn wanted to act in it—and direct it himself.

Interestingly enough, Tony eventually lost interest, and George came back to me, smiling, to let me know that David Merrick was now going to produce it, with Christopher Plummer. In my first meeting with David, we shook hands on a deal to direct it. Some weeks later, in Boston, I picked up a *New York Times* to discover Tony Richardson listed as the director of the Broadway-bound production of *Arturo Ui.* When I rang up Merrick to ascertain what had happened to our "deal," he informed me regretfully that Tony had insisted on directing *Arturo* as a precondition to doing *Luther* with Albert Finney, which Merrick also wanted to produce. I must give David some credit, however; he said he'd make it up to me, and he did, later offering me the first Broadway *Look Back in Anger*, which I unfortunately could not do because I was about to direct something else at that time. George and I, I'm afraid, never met again.

There's also the time that David Susskind, my old University of Wisconsin classmate, offered me a TV directing job. David was evidently too embarrassed to admit his plebeian Wisconsin association; he always claimed Harvard where, I believe, he had attended the business school for a few weeks one summer. He once called me into his elaborate Talent Associates office, lush with teak and leather, although they hadn't managed to round up the remainder of the $750 still owed me for my *Godot* production. On a large blackboard half a football field away from his desk were displayed the titles of a dozen or so contemporary works of fiction he was going to produce, definitively, for America's TV public. "Which one do you want to do?" he proclaimed, expansively. Without hesitating, I picked *The Citadel*, one of my favorite novels, and one I had seen Robert Donat do fairly well in a British film some time before. I walked out of David's door, trying to think who could possibly play the Robert Donat part. Over my shoulder, I heard David's parting words, "Wonderful! I'll be in touch." I never heard another word.

In a game where the stakes are so high and the pressures so great, where so many people are grabbing for that same loaf of bread, betrayal—I must reluctantly admit—is not just the name of a play by Harold Pinter.

But 1962 was to bring not only betrayal but my greatest opportunity. Early in the year, the educational television station WNET had approached a number of directors and playwrights with the idea of doing a series of programs called "Playwright at Work." The idea was that each director would take a short work and put it on without any previous discussions with its author; then, at the end of the program, the author would tell him what he had done right—and wrong. It was an idea not without its problems and pitfalls, but interesting enough. Would I like to do a program? And did Edward, by any chance, have a new short play?

Edward didn't, but he was just finishing up the first scene of a new long one. He was willing for me to work on it. In consultation with him—but never getting on to any questions about the script—I cast Shepperd Strudwick and, after a long search through various Studio and non-Studio actresses, Peggy Feury. I couldn't tell much about the play that was to come—the script I worked with didn't even have a title—but the scene obviously did have its own validity; the dialogue crackled, the people were real, the "battle game" of marriage very clearly fought out in those fifteen pages before whoever or whatever was to enter. I studied the scene, as best I could, talked it over with Edward in front of the camera, and then forgot about it until it was shown a year later.

I've never forgotten it since.

WHO'S AFRAID?

1962

One day in the late spring of 1962, I had sat at one end of producer Richard Barr's kitchen in his apartment just off Eighth Street, with Richard at the other end, both of us reading a new play by Edward Albee with a mysterious title, *Who's Afraid of Virginia Woolf?* It was the same untitled play whose first scene I had read and worked on almost a year earlier, and I still thought it might be about someone who wanted a room of her own. As we sat there, with Richard handing me a few pages at a time of what seemed to be an endless collection, I soon discovered otherwise.

I remember vividly the hand-to-hand passage and piling-up of those papers in that steadily darkening room, page after page of Edward's lightning-like words exploding in my brain. How many pages? Could it last? I felt as though I were being hit over the head with a succession of concrete blocks, and yet I didn't want them to stop hitting me. I had a headache, and yet I wanted to stand up and shout out the window. At that time, I had never seen or read Strindberg's *Dance of Death*, yet somehow it was Strindberg of whom I kept thinking. Strindberg and O'Neill—and Edward Albee, who was piercing the darkness with these unexpected, pulsating flashes of light. Those two marriage partners, Martha and George, were like dinosaurs battling on the cliff of emotional survival. When all the pages had been gathered, George and Martha huddled close in their pain, Richard and I tiptoed out to his living room, sat down, and could hardly say anything. Richard had already called the play "remarkable." Maybe too remarkable, he added, for Broadway. Now I thought, all too ruefully, he might be right. After a while I called Edward to tell him that I had read his new play and loved it.

Some of the notes I later wrote for myself in my director's script evoke the play's basic texture: "A dark legend of truth and illusion"; "a modern parable, with musical structure and rhythms"; "a portrait of people drowning and grasping for straws of awareness, of understanding, of communication." They are all hurt. Martha is hurt and wants to lash out to hurt back; George is hurt and has to fight back in order to survive. Nick wants to hurt others before they hurt him—he's out to get all he can. And Honey just tries not to get hurt anymore. In rehearsal, I would tell the actors that they were not in a realistic play—otherwise they'd all be flat on the floor. "Try to make the largest possible choices," I would say. "These are not little people but giants battling on the cliff."

All that spring and summer, the fate of the new play remained as inscrutable as its title, which, I was eventually to learn, had come from Edward's seeing the question scrawled on a bathroom wall in a Village bar. Edward had just become involved, actively and enthusiastically, with the Actors Studio. The Studio, then at the height of its glamour period, with such superstars as Marilyn Monroe and Paul Newman regularly in residence, and with international visitors like Laurence Olivier and John Gielgud, was about to launch itself as a producing theater. This was a step that the Studio's artistic director, Lee Strasberg, had always avoided, the memory of the Group Theatre's fall remaining too strongly fixed. But the pressures were strong, from both within and without, and Lee had finally given in.

Besides, he now had a play of prime quality, and plenty of actors to play each of its four roles. *The Zoo Story* had had its first showing there, and then gone on to success outside. This time Edward's new play would be done, and done right, by the one organization best equipped with talent and understanding to bring his work to the world. Geraldine Page was selected—by Lee—to play Martha, and Eli Wallach, George. Evidently, I was going to direct it—although no one ever told me directly, or talked to me about whether I approved of the casting. (I did.) There was talk about Lou Antonio or Ben Piazza for Nick, and a young Studio actress unknown elsewhere, Lane Bradbury, would play Honey. Since Gerry Page was pregnant, we couldn't go into rehearsal until the following January.

This scheduling was fine with me because I was concurrently involved with a Pinter double bill, *The Dumbwaiter* and *The Collection*, slated for off-Broadway in the fall under the sponsorship of a new lady producer, one Caroline Swann, whom I had not yet met. Harold, with whom I had remained friends since our original meeting in London, wanted me to direct, and Caroline seemed most responsive to the idea. I had signed a contract; and while Harold was in New York attending to the Broadway opening of *The Caretaker*, which had come over from London, we met several times to talk about the two plays. He liked the idea of my trying out *The Dumbwaiter* at Milwaukee's University of Wisconsin, where I was going to be in June. *The Collection* had just been done at London's National Theatre, and Harold had some thoughts and some changes to talk over with me. My career seemed suddenly to be in high gear. Pinter in October, Albee in January. Not bad.

As usual, there's many a slip. . . . The Studio, about to embark on production, had just persuaded that optimistic Broadway impresario Roger L. Stevens to serve as fund-raiser. Producer Cheryl Crawford had also come aboard to organize and manage. Lee was a terrific apostle of "the Method" but a totally inept administrator. The Studio's books, budget, and general administrative structure had to be taken seriously in hand before we went into production, and Cheryl set herself to the task.

Fate's Mona Lisa smile soon made itself evident. Cheryl did not particularly admire Edward's new play; besides, she said, it had too many dirty words in it—although I had some difficulty then, as I still do, in finding them. And Roger, after his initial reading of the script, called it "a dull, whiny play without a laugh in it." Roger is well known for having produced more successful plays than any man alive, but not necessarily for having read them. So Lee remained the only one of the Studio's ruling triumvirate who wanted to produce Edward's play.

When the chips were down, Lee could have insisted that the Studio put on the play even though both Roger and Cheryl demurred. He was, after all, not only artistic director but the Studio's guru, god, and godfather. But Lee's Achilles heel, here as always, was that he wanted success and feared failure. His colleagues' negative vibrations rubbing off on him, he began to question his own. In the crunch, he made the decision to back off—eventually settling on a less adventurous and safer revival of O'Neill's *Strange Interlude* for the Actors Studio Theatre's postponed debut. The membership's reaction—except for Gerry Page, who had never been enthusiastic about the play—was one of shock and dismay. In the hallways there were mutterings of meetings, petitions, even outright revolt, but Lee's psychological and moral hold on us was too strong. I often ruminate on the difference both for the Studio itself and for the entire American theater had Lee, in the particular case of *Virginia Woolf*, had the courage of his own taste. Might we have had, back in 1962, a real permanent "theater" in New York City?

The almost last-minute withdrawal of the Studio from its commitment to his play embittered and estranged Edward. It also gave Richard Barr the opportunity he had sought but was too much a gentleman to grab. Once the play came back to him, Richard was not himself sure that Broadway was ready to accept its outsized intensity and shock values. He and his new partner, Clinton Wilder, a wealthy young theater buff but no relation to Thornton, toyed with various ideas. One was simply to do the play off-Broadway—but then, it would be harder to get top actors for the cast. Another idea was to do simultaneous productions off-Broadway and on. If one didn't succeed, perhaps the other might. This alternative soon succumbed to various practical realities, chief among them the problem of getting a theater. The Shuberts had not seen fit to assign one of their many theaters to Edward's play; it obviously had no chance of becoming a success. Nor was any playhouse belonging to Roger Stevens' organization available. Only Billy Rose, persuaded by a perceptive production assistant, Malcolm Wells, that this new play with the strange long title "had something," offered us his theater. Evidently Malcolm had, without permission, read Roger's copy of the play. I'm not sure whether Billy ever did.

The Billy Rose Theatre, as it was then called, was considered too large for a straight play and too small for a musical. Besides, it was located on Forty-first Street, several blocks from the splendors of Forty-fourth and Forty-fifth; presumably most theatergoers could not or would not venture that far south. Still, it was a theater that was ours for the rental, including for rehearsals, and Richard and Clinton took it. Along with the insurance policy that Billy appended: we could have his theater only if we would agree to approach major stars to play Martha and George. Someone like, say, Katharine Hepburn and Henry Fonda.

All of us, from Edward to myself, had been talking only of Uta Hagen and Richard Burton. Uta wasn't sure, after her recent Broadway experience with *A Month in the Country*, that she wanted to work again in the commercial theater—ever. Burton was not available. Katharine Hepburn was not a bad idea, though Uta was a much better one. We dispatched a script to La Hepburn in Hollywood. She read it immediately and returned it forthwith with thanks, saying that she wasn't good enough, bless her. Henry Fonda worried us; after we had gone through a list of about fifty unavailable, uninteresting, or unsomething else names, we sent the script to his agent, name unmentionable. The unmentionable read it, decided that it was too dreadful even to submit to his client for a reading, and never forwarded it to Fonda. "Hank" later fired the agent. And he subsequently stated, orally and in a letter to me, that his greatest single artistic regret was that "I never got to play George." He would have been fine.

Somewhat off the hook with Billy, we applied pressure on Uta. I had briefly crossed paths with her at the Unviersity of Wisconsin before she ran off to join the Lunts as Nina in their *Seagull* back in 1938. I was selected to woo her back from her self-imposed exile as a successful acting teacher at her husband's, director Herbert Berghof's, Studio on Bank Street during the week and an active gardener around their Montauk house on weekends. She finally consented to read the script—out there. Remembering my collision with Herbert on *Godot* and his problems keeping the tape straight on *Krapp's Last Tape,* I wondered what Uta's reaction to me as director would be.

Richard telephoned Uta out in Montauk one day, and I spent, I think, about five hours talking her into accepting. She had evidently had a bad time with one of her directors, Michael Redgrave; quite apart from my "entanglements" with her husband, whatever she had heard about my methods and personality had not entirely reassured her that I wouldn't be equally impossible. At one point, she asked me if I carried a riding crop to rehearsals (evidently Redgrave did), or had ever hurt an actress physically. I explained that no matter how difficult I might be, the only whip I ever carried to rehearsals was a verbal one. And, besides, my only course of action in this particular case would be to love, honor, and obey her at all times. She was a great actress. She was ideal for the part. She would be absolutely wonderful. Edward had practically written the play for her—even without knowing it. I had seen her in everything from *The Seagull* through *Othello* and *Saint Joan,* and there was no one in the world at this specific moment who was more "right" for Martha than Uta was. At the end of our conversation, having really wanted to play the part after she had read the first four pages of Edward's script, Uta took a deep breath and agreed. Richard and I did a little dance around the phone, and then went back to casting George.

We had gone through every actor in the United States and England who was even remotely possible, starting with Richard Burton and ending up with Robert Flemyng, whom both Richard and I had liked in his seasons with John Gielgud in *The Importance of Being Earnest* and *Love for Love.* Flemyng at one point in our long-distance negotiations accepted but at the last moment—luckily for us, as matters turned out—changed his mind. We were desperate.

Somewhere, from the depths of my subconscious, I remembered an actor named Arthur Hill who had played the father in the James Agee/Tad Mosel *All the Way Home.* He didn't seem ideal for us, but he was around fifty, male, with male strengths and weaknesses, and available. Of all our group, Richard alone knew his work, and was able to persuade Edward that Arthur Hill was worth going after. Hill was in London finishing up a movie. We sent him the script and, after the usual period of nail-biting silence, the word came back that he had accepted. No one was exorbitantly enthusiastic, notably Billy, but we had our George.

For Honey, we went back to our original Actors Studio cast for Lane Bradbury, a sweet-faced and attractive brunette, whose work I had seen only in class. And for Nick, Edward's suggestion was another Studio actor then beginning to "make it," Robert Lansing. I thought Lansing a bit too bland, but he was certainly suited in physical appearance and feeling to play the tough, cynical, attractive stud on the make. Interestingly enough, we lost Lansing almost at once in a disagreement over billing. I have never, I think, lost an actor because of salary problems but have done so many times when a question of billing could not be resolved. Actors, it seems, care more for their status than for their pocketbooks. I suppose in a world where image is more important than reality, it's hard to blame them. And I was actually relieved when Bob Lansing decided not to come along with us. Especially since I had had a Nick up my sleeve all the time.

While I was away the previous summer, directing that Stanford production of Brecht, I discovered that George Grizzard, one of my favorite actors, was coming west. From the first time I had read *Virginia Woolf,* George had seemed to me ideal for Nick—except that he was not the hefty bruiser suggested by Edward's description. I told George I had a new play by Edward Albee for which he might be right, and suggested that he stop off to see me in Palo Alto. He did so and immediately took off with the script to some beach. He returned a few hours later, rhapsodic about the play but not entirely sold on the part. George had been or was about to be cast as Tyrone Guthrie's *Hamlet* in Minneapolis the following summer, and felt that he was on his way to the attention and acclaim which he'd worked for so long. He was very cautious about what he would do in between.

After we lost Bob Lansing, I once more brought up George's name to Edward, explaining that I was not sure if he was either interested or available; that was always the ploy to make an actor seem more desirable. In Edward's opinion, George was too light of weight, too small physically. The text spoke of a fullback, and that's what Edward wanted. I suggested that George was handsome, tough, aggressive; he might be able to do something more subtle with the role. "Why couldn't Nick be, after all, a halfback?" Richard and Clinton seemed to concur, especially since the horizon was not teeming with fullbacks who could act. Edward finally gave in on one end—and George, not too enthusiastically, on the other. I'll never forget the way Edward looked at me when he finally said yes.

"You'd better be right, Alan!"

Which meant that if George didn't deliver, it would be my scalp. As usual. Or Arthur. Or anybody. Casting is a large part of a director's job, it has been said, and I agree. Fifty percent, or eighty percent, or whatever percent. If you have a good script and you cast it well, it'll be good on stage. If you don't, it won't. You're a director and not a magician, I always say to myself, as well as to the cast. "Dear George, please, please deliver! Dear Arthur! Dear Everybody!"

Another problem loomed larger and larger as the summer kept coming in. That switch from the Studio and a pregnant Geraldine Page meant we didn't have to wait until January; we could go into rehearsal and open early in the following season—as soon as Arthur's film was over. Barr and Wilder as well as Billy Rose decided on an October opening. I was already contracted to Caroline Swann for her Pinter project in October, though we had no cast, no theater, and not yet all the money. When approached, however, on how best to settle this directorial dilemma, the good Caroline would not budge. Nor, on their side, would the Messrs. Barr, Wilder, Albee, or Rose. My attorney, Robert Montgomery, of the prestigious firm of Paul, Weiss, Rifkind, Wharton, and Garrison, tried every wile and gambit in his extensive repertoire; the lady was unmoved. At the time, I preferred an attorney to an agent, believing that lawyers at least tend to earn their original fee while agents don't always justify their continued ten percent. Edward ultimately "warned" me personally that if I didn't get the matter settled, he'd have to consider getting someone else to direct.

At one low point, I had just about made up what was left of my mind to choose the Pinter over the Albee, being dissuaded only by Harold's own plea to me not to give up something as powerful—and potentially successful—as *Virginia Woolf* for his one-acts. I had let him read Edward's script, and he confessed himself totally in awe.

Working overtime, Bob, together with Caroline Swann's general manager, Paul Libin, managed to rescue me at almost the last moment. For a price, of course. I would have to agree to direct the Pinter plays without any fee, collecting whatever weekly royalty payments would accrue if it ran—after it paid off. In effect, I was giving Caroline several thousand dollars. In return, she agreed to postpone a production that couldn't open anyhow on schedule because it lacked a theater, actors, and some of its money. But I could now legally do both shows, *Virginia Woolf* in October and *The Pinter Plays* (as the bill was now called) afterward, whenever. I breathed again. Harold Pinter, by the way, was outraged when he heard about Caroline's deal with me. Edward and Richard and the rest were immensely relieved.

Our "Evening Company" set, we proceeded to put together our "Matinee Company." This was mainly Uta's idea. She felt that since *Virginia Woolf* was almost four hours long, and the role of Martha required such physical and vocal strength, she would not be able to play two performances in one day. The producers were, ultimately, willing to confine our performances to six per week; Billy Rose was not. He was not about to have his theater take a weekly percentage of a smaller gross. Richard decided that instead of hiring regular understudies he would get actors who would play the matinees on a regular basis. We were fortunate enough to get Shepperd Strudwick, who had played George in the original television scene the year before, and Kate Reid, the noted Canadian actress whom I had seen perform many times. We also got Ben Piazza and Avra Petrides as an alternate Nick and Honey. And we had Jimmy Karen, one of our most reliable off-Broadway stalwarts, standing by for *both* George and Nick; I don't think there's another actor in the Western world who could have managed that trick.

That matinee business had a fascinating sidelight, of which I became aware only many years later. Evidently Uta, deciding she didn't want to share the matinees with another major actress, at some point told Richard she wanted to play all eight performances. When Richard, explaining that he'd already hired another actress, spent a lot of money on publicity, and had grown fond of the idea, told her she couldn't—Uta went to Equity. Equity ruled that an actress had the right to play all eight performances if she wanted to. Everyone got angry and stuck to his or her guns. The impasse was settled only when Richard agreed to give Uta a share of the production's profits, which of course have gone on for years and years, in fact are still doing so (although I never got any part of them). In effect, Uta got paid more for playing less. Bertolt Brecht, if not Karl Marx, might smile.

The "Matinee Company" was a good public-relations angle, and it kept our Wednesday and Saturday audiences from feeling they were being downgraded. Actually, they were seeing a different but equally valid version of the play. Kate Reid may have been a bit coarser than Uta but even more vulnerable at the end; Shep Strudwick's pain and anguish in the second act "games" sequence has never, in my opinion, been matched.

Much of this happened before I took off for my summer in Milwaukee and Stanford. All these shenanigans were forgotten once I was safely back from the West. Even before leaving, I had met with Bill Ritman to discuss the setting and costumes. And while I was away, Edward had contributed a few thoughts, some of which Bill had passed on to me. When I got back, I discovered that one or two of my ideas had survived. I wanted the set, for example, to be less realistic than more; Edward and Richard—then as generally always—wanted the opposite. Bill, a quiet and congenial fellow with nerves of steel, managed to give us a realistic set that suggested both a cave and a womb. And I was able, ultimately, to fill George's professional living quarters with a few specific artifacts from my own. Never liking the fake "spines" that passed for books on most Broadway sets, I brought a suitcase full of books from my own study to each rehearsal. Jean's father's metal newspaper rack, with space for each day's paper, also came in handy. It proved so suitable that the prop man built an exact copy.

Uta, of course, had ideas of her own about almost everything, although she took her time before imposing them on us. Before rehearsals started, we met once in Sardi's, at her suggestion, to talk about her part. Over the cannelloni, she confronted me with a notebook full of her jottings, most of them totally formed in her mind and not negotiable. She did most of the talking and I listened, soon realizing that she had taken my promise to "obey" her literally. I'm sure that she knew exactly what she wanted to do at almost every moment of her role long before we had that meeting. And I knew she was so well cast and so aware of the character she was playing that there would be very little to disagree about. We talked about the imaginary child, but I was never able to satisfy her on that point—and, indeed, it was the only deep disagreement we ever had in rehearsal.

Uta explained that she liked getting up on her feet as soon as possible, which meant to me that she wouldn't mind my working out the physical movement without a long period of around-the-table probing. Uta seemed to me to have done enough probing of her own. And she had definite ideas about costuming, some of which we had to beg her to change all the way up to opening night.

Our plans for the start of rehearsals were disrupted by the totally unexpected news that Arthur's film was running overtime and his arrival would have to be delayed an indeterminate period. Nor could we postpone our opening at the other end because Billy Rose kept telling us he'd give the theater to someone else if we did. So we knew we had a very short rehearsal period for a very long play.

Just before everyone could commit suicide, Arthur arrived, a few days earlier than feared. He seemed to be perfect casting for George, tall, determined, and sharp one moment, then shy, sensitive and frightened the next, half-sorry he'd even accepted the job. He was terrified that he'd never even be able to learn his lines, which seemed more numerous than Hamlet's.

We held our first reading in Uta's comfortable Old World apartment off Washington Square, which seemed an apt setting for a play about academic life. It was very low-key, not at all like a Broadway rehearsal. Edward welcomed everyone and told them how happy he was that they were all there. I gave them my usual spiel about a great play and a good cast making a good director; I told everyone to ask me whatever they wanted to even if I couldn't answer at the moment, never to take me literally, and not to worry if I changed my mind on something once in a while. I said that no matter what, critics and audiences would have to respect the material. Then we read it.

That was the first time I had heard Edward's words read aloud since an afternoon some months earlier, when Edward and Richard and a couple of actors had read through it at Edward's house—putting half the listeners to sleep with its seemingly interminable speeches, and making me think favorably of going off to do Harold Pinter. This time it was a blockbuster. With four real actors really acting it, the play exploded like a sudden storm, one stroke of lightning, one thunder clap after another. First readings tend to be misleading; they are usually either better or worse than the play in question. This time there was no doubting. It was what Audrey Wood called "magic time": language, life, and truth all blended into an emotional wallop that was as tangible as pain.

Moments later, I found myself alongside Uta in her kitchen as she was pouring coffee. "It's a disaster," she murmured, out of the corner of her mouth, without looking in my direction.

"Who? What? What was a disaster?"

She looked at me, amazed. "*He's* a disaster," she said, gesturing toward the living room and Arthur Hill, her costar.

I was as stunned as I was bewildered. I had thought that Arthur had proven amazingly effective, especially considering his state of nerves and his obvious exhaustion. Uta felt otherwise from the time she first set eyes on him. By the time we broke up that day, she had told everyone except Arthur that he was impossible and that we should replace him immediately with her own real-life husband, Herbert Berghof. Herbert was a fine character actor whom all of us knew, but he was all wrong for George, too old, too strange, and the possessor of a strong Viennese accent. Nevertheless, Uta persisted: Arthur should be replaced and Herbert hired. I'm not sure that she didn't have this in mind even before she ever saw poor unknowing Mr. Hill.

We were certainly not going to replace Arthur with anyone—he was doing too well. But a few days into rehearsals, we did have to make a change. Edward, along with the rest of us, came to the conclusion that we'd made a bad mistake with Lane Bradbury. Lane was a lovely actress but her quality was all wrong for Honey. I hated changing someone so soon in so small a cast—any cast—and tried to rationalize Lane's seeming colorlessness. Edward insisted, taking all the blame. When we began to explore possibilities—and we knew we had very little time—I thought of the young actress whom I considered the most talented and exciting personality I knew: Melinda Dillon. Melinda had decided to leave the Arena Stage and was rattling around New York, not getting past many doors. Edward had never heard of her. Luckily, however, Richard had seen her in my production of *The Caucasian Chalk Circle:* he thought she was great.

In great secrecy (which never works) we called Melinda in to read. She was reluctant because, as she always said, she read badly and never could get a part by auditioning. I explained that both Richard and I wanted her, but that Edward would not agree to hire her without some kind of audition. She gave in, reluctantly. After spending some time with the script, she showed up at the stage door of the Billy Rose, scared to death, overdressed, her hair a total mess. Determined that she wasn't going to get the part anyhow, she was simply showing us she didn't care.

Without letting Edward catch a glimpse of her, I sent her home to put on something simple, fix her hair, and wash the excess makeup off. An hour later she returned, scrubbed clean and shining; she read five lines, and we all knew that we had found our Honey—even Uta, when she got to see Melinda, who started out in total awe of her. Uta could tell that she was going to be good—perhaps a little too good.

No sooner were we all applauding ourselves on our new milk-fed Honey than I got a message to call George Grizzard at home. Late one night, calling from a public phone booth in Shubert Alley, I finally reached an angry George, who informed me he was leaving the show. Why? What was wrong? Everything was going so well; Edward had forgotten all about his original fullback image; Uta adored him. How could he possibly want to quit?

At first, George didn't want to tell me; but, finally, the truth came out. Bitterly, feeling betrayed by us all, me especially, he poured out the nature of that betrayal: we had changed our Honey without asking or even telling him, and to compound our felony had gotten one several inches taller than himself. He was now the shortest person on that stage. So far as George Grizzard was concerned, we had injured his deepest self, insulted his self-image, emasculated him; he had no intention of going on in the role. Oh, yes, Melinda was just fine, lovely, great, a terrific comedienne, but too tall.

Having known George for almost twenty years, ever since he first "crawled on" for me, as a high school student, in the Catholic University *Lute Song*, I could hardly believe his words or the vehemence with which he spoke. I had forgotten how sensitive George had always been about his height. From the moment he gave himself to the theater, he had wanted to be a leading man, he saw himself as a leading man; and he always wound up playing a character role. The romantic sexy leading man he saw himself as could not stand having a mate towering over him.

I spent endless hours—in that lonely, isolated phone booth, pouring in dime after dime—talking George back into staying with us. I coaxed, cajoled, flattered, pleaded. We'd even get him a pair of Adler's elevator shoes. Fortunately for us, he probably wanted to be talked back. He needed to be shown we all loved him, wanted him, cared for him, whatever his height. So he came back—to complain, almost without stop, about his role being unwritten, his sentences never completed, no logical reason why Nick would stay in Martha's house to take all those insults. As well as to give a wonderfully skillful and modulated performance—using every one of those dots he hated so much—and to grow more than fond of Melinda Dillon in spite of her being so tall. I always felt that our real George deserved every prize there was for his performance, although it was Uta and our stage George who got them.

Harold Pinter and A. S., New York City, 1962.
(Henry Grossman)

The Dumbwaiter: John C. Becher and Dana Alcar, 1962.
(Friedmann-Abeles)

A light moment during rehearsals of *Uncle Vanya* at the Arena Stage: A. S., Nancy Martin, Ray Reinhardt, 1962.
(George de Vincent)

Discussing *The Ballad of the Sad Café*: A. S., Edward Albee, Roscoe Lee Browne, Michael Dunn, William Prince, Lou Antonio, Colleen Dewhurst, 1963.
(Henry Grossman)

The "ship house" at Hastings-on-Hudson, New York, ca. 1964.

A. S., David, Vickie, and Jean Schneider, Hastings-on-Hudson, 1964. A very formal family pose for the amusement of friends.
(© Alix Jeffry, 1964)

(opposite) *Film:* A. S. in hat, at left; Buster Keaton in hat, at right; Samuel Beckett looking down from above. 1964. *(© Alix Jeffry, 1964, Harvard Theatre Collection)*

Samuel Beckett and A. S., New York, 1964. *(© Alix Jeffry, 1964, Harvard Theatre Collection)*

Rehearsing *Tiny Alice:* Irene Worth, A. S., John Gielgud, 1964. *(© Alix Jeffry, 1964, Harvard Theatre Collection)*

A. S. and Edward Albee on the set of *Tiny Alice*.
(© Alix Jeffry, 1964, Harvard Theatre Collection)

At a party at Joe Allen's restaurant after the opening of *A Delicate Balance:* Tharon Musser, Joy Small, Bill Ritman, 1966.
(© Alix Jeffry, 1966, Harvard Theatre Collection)

Play: Frances Sternhagen, Michael Lipton, Marian Reardon, 1964.
(© Alix Jeffry, 1964, Harvard Theatre Collection)

A. S., Tennessee Williams, Kate Reid, Margaret Leighton at a discussion of *Slapstick Tragedy*.
(Friedmann-Abeles)

Slapstick Tragedy: Zoe Caldwell, Kate Reid, Margaret Leighton, 1966.
(Friedmann-Abeles)

A. S. with family: Vickie, David, Jean, Vickie's husband,
Robert Swift, Christmas 1983.

Right up to our first preview, Uta never relented in her campaign to replace Arthur, a campaign that we were terrified might eventually register with him. He was frightened enough of his own inadequacies. He and Uta, like Viveca and Eugenie, Helen and Mary, Bert and Tommy, were at opposite poles of the acting spectrum. Uta worked from inside, but with exceptional control of her physical self. She always knew exactly what she was doing onstage, and what effect it was having on the audience—even as she never lost hold of her inner impulses and instinctive grasp of the moment's truth. Arthur, on the other hand, was what Method-trained actors always contemptuously term "a technical actor." Each move, each gesture, came from outside, studied and deliberate. Yet his own sense of reality was so strong and so sincere that whatever he chose to do, no matter how externally imposed, seemed real and organic to his audience. In this he resembled someone like Laurence Olivier, who was always blamed by Sanford Meisner and Lee Strasberg and their disciples for being an "indicator" and not an actor, and yet who always gave a performance which managed to be immensely "real" as well as highly theatrical.

Arthur would, for example, literally spend hours working out exactly on what syllable of a word he would pick up a glass, fondle an ice cube, or hand someone a completed drink. He had endless business pouring drinks for everybody in both Act One and Act Two. Always, however, he seemed to be doing it spontaneously and freely, no matter how rigidly he had worked to get that feeling. His sense of reality was as sure as Uta's—sometimes even surer—even though it came entirely from outside rather than inside, as it always did with her. But it was only when Herbert came to see our first invited preview and told Uta not only how believable Arthur was but also how well he complemented her own believability that she relaxed into accepting him as her partner.

Our rehearsal period being inordinately short, we spent every legal minute of our daily seven hours working, and lots of nonlegal ones in the bar next door to the Billy Rose going over the notes that my redoubtable assistant, Joy Small, had managed to write legibly in the darkness. Counting the first two days of readings, we had less than three weeks prior to our first preview. As I remember, I blocked the show in nine or ten days. The rest of the time was spent in polishing, as well as technical and dress rehearsals. We could not possibly have managed in the time available had not Richard and Clinton arranged for us to be on stage almost from the first day, rehearsing on our set with the actual props, something unheard of in the Broadway theater, before or since. We even managed to change a sofa when we decided our first one was too small. Clinton lent us his.

The producers had to pay for a complete theater crew, but it was well worth the cost. We could not have done the show in the normal manner, that is rehearsing in a rehearsal room or on a bare stage, with the setting and props brought in only at the last minute. Although the first act was almost twice as long as normal—eighty-four pages—I staged it in three days, coming home sweating blood. The other two acts, ninety-five and seventy-three pages, respectively, got on their feet at the same rate. We figured the show to be just under four hours when we started; by the time we opened, it ran about three and a half.

Edward and I followed the same pattern we had set in *American Dream*. He let me stage each scene without being around. Then he would come in, fresh, to look at it and give me his thoughts. Prior to rehearsals, of course, we had spent many hours and days together, with me asking him dozens of questions, sometimes not even to get the answers but to start him talking or thinking. We had already made a few small cuts; more were to follow during rehearsals. Most people think that a director is always making a writer cut out something he doesn't want to. In our case, I can take credit for persuading the author *not* to cut George's "Bergin" speech about the pain of growing up, even though Edward confessed he wasn't sure what specific relevance it had in the particular scene. I told him it was too good to cut regardless of its relevance. There was another speech of George's at the end, summing up the meaning of the evening, which I hated to see go; but this time I agreed with Edward that it held up the last scene too much. (Maybe he'll use it in another play some day.) The largest cut we made was some eleven pages at the very begining of Act Three, a long scene between George and Honey, which was interesting and funny but obviously delayed the action. Edward came in one day and presented us with a new opening which cut right to Martha's entrance. Everyone except Melinda was very happy. Arthur didn't mind having eleven less pages to memorize.

I'll never forget the day I'd finished staging the first act, and we were showing it to Edward and the producers. Richard, bless him, shot up from his seat, beaming. "I think it's excellent work," he said. Clinton was noncommittal but smiling, as usual. We all looked over at a slightly nervous Edward Albee, in baggy sweater and dirty tennis shoes, roaming around the back of the auditorium all by himself. After a few unspoken dots, his head slightly turned, he said: "Well . . . it's not at all the way I had seen it."

I turned pale, inside as well as out. "What was wrong?"

"I'm not sure. It's all different."

Richard, bless him, came in with, "Well, I loved it!"

"Okay," I persisted. "What's different? What's one thing different? What don't you like?"

Edward prowled up and down the aisle a moment. "Well, I think Honey and Nick sit down too soon. I didn't see them sitting down that soon."

"Oh," I said, "I think I can handle that. What else?"

"I don't know," Edward replied, looking away. "I'll think about it."

Through all this council-of-theater, the actors were milling about on stage, pretending nothing was happening. Richard smiled up at them, as a good producer should (but doesn't always). "Edward," I whispered between my teeth, "for chrissakes, go up there and say something nice to the actors. Anything. You don't have to mean it. They need it." Which he proceeded to do, bounding up onto the stage like a cat and spreading enthusiasm, like butter, onto their expectant, imploring selves.

Afterward, having told everyone how well everything went and how much Edward had loved it, I asked Nick to spend a little more time admiring the abstract painting over the fireplace before he and Honey sat down. George liked the idea. So did Edward the next time he saw Act One. "You changed the whole thing," he said. There's the difference between directors and playwrights, right there.

And so it went. Act Two seemed reasonably "there" to Edward when he saw it a few days later. I was especially pleased with my "chess game" between George and Nick, but Edward took the whole scene, an extremely subtle and difficult one to build, for granted. Act Three was more troublesome, especially Uta's deepening struggle to hold on to the imaginary child that George insisted on killing. Uta just would not go far enough in opening herself up. Only once, in a preview, after Edward and I had spent an hour with her in her dressing room imploring her not to hold back, did she let her insides really spill out. Her emotion was so strong, the scene was electric. We rushed back to tell her, but she refused even to talk to us. Nor did she ever play the scene with such intensity again. Months later we discovered that Uta herself had once lost a child. She could not suffer the pain of revealing herself that openly night after night.

Almost twenty years later, at a Dramatists Guild symposium, Uta blamed me publicly for never solving her problem of how to deal with that imaginary child. I'm sure she was right. And wrong. I told her at the start of rehearsals that George and Martha were not insane; they were always aware of their fantasy. Nor did they keep toys around, something she said she would have wanted. The child was, in Edward's own words, a "beanbag" for them to throw at each other, a way of getting at each other indirectly. Many of our critics later refused to accept the device. They could not believe that two intelligent adults, one of them a professor, could come to depend on such unreality to give meaning to their lives.

But life, as always, fools us. Years later, I heard—though I have no way of being sure—that Alfred Lunt and Lynn Fontanne had made up an imaginary child just as the two people in Edward's play had done. I wondered if there were any toys in their house in Genessee Depot, Wisconsin. As for my differences with Uta—differences of which I was happily unaware during rehearsals—I doubt that whatever I could possibly have told her about the child and her relationship to it would have satisfied her.

All during those rehearsals, I thought that I was at least doing tolerably well with Uta. She responded to most of my suggestions, beginning with the business I gave her in the first scene of cleaning up the place while carrying on her conversation about the guests with George. We improvised and improvised until a pattern that she could cope with emerged. She seemed to like most of my staging ideas, and carried them out beautifully. Wherever she didn't agree or felt uncomfortable, I always looked for and sometimes found an alternative. Where she felt strongly about a piece of business or a move of her own, I rarely challenged her. And it was only in that scene dealing with the child in Act Three that we really had trouble deciding on specifics. We tried many things and were never entirely happy with any choices we made.

Right at the beginning of rehearsals, Uta told me that her performance needed six months to find itself. In my opinion, she was brilliant on opening night—a night she claims she does not remember—and even more brilliant six months later. Toward the end of our New York run, she seemed to lose some of her spontaneity. Once or twice she refused to play with one of our matinee Georges when Arthur was ill.

I have often said that never have I worked with anyone more talented than Uta Hagen, or more capable of greatness. In any other theatrical society she would have been not just a star but a great lady of the theater. In the last twenty years of our own theatrical miasma, she has played only a handful of roles, never coming near her accomplishment in *Virginia Woolf*. That is a pity. And, speaking personally, it is also a pity that after twenty years she still seems to harbor a grudge not only against the author of the play in which she was able to give so striking a performance, but against the director who, at the very least, did not get in the way of her being able to give it.

Arthur posed for me exactly the opposite problem to Uta's. He begged for help, he demanded help, he needed help. Seemingly for every moment, every line, every move. I spent hours in and out of rehearsal guiding him, encouraging him, making him feel that he was a match for Uta. I gave him an endless string of Joy's notes, although he always asked for more. I would drill him over and over in his moves until they became part of his motor mechanism. He had to repeat things many times before he was able to get them right. More than anything else, I had to build his confidence in his own talent and ability. He was always willing to do anything I asked him, logical or crazy, right or wrong. Or willing to change whatever he was doing. And for that willingness I admired him and treasured his presence among us.

Interestingly enough, Arthur—for entirely different reasons—has also never been able to equal his *Virginia Woolf* achievement. A family man first and foremost, he left New York soon afterward, taking his family out of the theater's unsettled rhythms to the regularity of Hollywood's films and television. The roles he now gets out there have kept him working, established as either bland/sincere or Establishment/hypocritical. That is a loss to the American theater because onstage Arthur Hill, mature and attractive as he was and is, could give us something we do not have. That pram in the hallway does indeed remain the enemy of art.

Our rehearsals, under Richard's and Clinton's civilized guidance, proceeded, relatively speaking, without the agonies normally associated with every Broadway show. United by our faith in the play, and in our unspoken certainty that the rest of the world, critics and audiences, could not possibly appreciate it as much as we did, we worked hard and huddled together daily for warmth. We broke for twenty minutes each afternoon for tea and Uta's stories, related in a husky voice which could be heard a mile away. After rehearsal, there was the bar next door, with or without notes for Arthur. And sometimes the stage crew, Mel and Eddie and Barry, would let us go up onstage without penalty to work over some of the sections that troubled Arthur the most. Once he had gotten them, it would take an earthquake or a tank to shake him.

George kept asking Edward for a few lines and a big speech or two, something to atone for all those unfinished sentences and rows of dots. After he had accepted Melinda's dimensions, he became firm friends with her. And, throughout, he did everything possible to share in Uta's overall aura. I'm not sure how he felt about Arthur. They didn't seem to have much to talk about, although on stage they never missed an opportunity. That "chess game" at the beginning of the second act—with each player successively taking a pawn, then a bishop, then a rook, and then giving the mate—was one of the scenes that I knew would always stay on track. Melinda, whose New York debut this was, seemed throughout the proceedings to be surrounded by a slight haze made up of equal parts of admiration for Uta, an obvious crush on George, fear of her own fate, and her usual tinge of creative hysteria.

The audience at our first invited preview (of which we had five) consisted mainly of actors and other theater people, the ones normally kept away at all costs for fear of their spreading unfavorable word. From the time our curtain went up, their reactions convinced us that we had, in Richard's words, "something interesting and original," and that all would be well once we had opened. The excitement grew until by the end it enveloped us in a tumultuous curtain call. With each preview, the excitement and, better still, the business grew. We had had practically no advance sale. By the time we got to our five low-priced public previews—Billy Rose took out an ad inviting secretaries and telling them to suggest that their bosses stay at home—there was hardly a seat to be had.

Opening night, Saturday, October 13, 1962, was the most exciting night I've ever had in the theater. Even before the curtain went up, there was a buzz and hum throughout the audience that had nothing to do with friends or relatives. The audience seemed to have a sixth sense that they were in for something special. Even the "regulars," jaded and cynical as they tend to be about anything short of an atomic explosion in the adjoining seat, seemed to be actually alive.

With Uta's "Jesus H. Christ" entrance, I felt the audience fused into rapt attention, punctuated by machine-gun bursts of New York laughter. And two minutes into the performance, the actors on stage unable to produce anything other than perfection, I knew—from my usual pacing position beside the playwright at the very back of the orchestra—that nothing could stop us. Whatever happened tomorrow or next day, that audience was as one, absorbing Edward's "dark legend of truth and illusion" into their blood and bones. It was absolutely terrific to be part of that communal experience, to watch and listen and feel eleven hundred people transported and transformed, knowing that it was their own guts that were being kicked around on that stage.

When the last curtain finally came down, three and a half hours—or three eons—later I waited for the applause to end, which it wouldn't, then tore backstage through the pass door to congratulate or rather just hug everybody. On the way, I passed someone with a worried look, a middle-aged Gluyas Williams character telling his Helen Hokinson companion not to be fooled by the audience response: "I wish I could get out of my investment." Even though I'd made it a rule never to invest in any show I'm directing—or any show I'm not directing—I almost stopped in my tracks to tell him that I'd be glad to take whatever he had.

After any opening, it's bad enough to wait up four or five hours for the notices, usually pretending to enjoy the company and the drinks, at Sardi's. Opening on Saturday night—which we did for some now forgotten reason—meant that we had to wait for almost twenty-four. Nor were there any television reviews at that time to serve as poisoned hors d'oeuvres. The cast, I believe, had a sort of informal party at Sardi's. That is, after everyone had had a few drinks—sans notes—at the bar next door. After all that, I could barely wend my way up north toward my friendly little hamlet of Hastings-on-Hudson. I opened Edward's opening-night present, a newspaper headline stating SCHNEIDER ESSENTIAL TO STAGE TRUTH—E.A. His accompanying card explained, in Edward's scrawl, "The enclosed sentiment is no shit." (A prized possession, it now hangs in my bathroom.) Next morning, I slept into the afternoon, pretended to read the Sunday *Times*, kept my eyes on every clock in the house hoping one might conceivably get ahead of the others, and drove back into the city. Jean and I had been invited to Clinton Wilder's elegant town house on the upper East Side to gather at about six o'clock with Richard and Clinton and Edward and Bill Ritman and Howard Atlee, our always calm press agent, to wait for the Monday morning reviews to trickle in Sunday night. Billy Rose, who had somehow traced our whereabouts, joined us. We sat down to drink a bit, munch a bit, and wait for our spies in various newspaper printing plants to give us the news of our fate, a few minutes ahead of everybody else. Every press agent, it seems, has at least one someone whom he pays off generously to provide the news of a critic's opinion ahead of press time.

Just after seven, Howard was able to get to his man at the *Daily News* and was about to write down the review in longhand as it was read to him via Alexander Graham Bell's boon to the theater. At which convenient point, Richard said to Billy, "You used to be the champion shorthand writer in the world. Get on the phone and do your job!" Billy grabbed the receiver and a pencil and started to take down John Chapman's not ordinarily immortal words. I remember Billy's face, somber enough in normal repose, getting sadder and sadder, his mouth clamped around a huge cigar which kept drooping further and further earthward. None of us knew shorthand, but we could follow the movement of the cigar and interpret Billy's occasional grunts. It was clear not only that Mr. Chapman did not like us, but he did not like us in six figures. When Billy read us Chapman's headline, "For Dirty Minded Females Only," we knew the rest. Robert Coleman's verdict, in that other bastion of middle-class morality, the *Daily Mirror*, which came in a few minutes later, was even worse: "No red-blooded American would bring his wife to this shocking play."

The atmosphere in Clinton's warm living room suddenly became extremely chilly, Billy's cigar even more acrobatic. "I told you guys that furniture was lousy," he scowled. "You can't have a hit with that no-good furniture." We looked at each other.

Clinton, ever the gentleman, discovered at this moment that the food was ready for serving. Richard, a trifle less contained, left the room for a walk around the block and then went upstairs to lie down. Unable to read shorthand and not quite believing all this was happening, I held on to Jean's hand for comfort. We shall all be eternally grateful to Edward, who pretended the virtue of calmness even though I'm sure he had various vices on his mind. "Let's wait for the real reviews," he said, meaning the two more intellectually accepted morning papers, the *Times* and the *Tribune*.

Somehow, we all survived to read Taubman and Kerr the very moment our ubiquitous Howard Atlee brought them through the door. Neither wrote exactly what we would call a rave. But they seemed positive enough to keep us breathing. "A wry and electric evening in the theater," said Taubman. Walter Kerr, after several columns of rather turgid qualification, added: "But it must be seen." Which is, of course what got into the quote ads.

The rest of the reviews, which we read the next day, were more favorable. Apart from a few of the intellectual weeklies, which blamed Edward for not doing things he hadn't set out to do, responses ranged from respectful to strongly positive. And even the ones that had reservations of one sort or another, managed to say enough to get people interested in buying tickets. People who wouldn't come to see *Who's Afraid of Virginia Woolf?* as a play of ideas about the failure of American marriage, or a philosophical drama dealing with the ambiguous conflict between truth and illusion, came to see us because we were a "dirty" play or because someone told them there were sexy scenes, Uta Hagen touching the inside of George Grizzard's thigh. I remember how carefully we worked on that one.

On Monday morning, I journeyed down to Forty-first Street to discover a line stretching out a fair distance from the Billy Rose Theatre, and Sam Zolotow, the *Times*'s inevitable leg-man and super-sleuth, noting down the size of the line as well as my lurking presence. I decided that, in spite of both Mr. Chapman and Mr. Coleman, a lot of red-blooded American males and some non-dirty-minded females were going to be in our audiences for weeks or maybe months or perhaps even years to come. Suddenly, I realized that I was forty-four years old, almost forty-five, and I was finally going to make a living in the theater. Or if not a living, at least that temporary killing, which my playwright friend Bob Anderson had told me was easier.

ABC OF SUCCESS: ALBEE AND BECKETT AND THE CHERRY LANE

1962–1964

For the next two years I spent a lot of time, in various places, with various Georges and Marthas, working to produce results not exactly similar but equivalent to the originals. We had a matinee company—headed by Kate Reid and Shepperd Strudwick—which had to go on with less than two weeks of rehearsal. Eventually, I believe, in all the companies there were nine Marthas, including Nancy Kelly, Elaine Stritch, Mercedes McCambridge, and Vicki Cummings, and seven Georges, including Donald Davis, Henderson Forsythe, James Karen, and Bill Gibberson. Later, in London, Constance Cummings took over from Uta, and Ray McAnally and Jerome Kilty from Arthur.

People want to know who was the "best," but the combinations in Edward's characters were seemingly infinite. If I tend to remember Uta more than any of the others, that is understandable. She played Martha originally and for the longest time, 665 performances in New York and a few hundred more in London, and her recording always comes alive in the hearing. Yet I cannot deny that each of her numerous successors carried an echo of her own.

No one ever matched Uta's virtuosity and power; Kate got more humor, perhaps, and more humanity into the first act; and Nancy wrenched a few more tears from the third. Shep, always the gentleman and always willing to try anything, couldn't get all of Arthur's dry humor. But the pain he was able to express in that tough driving second act eventually came to move me more than anyone else's. Uta simply refused to play with Donald, my original Krapp, whom she considered a lightweight;

whenever Arthur was out and Shep not available, we had to ask Kate to play. Actually, Donald was not lightweight at all, merely different. Uta's tastes in partners—as evidenced in her original feelings about Arthur—were always intensely personal.

At the Tony Awards that spring, I spent a hideous evening during what should have been a celebration. Not because I was worried about winning the Best Director award—I was sure that veteran George Abbott would be the one—but because I was terrified that should only one of our two stars, Uta and Arthur, win, the other would be impossible to deal with and the whole production would collapse, bringing down my royalties with it. After Uta was announced as Best Actress very early on, I trembled for what seemed forever until Arthur emerged as Best Actor. Only then could I relax. The rest of the evening was anticlimactic: Edward Albee for Best Play, Richard Barr and Clinton Wilder for Best Production, even Alan Schneider as Best Director. Anyhow, by the time they got around to me, the television portion of Alexander Cohen's magnum opus was over. My mother and my two kids, watching a television screen, never got to see me, which shows how important the director really is. Dame Edith Evans once responded, when asked if she found a director useful to her during rehearsal, "Yes, of course." She added in that marvelous rangy voice of hers, "Especially to fetch a script I've left in the car."

Uta's performance onstage changed and deepened until it was beyond challenge. On opening night, I thought that what she was able to do was already terrific; six months later, as she had predicted, she was even stronger, every moment true and fervently alive. Even now the recording, made on a marked-out floor plan at CBS Studios, with the actors moving around as they did onstage, strikes me as the most spontaneous and exciting recording of a stage play I have ever heard. Uta hated the entire proceeding and complained at every moment, but gave a remarkable performance, especially considering the fact that she had a bad cold. From her first offstage laugh—sounded at a pitch Chaliapin would have found difficult to achieve —Uta was magnificent. Going into our second season, she may have tired, but then when we went to London in January 1964, she managed to reach even greater heights. To persuade her to come to London, we had to give her casting approval; she successfully vetoed a succession of excellent young actresses for the role of Honey, including one whom she turned down because, in her reading, the actress mispronounced the word naked as "nekkid."

Our British coproducer, Donald Albery, had Edward submit his text to the Lord Chamberlain for approval, and the script came back with some eight pages of prescribed cuts. Edward, of course, reared back and said, "No way!" For weeks negotiations and pages went back and forth across the Atlantic—here a cut accepted, there a line restored. The Lord's name could not be used in a disrespectful manner—"Jesus H. Christ" was grudgingly adjusted to "Mary H. Magdalene." "Screw you!" had to stay, Edward insisted, or no London production. The Lord High Chamberlain evidently proved willing to allow that one.

The absolute impossibility and sticking point was George referring to Martha as her father, the college president's, "right ball." On this one, his Lordship was adamant. George, he suggested—presumably seriously—could say "right testicle"; or, if that choice didn't scan properly for the author, "right nut"; but absolutely and definitely not "right ball." Of course, added the Lord High Executioner, we could just cut the entire line. But Edward decided he had cut enough. Eyeball to eyeball, excuse the expression, neither side would budge. Then, just as we began to think there would be no London production, Edward suddenly remembered an old Southern expression, "right bawl," meaning a good cry, which someone in his family had used. He would change the entire meaning of the line from "right ball" to "right bawl." To our collective delighted amazement, the Lord Chamberlain accepted. Arthur-George would refer to Uta-Martha as her father's "right bawl"; all transatlantic harmony was restored; smiles returned on all sides. Edward and I sailed, Arthur and Uta flew, to London.

Even with our smash success in New York, we were nervous about going to the West End, where coproducer Albery had not put us in his New Theatre in Leicester Square but had shunted us off to the cavernous Piccadilly. No serious American play had made it in London since the war—not *The Glass Menagerie*, not *Death of a Salesman*, not *Streetcar*. What would happen with this one, right bawl and all? We rehearsed, neither too long nor too strenuously, with tea breaks whenever possible. We had planned only one preview—primarily for the staff and crew, who were most respectful and efficient. The evening laid a flock of eggs, produced very few laughs, and resulted in a general letdown of our enthusiasm. What was wrong? Richard and Edward and I walked most of the night from Piccadilly along to the Strand, trying to figure out the answer to that question. The atmosphere was colder than the temperature, thicker with gloom than the wafts of London fog through which we walked. Had we rehearsed enough? Too much? Should we have slowed down our tempo for British audiences? Were they not understanding the words? With the show opening the next night, there wasn't much we could change. And I particularly did not want to alarm the actors with our own insecurities. It was all in the laps of the gods—and our audiences.

After a not too pleasant twenty-four hours, we opened with nothing changed from the night before—except the audience. The gods laughed as much and in the same places as they had done in New York. Uta and Arthur had never been better—even though Uta was so nervous that she said "Jesus H. Magdalene" on her first entrance. The audience ate it up, relishing every jarring note from those crazy Americans. Most of the reviews were favorable, although Harold Hobson, in the Sunday *Times*, disappointed me with his qualifications about the text. What had happened the night before? Really nothing. We had just forgotten that the audience had been made up mostly of lower-middle-class friends and relatives of the crew, who were nervous about some of the sexual references and overt male-female hostility, and were therefore afraid to laugh. Sophisticated Londoners, language differences and all, latched on to us no differently than had sophisticated New Yorkers; they kept us going more than a year.

Uta and Arthur had agreed to stay only twelve weeks, after which a too ladylike Constance Cummings and Ray McAnally took over. But each night during those twelve weeks, the working actresses of London stopped in after their own performances (our running time was considerably longer) to stand at the back and watch Uta play the third act. I always got a great thrill to see Peggy Ashcroft or Celia Johnson or Joan Plowright, their faces as rapt as schoolgirls, watching and listening to an American actress creating dynamic dramatic reality. Two decades earlier they had come to watch, for the same reason, the Group Theatre's celebrated ensemble performance of Odets' *Golden Boy*, with Luther and Stella Adler, Lee J. Cobb, Elia Kazan, and Sanford Meisner. The British theater would never be the same because of that performance; nor would it be the same after they had seen Uta and Arthur in Edward's play. A good many British actors and directors have told me that, and Royal Shakespeare stalwart Alan Howard admitted his debt in an interview many years later. Talent—or influence—doesn't only travel one way across the Atlantic, though in our awe over manners and diction we sometimes forget that.

With the artistic and commercial success of *Virginia Woolf*, my New York career was catapulted to a new stage of confusion. Not that I was actually making as much money as everyone thought I was, or as I myself had fantasized. We never sold out completely in any week of our run, although we did well. The theater's weekly grosses were under $40,000, and my one percent gave me a good though not a great return. But the elevation of the opportunities offered to me was both sudden and dangerous. For the first time in my life, there was no limit to the level and scope of the offers coming in, stage, screen, and television, with all sorts of star names and prospects. Had I been inclined (or able) to play the commercial game I could have made a fortune. At the very least, I could have transformed myself into the equivalent of a Gene Saks, a Robert Moore, a Herbert Ross. Instead, I chose—partially consciously and partially instinctively—to pay little attention to all the hoopla swirling around me, and go on directing wherever a decent script came along, off-Broadway, in the regional theater, or from Edward Albee.

First of all, right after my evening and matinee companies of *Woolf* got going, I had to deal with the delayed *Pinter Plays* and my "blackmailing" producer, Caroline Swann. Whatever my feelings about Caroline, I was not about to let Harold Pinter go on without me. Even though we did not yet have a theater, I proceeded to Greenwich Village to cast and rehearse *The Dumbwaiter* and *The Collection* with Dana Elcar, John C. Becher, Henderson Forsythe, and others, all former friends and colleagues. We worked together for a couple of weeks in some freezing Village loft until Caroline managed a deal with the Cherry Lane Theatre, which was my favorite small playhouse. Bill Ritman's designs somehow made the Cherry Lane's postage stamp of a stage seem large enough not only for *The Dumbwaiter*'s basement setting, but for all the exterior and interior spaces demanded by *The Collection*. From the beginning, *The Dumbwaiter*'s mysterious menaces seemed manageable; the show looked tight, funny, and powerful. But *The Collection*'s tone and stylistic nuances kept eluding us all. We awaited Harold's arrival toward the end of rehearsals with an equal measure of anticipation and concern.

Harold finally came over, and loved the cast, the theater, and New York. Only his *Caretaker* had been done in New York, and, though greeted favorably, it had not been a commercial success—in spite of excellent performances by Donald Pleasence, Robert Shaw, and Alan Bates. Then as now dressing impeccably, speaking and looking like a Pinter character, and radiating charm, he told us that *The Collection* was going to be just fine, but he was very worried about *The Dumbwaiter*. Everything in it was too obvious.

In the week or so that Harold was with us—he had to leave before we opened—he was helpful and understanding on all counts. His having been an actor made it possible for him to be specific about what was "right" and "wrong," and about what he wanted from the performance. He also knew much more about the process of rehearsal, about the way in which actors and directors worked, than did Edward. Edward would tend to give line readings or specific instructions about staging; Harold knew better. He made suggestions about props or costumes but never imposed himself, and tried very hard to bring Caroline and me together. He kept reminding me that he had been the one urging me not to give up *Virginia Woolf* in order to keep myself free for the original dates for *The Pinter Plays*. I was most grateful to him for that. The actors loved him, and so did I. When we said our farewells for his flight back to London, I felt I was parting from a warm friend.

We opened to rave reviews and another two-year run—but, as it turned out, no financial reward for me. Dana and John C. seemed fine to me; their audiences were sufficiently mystified by what was going on between them to have pleased Harold. Off-Broadway's vagaries provided us with a constant parade of performers succeeding each other, and years later, I would meet actors who told me that they had appeared in one role or another of *The Pinter Plays* in one or another of the theaters in which it played, and I had forgotten or not known them in the first place.

Caroline Swann, although she kept my name off the *Pinter Plays* poster (the first and only time in my New York career), continued her surface politeness and friendliness. A year later, she offered me another off-Broadway Pinter double bill, this time *A Slight Ache* and *The Room*, and this time including both fee and royalties. I accepted her offer, but because of a conflict with a new Albee play became unavailable before the contract was signed. In the spring, *The Dumbwaiter* and *The Collection* got me my first—and last—Obie Award alongside my Tony for *Virginia Woolf*. Since I was sailing off to Europe at the time, John C. Becher, a good friend, accepted for me.

The Pinter Plays opened at the Cherry Lane on November 26, 1962. As soon as they started their run I returned to my first love, the Arena Stage. Zelda had sent me regular offers to come back as her associate director. I had resisted, feeling that my appearances at the Arena would tend to be more effective if they didn't occur too often. Besides, those five plays I had directed there the season before had burned me out. And I was bombarded with offers of all kinds all the way from New York to Hollywood. Nevertheless, for some reason not entirely clear either then or now, I went right back to the Arena again to do three productions. Maybe it was, as I kept telling people over the years, my favorite place in the world to put on a play.

My first production was a reasonably effective version of Tad Mosel's *All the Way Home*, which Tad saw and liked. After that came my third attempt at *Othello*, this time with Brock Peters, Ray Reinhardt, and Inga Swenson, which didn't seem any better than the previous two times I had tried it at Catholic University, even though I had much better actors this time. Brock was extremely willing, but he lacked the necessary drive and sexuality; Ray was a little sluggish; Inga was lovely, a rare Desdemona. I ended the season—and, temporarily, all relationship with Zelda—in May 1963 with a *Threepenny Opera* of which I am still proud, although I wasn't proud of my behavior in a very difficult and painful rehearsal period. Apart from the normal hassles with designer, producer, and actors, I never got along with the musical director, who expected a much more conventional *Threepenny* than I was willing to accept. I was generally exhausted after a year of exhaustion, and kept driving the actors as well as myself into the ground. The show was difficult technically, and my old technical director friend-and-foe Henry Gorfein wasn't, at least in my opinion, being any more helpful than usual. I resigned on about a half-dozen separate occasions, each time after telling Zelda that she was running a second-rate theater, and that I would never come back again. The production itself, after all the fireworks, turned out to be first-rate—with Roscoe Lee Browne stealing most of it as an ingratiatingly sensual Streetsinger. Barely able to stand up, I sailed off to Europe to see the Berliner Ensemble do *Arturo Ui* and *Coriolanus*. As a parting gesture to my *Threepenny* cast and Zelda, I put a farewell note on the callboard: "Next Week, East Berlin!" It was a lot of pun.

The summer over, I returned to Edward to direct the National Touring Company of *Virginia Woolf*, starring Nancy Kelly and Shep Strudwick, which opened to acclaim in Boston in September. Almost on the next day, I was at work on Edward's adaptation of Carson McCullers' novella *The Ballad of the Sad Café*. The weeks and months after *Virginia Woolf*'s first reception brought Edward and myself as close together personally as we were ever to be. The night after the opening, the two of us had dinner at his new Tenth Street apartment, watching the television showing of *Woolf*'s first scene on Channel 13's "Playwright at Work" series, which had been taped the year before.

Not naturally gregarious, although sociable enough when comfortable, Edward would call me often, just to talk about the show, or to exchange tidbits about what was happening in the theater. He was always generous about my contribution to his plays. While basically withdrawn and private, and while he rarely shared his deepest self with anyone, Edward seemed open and frank enough that I felt close to him. Once at a big theater party that Jean and I gave in Joy Small's apartment to celebrate my New York productions, Edward arrived very late and almost embarrassingly solicitous of my welfare and person. He was a bit tipsy, and had brought along with him an equally affected Tallulah Bankhead, with whom he had evidently been playing cards. I was alternately touched and uncertain about how to deal with him.

Carson's relationship with Edward was always a mysterious one to me. She was already suffering from a disease that had twisted and wasted her entire body. She was totally stagestruck, even after two previous experiences with the theater's attempts at translating the delicate reverberations of her writing to the stage. *The Member of the Wedding* had succeeded; *The Square Root of Wonderful*, despite its evocative title, had not. Edward and I went out to her riverview home near Nyack, across the river from my place in Hastings, to talk to her about Edward's adaptation. I felt that she didn't really like Edward's script but that she respected his theater sense and craft. I respected that sense and craft also—how could I not?—but felt that *Ballad* had been constructed too rapidly, without carefully considering its structural and stylistic problems. Edward's adaptation contained some beautiful scenes and some exquisite speeches, but the whole piece didn't seem to connect. The wedding section was especially sketchy and unsatisfying. And Edward's insistence on a black narrator had nothing to do with anything else.

Colleen Dewhurst was our first and only choice for Amelia, and Colleen was eager to do the role. She did have some qualms about me, because she thought I had turned her down for the part of Jocasta in my *Omnibus Oedipus*. I had to spend time reassuring Colleen that it had really been Walter Kerr, our adapter and editor, who had made that decision on the basis of not liking her work in *The Eagle Has Two Heads* off-Broadway. For Marvin Macy, we could have had John Cassavetes, who read for us; but Edward preferred Lou Antonio, who was then about to break through as a successor to Marlon Brando although he never did. After exhaustive searching, we found our third member of Carson's love triangle, the dwarf, in Michael Dunn, who had once played in Richard Barr's off-Broadway production of Ionesco's *The Killer*. From the first, Edward wanted Roscoe Lee Browne for our Narrator. I suggested William

Prince for Henry Macy, and Bill accepted what was a very small though vital role. Roscoe, of course, was delicious, but his casting confused things. All through rehearsals, I kept thinking that the brother, Henry Macy, should be telling the story instead of an impersonal Narrator, no matter how attractive or witty. Edward, I believe, eventually came to agree with me, and he later suggested this change for future productions. Roscoe was too much of a delight to relinquish.

For some reason, something to do with obtaining the rights, a producer other than Richard Barr was involved, Lew Allen. Lew is a fine gentleman with excellent experience and taste. He supported Edward and me all along the way, perhaps even in those cases when he should have overruled us. Ben Edwards' setting was expressive and poetic, as was Jean Rosenthal's lighting. Edward complained about the latter throughout technical rehearsals, making Jean change it every day and driving her up her very special wall. The big fight scene at the end caused us all sorts of problems. We tried it every possible way: realistically, with a real fighter hired to help; then balletically choreographed; then a combination of fist fight and wrestling match. The final product, though effective enough with the audiences, was a hodgepodge.

I alternately loved and hated the show. I welcomed the opportunity to fill the stage with movement and spectacle, which I hadn't had in New York since *A Long Way from Home* and *The Skin of Our Teeth*. But its unwieldy mixture of styles, the holes Edward had left in its narrative thrust, perhaps just the difficulty of realizing Carson's diffused pastel images, made me feel we were never going to get what Edward wanted. And Colleen, who had started out being completely cooperative, decided somewhere along the line that Edward and I were trying to make her look and act like a lesbian. Nothing could have been further from our minds. The best thing about the production, I sometimes thought, was Leonard Baskin's poster—that shadowy figure balanced atop that mysterious head. How I longed for something of Baskin's control over his materials! If only Colleen's head could be as serene! If only Michael Dunn's gyrations could be as perfectly poised! If only . . .

Still, through some mysterious and redemptive chemistry of the theater, we almost made it. We opened at the Martin Beck on October 30, 1963. The reviews were mixed, but the ones that liked us were so rhapsodic and lyrical that they almost carried us to the top. Best of all, most theater people appreciated the show, including, of all people, a most enthusiastic Joshua Logan. I didn't think Josh knew I was alive. We managed to eke out slightly more than a hundred performances, and might have gone on a bit longer if not for cast dissension and general unwillingness on the part of Lew Allen and his associates to take the chance. I can't blame them. But for years afterward, people would mention the show to me, especially the scenes in which Michael Dunn appeared—or the big fight scene. It was another one of those artistic "success-failures" with which my career is liberally sprinkled.

Shortly after the start of *Ballad*'s run, my father died. He had been having a rough time for about five years, ever since his first heart attack in Israel in 1958. Dad had spent time in hospitals in Israel, Switzerland, and the United States, alternately for a heart condition, leukemia, and emphysema. In between, he had sold the house in Bethesda and moved to a New York City apartment in order to be near Jean and me and the grandchildren. After we moved out of the city to Hastings-on-Hudson in 1959, we still managed weekly visits to my parents, in either New York or Westchester. Dad continued to see my shows for as long as possible, but whether he understood them much, I doubt. He always found the proceedings "interesting," and was amazed that all the actors were able to remember all their lines. With *Virginia Woolf*, he admired the performance but, I'm sure, was more than a little nervous about the way it portrayed marriage.

Dad entered the Veterans Hospital in West Haven, Connecticut, for observation and treatment; Jean and I and my mother, then staying with us, had visited him several times early in *Ballad*'s run. Once he had held my hand hard and told me that he was glad to have lived long enough to see my life a success. He was referring, of course, to the production of *Virginia Woolf*. I remember holding onto him and saying, as quietly as I could, that my life had been a success the day I married Jeannie. He understood, but that was not what he meant. To him, even at that late hour, the material aspect of life counted most.

One night, the hospital rang to say that Dad's condition had worsened; we had better come right up. We drove, tight-lipped, through a steady rain to find him in his last stages. The leukemia had weakened him beyond repair; he had difficulty breathing. His huge hulk of a body, once so strong, lay helpless on the bed. But it was mostly his personal dignity that was suffering. The nurses, overworked and underpaid, cared little for his pain, even less about keeping him comfortable. I came into the room once to find him suffering great physical discomfort, which could have been ameliorated in a moment if anyone had cared. They didn't, or hadn't the time to. With my father lying almost unconscious on the bed, I could not restrain myself from telling the nurse off about her unwillingness to respect his past status and worth. My temper, as always, burst out much too strongly in its reaction to unfairness and injustice on the human level. All I could think of was that I would never subject myself to this kind of institutional inhumanity.

He died that same night, my mother and I holding his hands until the end. With all our differences and all our fights, my father's loss opened up caverns of emptiness inside of me, which it took many months to fill again. Samuel Beckett wrote me a solacing letter, which I have kept and referred to many times. Sometimes when the father of a close friend dies, I feel impelled to share it. I know how much that letter has meant to me over the years, and I hope Sam won't mind my sharing it now with a larger audience. "My very dear Alan," Sam wrote, "I know your sorrow and I know that for the likes of us there is no ease to be had from words or reason and that in the very assurance of sorrow's fading there is more sorrow. So I offer you only my deeply affectionate and compassionate thoughts and wish for you only that the strange thing may never fail you, whatever it is, that gives us the strength to live on and on with our wounds."

My father died on November 12, 1963. Ten days later I was having lunch with Richard Chandler, a young protégé of Cheryl Crawford's, at a French restaurant on Fifty-third Street. After lunch I was scheduled for understudy rehearsals for *Virginia Woolf* at the Billy Rose. When one of the waiters told us that President Kennedy had been killed, I walked right out and down to the theater to postpone the rehearsal.

President Kennedy was killed on Friday. I was supposed to give a talk in Buffalo that Sunday to some theater group. When I rang up to see if they still wanted me to come, they said yes; it was important to go on with things, "the things of the spirit," as they put it. My heart far from my body, I flew up to Buffalo Saturday afternoon, and was met at the airport by a young director, Melvin Bernhardt. He later became my assistant on a number of shows and went on to become a successful director. Mel had asked me to stay with him while I was in Buffalo. The next morning, prior to my going out to give my talk about the importance of the theater in times such as we were then experiencing, Mel and I were watching Lee Harvey Oswald being transferred from one prison to another, when a chunky figure appeared in the frame and shot Oswald. The whole thing took seconds and seemed totally unreal. Although I have read every word I could find on that sad moment of our history, I still do not think that we know what really happened that day in Dallas.

My talk about the importance of the theater in such times, this time, was called off.

I came back to New York, wondering what was to happen next, glad that my father had not lingered on to see this day. Two months later, in January, Jean's mother, Emmy Muckle, who had come from England to stay with us, also died. I remember my son, David, then almost five, asking us if everyone was going to die. It was not a good time.

My 1964 opened on January 4 with a double bill of Beckett's *Play* and Pinter's *The Lover* again at the Cherry Lane. I was very happy to be there again, especially with these two playwrights. The producers were once more Messrs. Barr and Wilder, now joined by Edward Albee, collectively known as Theatre 1965, for whom I had now become in some informal but nevertheless tangible way "most favored director." Harold had specifically given them *The Lover* for me to direct with Sam's play. I had read *Play*, which soon became known as *Last Year at Marienbad* in urns, sometime earlier and had found as fascinating as it was mysterious. The summer before, on my way to the Berliner Ensemble, I had journeyed with Sam from Paris to see its premiere production in Ulm, Germany.

We cast both plays with off-Broadway and Arena actors with whom I had previously worked—Frances Sternhagen, Marian Reardon, James Patterson, Michael Lipton, and Hilda Brawner (now television's Hildy Brooks). I was back in my native habitat on Commerce Street, happy as a lark with my favorite playwrights and my favorite producers. However, a day or two into rehearsals, I discovered that Jimmy Patterson, with whom I had worked so well in *The Collection*—and who had been Harold's first choice for the role of the husband in *The Lover*—was in some sort of traumatic "emotional state" and could neither learn the lines nor respond to direction of any kind. Reluctantly, after several days of trying, I gave Jimmy's part to Michael Lipton, who was also playing the Man in *Play*. Mike wound up doing very well in both plays. In the meantime, Marian was having trouble acting while she was stuck up to her neck in an urn. Frances was holding us all together.

On top of all this, came trouble from my favorite producers. According to Sam's exact instructions, *Play* was to be played through twice without interruption and at a very fast pace, each time taking no longer than nine minutes. The idea was that whatever references the audience didn't get the first time—most of them—would be absorbed the second time around. My producers, all three of them, objected strongly to Sam's idea. That was all right for less sophisticated audiences, in Ulm or elsewhere. But in New York . . . (Maximal pause. Stern looks.) A couple of their friends who had seen our early previews had made rude remarks about how Mr. Beckett was insulting their intelligence.

Having gone through some unhappy experiences with other producers objecting to Mr. Beckett's specific stage directions, I tried to explain that Sam had something very specific in mind when he demanded that repetition. It was not just a matter of additional information; it was a tonal matter, a question of rhythm, of establishing a circular pattern. My producers remained unmoved. They informed me that if I didn't get Mr. Beckett's permission for the actors to say the lines only once, speaking much more slowly, they would take it on themselves to make the change. Or they would cancel *Play*.

For the first and last time in my long relationship with Sam, I did something I despised myself for doing. I wrote to him, asking if we could try having his text spoken only once, more slowly. Instead of telling me to blast off, Sam offered us his reluctant permission. Years later, I learned through a mutual friend that Sam had felt hurt and betrayed by me—as well he should. I should have resisted or quit or anything but give in to the producers' wishes. Why Sam continued to have faith in me after that, I shall never know.

Inevitably, *Play* came off the better of the two plays. Although we were far head of our time, and although neither the actors nor I really knew how to do it as well as I—and many other productions—have done with it since, the play proved highly effective in the theater. That effectiveness came mainly from the fourth actor in the cast, the beam of light, darting instantaneously from one urn-topping face to another. That special magic was accomplished with dispatch and verve by our tiptop stage manager, Bob Currie, manipulating a remote control mechanism rigged up after seemingly hundreds of hours of hard work and imagination by our resident electronics genius, Gary Harris. That light made up for a lot of our deficiencies, including not having the right makeup for the actors' faces, makeup that would have made those faces look like charred ashes, part of the urns.

Our first-nighters may have been baffled; they were also intrigued. One of them, Virgil Thomson, came out beaming, explaining it to everyone as a soap opera. Someone else said that it reminded him of

Noel Coward. I even got the producers to let me put back the repeat, just a tiny bit slowed up. *The Lover,* which had seemed so accessible in its early stages, turned out to be much more baffling, although Mike and Hilda were excellent. I went off to London to direct *Virginia Woolf,* feeling I had managed to betray both Beckett and Pinter in one evening. All I had left was Albee.

TINY ALICE IN WONDERLAND
1964

It was Albee, triumphant on both sides of the Atlantic, who kept me working most of that year. Returning from London, I directed another version of *The American Dream*—not nearly so well cast or performed as the original, but seemingly as acceptable to its audiences, its authors, and the critics. This, over my strong objection, replaced *The Lover* on the Cherry Lane's double bill. The national company of *Virginia Woolf*, starring Nancy Kelly and Shepperd Strudwick, covered the Continent; and, in August, we added a bus-and-truck version, with Vicki Cummings and her real-life husband, Bill Gibberson.

Vicki, an accomplished light comedienne, was desperate to prove herself as a serious actress. Eager and willing to do anything, she practically begged for direction. I kidded myself that she was adequate. I knew the rest of the cast was not, and kept wondering why the producers, Edward, and I were so willing to descend from the heights. The answer, of course, was that the towns and theaters sheltering bus-and-truck tours in the mid-sixties did not count—only the dollars they brought in.

My portion of those dollars enabled me finally to exchange my little Hastings-on-Hudson cottage, where I had lived since *The Summer of the Seventeenth Doll*, for a very grand raw-wood-glass-and-stone contemporary overlooking the Hudson River, with a view on clear nights of the Empire State building. We had been driving past the house for years, admiring its textures and the thrust of its front porch, jutting out from a steep hillside like the prow of a Viking ship—the "ship house," we called it. One day, when our ailing parents—Jean's one and my two—descended on our increasingly cramped cottage, we drove past to see a charred mass of debris in place of our "ship house." We bought the debris, had it rebuilt by the original architect, a disciple of Frank Lloyd Wright, and lived in it happily for the next fifteen years. Only my mother survived long enough to share it with our two growing children, Vickie and David. Even the address was symbolic. We had moved from Flower Avenue to the corner of Hollywood and Scenic.

In the fall of 1964, I started the mysteriously titled *Tiny Alice*. Edward had been working on it a long time and talking about it since our days in London. The rumor was that he was writing it for John Gielgud, and that was enough to keep favorite producers Richard Barr and Clinton Wilder, and "most favored director" Alan Schneider, panting with anticipation.

In late September or early October, Richard informed me that the script was ready. He had read it, but wasn't talking. My reaction to the first scene—that caustic, coruscating, intellectual sparring match between the Lawyer and the Cardinal—was that it represented Edward at his best, venom and wit perfectly blended. I was so excited, I could hardly bear to turn the pages. The rest of the play, however, came as a letdown. Always tantalizing because of Edward's theatrical imagination and powerful language, it got murkier and murkier, ending in a scene I had difficulty believing on any level. I reported my reaction to Richard: "I . . . love it. It's fascinating although I'm not sure I got it all . . . but . . . do you think the Cardinal a large enough role for John Gielgud?"

A moment of silence on the other end of the line. Then, Richard's slightly strained voice. "John is playing Brother Julian." I gulped, inwardly. Julian was supposed to be a young man, an innocent, a Dostoyevsky or Graham Greene "naif." Wasn't John too old? What about Marlon Brando or Montgomery Clift? Richard explained patiently that Edward had written the play specifically with John's qualities in mind, his diffidence, his quizzical innocence. "We" all agreed on that. Of course, if I did not . . .

Eventually, the idea of John (then about sixty) playing a youthful sexually obsessed priest was accepted by everyone—except John. I met with him before rehearsals to find out how he wanted to work. The idea of "directing" John Gielgud in any conventional manner seemed preposterous. I discovered at once that John was absolutely terrified. Edward had told him about the play before it was written, had shown him a few scenes, and had persuaded him to accept the role before he had read the entire script—something he had never done before. He was baffled by the play itself, totally puzzled by the character he was supposed to play, and completely bewildered by what he called "surrealist theater," by which he meant the plays of such writers as Samuel Beckett, Harold Pinter, and Edward Albee. Someone had suggested that he had to immerse himself in this new form of playwriting that seemed to be taking over our stages; but ever since he had read *Tiny Alice,* he had wanted to get out of doing it. But his promise to Edward kept him steadfast. What John wanted from me was clarity and reassurance that there was a play here. In addition, he kept warning me, "I always try all sorts of things, so you mustn't get too worried." But it was mainly reassurance he wanted. As if I had any to spare.

John's insecurity was alleviated somewhat by our casting of Irene Worth as Miss Alice. He knew and admired her, and her willingness to accept the role gave him confidence. Although I was nervous at first, having heard for years how difficult and demanding Irene could be, I soon discovered that she was generous, good-natured, and perceptive. I was also pleased that Edward and the producers took my suggestion of William Hutt, a Canadian actor who had not previously been seen in New York, for the Lawyer. John Heffernan, Edward's choice, played the Butler; and, after much searching and indecision, we cast an English performer, Eric Berry, as the Cardinal. American actors, it seemed, were great at playing taxi drivers and waitresses, but we had to go elsewhere for the upper classes.

The rest of our Albee-*Woolf* team remained intact. Bill Ritman, guided not too gently by Edward, provided us with a massive and impressive Gothic setting—complete with a huge detailed model of that setting dominating center stage. Mark Wright, our ever smiling production stage manager, kept us under control. Joy Small was there to take—and give—notes in the dark. Martin Aronstein joined us to provide the necessary magic in the lighting, and Mainbocher dressed Irene beautifully. All of us, each one with an entirly different perception of the play, felt that we were involved in bringing to life a major work of art.

What that work was specifically saying, or how to make whatever it was saying clear, none of us was entirely sure—including, I believe, Edward. Still in his mid-thirties, he had written his "big, philosophical play," his *Lady from the Sea*, his *Dream Play*, his *Tempest*. Perhaps if he had waited to rewrite it once or twice before we went into rehearsal . . . but he would not. So it remained what the notes I kept jotting down in my script as I read and re-read the play suggested: a "metaphysical mystery," a "parable or allegory," a "modern morality play dealing with reality and illusion, essence and symbol, the tangible and the abstract." On and on I went, filling pages with my ideas, with not an idea how to make them work on stage.

Richard kept saying the play was crystal-clear. Modern man, seeking answers to a noncomprehensible existence, substitutes symbols—including a personified abstraction he calls God—for reality, then mistakes the symbols for reality itself. To which I added that this is a corrupting, but necessary, state of affairs; anyone—like Julian!—who challenges that corruption must, therefore, be destroyed or the "system" will collapse. The abstract is incomprehensible; only its concrete representation is graspable. That representation, of course, is not the same thing—any more than Plato's solid table is the same as his "real" table. Any "reality" we seek to grasp is an illusion. Q.E.D. And no wonder the Shuberts would not give us a theater!

By the time rehearsals started, I had over a dozen pages of notes, intelligent, articulate, and largely irrelevant. Nor did my opening rehearsal remarks help much. Usually, on that all-important first day, I try to make everyone as comfortable as possible. Sometimes I formulate a statement of what I think the play is "about," or discuss its characters, language, or tone. But I don't normally make a speech. Here I remember vividly making a long one. Something about the play, like all of Edward's work, existing on various levels, and that we should not worry if everything was not immediately clear. Since actors cannot act either symbols or abstractions, we should concentrate, as in Beckett, on what I called "the local situation" and let the overtones fall where they may. Who were the people and what were they doing? Edward's play was like a poem written in a dream, rich in images and echoes. Everything didn't have to fit logically and tightly. We should just let the words and the scenes flow over and through us, grab on to things that were clear, and trust the playwright. I didn't dare mention trusting the director.

No one burst into applause, but we got through the reading, excited mostly by Bill Ritman's carefully constructed model. Everyone, especially John and Irene, plunged into the task of making the play have some kind of sense. Since we were once more to be in Billy Rose's theater, Billy had given us rehearsal space in the Ziegfeld, where he had his office. (I'm sure he didn't recall his meeting with me fifteen years earlier in that same office.) That vast, bleak, freezingly cold room somewhere in the upper darkness of the Ziegfeld seemed a fitting locale for our "metaphysical mystery."

Almost at once, Bill Hutt—saturnine and urbane—and Eric Berry—overly pompous though he was—made that first scene electric. John, still terror-stricken and alternating between elation and despair, managed to make me forget he was miscast. Irene was marvelous in her transformation from old crone to the radiantly beautiful Miss Alice. Their seduction scene became pure music, and I've always regretted that there is no recording made of it. The rest of the play, however, from the time the three coconspirators pulled the rug out from under Julian to that interminable and almost unbelievable death soliloquy, grew in confusion.

John wanted to withdraw almost daily, and was sustained mainly by post-rehearsal brandy and Irene's good-natured joshing. Pleas to Edward to rewrite and clear up at least some of the confusion went unanswered. I don't think he knew what to do. The one scene he did work on, in which the Lawyer and the Cardinal exchanged roles and talked about "the mouse in the model," trembled on the edge of clarity but never reached that happy state. I kept plodding through a darkness only occasonally lit by someone's candle.

As often as possible, we stopped to drink tea and tell theater stories, a practice that I've always felt accounts for the British theater's continued excellence. John and Irene had an abundant supply. But as the days went by, John told fewer stories and complained more about the elusiveness of his role. And although Irene alternately comforted and poked fun at his anxieties, telling him about her experiences with T. S. Eliot's *Cocktail Party* and *Family Reunion*, and urging him to "get on with it," John's confidence and will both weakened. He refused to let that weakening affect his work. He experimented with moves and positions, and kept refining his speeches. But I could see that he was becoming increasingly concerned about the script, especially his later scenes. He begged Edward to cut the long final monologue. Once Julian was shot, he felt, the play should end as quickly as possible. Edward insisted on waiting until previews. The atmosphere at rehearsals alternated between manic and depressive.

Increasingly unhappy about Eric Berry's pompousness as the Cardinal, Edward persuaded the producers and me to audition another actor, Richard Dysart, newly arrived from Hollywood. On our day off, one gloomy Sunday afternoon, I drove in, reluctantly, from Hastings, to listen to a nervous Dysart. I immediately wanted to hire him, but no one else did; we made the decision to stick to Eric Berry. I drove back to Hastings slightly depressed, then piled the family into our Volkswagen for a Chinese dinner. At the last minute, my mother decided not to go. Jean and David piled in the back, Vickie in the front seat. The evening was foggy, my concentration equally so. In the fog, I misjudged a curve and plowed into the side of the road. I was going about twenty-five miles an hour; nevertheless Vickie—not wearing a seatbelt—went through the windshield. Through my panic and horror, I waved down a passing car and took Vickie directly to her pediatrician, who, as it happened, lived nearby. We then took her to our local hospital in Tarrytown, where I spent the longest night of my life, not sure whether Vickie would ever see or hear again. I hardly noticed that Jean had, in her attempt to hold on to our five-year-old son during the crash, suffered a broken arm.

At rehearsals next day, I appeared before a most sympathetic and supportive cast. Everyone felt the weight of *Tiny Alice*'s "curse" on us, though they knew little of the actual circumstances. Irene, who had been wonderful at holding everyone's hand, did wonders with mine. And after each day's rehearsal, I drove to the hospital—to be sustained by Vickie's little-girl cheerfulness and her physician's optimistic reports. The world could still be bearable in spite of symbols, abstractions, and the forces of evil. We went into previews at the Billy Rose, my mind mostly on a nine-year-old daughter lying in a bed in a hospital thirty miles away.

As with *Virginia Woolf*, we attracted an immediate audience, perhaps not as enthusiastic, but seriously attentive. At the back of the house, his head rarely turned toward the stage, our author stalked back and forth nightly, greeting me in the morning with scattered line changes, transpositions, notes for the actors. Each day also, we took a line or two out of John's final speech. John continued to hope that Edward would spare him his ordeal; he remained scrupulously faithful to the author's daily last-minute pruning, threading in the cuts each night. The audience never sensed his agony. Any American actor would have told Edward to go fly a kite, or something much stronger. John bore his cross, literally and metaphorically, each night.

Audiences, however, savored the performances even if they might have been confused by the play. Business grew, as did our morale. At one preview, in the midst of enthusiastic applause at the end, I saw a handsomely dark young man standing up and booing fervently. Working my way to his side, I asked what bothered him. "Edward Albee hates life!" he shouted at me. "I can't stand him!" I was surprised to recognize Roy Scheider, then not yet established as a star but clearly on his way.

We opened on December 29, my daughter and wife both well on their way to complete recovery, the play as polished as it could be. Our reviews were better than any of us expected. The *Times*' Taubman spoke of "boldness and wonder" and pronounced us "the kind of exhilarating evening that stretches the mind and the sensibilities." He lauded the performances and production. Richard Watts told readers that it had "a steady theatrical fascination and is brilliantly acted in a handsome production." Other critics referred to us as "electrically alive theater," "a theatrical wonder," "staggering." John, relieved and grateful—as were we all—couldn't believe what he read.

The reviews also stressed the play's fundamental inscrutability, and tended to frighten off potential audiences. In previews, people had been content to figure things out for themselves. Now they were being told that *Tiny Alice* was impossible to understand. Edward, overreacting, called various press conferences to explain how clear and simple his play was. The critics then began to accuse him not only of obscurantism but pretentiousness as well. The feud soon grew hot and heavy on both sides—to the ultimate detriment of the production. We lasted 167 performances, with John and Irene deepening and enriching their work, and finding more truth and musicality. I felt proud to have been part of the *Tiny Alice* expedition, and was sorry that its ending had to be soured with so much misunderstanding and recrimination.

On a more personal and artistic level, I was disappointed by the critics' response—or lack of response—to the last scene, in which the moving presence of "Alice" is made powerfully evident. As "Alice" proceeds closer and closer to the room where Julian lies dying, the lights in the model go out one by one. Then, as the tiny light is extinguished in the room that represents the actual room where the scene takes place, the room's lights go out, the doors open, and the thumping sound, which has been growing and growing, becomes unbearably loud. "Alice" is as "felt" as anything unseen can be. No matter how many times I watched the scene, it moved me and made my blood ring. Not one critic referred to Alice's presence; and the only ones who mentioned the thumping thought it was Julian's heartbeat. Shades of clattering radiators!

Gossip columnists, then in their heyday, trumpeted that John Gielgud, the eminent British classical actor, didn't understand one word of whatever he was saying. Whatever John's hesitations, that assertion was completely untrue. The confusion lies in the many-layered meaning of the word "understand," a subtlety that often estranges me from some of my more learned academic colleagues. I maintain that John, in his actor's sensitivity to the character of Julian, in his awareness of the structure and development of each scene, in his abilty to make Edward Albee's language alive and resonant with meaning, in his own way "understood" the play as well as any critic or any scholar. Perhaps he could not write a book about it, or analyze it in intellectual or philosophical terms. But he could act out its truth and beauty on a stage, and have it make theatrical sense. If that is not "understanding," I don't know what is.

I treasure John's response when he heard that Edward was lecturing on the "meaning" of *Tiny Alice*. "Ah," he said, with his playful tremolo of a smile, "I'll *not* be there." When he needed to be there—frightened and uncertain of this "surrealist play," too old to be playing Julian, and without much help from Edward—he was shining through the play's darkness. I shall never forget his gentleness and gentility.

THE SAM AND BUSTER SHOW

1964–1965

In a year so devoted to Edward Albee, I did go off elsewhere twice; once to do *The Glass Menagerie,* at the Guthrie Theatre in its second season, and once to direct a Beckett film, called *Film,* with Buster Keaton. Neither experience turned out exactly as promised.

From the time I first became familiar with Tyrone Guthrie's work as a director, back in the mid-forties, I was fascinated by him as the theatricalist director par excellence. When I first saw Guthrie's Theatre Guild production of Andreyev's *He Who Gets Slapped,* I could hardly keep from shouting with joy. Here was Theater, done with magnificent imagination, taste, and flourish. No movie could come close to that experience. I wrote Guthrie a fan letter and etched his name in my memory book. No answer came.

In 1949, in Scotland, I saw his *Satire of the Three Estates,* a version of Sir John Lindsay's sixteenth-century morality play that seemed to me a combination of *Henry* V and the Marx brothers. Again, Guthrie demonstrated the theater's magical ability to express the deepest truth without attempting to create the illusion of life; to be itself instead of trying to be something else. I spent the rest of my summer in England trying to catch up to him. Did he need an assistant, any kind of an assistant? This time he finally answered me: no, thank you. He was flattered, but why did I want to waste my valuable time watching him move actors around.

Over the years, I journeyed far and wide to do precisely that. In 1953, Zelda Fichandler and I drove to Stratford, Ontario's new thrust stage, to see the opening night of *Oedipus the King.* My first view of the tent included a glimpse of what seemed to be an eight-foot-tall Tony Guthrie emerging from backstage, carrying a basket of props. Zelda and I spent some hurried hours persuading Tony to direct *Volpone* at the Arena, which interested him because the audience sat on all four sides. (He never came, his mother's death scrapping his plans.) In Philadelphia, Thornton Wilder introduced us when Tony was directing the pre-Broadway production of *The Matchmaker.* I saw his *Tenth Man* on Broadway and loved his modern-dress *Troilus and Cressida,* set in the time of the Franco-Prussian War. I went four times in two weeks to an almost empty Winter Garden Theatre to watch his arrows fly across the stage in *Tamburlaine.*

I would have flown as fast and as freely as those arrows to go anywhere Tony asked me. So when, out of a clear blue sky, he rang to ask me if I would direct *The Skin of Our Teeth* at the Guthrie, I said yes before I'd even asked "when?" or "how much?" The year before, I had attended the Guthrie's opening night festivities, and seen his modernized *Hamlet,* with George Grizzard, late of *Virginia Woolf,* as the Dane. Guthrie was my favorite director. *Skin* was one of my two or three favorite plays. I was ecstatic. My only condition was that he let me watch rehearsals of his *Volpone.* He laughed.

Some weeks later, just after I had figured out how to do *Skin* amid the Guthrie's vast asymmetrical spaces, Tony called again, his voice a bit subdued. The Guthrie's budget had been cut; instead of *Skin,* they were doing *The Glass Menagerie.* I loved Tennessee's play, had done it in my first Arena Stage production—which I sometimes considered my best work. But *Menagerie* seemed ill-suited to the Guthrie's solid wood steps and enormous reaches. The play needed intimacy, transparency, fragility. Tony persisted. I resisted, but finally gave in—as he knew I would. I couldn't have Tanya Moiseiwitsch for scenery and costumes, of course. Tony was keeping her too busy, but someone named Lewis Brown, who was "wonderful." Could I have George Grizzard for Tom? Lee Richardson for the Gentleman Caller? A decent Amanda? "Yes, of course!"

Little turned out as planned. Lee Richardson played Tom instead of George, who was too busy doing Mosca in *Volpone* and I'm not sure that Lee, though effective enough, was ever happy in the role. Ruth Nelson, one of my early Group Theatre heroines, was a touchingly sad Amanda but somehow not "large" enough. Lew Brown's settings and costumes were far from "wonderful." And I got to only one rehearsal of *Volpone,* at which not much happened. In my own rehearsals, I kept thinking how much more effective and beautiful my Arena production had been. At the same time, everyone from the actors to the composer resented my slightest attempt to recall that experience. I kept feeling I had lost the way I knew, and I couldn't find another way. It was an unpleasant six weeks, even (or, especially) with Tony on the premises. The reviews, surprisingly enough, were respectable, Elliot Norton saying that it was the most faithful production of *Menagerie* since the original. I left Minneapolis without a trace of regret on anyone's part—not to be asked back for almost twenty years. I still consider Tony an extraordinary director, whose imagination and artistic philosophy seriously shaped my own.

On several occasions various Guthrie board members approached me to see if I was interested in being considered in the search for Guthrie's successor. I wasn't because I had already committed myself to the artistic directorship of a nonexistent theater, the Ithaca (New York) Festival Theatre, which had ideas about a summer festival akin to Stratford's, featuring Greek classics instead of Shakespeare. The Ithaca Festival never materialized and neither did my Guthrie candidacy.

The final weeks of my Guthrie sojourn were made both bearable and unbearable by a growing absorption with my first venture into non-TV film—a short silent written by Sam Beckett and containing more technical problems than several normal feature-length scripts. Among its eccentricities, the film contained a sequence involving a cat and a dog. John Cromwell, Ruth Nelson's husband, and an experienced director, read the script and told me the dog would be no problem, but that I was sure to have trouble with the cat. He was wrong, as was almost everything else in Minneapolis that summer.

Starting out as part of an ambitious project for Beckett's publisher, Barney Rosset of Grove Press, Samuel Beckett's *Film* was one of a commissioned trio of short films by avant-garde writers, the other two being by Pinter and Ionesco. (The others never got done; Pinter turned his into a television script, the Ionesco still languishes.) The script had appeared in the spring of 1963 as a fairly baffling—when not downright inscrutable—six-page outline. It was accompanied by pages of addenda in Sam's inimitable informal style: explanatory notes, a philosophical supplement, modest production suggestions, a series of hand-drawn diagrams. They described, in detail, his principal characters O and E, the question of "perceivedness," the angle of immunity, and the essential principle that "*Esse est percipi*": to be is to be perceived. All this was composed with loving care, humor, sadness, and Sam's ever-present compassionate understanding of man's essential frailty. I loved it, even when I wasn't completely sure what Sam meant. And I suddenly decided that my early academic training in physics and geometry might finally pay off.

Came then almost a year of preparation: I read and reread the "script," which, of course, had no dialogue (with the exception of one whispered "shhhh"); asked Sam a thousand questions, largely by mail and eventually in person at his Montparnasse apartment; and tried to visualize the varied demands of those six tantalizing pages. Gradually the mysteries and enigmas, common denominators of all new Beckett works, came into focus. The audacity of his concept—a highly disciplined use of two specific camera viewpoints—emerged from behind all the seeming ambiguities of the technical explanations. I began to work out a tentative shooting script.

What was required was not merely a subjective camera and an objective camera, but two different "visions" of reality: the perceiving "eye" (E) constantly observing the object (the script was once titled *The Eye*), and the object (O) observing the environment. The story of this highly visual film was simply that of O's attempt to remove all perception, an attempt that ultimately fails because he cannot get rid of self-perception. At the end, we would see that O = E. Q.E.D.

What became clear was that whenever the camera was O, it would, of course, not see or show any parts of O. Whenever the camera was E, it would always have to stay directly behind O, never revealing O's face until the very last shot of confrontation between the two. What star actor would be willing to play a part in which we would only once see his face? What cameraman would accept such a limited range of camera placement?

From the beginning, in keeping with Sam's feeling that the film should possess a stylized comic reality akin to that of a silent movie, we thought in terms of Chaplin or Zero Mostel for O. Chaplin, as we expected, was inaccessible; Mostel unavailable. We hit upon Jack MacGowran, a mutual favorite. Jackie was a delicious comedian and had performed Beckett's plays widely in England and Ireland. Luckily, Jackie had just been acclaimed in the small but juicy role of the Highwayman in *Tom Jones* so that he was suddenly "salable." We went after a cameraman and the technical crew. Since we couldn't get financial backing for all three films, we decided to do the Beckett segment first and use it as a sample of things to come. We also picked our shooting date and location: June 1964, somewhere in Greenwich Village.

Best of all, we finally persuaded Sam Beckett to make his first visit to New York for the shooting. Sam didn't want to come. New York would be too loud and too demanding, too many interviews and cocktail parties. He preferred the quiet of Paris and his country retreat at Ussy. But for our sakes, he came.

In the usual fashion, things began to happen. First, even before we got started, the budget had to be revised upward. We lost our director of photography to some Hollywood epic. The owners of the small New York studio where we were going to shoot our single interior got cold feet. Jackie went off to do a feature film, which made his summer availability uncertain. I got increasingly nervous and kept asking for more preparation time. Production costs kept going up.

With the rest of us suffering various degrees of panic, Sam reacted to all developments with characteristic resilience and understanding. From Paris he responded to our desperation over the sudden casting crisis by suggesting Buster Keaton. Was Buster still alive and well? (He was.) How would he react to acting in Beckett material? (He'd been offered the part of Lucky in the original American *Godot* some years back, and had turned it down.) Would this turn out to be a Keaton film rather than a Beckett film? (Sam wasn't worrying about that.)

Off went the script (?) to Keaton, followed a few days later by my first voyage to Hollywood to woo Buster. It was a weird experience. Late one hot night, I arrived at Keaton's house, in a remote section of Los Angeles, to discover that I seemed to have interrupted a four-handed poker game. Apologizing, he told me that he was playing an imaginary game with long-since-departed Irving Thalberg, Nicholas Schenck, and somebody else, which had been going on since 1927. He added that Thalberg owed him over two million dollars (imaginary, I hoped). We went on from there, with me suddenly realizing that everything in the room harked back to circa 1927. Keaton had read the script and was not sure what could be done to fix it. His general attitude was that we were all, Beckett included, nuts. But he needed the money, $5,000 for less than three weeks' work, and would do it. Yes, he remembered the *Godot* offer, but he didn't understand that script either.

Keaton made no effort to disguise his general bafflement. The script was not only unclear, it wasn't funny. He suggested some special business with his walk or perhaps that "bit" where he kept sharpening a pencil and it got smaller and smaller. I said that we didn't normally pad Beckett's material. Then he told me, confidentially, that he had made a lot of movies in his time and didn't see how this one could play more than four minutes. Even if we stretched that cat and dog business. He'd be glad—for a fee—to supply some ideas. From 1927.

On the way home, I worried considerably about Keaton; but, like Everest, he was there and, with Sam's encouragement, we got him.

Our casting complete, we needed a great photographer and an editor without too strong an ego. With time at a premium, we were fortunate enough to persuade Academy Award–winning director of photography Boris Kaufman and editor Sidney Meyers that Beckett had not lost his mind in confining those camera angles so rigidly. Sam arrived, late in June, for our first big weekend production conference at Barney Rosset's pool in East Hampton. He was taken from J.F.K. to East Hampton in a privately hired plane, which, to our horror, turned out to be hardly large enough to contain his long legs. We talked, walked, and sat. We also played tennis. Sam explained the necessary camera positions and angles in the face of some highly sophisticated arguments about the flexibility of the film medium, and I revised the rough shooting script into an exact one.

In New York, as we continued to talk, walk, and occasionally sit down, Sam decided that the city wasn't as bad as he had feared; he especially liked the Village, and managed a special pilgrimage to the Cherry Lane Theatre, home for so many of his plays. We scouted locations and eventually found one to Sam's liking. It was an about-to-be-knocked-apart wall in lower Manhattan rather than one of our more accessible choices.

A few days before shooting was to start, Keaton arrived in Manhattan. I took him to pick out his costume and eye patch, showed him the city, and, ultimately, brought him to the author. That meeting of Beckett and Keaton, one afternoon in the latter's hotel suite, was one of those occasions that seem inevitable before they take place, impossible when they do, and unbelievable afterward. Sam was expectantly looking forward to Keaton's arrival; he had known and respected his work since the old silent days. Keaton, aware of Sam's standing as a playwright and novelist, was intrigued, but didn't really know what to make of him.

When Sam and I came, Keaton was drinking a can of beer and watching a baseball game on television; his wife was in the other room. The greetings were mild, slightly awkward without meaning to be. The two exchanged a few general words, most of them from Sam, then proceeded to sit in silence while Keaton watched the ball game. I don't even think he offered us a beer. Not out of ill will; he just didn't think of it. Or else maybe he thought that a man like Beckett didn't drink beer.

Now and then, Sam—or I—would try to say something, to show some interest in Keaton or just to keep the nonexistent conversation going. Keaton would answer in monosyllables and get back to the Yankees—or was it the Mets?

"Did you have any questions about anything in the script, Buster?"

"No."

(Pause.)

"What did you think about the film when you first read it?"

"Well . . ."

(Long pause.)

And so on. It was harrowing. And hopeless. The silence became an interminable seventh-inning stretch.

They had nothing to share. All of Sam's goodwill and my own flailing efforts to get something started failed to bring them together on any level. We didn't talk much about Keaton that evening. Although I tried to recall all the high points of his performances in *The Navigator* and *The General*.

The meeting was a disaster.

Just before we left, Keaton made some comment about his old flattened-down Stetson being a trademark, and mentioned that he'd brought several of them along, in different colors, to use in the film. (The script called for slightly different headgear.) While I was figuring out how to react, Sam replied—to my surprised delight—that he didn't see why Buster couldn't wear his own hat in this one. He then proceeded to demonstrate how a handkerchief worn inside of it (to hide his face from E in that first sequence of running along the wall) might prove more interesting than what was originally called for.

On Monday morning, July 20, we traipsed down to begin shooting in the shadow of Brooklyn Bridge. Much hoopla: lots of reporters, hordes of onlookers, Alain Resnais. The sequence was a tough one: light problems, traffic problems, actor problems (two supporting actors were held up in traffic), and camera problems. There were also beginning-film-director problems, such as my ignorance of the strobe effect that causes the background to undulate on a pan shot. I went right on panning the extras up and down our water-soaked street. Everybody kept saying friendly things to me, and there was a general feeling that we were making progress, though I kept having my doubts.

The one thing I was sure of was that Buster was magnificent. He was totally professional; patient, unperturbable, relaxed, helpful. He must have been over seventy, but he never complained when we asked him over and over again, for one reason or other, to run along that obstacle course of a wall in the broiling heat. Nor did he object when we kept adding obstacles that would have stopped a steeplechaser. Nor did he nag us when something went wrong, which happened sixty percent of the time, or when we didn't do something the way he did it in 1927. He didn't even mention 1927 that day. He didn't smile either, but then he smiled rarely, offscreen or on.

I finally went home, drained, five pounds lighter, six years older, but relatively happy about moviemaking. And radiant about our choice of Buster.

The second day we were shooting in a hallway and up some stairs. There was no room for anything or anyone. The lights were inadequate. The camera couldn't move in the direction or at the speed we wanted. We had to keep restaging Keaton's main action in the sequence. Even then, something was wrong with the timing, and Sidney kept saying we should be shooting it differently. The hallway was packed with technical people, and I couldn't ever get the proper setup. It was hotter than a steam room. Everything took forever. We must have used up half of the budget on overtime, not to mention all of our energy and willpower.

Worst of all, we saw yesterday's rushes. I thought at first that they looked pretty good—after the first day's madness any exposed film inevitably seemed to me of Academy Award caliber. But the timing was all off, and I cursed the jiggling dolly and the rough roadbed. Maybe there were possibilities, I thought.

I was the only one. Everyone else, from Sam to the producer, suffered glum despair. The lighting was gloomy. The performances, except for Buster's, were terrible. The group scenes suffered so badly from that strobe effect that they were impossible to watch. In everyone's opinion, none of the scenes involving the other actors were even remotely usable. And the budget would not permit our going down there again to do everything over.

Again, it was Sam who saved the day, this time the night. Piercing through what was beginning to be an atmosphere full of rancor and bitterness, Sam quietly proposed the ultimate solution: eliminate the entire sequence. That made great sense, he thought. He had never been sure all those people belonged in that opening anyway. They gave it and the film a different texture, opened up another world. Besides, it removed that damned strobe effect, which was rapidly becoming the star of the picture.

Sam was incredible. People always assume him to be unyielding, but when the chips are down, on specifics—here as well as in all his stage productions—he is completely understanding, flexible, and pragmatic. Far from blaming anything on the limitations and mistakes of those around him, he blamed his own material, himself. He had no recriminations for me or anyone else. He was even prepared to eliminate an important segment of his film. I was ready to quit, kill myself, cry, do it all over again on the sly, anything!

For the next three weeks, we shot in our one interior. That was a lot easier—and better. Besides, the rushes of the hallway scene from the second day weren't too bad. The actress who played a flower lady was beautiful. Most of the time we just put the camera at eye level directly behind Buster and stuck there with him—or tried to. Every foot of his shambling gait, every rise from the rocker, every twist to cat, dog, or parrot, goldfish, door or window, we moved with him. Cursing and sweating and wondering why, we seemed to shoot more 180-degree and 360-degree pans than in a dozen Westerns. Our apparently simple little film was not so simple, technically as well as well as philosophically.

Buster and almost everybody on the crew made a few corner-of-the-mouth remarks about his face being his livelihood all these years and here these idiots were knocking themselves out to avoid it. In fact, when even a fraction of profile did get in, we immediately did another take, no matter how good the previous one had been. But Keaton's behavior on the set was as steady and cooperative as it had been that first day. He was indefatigable if not exactly loquacious. To all intents and purposes, we were shooting a silent film, and he was in his best form. He encouraged me to give him vocal directions during the shot, sometimes starting over again without stopping the camera if he felt he hadn't done something well the first time. (Nor did he believe much in rehearsal, preferring the spontaneity of performance.) Often when we were stumped over a technical camera problem, he came through with suggestions, prefacing his comments by explaining that he had solved such problems many times at the Keaton Studios back in 1927. He ate lunch with us each day and talked about how films were made back then—no script, an idea about a character in trouble, a series of improvisations and gags to get him out of trouble, the end—but never a direct comment on this one.

About the fourth or fifth day, with the sequence at the window, sidling up in his greatcoat and scarf to pull aside the gauze curtains with his own poetic combination of grace and awkwardness, he caught on that there was more here than had previously met his inner eye. Maybe we had something, and this wasn't just for the dough. "I'm beginning to catch on to this Shakespeare stuff," he told us. He didn't exactly hop up and down, but we could see that he was getting interested.

By the time we finished up with the animals, Buster was in his element. This was straight slapstick, a running gag, the little man versus a mutely mocking animal world. Everyone had agreed with John Cromwell that dogs were dependable performers and could, with training, do almost anything; cats, on the other hand, tended to be highly erratic and usually wound up as total nuisances. As our menagerie turned out, the alley cat performed splendidly, doing exactly what it was supposed to do; but our dog, a rather shy chihuahua, started timidly then froze up completely. On one of the early takes, Buster had been so anxious to get rid of him that he dropped him behind the door too roughly. The dog never recovered its equilibrium, and we lost a fair portion of ours. Nothing was wrong with it physically; it just didn't trust Buster, or filmmaking. (Moral: Always have understudies for the animals.)

We spent the better and worse part of a day on that sequence, with lots of laughs from the onlookers. Some of the outtakes, with Buster making faces at the animals and breaking up, were funnier than anything in the film. Because of the rigid dichotomy of the two visions we couldn't just cut anywhere and then splice parts of two takes together. Each take had to go till the end of the shot.

Here again, Buster was patient and understanding, although the chihuahua didn't think so. So was Sam, who learned more and more about the vagaries and vicissitudes of making a film. He was always there, watching from above the set, unobtrusive but dominant, eager to answer, to look through the camera, to help with a move. He sat there for hours, motionless and intent, his elbows akimbo on the light rail, staring down at us through his spectacles like some wise old owl contemplating a bunch of frantic beavers building some nonsensical mud-stick dam.

After our crew began to accept the fact that we were not going to shoot closeups of Buster's lovely deadpan visage, or have him tap-dance to make the script more interesting, the camera-behind-his-back technique grew smoother. Along the way we hit upon some happy accidents. The rocker we were using happened to have two holes in the headrest, which began to glare at us. Sam was delighted. A folder from which photographs were taken had two eyelets, well proportioned. Another pair of "eyes" for O to avoid.

Once the original opening sequence was eliminated, we had decided to open with a huge menacing closeup of Buster's closed eye, held as long as possible and then opening to reveal the pupil searching and then focusing. Then we cut to Keaton running along the wall. The texture of Buster's eyelid was beautifully reptilian; he was willing to sit for interminable periods of time, with dozens of lamps blazing at him, for us to get several good shots of his eye, open and closed. He sat patiently in his dressing room reading or playing cards, always ready for another take. Always behind his silence somewhat amused by it all.

He was surprised, but also pleased, that the running time of the film had gone past his estimated four minutes. And he knew by the time we were finished that it all "meant" something, even though he still was not sure exactly what. What I remember best of our final farewell on the set was that he smiled and half-admitted those six pages were worth doing after all. Ultimately, that "Shakespearean stuff" had reached him.

Sidney proceeded to do a very quick very rough cut for Sam to look at before taking off for Paris. And that first cut turned out to be not far off from what we finally used. The editing was painstaking—and painful, Sidney always gently trying to break the mold we had set in the shooting, and Sam and I in our different ways always gently holding him to it. There was no question of sparring over who had the legal first cut or final cut or whatever. We talked, argued, tried various ways, from Moviola to screen and back again, to make it come out as much the film that Sam had first envisioned as we could. Sometimes I loved it, and sometimes I hated it. Remembering all the things I didn't do or did badly. Feeling that the two-vision thing never worked and that people would be puzzled (they were). Seeing all sorts of technical bloopers. Laughing—and crying—over that bloody chihuahua. Yet, the film undoubtedly took on an ambiance, a strange snow-soft texture, that gave it depth and richness. Like an abstract painting—or one of Beckett's plays—it grew on the perceiver.

We had difficulty marketing the film. No one wanted it. No one wants shorts anyhow, and this one they didn't want (or understand) with a vengeance. Nor did showing it around help get us money for the other two films that were to complete the original omnibus. We stopped showing it. What had started out as a trilogy became a lone, very lone, piece indeed.

Then, in the summer of 1965, came an unexpected offer from the New York Film Festival. Amos Vogel had seen a print somewhere and thought it was worth showing—as part of a Keaton revival series. Already the film was becoming Keaton's and not Beckett's. I fought another losing battle to keep it from getting sandwiched in between two Keaton shorts, a standard one he'd made some years earlier and a new railroad promotional. Both were funny if not great, and they were the expected Keaton. I dreaded what would happen when the unexpected Keaton came on. Then *Film* began—with me crouched underneath my balcony seat at the top of Philharmonic Hall (I haven't been back since). The professional film festival audience of critics and students of film technique started laughing the moment the credits came on, roaring at that lovely grotesque closeup of Buster's eyelid. I could hardly stand it. A moment later they stopped laughing. For good. All through the next twenty-two minutes they sat there, bored, annoyed, baffled, and cheated of the Keaton they had come to see. Who the hell was Beckett? At the end they got up on their hind legs and booed lustily. I thought of Godard and Antonioni and a few others at Cannes, wept, and ran.

The critics, naturally, clobbered us or ignored us. One of them called the film "vacuous and pretentious," the exact two things it wasn't, and even told us how stupid we were to keep Keaton's back to the camera until the end. As to the "message"—*esse est percipi*—not one had a clue.

Sam and I survived the experience (he's absolutely marvelous at doing that; I'm not) and eventually *Film* was shown at various European film festivals, getting lots of coverage and winning numerous prizes. Wherever it was shown, sometimes even with other Keaton films, it received respectful attention and at least partial understanding of its intention. It began to have occasional public showings, mostly for university audiences, and developed an underground audience of Beckett or Keaton fans.

Four years after it was shot, *Film* was finally shown in New York for the general public in a program of shorts at the Evergreen Theatre and received generally favorable reviews. Since then it seems to crop up regularly all over the place. Hard as it is for those involved to appreciate the process at the time, that's par for the Beckettian course. Almost all of his stage, radio, and television pieces are first slammed, derided, ignored. A few years later they are hailed as classics. So *Film* keeps getting seen—and talked about—all over the world. I've even been stopped on the street, on trains, in theater lobbies by youthful lovers of Beckett, who have seen it somewhere and are eager to talk about it.

I was told once that British director Peter Brook had seen it and said that half of it was a failure and the other half a success. I'm inclined to agree with him, although I'm not sure we'd both pick the same half. In fact, I change my mind about which half I like every time I see it.

STILL PROMISING—AND STILL UNFULFILLED

1965–1966

With the sixties exploding in unfamilar directions around me, I found myself more and more staying near the familiar haven of Theatre 1964, Theatre 1965, and Theatre 1966, and their most promising playwright, Edward Albee. After *Dream* and *Woolf, Ballad*, and *Alice*, differing as their fortunes had been, all of us connected with those productions seemed to take for granted our continued association, if not exactly partnership. Offers from external sources—commercial, artistic, Californian, European—poured in. Always finding it difficult to turn down any opportunity, I tried to keep myself involved, but available for what the Messrs. Barr, Wilder, and Albee might come up with.

Early in March 1965, Theatre 1966 was planning *Do Not Pass Go*, a two-character play about a sadomasochistic relationship in a grocery stock room, by Charles Nolte, a member of the Playwrights Unit that Edward and Richard and Clinton had set up from *Virginia Woolf* profits. I responded to the script, welcomed the return to the Cherry Lane, and felt at home with the entire setup. In the end the overall response was not unfavorable—"one of the better new plays presented this season . . . on or off-Broadway" (*Times*), "curious, macabre, strangely moving" (*Journal-American*)—but somehow, perhaps because of casting problems, the experience didn't seem worth the effort. I went back to waiting for Albee.

A month later, Barney Rosset called me in anguish about NBC's television version of Beckett's mime play, *Act Without Words, II*. Evidently the director had changed it all around. Barney was insisting that NBC do it over. Would I direct it? After my experience with the television *Godot*, I wasn't exactly tingling with anticipation. NBC had signed two fine actors, Donald Moffat and McIntyre Dixon, but neither one was experienced with Beckett. I myself had not yet attempted a Beckett pantomime. We would have only a few days for rehearsal and shooting. And NBC was not happy with the additional cost of redoing the show. Reluctantly, I agreed. I stuck strictly to the text, kept the camera more or less stationary, and came up with a reasonable renditon of *Act Without Words, II*. I felt pleased with the results, and so did Barney. I never heard anything from anyone at NBC; theirs was an act without words, III. The program came and went without much response. I suppose the tape languishes, forgotten, somewhere in the NBC archives.

In June, I was once more back with Theatre 1966 at the Cherry Lane, this time directing both halves of *Krapp* and *Zoo*. The reviewers liked this version as much as or more than the original. I didn't. Theatre 1966 didn't seem quite as exciting as Theatre 1965.

Which is why, I suppose, I began to look more favorably on two other producers with possible Broadway projects, which kept being scheduled and then postponed, scheduled and postponed. Tanya Chasman, a cheerful lady with film connections trying to break into the theater, wanted me to direct a new play by a young British writer, Joe (*not* Joseph) Orton. It was called *Entertaining Mr. Sloane* and had just won the *Evening Standard* award as best comedy. I found Joe's play funny and touching, a real original of black humor. At the same time, I found its frank and even brutal view of lower-middle-class morality, as well as its bisexual hero, unlikely to make it a candidate for Broadway. Money-raising problems, casting difficulties, and State Department refusal to let the author into the country on grounds of moral turpitude delayed the production. It seems that Joe, in his errant youth, had defaced some library books, winding up in jail for his literary offense.

The other production that kept appearing and disappearing on the horizon was something called either *Slapstick Tragedy* or *Slapstick Tragedies*, depending on author Tennessee Williams' mood of the moment. *Slapstick* actually consisted of two separate and stylistically different one-acts, *The Mutilated* and *The Gnädiges Fräulein*. Tennessee had evidently set his sights on me after seeing *Virginia Woolf*, which he adored; he'd written a note to someone saying that Edward's play was almost good enough for him not to be jealous. After *Tiny Alice*, he wooed me openly.

He'd forgotten, of course, our doorstep meeting when I desperately wanted him to see *The Long Goodbye* at Theatre Inc. Nor did he answer my invitations to see any of my three *Menagerie* productions.

Suddenly finding myself the object of pursuit by Tennessee Williams instead of vice versa, I felt flattered—with reservations. I had strong doubts about *The Mutilated*, which seemed a replay of his standard wounded ladies. But I loved *Fräulein*, finding it wildly funny and deeply touching in its almost absurdist treatment of the artist's brutalization by society. I agreed to make myself available if and when the would-be producers, Charles Bowden and Lester Persky, got the money.

In the midst of all this uncertainty, I found myself down at the Cherry Lane watching Madeleine Renaud and Jean-Louis Barrault performing two weeks of *Happy Days* in French—to great acclaim from critics who hadn't understood it in English. I then followed with two weeks of Ruth White and Johnny Becher in English. Madeleine was wonderful in the serious moments and moods, but almost lacked humor or variety. Barrault, as expected, was brilliant with Willie's pantomimic details. Ruth, less fearful than before, was as winsome and ebullient as ever. Many people regretted that the nature of the American theater, especially the second-class status of off-Broadway, kept the Lunts from being interested in following in the footsteps of the Barraults. But Ruth, I felt then and now, could not be surpassed.

Early in the fall, *Entertaining Mr. Sloane*'s producers had finally raised their money, Joe Orton's morals had been suitably attested to, and an entirely British cast was lined up, including Dudley Sutton from the original London cast in the title role; Lee Montagne, a fine young character man, as the brother; George Turner, an American of English origin, as Dadda; and Sheila Hancock, a delightful English comedienne for Kath, the one female role—we went into rehearsal. Joe turned up just in time. A cherubic, grownup ragamuffin, he turned out to be endearing but often exasperating. He stayed in a Times Square hotel and cruised the local streets nightly, picking up anything that moved. I was sure that we would find his body stuffed into an ashcan on Forty-fifth Street, where the Lyceum Theatre was located. But he was completely friendly and cooperative, responded cheerfully to suggestions about cutting or rewriting his script for American consumption, was highly supportive of my work at rehearsals—and grew fond of Jean, who had him up to Hastings for dinner as often as possible. I decided he was the most amoral person I'd ever met, a true innocent unaware of his own capacity for depravity; we got along swimmingly.

Sloane was exciting and satisfying, my first liberating directorial task in more than a year. The Lyceum, not considered especially desirable because it was east of Broadway, was an attractive, comfortable theater; it evoked fond memories of *Anastasia*. The cast was excellent, especially Sheila Hancock—much superior, in Joe's opinion, to the London version. Everyone pulled together for the play, as had the actors in my first *Virginia Woolf*. Although we had little advance publicity or action at the box office, audiences and enthusiasm built immediately after our first preview, as with *Woolf*. The night before our official opening, we turned away nearly five hundred people. I thought we might have a chance.

That opening, October 12, 1965, Columbus Day, will, I'm afraid, live in infamy. Everything started out fine. The audience came in buzzing, so evidently our word-of-mouth was favorable. Howard Taubman, the *Times* critic, arrived early and without his usual female companion. He sat down in his aisle seat, every few minutes looking ostentatiously at his watch. Opening night curtains always go up at least ten minutes later than scheduled, but this one promised to be even more delayed because our press agent insisted on waiting for the *Tribune*'s Walter Kerr and the *Post*'s Richard Watts, who, rumor had it, were having dinner together somewhere nearby. As the minutes went by, and Mr. Taubman's impatience grew, we finally located the two tardy critics at a restaurant next door. They strolled in at least twenty minutes after the announced curtain time. The press agent asked me to explain to Taubman why we had waited so long. Much against my judgment, I apologized as politely as possible. Taubman turned to me and said, in an absolutely icy voice: "Am I my brother's keeper?" That was a preview of coming detractions.

The show went well. The audience was enthusiastic. The reviews were awful. Not only Taubman's, which slammed the play, hated the performances and direction, and came close to accusing Sheila Hancock and me of outright obscenity. To this day, I don't understand why most of the critics were so viciously negative. Perhaps they resented the casual manner in which the play exposed the hypocrisy of middle-class morality. Perhaps Joe was ahead of his time in his acceptance of bisexuality. Only a few of the reviewers were willing to accept Joe's open disdain for conventional morality. Most of them saw the play as a direct attack on our eternal values and institutions, and were determined to destroy it. I wrote the only letter I have ever written to a drama critic, a long one to Howard Taubman, suggesting that he had every right to question the talents of those persons who had contributed their aesthetic tastes and judgments to the play—but not their morality. After all, an actor sympathetically portraying Iago or Richard III did not thereby deserve to be jailed. The letter helped me feel a bit better, but it did not stop *Entertaining Mr. Sloane* from closing almost immediately. Very few of the crowd of five hundred, desperately milling about our box office, hoping to snare tickets the night before our opening, came back to try again.

Joe did everything to make us feel that the response was his fault rather than ours. I told him that only Samuel Beckett had ever said anything like that to me before, and he was genuinely pleased. When his diaries were published after his death (he was stabbed by his lover, who had become afraid of losing him), the excerpts on his New York *Sloane* experience reflected his positive feelings. I was shocked to learn of his death, just as he was beginning to be recognized, and retain fond memories of an extraordinary comic talent. I think that *Sloane*, whatever the flaws of my production, is a fine and disturbingly funny play. And I consider his *What the Butler Saw*, which I directed twice outside New York, the wittiest farce in the English language since *The Importance of Being Earnest*.

Two weeks after *Sloane* opened, I was in Ann Arbor, Michigan, directing another new play, Archibald MacLeish's *Herakles*, which he had written for the then active and successful APA (Association of Producing Artists), of which Ellis Rabb was artistic director. *Herakles* received mixed reviews, played out its Ann Arbor existence with the rest of the APA's repertory, and never came to New York. Archie was bitterly disappointed, and spent years trying to rewrite it. He was a gentleman through all this, as always, fascinated by the theater, and yet somehow too immersed in literature and ideas to create the theatrical thunder and lightning that he visualized. We remained friends and avid correspondents—though never again onstage colleagues—until he died.

My other Broadway venture, Tennessee Williams' *Slapstick Tragedy*, also materialized at about this time, the producers having gotten their money and the Longacre Theatre, no less ancient though even less "desirable" than the Lyceum. Opening night would be February 22, 1966. We stumbled past a variety of casting ideas, starting with Ruth Gordon and Leueen MacGrath, and ending up with Margaret Leighton and Kate Reid as the odd female couple in *The Mutilated*. Maggie also played the title role of the ravaged artist who had her eyes plucked out in *The Gnädiges Fräulein*, with Kate playing Molly, one of her two critics. Tennessee later wrote that he wanted the Fräulein played by a singer, someone like Lotte Lenya, and that he thought of Maureen Stapleton for Molly; he never mentioned these suggestions to me. At the time he seemed quite happy with our two leading ladies, and wanted Margaret Braidwood, a lesser known but very talented comedienne, to play Polly. The rest of our cast—Ralph Waite, Jon Voight, my old Catholic University student Louis Camuti as the Cocaloony Bird—were picked by me with Tennessee's benediction, but without his direct participation.

At almost the last moment I discovered that Zoe Caldwell—whom I had adored at Stratford and the Guthrie—was in New York, unknown and unrecognized, currently understudying Anne Bancroft in *The Devils*, and miserable. Zoe, a mad, deluxe Australian pixie, would be ideal for the part Margaret Braidwood was supposed to play. Tennessee, disturbed by my tampering with his choice, was unwilling to meet Zoe, of whom he had never heard. I finally was able to persuade him, but he insisted on her auditioning. Zoe categorically refused to audition, saying that she was no good at readings. Not exactly sure what was going to happen but determined to bring the Monitor and the Merrimac together, I inveigled Zoe to Tennessee's apartment for tea. Five seconds after he had met her, he was eating out of her hand and had totally forgotten his previous insistence on auditioning and Margaret Braidwood. Zoe made her Broadway debut as Polly and won a Tony for the role.

Jon Voight dropped out to do a film, and we wound up with his look-alike, James Olsen, who was equally good as the blond Indian Joe. Double-jointed Louie Camuti was so spectacularly effective as the Cocaloony Bird that Tennessee marveled at our good fortune in finding him. That good fortune, however, did not survive rehearsals. Louie ended his Broadway career before it began after falling down some steps in the dark and breaking his leg. We opened with him in the hospital and his understudy on stage.

Disappointing as was the loss of our big bird, there were other matters I regretted even more. For years I had admired and loved Kate Reid, from her London *Rainmaker* to her New York *Virginia Woolf*, always finding her easy and fun to be with. I adored Zoe, whether she was doing Brecht or Shakespeare; she always evidenced a vitality and zest that were immensely attractive. In rehearsals, I was prepared to do anything to keep those two happy. Much to my horror, I found, almost from the first day, that whatever I did or didn't do made both of them deeply unhappy. Maybe I made too many demands. Maybe I took their friendship too much for granted and treated them too disrespectfully. Maybe they were both inordinately afraid of their roles, or of the play's peculiar style and texture. I had no trouble with Margaret Leighton, whom I'd never met before. She threw herself into her part—bizarre and unpredictable as it was—with complete willingness. Kate and Zoe, obviously disturbed and hampered by my attempts to suggest specific comic business, withdrew into an unreachable world that I entered less and less—and with greater and greater trepidation. Pursued by Furies on all sides, I thanked the Fates for Maggie—and her lightly off-color stories during our daily tea breaks.

Tennessee came to rehearsals occasionally and seemed to enjoy them more than I did. He added and subtracted a few lines, and kept rewriting the lines spoken by *The Mutilated*'s chorus, whose physical disposition was baffling me daily; I needed—and lacked—a choreographer. We were all happy with Ming Cho Lee's two settings, especially the wind-blown slant of the hut for *Fräulein*. Maggie Leighton alternately tore us apart onstage and made us laugh offstage. Kate and Zoe—despite our difficulties—were as madly funny as the Marx Brothers.

Fräulein, a surrealist romp about the position of the artist in our society, seemed very real to all of us. *The Mutilated*, another in Tennessee's series of studies of the poor and lonely huddled together in some fleabag hotel, seemed contrived, even though it was occasionally touching. The critics, of course, disagreed. They hated *Fräulein* with a vengeance, not even allowing the performances to soften their response to Tennessee's daring to write something akin to Ionesco or Beckett. *The Mutilated* they didn't mind so much; it was familiar.

The reception bothered me, but not nearly as much as Tennessee's reaction. For months he had been after me to do his plays. He had praised my work with both Beckett and Albee. He expressed a real kinship with me. All during rehearsals he kept telling me I was on the right track. And on opening night, as the curtain fell on less than tumultuous applause, he grabbed me and kissed me with some passion on both cheeks, telling me—with great liquid tears in his eyes—"No one! No one has evuh suhved mah wuhk moah faithfuhly!" After the reviews came out, I never saw him again. Nor did he return my phone calls. In Tennessee's autobiography, he refers to me, only once and briefly, as an untalented, smiling little man who always wore a red baseball cap. Let me say in return that Tennessee seems to have been a talented but unhappy little man, everlastingly pursued by demons he had himself created and never been able to dispel. After my experience with him—and the two ladies—I can no longer get starry-eyed about a new association with any theater great whom I have previously worshiped from afar. And I have long exchanged my baseball hat for a Russian student's cap.

The failure of both *Sloane* and *Slapstick* to please the critics or attract an audience led me to one of two conclusions: either I was incapable, as a director, of making these plays succeed, or Broadway was becoming impossible for the kind of material I most appreciated, and with which I felt most at home. Neither alternative was palatable.

Once more I was to find myself back with Samuel Beckett and Edward Albee—and within the forgiving heart and arms of Theatre 1966, soon to become Theatre 1967.

TO ALBEE OR NOT TO ALBEE

1966

After *Slapstick*'s quick demise, temporary relief came in the guise of an offer from Public Television's Channel 13 to direct another Beckett. This time, it was *Eh Joe?*, which he had written especially for television. I accepted enthusiastically and immediately went after George Rose—a British actor living in the States—whom I had once seen play a riotous Dogberry at Stratford-upon-Avon, and considered suitable for any Beckettian victim. I also pursued the possibility of luring Rosemary Harris to do the offscreen woman's voice.

Rosemary turned out to be a dream—enthusiastic, cooperative, lovely, her vocal musicality captivating. George, right from the start, hated everything: Beckett's play, the camerawork, my ideas, his role, me. He complained about everything, remained unresponsive to every suggestion, and wound up antagonizing the entire staff and crew. Since the show consisted of a slowly enlarging shot of Joe's face as he listened to his memories, there was very little I could do to focus elsewhere. The finished product was competent but undistinguished. Only Rosemary's magical vibrations remain to cheer me.

The year (1966) was distinguished at both beginning and end by my work on two works by Edward—one an adaptation and one strikingly original—which produced widely differing results.

Once before, after his *Woolf* triumph, Edward had chosen to take the pressure off his needing to come up with something "bigger and better" by doing an adaptation (Carson McCullers' *The Ballad of the Sad Café*). The response, though mostly negative, had not discouraged him from doing the same after the *Tiny Alice* hoopla. This time he chose James Purdy's *Malcolm*, another cult novel, peopled with exotic and even bizarre characters, as well as highly theatrical situations and locales. The theme was Edward's favorite: the corruption of innocence. The question was whether Purdy's special brand of phantasmagoria could be transported to the stage without becoming too literal.

I liked parts of the script and relished the challenge of its highly seasoned theatricality. But I didn't know if it held together and didn't know how to direct it to have it hold together. And I never did—from our first conferences to the rise of the curtain on opening night, January 11, 1966. Bill Ritman's elaborate and complicated set included treadmills that never worked, and the confusing and inconsistent lighting didn't help. Why did I stay on? Because it was Edward. And because Richard and Clinton and Mark Wright and Joy Small were there.

The Shuberts had finally provided one of their own theaters for an Albee play—the Shubert itself, probably the most sought-after theater on 44th Street. In the dark reaches of that precious but cavernous space, the wings of our efforts beat hollower and hollower.

People who are not in the theater inevitably ask theater people who happen to be associated with an obvious failure whether they knew all along that they had no chance. In the case of *Malcolm*, I think we did. But we kept pretending that we didn't; that in the theater *anything* is possible. Half of me kept thinking that the actors or the lines or those wild costumes might, at the last second, provide a magical transformation. Half of me kept hoping that the producers would finally get Edward to agree to cancel the opening. The third half of me just kept trying to get the treadmills to work.

Previews weren't too bad. People actually laughed—and stayed in the theater. Two nights before our official opening, I would have bet we had an even chance. I was as wrong as I could be. When the notices came out, they were exactly as expected: disastrous. Surprisingly enough, the *Times*'s Stanley Kauffman, a new occupant of its critical throne, thought the production was "exquisite" and said that the playwright had never been better served. He had, however, serious reservations about the play. Other critics were harsher: "An elaborate bore" . . . "Edward Albee Has a Catastrophe" (this from his most consistent supporter, Richard Watts) . . . "Tiny Albee." There were lots of others. We closed in a week, our closing preceded by a black-bordered announcement, composed, paid for, and signed by Edward: "To those who have come to see *Malcolm*, my thanks. To those who were pleased, my gratitude. To those who were disappointed, my apologies. See you next play." I felt sorriest for James Purdy, innocent of our deed but somehow sucked up in it. Purdy never blamed any of us publicly, and I often wondered what he thought of it all. It was the kind of experience that makes you want to quit believing in the theater.

But believe I did when Edward sent me the unbound pages of his next play, *A Delicate Balance.* I took the manuscript out on the porch of my Hastings ship house one windy spring afternoon, almost losing some pages to the Hudson River. *A Delicate Balance,* about which I had heard nothing before that afternoon, was the opposite of *Malcolm.* It was an original, and Edward's most mature play, almost Chekhovian in its nuances and tones. I loved it, reveled in it, and had no sooner come to the end than I proceeded to read it again, savoring the language even more the second time around. I called Edward and Richard immediately to tell them how pleased I was that they had asked me to direct.

The producers and I were keen on asking Lynn Fontanne and Alfred Lunt to play Agnes and Tobias. They were perfect casting, and I welcomed the opportunity of working with the Lunts. Edward seemed less enthusiastic about the idea, but not unwilling. The Lunts, apart from their prowess as performers, were box-office magic. We dispatched the script to their hideaway in Genessee Depot, Wisconsin, and kept our fingers crossed.

Their answer came back sooner than it usually does from stars who are sent scripts and dawdle for weeks or months before reading them, much less replying. Yes, the Lunts would be interested in appearing in Mr. Albee's play. They had, however, two conditions. They wanted to start the production in London, where they felt safer and more at home; two, they would sign only for six months. Richard and Clinton were, I believe, willing to accept those conditions. So was I. Edward was not. We begged him to change his mind. But Edward was determined to assert his writer's prerogatives. He didn't enjoy having anyone make conditions, even the Lunts. My dream of working with Alfred Lunt and Lynn Fontanne vanished, to be replaced by a mirage of John Gielgud and Irene Worth and the possible reality of Hume Cronyn and Jessica Tandy.

By the fall Hume and Jessie had accepted. Bill Ritman's design took delicate shape, a bit grandiose, which was what Edward wanted. It was always gratifying to work with Bill, who had become a good and faithful friend. All the old reliables, among them Mark Wright and Joy Small, were assembling. Only the Billy Rose Theatre, otherwise engaged, evaded us. We settled on the Martin Beck, much too large for Edward's play, though we refused to admit that. We battened down the rest of the casting. Marian Seldes as the daughter was everyone's idea; she had understudied Irene Worth in *Tiny Alice*. Henderson Forsythe, as Harry, Agnes and Tobias's best friend, was mine; I always tried to find a part for Hank in every play I directed. After we had thought of and abandoned a dozen ideas for Agnes's wise-cracking—and wise—sister, Claire, Rosemary Murphy's name came up. Rosemary had been one of my earliest drama students at Catholic University, struggling in the chorus of Sophocles' *Electra*, but I had never worked with her since. We read Rosemary and took her, a bit cautiously. Apart from Hume and Jessie (and Hank) it was not a cast with whom I felt secure.

We had our first rehearsal at Edward's house, everyone reasonably relaxed, admiring Bill Ritman's final model of the set. I wore my red baseball cap and talked a bit about *A Delicate Balance* as a play about the daily struggle between our sense of self and our social responsibility. It was poetic, sophisticated, and "relevant"—without being obvious or conventional. This was clearly a nut worth cracking. "Oh, yes, what exactly were Harry and Edna afraid of?" I said. "Let's get into rehearsal and find out."

Despite everyone's inner tremors, rehearsals seemed to go smoothly. Hume and Jessie were charming. From the time I settled Agnes down in a comfortable spot on the sofa for her lengthy constantly-interrupted-by-herself speech, and then worked out in precise and well-timed detail Tobias's business with her drinks, I found myself—much to my astonishment—working easily with our two stars.

Our only real problem was that Ro Murphy was floundering around as Claire, and Edward threatened to replace her—with or without my approval—if she didn't get on track. I actually liked her and felt that her unevenness came from inexperience and insecurity. I spent extra time with her and did everything possible to build her confidence. Several times, we almost let her go, but eventually she came through with a truthful and alternately comedic and moving version of Claire. Even Edward agreed. Up until years later, when I heard Ro had been deriding my ability as a director on some West Coast talk shows, I thought she had appreciated the help I gave her.

The closer we came to our opening, the more I grew to love the play and appreciate the performers. If *Virginia Woolf* had been a brass band, *A Delicate Balance* was a Vivaldi quartet, its tones more muted but ringing out, rich and resonant. Jessie's understanding of her character was almost instinctive; her voice, as well as every move she made, was like music. And Hume, going from concern and apprehension to bedraggled despair, constantly surprised us.

Our only real problem was Harry and Edna's arrival, when they announce simply that they are "afraid." I staged it, I thought, with both sublety and simplicity. Yet, at our first preview—much to everyone's astonishment—the audience laughed. Edward was shocked, as were we all. We tried cutting several of the lines that got the laughs. The laughs just shifted. We worked with the scene, Edward suggesting some changes in the staging and timing. The laughs continued. We considered replacing the actors. I'm sure Edward, behind the scenes with the producers, must have considered replacing the director. Finally, Richard bit the bullet and told Edward that perhaps the laughs were not entirely bad. Maybe they were the audience's way of dealing with tension, with the unknown. I'm not sure that I agreed, but anything that got rid of our own panic was welcome. The laughs remained, and we got to enjoy them.

As we came closer to our opening night, I began to worry more and more about the play's being "too good" for Broadway, too delicate for the grosser tastes of the commercial theater's audiences. There was no question of *A Delicate Balance*'s expressive grace, its language, its intelligence. And its cast was much stronger than I had originally thought. Hume's cat speech, which worried me because it seemed imposed and because it resembled the dog story in *Zoo Story*, was extremely effective. The climax of the play, in which Tobias zigzags between ordering Harry out of the house and imploring him to stay, was riveting. And, I thought, the last elegy—those three ladies facing the future dawn—had classical strength. And yet I worried. Previews were going well, but they were not like *Virginia Woolf*'s.

On opening night, September 22, I felt the audience was somehow aware it was sitting in on theater history. Although the response, as in previews, could not match the thunderclap intensity of that first head-on collision with a new writer, it filled the Martin Beck. Then the reviews came out. Chapman of the *News*, rarely prone to eloquence, called it "A beautiful play, filled with humor and compassion and touched with poetry." Watts rebounded from his scorn of *Malcolm* to say that "*Delicate Balance* is not only a brilliant and searching play, but a strangely beautiful one." Other critics joined the chorus. Even *Variety*, that dour Bible, agreed that "Edward Albee has returned to successful form . . . an absorbing evening for followers of serious theater. . . . Edward Albee's most mature, most ambitious play."

Everyone liked us. Almost everyone, that is. Walter Kerr, the new daily critic for *The New York Times*, felt the play was too talky and too hollow, that it dealt with "a condition rather than an action," that it was "speculative rather than theatrical, an essay or an exercise when it might have been an experience." Walter analyzed it to death, sounding as though he was trying hard to rationalize a personal distaste.

I came home with Jean after our opening, saying that if this play—this level and quality of dramatic writing—did not survive because of Walter Kerr's abstract and intellectual ideas about playwriting, it would not be possible for me to work in the New York theater—so long as Walter was critic for the *Times*. All the work, all the beauty of my experience with the play had ended with the taste of ashes.

Despite Kerr's reservations, we lasted for 132 performances, to reasonably full and appreciative audiences. Afterward, we embarked on a successful national tour, with a somewhat different cast though, fortunately, still including Hume and Jessie. We started at the Coconut Grove Playhouse in Miami—my first return there since *Godot* twelve years earlier. The Coconut Grove loved us. Neither Hume nor Jessie received a Tony Award, though Marian Seldes got one as Best Supporting Actress. I had been nominated, my third nomination since *Virginia Woolf*, but I knew I would not win, and I didn't. The following May, Edward Albee received the Pulitzer Prize, in place of the one denied him for *Virginia Woolf*. He accepted with alacrity, tossing off a few caustic cracks at the Pulitzer Committee's previous timidity.

But there was Walter Kerr, turning out those daily reviews—straight out of Aristotle via Thomas Aquinas. Walter Kerr did not like Ibsen or Chekhov, hated Samuel Beckett, and had strong reservations about Harold Pinter. I liked them all, but the *Times* never gave me equal time. That was a most indelicate balance, but I had to face it every day of my theater life.

FINALE:
THE RUNNING OF THE WATER
1966 On

With the success of *A Delicate Balance*, I was just forty-nine; I had been married to the same woman for almost fourteen years; my children were about to be twelve and eight; my bank account was growing, and so were my prospects. I was now an American director, established and known—the fellow who did those strange plays and sometimes made them work.

Robert Anderson's fairly conventional new play, or rather four one-act plays, had the strange collective title *You Know I Can't Hear You When the Water's Running*, a name that no one understood and everyone hated. Bob and I went back a long way together, as far as the Arena Stage and *All Summer Long*. A year previously he had sent me the first draft of his *I Never Sang for My Father*, which he was sure no Broadway producer would do, but to which I responded immediately. It reminded me strongly of my own problems with my father. Then Bob told me about another script called *Four Plays for Saturday Night*, at that time containing only three: *The Shock of Recognition*, *The Footsteps of Doves*, and *I'll Be Home for Christmas*. He had written them for something he called Paperback Theatre, an off-Broadway place where plays might be performed several times each evening in rotation—as in a movie house—without advance reservations and for low prices. Obviously, no one would pay Broadway prices to see four one-act plays, no matter how funny or moving. I told Bob it was a great idea but Equity wouldn't allow more than eight performances a week with the same actors. To double or triple cast would make costs prohibitive, and no producer would accept the idea of two- or three-dollar ticket prices. I also told Bob I couldn't be sanguine about a commercial production. Bob, as always, was idealistic. I wasn't—at least not about Broadway. But it was great to hear from him after all those years. Of course, I'd love to read *Four Plays for Saturday Night*.

I read them one afternoon, was mildly amused, and was even more certain that no Broadway producer in his right mind would take them on. Nevertheless, I told Bob I was his, whenever and wherever, and went off to Israel to do *The Cherry Orchard* for the Cameri Theatre in Tel Aviv. Bob's fourth play, *I'm Herbert*, arrived just as I was occupied with technical rehearsals in Hebrew. I laughed aloud and forgot about the whole thing. A week or so later, a cable from Bob announced a definite Broadway production of *Four Plays for Saturday Night* for fall or winter, depending on my availability. Audrey Wood, Bob's longtime agent, had sent the script to every established Broadway producer, all of whom had turned it down. Finally, in desperation, she gave it to two newcomers from television, Gil Cates and Jack Farren, who took an option. They had no money but were determined to get it. I called Bob to say that I could be with him the moment *A Delicate Balance* opened in the fall. But I never believed that *Four Plays for Saturday Night* would ever be done. Any night. On Broadway!

Once back in New York, I found time to meet the nitwits who thought *Four Plays* was commercial. Casting, of course, was our first line of defense. We decided to go after four big stars, two men and two women. Everybody agreed on Walter Matthau, who was an old friend of Bob's and supposedly interested. Bob wanted his wife, Teresa Wright, who was sure and unsure on alternate days, especially about playing the older roles.

Walter Matthau delayed, dodged, and finally disappeared somewhere in Beverly Hills. Eileen Heckart appeared, in combination with Teresa, but Heckie was interested only if she could play the wife in *Doves* —which was clearly Teresa's best role. Teresa remained torn. In the midst of this ring-around-the-rosy, I suggested Martin Balsam for Walter's roles, George Grizzard for the other male characters, and Melinda Dillon to go with Teresa. They were not exactly big star names, but good actors all. Marty—eventually—expressed interest, but only if he could play the actor rather than the producer in *Shock*. (He was smarter than all of us; he realized at once that it would be the actor—and his eagerness to take off all his clothes—who would get the big laughs in Bob's deceptively simple first play.) George was willing, but Bob wasn't sure he wanted him. I think Bob still felt guilty about not using George (who had been the lead in Arena's *All Summer Long*) on Broadway. Nobody was sure about Melinda, and Melinda was not sure about us. The ring-around-the-rosy continued as I went off to direct *Delicate Balance*.

When I returned, not much had changed. Marty's demands—including the financial ones—kept us all at bay. We went after David Wayne but stopped when we discovered he was asking a weekly salary (plus percentage) that made Marty a piker. We went after a comedian named Eddie Mayehoff, suddenly come to fame, but he stood us up, twice. Confusions and conflicts between Teresa and Heckie were increasing, with no hint of resolution, and there was now a question about the latter's availability. We had various differences of opinion over Joe Silver or John Randolph as the producer. George Grizzard still wanted to be with us, but was growing increasingly nervous about Bob's lack of enthusiasm for him. One stormy night I flew up to Buffalo, where George was playing Cyrano, to hold his hand and reassure him tearfully that we all loved—and wanted—him.

Bob and I also disagreed about offstage personnel. He wanted his favorite designer, Jo Mielziner. I admired Jo, but after my previous experiences with his assembly-line methods, I didn't. And I wanted my regular stage manager and confidant, Mark Wright. Bob didn't.

In the meantime, the name of our evening of plays had been changed to *The Shock of Recognition*, which to me suggested Greek drama more than American comedy. And our two amiable producers, Jack and Gil, were saddled not only with their own inexperience, but also with bad luck. Promised backing was withdrawn. Promised theaters were given to other plays. Another evening of one-acts, Saul Bellow's *A Wen*, opened and closed on Broadway, diminishing our own prospects. I began wondering whether I might not have been better occupied.

Somehow or other, by the time we got into rehearsal on January 30, everything had been decided, settled, worked out, resolved. We had Marty, Heckie, George, Melinda, and Joe Silver. Obviously not the "big stars" we originally planned, but a very decent group of actors. We had a designer I'd never worked with before, Ed Wittstein, doing the sets, and dear Theoni Aldredge for the costumes. We had Frances Sternhagen, whom Bob kept calling an "off-Broadway actress," understudying Heckie. We had my Mark Wright and Joy Small for the millionth time. And we had a general manager, Bob Kamlot, who kept telling me, "When you have a problem, talk to me. These producers don't know what they're doing." As if I didn't know by that time. Bob had finally gotten us a theater, the Ambassador, in a bad location and with too wide a stage, but with strong positive vibrations for me. My son, David, was "born" there on opening night of *Kataki*, eight years before. And we had a new title, *You Know I Can't Hear You When the Water's Running*, whose exact relevance to our subject matter was not clear, but which at least removed us from Greek tragedy.

We were able to rehearse onstage from the first day—always a great advantage. But most Broadway rehearsal periods tend to be equal. They start out with all the excitement of newness, partnership, and anticipation, and then, as egos intensify and nerves become raw, end up as total agonies. With this one, the agonies had begun before we started. And even on our first day, I knew that I was destined to be walking in a circle through mud. Apart from Marty's aloofness, George's insecurity, and Melinda's shy strangeness, I soon became aware of Heckie's basic toughness and Joe Silver's sullen unwillingness. Ed Wittstein and I had worked out what I thought was a charmingly theatrical way of having the actors change the scenery from play to play; Ed brought along a model on which I could demonstrate. The demonstration for our cast wound up with a dull thud. Joe Silver asked if the actors would get stagehand's salaries. He meant it. Even my old friend George took a crack at me: "Still up to your Arena tricks, huh, Alan?"

Heckie, who had been so easygoing and good-natured during our preproduction meetings, turned into steel, only grudgingly accepting my direction or Bob's rewrites. Onstage, she was dynamite—funny, true, spontaneous—but in rehearsal, I had a hard time budging her once she set something. George, as usual unhappy playing anything but the lead, and complaining about almost everything, was excellent as *Shock*'s idealistic playwright, just right as the salesman in *Doves*, and riotous as the old man in *Herbert*. Joe kept talking about "reality" and "truth" but insisted on facing downstage all the time, no matter where I placed him. And Melinda, who had been so immediately "right" as Honey in *Virginia Woolf*, gave us trouble all along. She was fine in the tiny part of Dorothy (*Shock*), and I loved her when I could hear her as the daughter (*Christmas*), but she couldn't find the character of the girl in *Doves* and began to cry, sulk, and threaten to quit. Melinda's understudy, encouraged by an agent, tried everything to get me to put her in.

It was Marty, naturally, who contributed my major agonies. He took only those directions with which he agreed, simply ignoring me at other times. And even when he agreed, he always gave the impression that he was doing me a favor. As he grew in his three roles, he put more distance between himself and the rest of us. His technique for achieving spontaneity required constant paraphrasing, repetition, colloquialization of Bob's lines, and yards of ad-libbing. He never said the same lines twice. Mark, as stage manager, eventually stopped correcting him, but Bob objected strongly, insisting on his words being said exactly as they were written. Not one day passed without Bob's coming to me to complain, "Marty's got to stop that!" Remembering Buzz Meredith's knees, I kept delaying the inevitable, telling Bob that this was just the way Marty worked, and that he would eventually get all the lines right. As rehearsals went on and Marty kept on getting them all wrong, Bob insisted that he or I confront him. One day I did, as glancingly as possible, just to test the murky depths of Marty's reaction. The response was immediate and clear: "Tell Anderson to go to hell! That's the way I work. If he doesn't like it, that's too bad!" I didn't tell Anderson.

In addition to the normal strains of rehearsal, we had the problem of dealing with separate plays. Working on four plays, no matter how short they are, is four times as difficult as working on one long play. Each play has its own tone and style. Nor do the plays ever progress at the same rate; we would be flung daily from exhilaration to despair. *Shock*, largely because Marty enjoyed his role and George was so good, shaped up quickly. *Doves*, with Marty and Heckie and Melinda pulling against each other, went in and out. *Christmas* remained a dull, amorphous mess. And *Herbert*, with George and Heckie struggling for lines and credibility, seemed rough and overly caricatured. The actors also worked at varying speeds, George and Heckie forging ahead, Melinda mired and erratic, Marty holding back or going off on various extremes. I finally couldn't stand his vacillations and asked him point-blank one day what he was doing. His "I don't know yet" triggered my furious response: "It's about time you did," which I followed up with "I might even be able to help you—if you'd let me!" Then, once launched, I went on much too long with one of my emotional diatribes about how we just *had* to set something, had to do *something* the same way twice in a row, had to say at least *some* of the author's favorite lines the way they were written. Marty looked at me in absolute shock, murmured "Lunch!" and walked out the door. I wasn't sure whether he was ever coming back. Or that I wanted him to.

Bob, luckily, knew nothing about the incident. Marty returned after lunch and a few drinks. We went on, largely as before. As usual, Bob was absorbed in tiny details. We cut and transposed and changed lines every day, chipping away at the dull spots, heightening the humor and the climaxes. My major concern was with the performances and the tone of each play. I was also trying to deal with the problem of unifying the evening and smoothing out the scene shifts. At various times, the producers or the actors or somebody would suggest cutting one of the plays so that the evening would consist of a trio instead of a quartet. I think suggestions were made to cut each of the plays, whichever was, at the moment, considered the "weakie," except for *Shock of Recognition*, which was always the "strongie." Just before previews began, there was increased producer pressure for Bob to drop *Herbert* because it wasn't funny. Bob and I resisted with a passion—although there were days when I would have tossed out *I'll Be Home for Christmas* without a qualm. Through all this, we were constantly undecided about the order of the plays, though we eventually stuck to our original sequence. Prior to previews, we also began hearing rumors that one of our producers had borrowed money on his life insurance to keep us rehearsing. We also heard that because our advance sale was so small, the other producer had to mortgage his house. I have always had my doubts about either rumor.

But even without such melodramatic beginnings, the show's birth was not easy. For our first paid preview, Heckie fell ill and couldn't play. Frannie Sternhagen went on with two hours' rehearsal, and in my opinion turned in a performance every bit as effective as Heckie's. Bob was grateful but refused to accept any revision of Frannie's artistic status. To him, she was still just an off-Broadway actress.

Heckie came back the next night. Pressures continued, unevenly applied, first to one show then another. But audience responsiveness—and numbers—grew, as did our hopes. Marty, despite his unpredictability and all the traumas of rehearsing with him, came into his own with an audience; he was uproarious, truthful, and full of surprises. The audience loved him, and so did the producers, and, eventually, even Bob and Alan. George and Heckie grew more and more secure, and Melinda's work seemed less fragmented. Our scene changes, "dissolving" one setting into another, usually got applause. The producers, mortgaged or not, were suddenly smilingly evident. Friends called to tell us that if this one didn't "make it," they were crazy. For the first time since we started, we began to hope—and worry harder.

With each preview, we seemed to get better and better, closer and closer. To what? There was nothing more to do but pray. I've never longed so fervently for previews to end and opening night to arrive. I just couldn't go through this four-horse race night after night, one horse getting ahead, one horse stumbling, one horse dragging, one horse something else. And me betting on all four to win.

The big day was March 13, a Monday, the only Monday opening I've ever had on Broadway. Nor did the significance of that particular date go unnoticed. Thirteen had always been a lucky number for me. Among other portents, there were thirteen letters in my name. Sam Beckett, the playwright who had changed my life, had been born on Friday the thirteenth. And *Virginia Woolf* had opened on October 13, 1962.

The day dawned wet and cold, the beginning of the rest of my life, as well as the ending of this chronicle. That afternoon, as is usual with all my theater openings, I got the actors together onstage to run through portions of each play. In reality, we were just huddling together that last time for psychological—and physical—warmth. Even Marty and Heckie went along with that.

A few hours later the audience joined us, friendlier and more human than any opening-night audience I'd ever seen. Richard Watts, who had arrived so late for *Entertaining Mr. Sloane*, was late again—this time waiting for a female companion, who finally showed up. They rushed down the aisle just as the curtain went up ten minutes past our scheduled time, par for the course.

Shock had never played better. George was strong and clear and passionate. Joe was as solid as stone. Melinda was charmingly modest and pert. And Marty was funny and sad, as always, but, for a change, totally in control. In spite of such sublimity, the initial response from the audience was cautious, held back, professional. But as the performance built and began to reach its climax, Marty glowing and radiating goodness, even that audience gave in. The curtain brought real applause, solid, sustained, end-of-the-evening-type applause. We chalked it up. One down and three to go!

Doves didn't come off nearly so well. The feeling and the laughs were there, especially Heckie's; *Shock* had loosened them up. But the pace kept faltering, and the performances—including Marty's—didn't have their proper edge. *Doves* was also much tamer than *Shock*—a game of tennis instead of baseball. The applause was decent, not great. There was a welcome buzzing and a very live atmosphere in the lobby during intermission.

Christmas started out with a bang, Marty and Heckie glowing with color and domestic truth. The laughs and the silences were equally intense. Several of Bob's lines got applause, which had not happened before. And at the curtain, the clapping went on and on until I thought it would never stop. Naturally, the weakest play got the best response.

Maybe they thought it was the last one; perhaps they had miscounted.

Finally, the change lights came on and we were into the transition to *Herbert*. Normally the funniest, it suddenly seemed frail, forced, uncertain. Most of the usual laughs came, but they didn't build or sustain as they usually did. The timing was way off. George was in reasonable form, but Heckie seemed especially jittery. Toward the end, she went completely askew with her lines, and only George's superb concentration and control pulled them out, relatively unscathed. The curtain calls were loud but not thunderous. It was not *Virginia Woolf*, but then how could it be? Bob Anderson came over to me, pleased and beaming nervously, though he did say that it was too bad about the way *Herbert* had gone, and that we had lost them somewhere past the middle of *Doves*. As if I didn't know!

For only the second time after an opening in New York (the first occasion was with *Kataki*), I attended a first-night party at Sardi's. By the time Jean and I got there, everyone was scouting rumors. The one most available was that Edwin Newman had been seen "laughing." We would only have to wait a couple of hours to find out who had been scowling. Gil and Jack had reserved Sardi's third-floor Belasco Room for us, and it was soon jammed with friends, relatives, well-wishers, hangers-on, and even members of the cast and crew. I couldn't find a place to sit and wound up on the floor, coping with a double Manhattan and a plateful of hors d'oeuvres. An amused press photographer rushed over to shoot pictures of this strange sight.

Somehow, from eleven to about eleven twenty, I survived the chit-chat around the single available television set, my stomach sinking lower and lower toward the floor, my mouth drying into a semi-fetid Sahara, as the sense-memory of similar times and places took over. Suddenly, without warning, the broad, square-jawed countenance of my old college classmate Ed Newman occupied the screen and told us all in definitive declarative sentences that it was "touching," "funny," and "successful." God had liked three of our four plays! (He didn't enjoy *Herbert*.) Two minutes later, whoever it was on CBS spoke, in less structured sentences, but even more glowingly. ABC followed. The decibels of hope were rising. For almost the first time in my theatrical existence, all three television critics were favorable! Now on to the printed word, four flights up in the office of our advertising agency. Impatient of elevators, I raced up the stairs.

The one familiar face, Bob Kamlot's, informed me that Chapman of the *News* was a rave. We had been worried about his known prudery.

I dashed downstairs immediately to reveal this world-shaking news to Jean and Bob Anderson and Gil Cates and Audrey Wood and anyone else who was nearby, all caught up in the beginnings of a contagion impossible to appreciate unless one has gone through an opening—or an election. Then upstairs again to learn that Kerr was writing "a long one." We would have to await his capsule version on WQXR at midnight. Our press agent, Harvey Sabinson, decided to telephone his old friend Richard Watts at home. Watts was still up. The conversation rambled in pleasant generalities for interminable minutes; then Harvey smiled broadly and lifted his left thumb toward the ceiling. Watts was a rave. We had the Southern states.

Like a forest fire racing through parched underbrush, enthusiasm spread over the tension. We had the *News*. We had the *Post*. Norman Nadel (the *World-Telegram*) was a shoo-in. (No one, by the way, had yet seen Nadel's notice; we were already—rightly, as it turned out—taking him for granted.) What about Kerr? Once more, I flew downstairs to report to Jean and the assembled multitudes. Then up once more for the midnight vigil, that familiar waiting for a Godot who, unfortunately, always came.

Finally, the twelve o'clock news: something about Viet Nam; Congressman Adam Clayton Powell's foibles; and then the capsule Walter Kerr, loud and clear, ". . . funny . . . entertaining . . ." As though released by a starter's gun, I spun on my heels and dashed down to my ever-faithful, eternally waiting Jean. "Kerr was good!" We were in.

Actually, in the morning's light Kerr's review was not all that favorable. But the rest of them definitely were. They were the best set of notices I'd ever gotten. Pleased and relieved as I was, such unanimously favorable responses for work that seemed less praiseworthy than much of what I had contributed with Albee or Beckett, ultimately brought a measure of pain. I felt the critics—except for the more intellectual ones, who did have reservations—were settling, as always, for the superficial and showy. *You Know I Can't Hear You* had been well done, and I was certainly proud of it. But neither its choreography nor its sense of life were on a par with what I had achieved with so many previous moments, in *Slapstick* or *Delicate Balance* or *Endgame* or. . . .

Obviously, neither the reviewers nor the public agreed. We stayed at the Ambassador for 775 performances, more than for any play I have done before or since. It was a real commercial success, the most resplendent I've ever had. Nor did I sneer at it as I pocketed my weekly royalties; they paid the bills and got my kids through college. Nor, despite my occasional reservations about its artistic merits, can I recall greater aesthetic pleasure than watching Marty in *Shock of Recognition* express his willingness to do *anything* for a part in that play for which he was auditioning, and observing his expertise in making the laughs roll out like thunderclaps. I used to come in at least once a week for as long as we were there.

Eventually, after about a year, Marty and Heckie and George gave way to Larry Blyden and Irene Dailey and William Redfield. We were terrified of being rereviewed because we knew that the quality of the show had declined. But Clive Barnes, newly on the *Times* in place of Walter, said the new cast was a superior one, thereby extending our run—as well as my low opinion of critics. Afterward, we did a national tour with Eddie Bracken and Ruth Manning, and a bus-and-truck with none other than Imogene Coca, who was great, and her husband, King Donovan. Marty took the Tony for best actor—without a nod in my direction. Bob's play was recognized as one of the year's ten best. *Four Plays for Saturday Night*, also known as *You Know I Can't Hear You When the Water's Running*, went down in history on two counts: it lowered the barriers on one-act plays being successfully presented on Broadway; and it was the first Broadway play that concerned itself seriously and organically with the issue of nudity—although no one appeared nude onstage.

At one point during our opening-night party, my old college-mate Howard Teichmann, the playwright who had dramatized *Miss Lonelyhearts* and made me miserable for weeks in Boston, came over to me to embrace me and tell me that this was the greatest moment of my life, that *You Know I Can't Hear You* was my finest directing job, that this was the night when I had moved to another, higher league.

"Like hell!" I answered Tike. "I can do this kind of show with one hand tied behind my back! The really good things I've done have gone by largely unrecognized and unrewarded. And I'm going to go right on doing them."

The next two decades of my working life were to prove me correct. *You Know I Can't Hear You When the Water's Running* did succeed in moving me to a plane of greater opportunities, many of them golden indeed. Hollywood and TV beckoned; I demurred. Neil Simon and Burt Bacharach and David Merrick offered me *Promises, Promises*, which I later enjoyed seeing but did not want to direct. The way of commercial success and celebrity lay open before me; I did not choose to follow it. That short story I had written in high school about the actor walking out on his Academy Award had come to life.

I cannot say that I was never tempted. Nor can I deny that there have been moments since when I have wondered about—and perhaps even regretted—my basic decision. But I have always cared more about good work than success or failure. I have always valued the exploration of innate quality over material rewards. And the years that followed this decision brought me more such explorations than I ever expected.

They brought me more of Samuel Beckett's best writing, more of Edward Albee, more of Harold Pinter. They brought me Edward Bond, Michael Weller, Lanford Wilson, Preston Jones. They brought me more of my first home, the Arena Stage, and of the Guthrie Theatre. They brought me the Juilliard Theatre Center, the Acting Company, the University of California at San Diego, the Theatre Communications Group, and growing involvement in the coming of age of the not-for-profit regional theater, the real American national theater to be, that "one theater" of which I dreamed almost half a century before.

More than that, these years have brought me to a sense that my life in the theater, arrived at so accidentally and erratically, finally had some shape and meaning. That is a reward that cannot be measured, only felt.

APPENDIX: PRODUCTIONS BY ALAN SCHNEIDER

PLAY	AUTHOR	LOCATION	DATE
Squaring the Circle	Valentin Katayev	University of Wisconsin	1938
A Night in the Country	Betty Smith and Robert Finch	Cornell University	November 1940
Jim Dandy	William Saroyan	Catholic University	October 29, 1941
Athalia	Jean Racine	Catholic University	March 4, 1942
Child's Play	Jacques Blanchard	Catholic University	August 20, 1942
The Romancers	Edmond Rostand	Catholic University	August 4, 1943
The Doctor in Spite of Himself	Molière	Catholic University	August 9, 1944
Lute Song	Kao-Tong-Kia (adaptation by Will Irwin and Sidney Howard)	Catholic University	November 19, 1944
The Tidings Brought to Mary	Paul Claudel	Catholic University	February 18, 1945
The Importance of Being Ernest	Oscar Wilde	Catholic University	August 5, 1945
Electra	Sophocles	Catholic University	November 30, 1945
That's Where the Money Goes	James Finchley, Jean Kerr, Joan O'Byrne	Catholic University	May 10, 1946
State Occasion	Clinch Calkins	Catholic University	November 29, 1946

PLAY	AUTHOR	LOCATION	DATE
You Can't Take It with You	Moss Hart and George S. Kaufman	Cain Park Theater, Cleveland	July 1, 1947
Sing Out, Sweet Land	Walter Kerr	Cain Park Theater, Cleveland	August 5, 1947
The Long Goodbye	Tennessee Williams	Theater Inc., New York	November 1947
A Long Way from Home	Maxim Gorki (adapted by Randolph Goodman and Walter Carroll)	Maxine Elliott's Theatre, New York	February 8, 1948
Make a Statue Laugh	Arnold Shulman	American Theater Wing, New York	1948
Lute Song	Kao-Tong-Kia (adaptation by Will Irwin and Sidney Howard)	Cain Park Theater, Cleveland	July 6, 1948
Reluctant Lady	Maurice Valency	Cain Park Theater, Cleveland	July 27, 1948
The Taming of the Shrew	William Shakespeare	Cain Park Theater, Cleveland	August 17, 1948
My Heart's in the Highlands	William Saroyan	The Barn Theater, Dartington Hall, England	July 1, 1949
The Real McCoy	John Finch	Catholic University	December 2, 1949
Oedipus the King	Sophocles	Catholic University	March 17, 1950
Born Yesterday	Garson Kanin	Cape Playhouse, Dennis, Massachusetts	July 3, 1950
Over Twenty-One	Ruth Gordon	Falmouth Playhouse, Coonamassett, Massachusetts	July 31, 1950
Harvey	Mary Chase	Falmouth Playhouse, Coonamassett, Massachusetts	August 7, 1950
Post Road	Wilbur Daniel Steele and Norman Mitchell	Falmouth Playhouse, Coonamassett, Massachusetts	August 14, 1950

PLAY	AUTHOR	LOCATION	DATE
Macbeth	William Shakespeare	Catholic University	September 30, 1950
The Madwoman of Chaillot	Jean Giraudoux (adapted by Maurice Valency)	Catholic University	October 27, 1950
Othello	William Shakespeare	Catholic University	March 2, 1951
The Glass Menagerie	Tennessee Williams	Arena Stage, Washington, D.C.	April 10, 1951
The Primrose Path	Robert Buckner and Walter Hart	Playhouse Theater, Houston	August 8, 1951
The Cherry Orchard	Anton Chekhov	Catholic University	November 30, 1951
Pullman Car Hiawatha	Thornton Wilder	The Neighborhood Playhouse, New York	January 30, 1952
Macbeth	William Shakespeare	Catholic University	March 21, 1952
The Hasty Heart	John Patrick	Arena Stage, Washington, D.C.	June 17, 1952
Desire Under the Elms	Eugene O'Neill	Arena Stage, Washington, D.C.	October 7, 1952
The Skin of Our Teeth	Thornton Wilder	Catholic University	December 5, 1952
Lady Precious Stream	S. I. Hsiung	Arena Stage, Washington, D.C.	December 9, 1952
All Summer Long	Robert Anderson	Arena Stage, Washington D.C.	January 13, 1953
Our Town	Thornton Wilder	Arena Stage, Washington, D.C.	March 16, 1953
Hide and Seek	Arnold Sundgaard	The Neighborhood Playhouse, New York	April 23, 1953
The Country Girl	Clifford Odets	Arena Stage, Washington, D.C.	May 18, 1953

PLAY	AUTHOR	LOCATION	DATE
My Heart's in the Highlands	William Saroyan	Arena Stage, Washington, D.C.	August 11, 1953
The Happy Journey	Thornton Wilder	Arena Stage, Washington, D.C.	September 1, 1953
The Miser	Molière	Catholic University	September 29, 1953
Othello	William Shakespeare	Catholic University	September 29, 1953
The Bad Angel	Joel Hammil	Arena Stage, Washington, D.C.	October 20, 1953
The Remarkable Mr. Pennypacker	Liam O'Brien	Coronet Theatre, New York	December 30, 1953
Summer and Smoke	Tennessee Williams	Arena Stage, Washington, D.C.	February 9, 1954
All Summer Long	Robert Anderson	Coronet Theatre, New York	September 23, 1954
Anastasia	Guy Bolton	Lyceum Theatre, New York	December 29, 1954
Tonight in Samarkand	Jacques Deval and Lorenzo Semple, Jr.	Morosco Theatre, New York	February 16, 1955
The Skin of Our Teeth	Thornton Wilder	Théâtre Sarah Bernhardt, Paris	June 28,1955
The Skin of Our Teeth	Thornton Wilder	ANTA Theatre, New York	August 17, 1955
Waiting for Godot	Samuel Beckett	Coconut Grove Playhouse, Miami	January 3, 1956
The Little Glass Clock	Hugh Mills	Golden Theatre, New York	March 26, 1956
The Trip to Bountiful	Horton Foote	The Arts Theatre Club, London	July 4, 1956
A View from the Bridge	Arthur Miller (revised version)	Arena Stage, Washington, D.C.	November 7, 1956
The Glass Menagerie	Tennessee Williams	The New York City Center, New York	November 21, 1956

PLAY	AUTHOR	LOCATION	DATE
The Enchanted	Jean Giraudoux	Boston University	May 3, 1957
The Circus of Dr. Lao	Gwyn Conger Steinbeck and Nathaniel Benchley	Edgewater Beach Playhouse, Chicago	July 9, 1957
Miss Lonelyhearts	Howard Teichmann	Music Box Theatre, New York	October 3, 1957
Endgame	Samuel Beckett	Cherry Lane Theatre, New York	January 28, 1958
The Summer of the Seventeenth Doll	Ray Lawler	Arena Stage, Washington, D.C.	April 29, 1958
Pullman Car Hiawatha *The Happy Journey* *The Long Christmas Dinner*	Thornton Wilder	Brooklyn College	May 15, 1958
The Deserters	Thaddeus Vane	England Tour	August 1958
Kataki	Shimon Wincelberg	Ambassador Theatre, New York	April 9, 1959
Epitaph for George Dillon	John Osborne and Anthony Creighton	Arena Stage, Washington, D.C.	May 5, 1959
Waiting for Godot	Samuel Beckett	Alley Theater, Houston	September 9, 1959
The Summer of the Seventeenth Doll	Ray Lawler	Players Theatre, New York	October 13, 1959
Clandestine on the Morning Line	Josh Greenfeld	Arena Stage, Washington, D.C.	November 24, 1959
The Cherry Orchard	Anton Chekhov	Arena Stage, Washington, D.C.	January 12, 1960
Krapp's Last Tape	Samuel Beckett	Provincetown Playhouse, New York	January 14, 1960
Detective Story	Sidney Kingsley	Boston University	February 24, 1960
Two for the Seesaw	William Gibson	Royal Poinciana Playhouse, Palm Beach, Florida	March 28, 1960

PLAY	AUTHOR	LOCATION	DATE
Twelve Angry Men	Reginald Rose	Bucks County Playhouse, New Hope, Pennsylvania	May 23, 1960
Measure for Measure	William Shakespeare	New York Shakespeare Festival, Central Park, New York	July 25, 1960
Rape of the Belt	Benn W. Levy	Wilbur Theatre, Boston	October 20, 1960
Twinkling of an Eye	H. W. Wright and Guy Andros	Actors' Workshop, San Francisco	January 11, 1961
The American Dream	Edward Albee	York Playhouse, New York	January 24, 1961
Krapp's Last Tape	Samuel Beckett	Arena Stage, Washington, D.C.	April 4, 1961
Uncle Vanya	Anton Chekhov	The Goodman Theatre, Chicago	April 16, 1961
The Bald Soprano *Pullman Car Hiawatha*	Eugene Ionesco Thornton Wilder	Hofstra College	May 12, 1961
The American Dream	Edward Albee	Cherry Lane Theatre, New York	June 1961
The Chairs *The Lottery* *The Dock Brief*	Eugene Ionesco Shirly Jackson John Mortimer	University of Wisconsin	July 25, 1961
Happy Days	Samuel Beckett	Cherry Lane Theatre, New York	September 17, 1961
The Caucasian Chalk Circle	Bertolt Brecht	Arena Stage, Washington, D.C.	October 30, 1961
The American Dream *What Shall We Tell Caroline?*	Edward Albee John Mortimer	Arena Stage, Washington, D.C.	November 28, 1961
Happy Days	Samuel Beckett	McCarter Theatre, Princeton, New Jersey	January 12, 1962

PLAY	AUTHOR	LOCATION	DATE
Endgame	Samuel Beckett	Cherry Lane Theatre, New York	February 11, 1962
The American Dream	Edward Albee	Cherry Lane Theatre, New York	March 1, 1962
The Burning of the Lepers	Wallace Hamilton	Arena Stage, Washington, D.C.	March 20, 1962
Uncle Vanya	Anton Chekhov	Arena Stage, Washington, D.C.	April 17, 1962
The Time of Your Life	William Saroyan	Arena Stage, Washington, D.C.	May 15, 1962
The Dumbwaiter *Pullman Car Hiawatha* *Act Without Words, II*	Harold Pinter Thornton Wilder Samuel Beckett	University of Wisconsin	July 10, 1962
A Man's a Man	Bertolt Brecht (adapted by Gerhard Millhaus)	Stanford University	August 9, 1962
Krapp's Last Tape *Zoo Story*	Samuel Beckett Edward Albee	East End Theatre, New York	September 12, 1962
Who's Afraid of Virginia Woolf?	Edward Albee	Billy Rose Theatre, New York	October 13, 1962
The Dumbwaiter *The Collection*	Harold Pinter	Cherry Lane Theatre, New York	November 26, 1962
All the Way Home	Tad Mosel	Arena Stage, Washington D.C.	March 12, 1963
Othello	William Shakespeare	Arena Stage, Washington D.C.	April 10, 1963
Threepenny Opera	Bertolt Brecht (music by Kurt Weill)	Arena Stage, Washington D.C.	May 14, 1963
Who's Afraid of Virginia Woolf?	Edward Albee	Colonial Theatre, Boston (national company)	September 12, 1963
Ballad of the Sad Café	Edward Albee	Martin Beck Theatre, New York	October 30, 1963

PLAY	AUTHOR	LOCATION	DATE
Play *The Lover*	Samuel Beckett Harold Pinter	Cherry Lane Theatre, New York	January 4, 1964
Who's Afraid of Virginia Woolf?	Edward Albee	Piccadilly Theatre, London	February 6, 1964
The American Dream	Edward Albee	Cherry Lane Theatre, New York	April 21, 1964
The Glass Menagerie	Tennessee Williams	Tyrone Guthrie Theatre, Minneapolis	June 1, 1964
Tiny Alice	Edward Albee	Billy Rose Theatre, New York	December 29, 1964
Do Not Pass Go	Charles Nolte	Cherry Lane Theatre, New York	April 13, 1965
Happy Days	Samuel Beckett	Cherry Lane Theatre, New York	September 28, 1965
Entertaining Mr. Sloane	Joe Orton	Lyceum Theatre, New York	October 12, 1965
Herakles	Archibald MacLeish	University of Michigan	October 24, 1965
Malcolm	Edward Albee	Shubert Theatre, New York	January 11, 1966
Slapstick Tragedy	Tennessee Williams	Longacre Theatre, New York	February 22, 1966
The Cherry Orchard	Anton Chekhov	Cameri Theater, Tel Aviv	July 20, 1966
A Delicate Balance	Edward Albee	Martin Beck Theatre, New York	September 22, 1966
You Know I Can't Hear You When the Water's Running	Robert Anderson	Ambassador Theatre, New York	March 13, 1967
The Birthday Party	Harold Pinter	Booth Theatre, New York	October 3, 1967
I Never Sang for My Father	Robert Anderson	Longacre Theatre, New York	January 25, 1968

PLAY	AUTHOR	LOCATION	DATE
Box Mao Box *Krapp's Last Tape* *Zoo Story*	Edward Albee Samuel Beckett Edward Albee	Billy Rose Theatre, New York	October 1, 1968
The Watering Place	Lyle Kessler	Music Box Theatre, New York	March 12, 1969
The Gingham Dog	Lanford Wilson	John Golden Theatre, New York	April 23, 1969
La Strada	Book by Charles Peck, Jr., music and lyrics by Lionel Bart	Lunt-Fontanne Theatre, New York	December 14, 1969
Blood Red Roses	Book and lyrics by John Lewin, music by Michael Valenti	John Golden Theatre, New York	March 22, 1970
Inquest	Donald Freed	Music Box Theatre, New York	April 23, 1970
Saved	Edward Bond	Chelsea Theatre Center, Brooklyn Academy of Music, Brooklyn, New York	October 15, 1970
Breath *Come and Go* *Marquettes*	Samuel Beckett Francis Warner	Voge Hall, Performing Arts Center, Toronto	November 23, 1971
What the Butler Saw	Joe Orton	University of Wisconsin	July 29, 1971
Waiting for Godot	Samuel Beckett	Sheridan Square Playhouse, New York	August 1971
Moonchildren	Michael Weller	Arena Stage, Washington, D.C.	October 29, 1971
The Sign in Sidney Brustein's Window	Lorraine Hansberry (revival with music)	Longacre Theatre, New York	January 1972
Moonchildren	Michael Weller	Royale Theatre, New York	February 9, 1972
Uptight	Günter Grass	Arena Stage, Washington, D.C.	March 17, 1972

PLAY	AUTHOR	LOCATION	DATE
The Foursome	E. A. Whitehead	Arena Stage, Washington, D.C.	November 3, 1972
Not I *Happy Days* *Krapp's Last Tape* *Act Without Words, II*	Samuel Beckett	Mitzi Newhouse Theatre, Lincoln Center, New York	November 22, 1972
Our Town	Thornton Wilder	Arena Stage, Washington, D.C.	December 15, 1972
Enemies	Maxim Gorki	Arena Stage, Washington, D.C.	March 16, 1973
The Love Suicide at Schofield Barracks	Romulus Linney	Boston University	April 25, 1973
Jabberwock	Jerome Lawrence and Robert E. Lee	Missouri Repertory Theatre, Kansas City	August 9, 1973
Krapp's Last Tape *Not I*	Samuel Beckett	Arena Stage, Washington, D.C.	September 18, 1973
Our Town	Thornton Wilder	Arena Stage, Washington, D.C.	October 24, 1973
Tom	Alexander Buzo	Arena Stage, Washington, D.C.	December 14, 1973
The Madness of God	Elie Wiesel	Arena Stage, Washington, D.C.	May 1974
Marat/Sade	Peter Weiss	State University of New York, Purchase	December 5, 1974
The Skin of Our Teeth	Thornton Wilder	Boston University	February 15, 1975
The Last Meeting of the Knights of the White Magnolia	Preston Jones	Arena Stage, Washington, D.C.	June 27, 1975
Waiting for Godot	Samuel Beckett	Stanford University	August 10, 1975
The Madness of God	Elie Wiesel	Lyceum Theatre, New York	March 1976

PLAY	AUTHOR	LOCATION	DATE
Our Town	Thornton Wilder	Arena Stage, Washington, D.C.	May 19, 1976
Texas Trilogy: *Lu Ann Hampton Laverty Oberlander* *The Last Meeting of the Knights of the White Magnolia* *The Oldest Living Graduate*	Preston Jones	Kennedy Center, Washington, D.C.	April 1976
Texas Trilogy	Preston Jones	Broadhurst Theatre, New York	September 21, 1976
Play *Footfalls* *That Time*	Samuel Beckett	Arena Stage, Washington, D.C.	December 3, 1976
The Cherry Orchard	Anton Chekhov	Juilliard Theatre Center, New York	February 24, 1977
Play *Footfalls* *That Time*	Samuel Beckett	Manhattan Theatre Club, New York	December 14, 1977
Mother Courage	Bertolt Brecht	American Place Theatre, New York	April 4, 1978
Antigone	Jean Anouilh	The Acting Company, Touring	September 1978
Loose Ends	Michael Weller	Arena Stage, Washington, D.C.	February 2, 1979
Loose Ends	Michael Weller	Circle in the Square, New York	June 6, 1979
The Great American Quiz Show Scandal	Louis Phillips	University of California, San Diego	November 8, 1979
The Lady from Dubuque	Edward Albee	Morosco Theatre, New York	January 31, 1980
The Happy Journey *Pullman Car Hiawatha* *The Long Christmas Dinner*	Thornton Wilder	University of California, San Diego	November 13, 1980

PLAY	AUTHOR	LOCATION	DATE
Rockaby	Samuel Beckett	State University of New York, Buffalo	April 8, 1981
Rockaby	Samuel Beckett	La Mama E.T.C., New York	April 13, 1981
Rockaby	Samuel Beckett	State University of New York, Purchase	April 16, 1981
Waiting for Godot	Samuel Beckett	The Acting Company, Public Theater, New York	April 22, 1981
Our Town	Thornton Wilder	Guthrie Theatre, Minneapolis	July 13, 1981
Rockaby	Samuel Beckett	National Theatre, London	December 1982
Pieces of Eight:		University of California, San Diego	February 10, 1983
The Unexpurgated Memoirs of Bernard Mergendeiler	Jules Feiffer		
The Black and the White	Harold Pinter		
The Tridget of Greva	Ring Lardner		
The Sandbox	Edward Albee		
The (15 Minute) Dogg's Troupe Hamlet	Tom Stoppard		
Come and Go	Samuel Beckett		
Foursome	Eugene Ionesco		
I'm Herbert	Robert Anderson		
Play *Footfalls* *That Time*	Samuel Beckett	American Place Theatre, New York	April 29, 1983
Ohio Impromptu *Catastrophe* *What Where*	Samuel Beckett	Harold Clurman Theatre, New York	June 11, 1983
Our Town	Thornton Wilder	University of California, San Diego	November 10, 1983
Rockaby *Footfalls* *Enough*	Samuel Beckett	Samuel Beckett Theatre, New York	February 16, 1984

PLAY	AUTHOR	LOCATION	DATE
Pieces of Eight		The Acting Company, Public Theater, New York	March 8, 1984
Victoria Station *One for the Road* *A Kind of Alaska*	Harold Pinter	Manhattan Theatre Club, New York	April 3, 1984
Ohio Impromptu *Catastrophe* *What Where* *That Time*	Samuel Beckett	Edinburgh Festival, Scotland	August 13, 1984
Ohio Impromptu *Catastrophe* *What Where* *That Time*	Samuel Beckett	Warehouse Theatre, London	August 27, 1984

WORKS ON TELEVISION

Pullman Car Hiawatha	Thornton Wilder	CBS, Color TV Experimental, Washington D.C.	1951
Oedipus the King	Sophocles	NBC-TV, *Omnibus*, NY	1956
The Life of Samuel Johnson	James Lee	CBS-TV, Sylvania TV Award	1957
The Years Between		CBS-TV, NYC	1958
The Secret of Freedom	Archibald MacLeish	NBC-TV, NYC	1959
Waiting for Godot	Samuel Beckett	PBS	1960
Act Without Words, II	Samuel Beckett	PBS	1966
Eh Joe?	Samuel Beckett	PBS	1966

FILM

Film	Samuel Beckett	Evergreen Theatre Productions	1964

INDEX